Islands of Australia's
Great Barrier
Reef

Tony Wheeler

Islands of Australia's Great Barrier Reef - a travel survival kit
1st edition

Published by
Lonely Planet Publications
Head Office: PO Box 617, Hawthorn, Vic 3122, Australia
US Office: PO Box 2001A, Berkeley, CA 94702, USA

Printed by
Singapore National Printers Ltd, Singapore

Photographs by
Great Barrier Reef Marine Park Authority (GBRMPA & pages 36, 41, 97, 117, 232)
Tony Wheeler (TW)
Mark Norman (MN & page 232)
Vicki Beale (page 45)
Bundaberg Tourism & Development Board (BTDB)
Queensland Tourist & Travel Corporation (QTTC)

Front cover: Reef Snorkelling (GBRMPA)
Back cover: Purtaboi Island, Family Group (TW)

First Published
July 1990

**Although the author and publisher have tried to make the information as
accurate as possible, they accept no responsibility for any loss, injury or
inconvenience sustained by any person using this book.**

National Library of Australia Cataloguing in Publication Data

Wheeler, Tony
    Islands of Australia's Great Barrier Reef: a travel survival kit.

    Includes index.
    ISBN 0 86442 031 5.

    1. Great Barrier Reef Region (Qld.) - Description and
    travel - Guide-books. I. Title.

    919.43

    text © Lonely Planet 1990
    maps © Lonely Planet 1990
    photos © photographers as indicated

Tony Wheeler

Tony Wheeler was born in England but spent his youth in places like Pakistan, the West Indies and the USA. A degree in engineering and an MBA did nothing to settle him down and he then joined the Asian overland trail with his wife Maureen in the early '70s and that first long trip resulted in *Across Asia on the Cheap*, which later changed titles to *West Asia on a Shoestring*. Tony and Maureen set up Lonely Planet Publications to publish that first book and have been travelling, writing and publishing ever since.

Lonely Planet Credits

Editor	Peter Turner
Maps	Ralph Roob
	Trudi Canavan
Design	Vicki Beale
Cover Design	Vicki Beale
Line Illustrations	Trudi Canavan
	Vicki Beale
Colour Illustrations	Trudi Canavan

Thanks also to Katie Cody for proofing, and Tamsin Wilson for additional maps.

Acknowledgements

Researching this book involved a number of trips up to the reef, sometimes by myself, sometimes with Maureen, sometimes with our children Tashi and Kieran as well. Additionally John Noble and Susan Forsyth visited a number of islands and conducted additional research while working on the recent update of *Australia – a travel survival kit*.

Thanks must also go to David Stranger for his expert assistance, to the Queensland National Parks & Wildlife Service and the Great Barrier Reef Marine Park Authority for their help and advice and particularly for access to their photographic library. I'd also like to thank the numerous reef enthusiasts I ran into while working on this book – they ranged from scuba divers and bushwalkers to round-the-world backpackers or simply dedicated lotus eaters! Finally I mustn't forget the divemasters at the various dive sites along the reef and the enthusiastic crew of the ship *Queen of the Isles*.

A Warning & A Request

Things change – prices go up, schedules change, good places go bad and bad places go bankrupt – nothing stays the same. So if you find things better or worse, recently opened or long since closed, please write and tell us and help make the next edition better!

Your letters will be used to help update future editions and, where possible, important changes will also be included as a Stop Press section in reprints.

All information is greatly appreciated and the best letters will receive a free copy of the next edition, or any other Lonely Planet book of your choice.

Contents

MAP LEGEND

BOUNDARIES

- — · — · — · — ....International Boundaries
- — .. — .. — .. ..Internal Boundaries
- . — .. — .. — ....National Parks, Reserves
- - - - - - - - ....The Equator
- . . . .The Tropics

SYMBOLS

- ◉ NEW DELHI ....National Capital
- ● BOMBAY ....Provincial or State Capital
- ● Pune ....Major Town
- • Borsi ....Minor Town
- ≙ ....Post Office
- ✈ ....Airport
- i ....Tourist Information
- ⊖ ....Bus Station, Terminal
- 66 ....Highway Route Number
- ⚑ ☩ ☩ ....Mosque, Church, Cathedral
- ∴ ....Temple, Ruin or Archaeological Site
- ≙ ....Hostel
- ✚ ....Hospital
- ☼ ....Lookout
- ⚐ ....Camping Areas
- ⊓ ....Picnic Areas
- ⌂ ....Hut or Chalet
- ▲ ....Mountain
- ⚑⚐⚑ ....Railway Station
- ⫽ ....Road Bridge
- ⊞ ....Road Rail Bridge
- ⊃⊂ ....Road Tunnel
- ⊃⊂ ....Railway Tunnel
- ⫟ ....Escarpment or Cliff
- ⫝ ....Pass
- ⌇ ....Ancient or Historic Wall

ROUTES

- ———— .....Major Roads and Highways
- - - - - - - - - ....Unsealed Major Roads
- ———— ....Sealed Roads
- - - - - - - - - ....Unsealed Roads, Tracks
- ══════ ....City Streets
- +++++++++++++++ ....Railways
- ═══●═══ ....Subways
- . . . .Walking Tracks
- - - - - - - - - - ....Ferry Routes
- ++ ++ ++ ++ ....Cable Car or Chair Lift

HYDROGRAPHIC FEATURES

..................................Rivers, Creeks
.........................Intermittent Streams
......Lakes, Intermittent Lake
....Coast Line
....Spring
....Waterfall
....Swamps

Salt Lakes, Reefs

Glacier

OTHER FEATURES

Parks, Gardens and National Parks

Built Up Area

Market Place and Pedestrian Mall

Plaza and Town Square

Cemetery

Note: Not all the symbols displayed above will necessarily appear in this book

Introduction

A reef such as is here spoke of is scarcely known in Europe. It is a wall of Coral Rock rising almost perpendicular out of the unfathomable ocean.

Captain James Cook, 1770

The Great Barrier Reef stretches for 2000 km along the coast of Queensland – an area of stunning natural beauty and great scientific interest. The reef starts around Gladstone and the Tropic of Capricorn and at first it is a wide scattering of individual reefs around 200 km out from the coast. As you move north the reef becomes more and more continuous and also closer and closer to the coast, while still containing a scattering of individual reefs in the inner lagoon. North of Cairns the reef really is an almost continuous barrier to the Pacific Ocean.

Along the reef there are many islands, most of them uninhabited. Some of them are true coral cays, tiny outcrops of sand and hardy vegetation gradually accumulated after a reef has stayed consistently above sea level. Other islands are larger 'continental' islands, the drowned mountain-tops of an ancient coastal range.

The islands have interesting vegetation and many are home for a wide variety of birds but it's the waters around the islands where the reef's real excitement lies. Nowhere else is such a diversity, and such a colourful diversity, of life found.

There are numerous islands along the reef where you can stay and the islands offer the widest range of possibilities imaginable. If you're after real seclusion try the exclusive small resorts like Bedarra or Lizard, or relaxed and quiet Hinchinbrook. If you want a big international resort with a wide range of activities you can head for Hamilton. If you're young and want to meet lots of other young people then Great Keppel is aimed right at you. If you're a scuba fan then islands like Heron, Lady Elliot or Lizard specialise in catering for your needs.

If you want to get away from small children Lizard, Orpheus and Bedarra ban them. If you don't want to – well Lindeman and South Molle take pains to cater for kid's interests. If you have lots of money to spare you can run through a fortune on fine food and expensive activities at some islands. If you're penniless you can get a national park camping permit and there are plenty of places where you can camp for nothing and there will be absolutely nothing to spend money on!

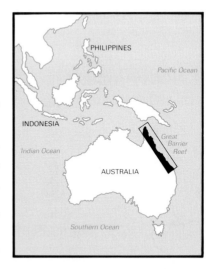

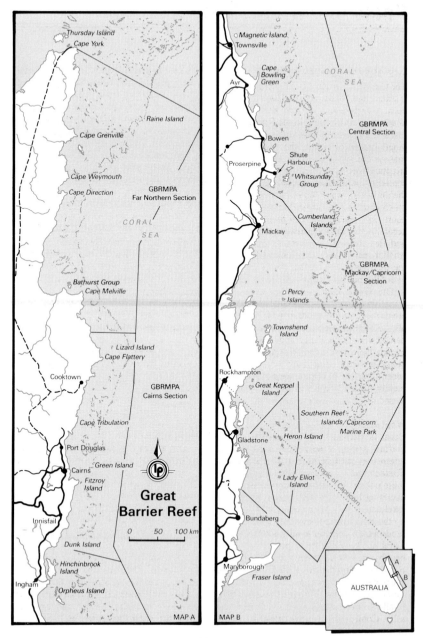

MAP A

MAP B

Great Barrier Reef

0   50   100 km

AUSTRALIA

Facts about the Region

THE GREAT BARRIER REEF

The Great Barrier Reef is 2000 km in length. It starts slightly south of the Tropic of Capricorn, somewhere out from Bundaberg or Gladstone, and it ends in the Torres Strait, just south of Papua New Guinea. This huge length makes it not only the most extensive reef system in the world but also the biggest structure made by living organisms. At its southern end the reef is up to 300 km from the mainland, but at the northern end it runs much closer to the coast, has a much more continuous nature and can be up to 80 km across. In the 'lagoon' between the outer reef and the coast the waters are dotted with smaller reefs, cays and islands. Drilling on the reef has indicated that the coral can be over 500 metres thick.

The Great Barrier Reef encompasses something like 2500 individual reefs which are actually named, more than 600 islands in all, 250 named continental islands and 70 named coral cays. Only about 20 of these islands have resort facilities although it is possible to camp on many of the islands. Most of the resort islands are partly or completely national park and the resort area is leased to the resort operators.

What Is It?

Coral is formed by a primitive animal, a marine polyp, closely related to the sea anemones and jellyfish of the family *Coelenterata*. The vital difference is that these polyps form a hard exterior surface by excreting lime. When a polyp dies its hard 'skeleton' remains and these gradually build up the reef. New polyps grow on their dead predecessors and continually add to the reef. Coral needs a number of preconditions for healthy growth. First the water temperature must not drop below 17.5°C – thus the Barrier Reef does not continue further south into cooler waters. The water must be clear to allow sunlight to penetrate and it must be salty. Coral will not grow below 30 metres

depth because the sunlight does not penetrate sufficiently and it will not grow around river mouths. The Barrier Reef ends around Papua New Guinea because the Fly River's enormous water flow is both fresh and muddy – two antagonistic factors for coral growth.

Reef Types

Basically, reefs are either fringing or barrier. You will find fringing reefs around many of the Great Barrier Reef's islands. Barrier reefs are further out to sea and usually enclose a 'lagoon' of deep water. The Great Barrier Reef is out at the edge of the Australian continental shelf and the channel between the reef and the coast can be 60 metres deep. At places the reef rises straight up from that depth. This raises the question of how the reef built up from that depth when coral cannot survive below 30 metres? One theory is that the reef gradually grew as the seabed subsided, and that the reef was able to keep pace with the rate of sinkage. The alternative is that the sea level gradually rose, and again the coral growth was able to keep pace.

Island Types

Let's admit right away that this book, like most books and articles about 'Barrier Reef islands' is not really accurate. Most of the reef islands are not really on the Great Barrier Reef at all, they're between the reef and the mainland. Of course there are real reef islands but in general they tend to be very small and the major islands are not actually on the reef. The islands covered in this book are islands on or within the Barrier Reef – Queensland has other islands such as Fraser Island or Moreton Island which lie south of the reef.

There are two types of islands along the Barrier Reef. The larger islands, like those of the Whitsunday group, are the tops of flooded mountains. At one time these would have been the high points of a range running along the coast, but rising sea levels submerged it. They have vegetation like the adjacent mainland. Other islands may actually be on the reef, like Heron Island near Gladstone, or may be isolated coral cays, like Green Island near Cairns. These are formed when the growth of coral is such that the reef is above the sea level even at low tide. Dead coral is ground down by water action to form sand and eventually hardier vegetation takes root. Coral cays are low-lying, unlike the often hilly islands closer to the coast.

Most of the islands, continental or cays, suffer from water shortages and building resorts has often required desalination plants, shipping in water or other expensive solutions. Only three islands with resorts – Dunk, Bedarra and Hinchinbrook – are moist enough to have rainforest cover.

THE HISTORY OF THE REEF

The history of the Great Barrier Reef is a comparatively short one by geological standards. At the time of the last ice age the sea level was probably over 100 metres lower than it is today. The continental shelf leading

out from the present coast to the outer Barrier Reef was dry land 18,000 years ago and islands like the Whitsundays were hills rising from this coastal plain.

Then the ice started to melt, the sea started to rise and by 12,000 years ago the coastal plain had become a submerged continental shelf. By 8000 to 9000 years ago the outer edge of reef, built up during previous cycles of thaw and freeze, was also submerged and by 6000 to 7000 years ago the sea had reached its present level. The reef, building on the base established by preceding ancient reefs, began to assume its present form.

The formation of the Great Barrier Reef is so recent that humankind was already on the scene by the time it started to form. It's thought that the ancestors of Australia's Aborigines started to arrive in Australia as long as 40,000 years ago and they certainly knew about the reef and made use of its islands. In some cases they actually lived on islands along the reef but at other times they made periodic forays out to the islands from the mainland. Shell middens, the accumulated

Reef walking & snorkelling (GBRMPA)

reminders of countless Aboriginal shellfish feasts, can be found on many Great Barrier Reef islands. Captain Cook, in the log of his pioneering voyage along the coast, commented a number of times about the Aborigines he had seen on the islands, sailing in their canoes between the islands or simply evidence he had seen that they had visited them in the past. Today there are few islands populated by Aborigines. One of the exceptions is Palm Island, in the Palm Island group north of Townsville.

With the arrival of Europeans little more than 200 years ago humankind's relationship with the Great Barrier Reef took on a new form as the reef was extensively explored and charted. For the first European navigators the reef was initially a fearsome place, Captain Cook was mightily glad to escape from its clutches, but soon afterwards even happier to return to its protection (see the Lizard Island and Lizard Island to Cape York chapters).

With the start of European settlement in Australia careful exploration of the reef became a necessity and in 1802 Matthew Flinders circumnavigated Australia and charted many previously unexplored areas of the coast. It was not until 1815, however, that Charles Jeffreys sailed the entire length of the Barrier Reef coast *inside* the reef. Phillip King continued the work of charting the coast and reef in 1819 and following his surveys the 'inside passage' soon supplanted the 'outside passage' as the safest and fastest route along the east coast. Further surveys continued in the 1840s and the advent of steamships and the completion of the Suez Canal in 1869 made the route around the north of Australia and inside the Great Barrier Reef a far faster and shorter voyage from Europe than the old route around the southern tip of Africa and the south of Australia.

Today a steady stream of cargo ships continue to move up and down the carefully plotted channels inside the reef but it was not until this century that the reef's potential as a tourist attraction began to emerge. E J Banfield's well known sojourn on Dunk Island at the turn of the century excited a great deal of interest in the reef islands and between WW I and WW II a number of popular island resorts were established, some of which still operate today.

To the early explorers the colourful and intriguing world beneath the surface was a complete mystery and although pearl diving became an important activity before the turn of the century it has only been since WW II that snorkelling and scuba diving have taken off as recreational activities. Today visitors to the reef come for a variety of reasons. They may be simply passing through on commercial ships, cruise liners or yachts. They may be actually working the waters of the reef in prawn trawlers or other fishing vessels. Or they may be there simply to marvel at one of the great wonders of the natural world. Keeping these conflicting demands in balance will be the greatest challenge into the next century.

Reef Management

In 1975 the Great Barrier Reef Marine Park (GBRMP) was established. It is administered by the Great Barrier Reef Marine Park Authority, PO Box 1379, Townsville, Qld 4810. In 1981 the reef was added to the World Heritage List by the United Nations Education, Scientific & Cultural Organization (UNESCO). The GBRMP is not a national park although the Queensland National Parks & Wildlife Service handles the 'in the field' management of the marine park.

The GBRMPA coordinates different activities and uses of the Great Barrier Reef and a complete zoning of the 344,000 square km of the reef has been completed. The zoning breaks the Great Barrier Reef up into six classes:

Preservation Zone Areas of the reef which are intended to be kept completely untouched. Entry is only allowed in an emergency or for permitted scientific research.
Scientific Research Zone Areas set aside exclusively for scientific research.
Marine National Park B Zone A 'look but

don't take zone' intended to be kept in a relatively undisturbed state. Fishing and shell collecting are not permitted.

Marine National Park A Zone Recreational use of these areas is permitted which means fishing with one line and one hook is allowed but not collecting.

General Use B Zone Reasonable recreational and commercial uses are permitted but not trawling or shipping.

General Use A Zone All reasonable uses are permitted including trawling and shipping. Mining, oil drilling, commercial spearfishing and spearfishing with scuba equipment are not permitted in these zones, or anywhere else in the Great Barrier Reef Marine Park.

Information on the GBRMPA zoning can be obtained from the authority. The GBRMPA produces a free quarterly newsletter titled *Reeflections* and a quarterly $25 video titled *Reef Report*. The authority also operates Great Barrier Reef Wonderland, probably the best aquarium in Australia, at its headquarters in Townsville.

CLIMATE

The Great Barrier Reef is completely in the tropics. It commences around the Tropic of Capricorn and extends 2000 km north from there so it's always warm, warmer as you move further north of course. The best season is probably over the southern hemisphere winter period from April to December except in the extreme south where it can be a little chilly at the height of winter, June-July-August. Cairns and north the water is pleasant year round, the Whitsundays and south you wouldn't want to spend too long in the water in the middle of winter, unless you were wearing a wet suit.

Over the summer it can sometimes be too hot for comfort and tropical thunderstorms can bring heavy rain. The reef islands are in the cyclone (hurricane) belt and every few years one does come by and cause some damage. If they're going to turn up then the summer period is the time they'll arrive. February and March, towards the end of the

summer, tend to be the wettest months and if you're unlucky you may get a string of rainy days in a row. The rain gets progressively heavier as you move north but the distinction between the dry season and the wet season also becomes clearer. By the time you get to the top of Cape York the wet season is very wet and the dry season can be completely dry.

The rainfall probably has more influence than the temperature, it's hard to enjoy a tropical island when the sky's grey and the rain is pelting down. Rainfall charts for Rockhampton (the Southern Reef Islands, Great Keppel), Mackay (the Whitsundays), Townsville (Magnetic Island, Hinchinbrook), Cairns (Dunk Island, Green Island), Lizard Island and Weipa (Torres Strait Islands) are shown. Note how the peak monthly rainfall is about 175 mm in Rockhampton, twice as high in Mackay or Townsville and nearly three times as high by the time you get to Cairns and Cape York.

When to Visit

Apart from the climate there's another influence on when to visit and that is Australian holiday patterns. During school holidays the resorts can be very crowded although, of course, the resorts which ban all children are less likely to be affected! The main annual holiday period is from mid-December over Christmas through to the end of January. This is Christmas, New Year and school summer vacation all rolled into one and although it's not the best time of year on the reef it can get crowded nevertheless.

Other school vacations come in two week bursts but because there's some variation from state to state the danger period is more like three weeks. Approximately the periods are around the last two weeks in April, the first two weeks in July and the last two weeks in September. Lots of families head north to escape the winter weather in southern Australia at these times, particularly over the July holiday.

FAUNA & FLORA

The Barrier Reef islands are fascinating places for anybody with an interest in wildlife whether it's strange and exotic sea creatures or the many species of birds that make the islands their home. The Barrier Reef would just be a very big breakwater if it wasn't for the colourful and highly varied reef life.

Reef Life

Coral reefs provide a home and shelter for an enormous variety of life. Most evident are, of course, the often fantastically colourful reef fish – but fish are only one of a host of species to be seen. Reef walks, glass bottom or semi-submersible boat trips, snorkelling or, best of all, scuba diving, will all help to open the door to the magical word below the surface.

Coral Coral is highly varied in its types but almost all the polyp skeletons are white – it's the living polyps which give coral its colourful appearance. During the day most polyps retract to the protection of their hard skeleton so it's only at night that the full beauty of the hard corals can be seen. Hard coral is, however, only half the story. There is an equally varied assortment of soft corals. Like hard corals they are animals which gather in colonies but they do not have the hard lime skeleton of their reef-building relations.

Fish The Great Barrier Reef has something like 2000 species of fish and this remarkable

Monthly Rainfall (mm)

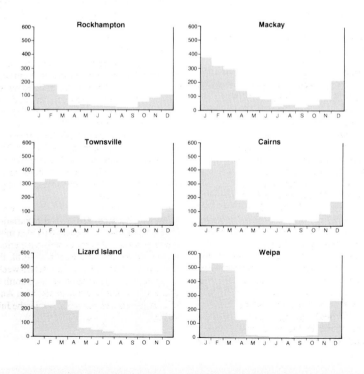

variety includes everything from tiny gobies, the smallest backboned animals, to huge whale sharks. Some fish are seen in the day while others shelter in crevices and caverns in the coral and only emerge at night. Some are grazers, others hunters. Some huddle together in groups for protection while other move around by themselves. And some are territorial, guarding their own patch of reef fiercely, while others are free ranging.

Echinoderms The widely varied group of creatures known as echinoderms includes sea urchins, starfish or sea stars, brittle stars, feather stars and sea cucumbers. It appears to be a curiously diverse group but they all share basic structural similarities.

Starfish are highly visible since they have few natural enemies and do not hide away during daytime. The Great Barrier Reef starfish include the notorious coral eating crown-of-thorns starfish.

Sea cucumbers, also known as trepang or bêche-de-mer, are also quite unhidden. (Gathering this oriental delicacy was one of Australia's earliest export activities.)

Crustaceans Hard shelled crabs, shrimps, prawns and lobsters are another colourful and diverse group of reef creatures. The variety of shrimps is particularly large and many of them engage in the symbiotic relationships which are of such interest on the reef. Several types of shrimps act as cleaners – removing parasites, dead tissue and other waste matter from fishes.

Molluscs Like the echinoderms, molluscs include members that scarcely seem to bear any relationship to each other. Molluscs include a variety of shelled creatures or gastropods, the oysters, scallops and clams known as bivalves and also the cephalopods, a group which includes octopus and squid.

The mollusc family includes the many clams which appear to be embedded in the coral. Their fleshy mantles are seen in a spectacular array of colours.

Nudibranchs or sea slugs are snails which have abandoned their shells and put on their party clothes. They're some of the most colourful and graceful creatures you can see on the reef.

While some of the shells found on the Great Barrier Reef are incredibly beautiful there are some varieties, such as the cone shell, which can fire out a deadly poisonous barb.

Whales & Dolphins Fish are not the only creatures to be seen swimming around the waters of the Great Barrier Reef. The inviting waters are home to dolphins which can often be seen sporting around boats. Huge humpback whales visit the reef on annual trips from Antarctica and their numbers are slowly recovering since whaling ceased in 1962. The shy and homely dugong are also found in shallow waters along the reef but they're a rare and now protected creature.

Reptiles Several types of turtles are found on the reef and there are a number of islands where they come ashore to lay their eggs. Sea snakes are another marine reptile which divers may meet.

Other Reef Life Like coral, sponges are an animal and their basic form has changed very little over hundreds of millions of years. The reef has a fantastic variety of worms, many of them colourful and strangely shaped creations totally unlike the typical terrestrial worm. Jellyfish found along the reef fortunately do not include the deadly box jellyfish or sea wasp which usually remains close to the coast. Jellyfish are coelenterates, part of the same family as coral and anemones.

Nudibranch (GBRMPA)

Island Life

Not all the life along the Great Barrier Reef is found underwater, the islands of the reef also harbour a great variety of life forms.

Island Flora The island flora varies with the islands found along the reef. At one extreme there are the vegetated coral cays, sandy islands recently emerged from the depths. Plant life here is limited and hardy but of great interest as you see life actually beginning. At the other extreme there are the rainforest islands where rich soil and heavy monsoonal rain cloaks the landscape in a jungle of deep, moist plant life. In between are the other continental islands where plant life is rich and varied but without the dense rainforest growth found on the moister islands. Several islands also have mangrove forests and this provides another interesting insight into the powers of nature to adapt to often hostile environments.

Birds There is a surprising variety of birdlife on even quite small islands. Some of the smaller cays support a small variety of birdlife but often in phenomenal numbers at breeding time. The Southern Reef Islands are particularly noted for their huge breeding populations and there are other islands, like Michaelmas Cay off Cairns, with similarly huge populations. Larger continental islands like the Whitsundays, Hinchinbrook or Dunk support a wider variety of birdlife.

Certain islands are closely linked with a particular type of bird and Heron Island even takes its name from the reef herons which are a familiar feature of the island scenery. The haunting 'wee-loo' call of the bush stone curlew is a familiar sound on many islands, particularly Magnetic. Over 200 species of birds have been sighted on Hinchinbrook Island while the nearby Brook Islands are noted for the huge nesting colonies of Torresian imperial pigeons. Dunk Island's bird population was closely studied by E J Banfield, Dunk's famous 'beachcomber', and this is one of a number of islands where

you can see the mound building megapode or jungle fowl.

Other birds that island visitors will soon recognise are the colourful but raucous little lorikeets; regular visitors to the lorikeet feeding tables which so many resorts provide. Jaunty little silvereyes are a feature on many islands where they shamelessly scrounge off the restaurant tables. The tiny hummingbird-like sunbirds are a delight wherever you see them.

Insects Dunk and Bedarra's most colourful fliers are insects rather than birds. On these islands of the Family Group the huge and bright blue Ulysses butterflies are a truly spectacular sight.

Animals The animal life on the reef islands is, of course, rather restricted but even some of the smallest islands manage to support some mammals. Flying foxes or fruit bats, one of the largest types of bats, can be seen flapping away over many islands at sunset; even Lizard Island supports a small flying fox colony. A number of islands, Hinchinbrook in particular, have wallabies while Magnetic Island has a large koala population and an extremely fearless collection of possums. Even Orpheus has its resident population of tiny bandicoots.

HOLIDAYS & FESTIVALS

As well as the school holidays when Australian families flock to the Great Barrier Reef islands (see the When to Visit section under Climate) there are also holidays, festivals and events directly related to the islands. Some of the main ones include:

April
    Hamilton Island Race Week features a series of yacht races.
October
    Heron Island Dive Festival brings together divers from all over the world for a week of scuba activity.
October-November
    Marlin season at Lizard Island peaks with the Lizard Island Black Marlin Classic from 30 October.

Crown-of-Thorns Starfish

The monster that ate the Barrier Reef – the crown-of-thorns starfish has managed to build itself a fearsome reputation since the early '60s. At that time it was noticed that the crown-of-thorns numbers were multiplying rapidly and that in certain areas it could prove a grave danger to the reef since the favourite food of this instantly recognisable starfish is living coral.

The crown-of-thorns is a large 'thorny', brown-coloured starfish. When it finds a patch of coral to its liking it turns its stomach out through its mouth, an activity known as 'stomach eversion', wraps it around the coral and digests the living coral polyps. When the stomach is drawn back in and the starfish moves on to the next tasty coral patch, all that's left is the limestone coral skeleton. A hungry crown-of-thorns can work its way through five square metres of coral in a year. The problem is made worse by the ability the starfish seems to have to send out a message that it has found a tasty coral reef and call in its relatives. Eventually huge numbers of starfish concentrate on one area and when this happens they start to feed day and night instead of hiding during the daylight hours.

Although it's undeniable that the Great Barrier Reef population of crown-of-thorns starfish has increased dramatically in the past 20 years nobody knows quite why or even if it is a real danger. Heavier than normal monsoonal rains have been postulated as one possible cause of the increase in numbers, shell collecting and reef fishing as another. A decline in numbers of triton shells due to shell collectors has been one favourite explanation, for the triton is one of the crown-of-thorn's few enemies. Tritons don't, however, depend only on the crown-of-thorns for food and they have never been very common.

The only way to combat the crown-of-thorns appears to be to physically remove them and over an area as great as the Great Barrier Reef that is clearly an impossibility. In any case after so few years studying the reef in general, let alone one of its many inhabitants in particular, it's still an open question whether the crown-of-thorns is a real danger. In a 1984 study of 178 reefs no starfish at all were sighted on more than half of the reefs. On the other hand some reefs had very large concentrations of crown-of-thorns starfish and in that case destruction of more than half of the reef was not unusual. In some cases over 90% of a reef had been destroyed. Meanwhile the studies continue and, from time to time, so do the newspaper headlines.

More information about the crown-of-thorns starfish can be found in the *Crown of Thorns Story*, a 44 page booklet available for $4 including postage within Australia from the Great Barrier Reef Marine Park Authority, PO Box 1379, Townsville, Qld 4810. A video with the same title is also available for $37 including postage. ∎

Crown-of-thorns starfish

Sea Urchins

The spiny sea urchins are another member of the *echinoderm* group which includes starfish and sea cucumbers. With a ball-like body covered in spines it is the sea urchin which gives the group its name, Greek for spiny *(echino)* and skin *(derm)*. The spines can vary considerably from the short blunt spines of the slate-pencil urchin to the long, sharp black spines of *Diadema* urchins. These spines will easily penetrate skin if the urchin is stepped on or handled and once broken off they are very hard to remove and will easily cause infections.

When an urchin dies the spines fall off and the circular 'sea egg' which remains makes a fine if fragile ornament. It's easy to see the five-armed star pattern on the casing which shows the urchin's relation to starfish. The sea urchin's mouth at the bottom is a complex structure known as Aristotle's lantern and with this the urchin grazes as it crawls across the sea bottom. Despite the formidable protection of its spines urchins hide away during daylight and come out to feed at night. Spines or not, some triggerfish will eat sea urchins and in some countries, but not Australia, sea urchins are a delicacy for human consumption. ■

Slate pencil urchin

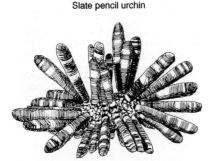

Sea urchin

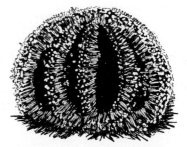

Stylophora pistillata
(GBRMPA)

Baler shell (GBRMPA)

Coral

Coral is usually stationary and often looks decidedly flowery but in fact it's an animal and a hungry carnivorous animal at that. Although a 3rd century AD Greek philosopher surmised that coral was really an animal it was still generally considered to be a plant only 250 years ago.

Corals are Coelenterates, a class of animals which also includes sea anemones and jellyfish. The true reef-building corals or Scleractinia are distinguished by their lime skeletons. It is this relatively indestructible skeleton which actually forms the coral reef, as new coral continually builds on old dead coral and the reef gradually builds up.

Coral takes a vast number of forms but all are distinguished by polyps, the tiny tube like fleshy cylinders which look very much like their close relation, the anemone. The top of the cylinder is open and ringed by waving tentacles which sting and draw into the polyp's stomach, the open space within the cylinder, any passing prey. Each polyp is an individual creature but they can reproduce by splitting to form a coral colony of separate but closely related polyps. Although each polyp catches and digests its own food the nutrition passes between the polyps to the whole colony. Most coral polyps only feed at night, during the daytime they withdraw into their hard limestone skeleton so it is only at night that a coral reef can be seen in its full, colourful glory.

Hard corals may take many forms. One of the most common and easiest to recognise is the staghorn coral which grows by budding off new branches from the tips. Brain corals are huge and round with a surface looking very much like a human brain. They grow by adding new base levels of skeletal matter and expanding outwards. Flat or sheet corals, like plate coral, expand out at their outer edges. Many corals can take different shapes depending on their environment. Staghorn coral can branch out in all directions in deeper water or form flat tables when they grow in shallow water.

Like their reef building relatives soft coral is made up of individual polyps, but they do not form a hard limestone skeleton. Without the skeleton which protects hard coral it would seem likely that soft coral would fall prey to fish but in fact they seem to remain relatively immune either due to toxic substances in their tissues or due to the presence of sharp limestone needles which protect the polyps. Soft corals can move around and will sometimes engulf and kill off a hard coral.

Coral catch their prey by means of stinging nematocysts. Some corals can give humans a painful sting and the fern like stinging hydroid should be given a wide berth. ■

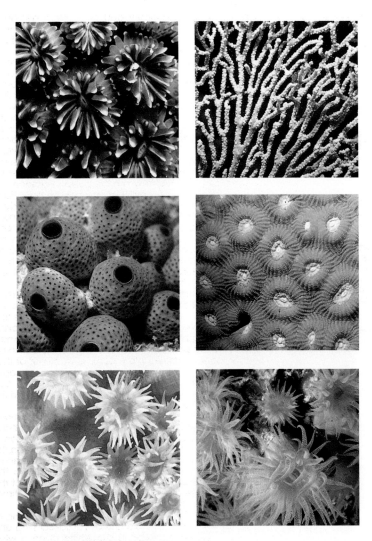

Top Left: Galaxea fascicularis (GBRMPA)
Top Right: Gorgonian coral (MN)
Middle Left: Ascidians (GBRMPA)
Middle Right: Fauki lizardensis (GBRMPA)
Bottom Left: Turbinaria peltata (GBRMPA)
Bottom Right: Daisy coral (GBRMPA)

Facts for the Visitor

VISAS

If you're coming to Australia from overseas you need a passport and visa unless you're a New Zealander. Visas are issued by Australian consular offices and the process is quick and efficient. The visas are valid for a stay of up to six months and this can usually be extended for a further six months. You'll usually be required to have an onward or return air ticket in order to be issued with a visa.

Embassies

Australian consular offices overseas include:

Canada
Australian High Commission, Suite 710, 50 O'Connor St, Ottawa K1P 5H6 (tel (613) 236 0841)
also in Toronto and Vancouver
Denmark
Australian Embassy, Kristianagade 21, 2100 Copenhagen (tel 26 2244)
Greece
Australian Embassy, 37 Dimitriou Soutsou St, Ambelokpi, Athens (tel 644 7303)
Hong Kong
Australian High Commission, Harbour Centre No 27, 24th floor, 25 Harbour Rd, Wanchai, Hong Kong (tel 5 731881)
India
Australian High Commission, Australian Compound, No 1/50-G Shantipath, Chanakyapuri, New Delhi (tel 60 1336)
Indonesia
Australian Embassy, Jalan Thamrin 15, Jakarta (tel 323109)
also in Denpasar
Ireland
Australian Embassy, Fitzwilton House, Wilton Terrace, Dublin 2 (tel 76 1517/9)
Italy
Australian Embassy, Via Alessandria 215, Rome 00198 (tel 832 721)
also in Milan and Messina
Japan
Australian Embassy, No 1-12 Shibakoen 1 Chome, Minato-ku, Tokyo (tel 435 0971)
also in Osaka

Malaysia
Australian High Commission, 6 Jalan Yap Kwan Seng, Kuala Lumpur (tel 242 3122)
Netherlands
Australian Embassy, Koninginnegracht 23, 2514 AB The Hague (tel (070) 63 0983)
New Zealand
Australian High Commission, 72-78 Hobson St, Thorndon, Wellington (tel 73 6411/2)
also in Auckland
Papua New Guinea
Australian High Commission, Waigani, Hohola (tel 25 9333)
Philippines
Australian Embassy, China Bank Building, Paseo de Roxas, Makati (tel 81 77911)
Singapore
Australian High Commission, 25 Napier Rd, Singapore 10 (tel 737 9311)
Sweden
Australian Embassy, Sergels Torg 12, Stockholm C, S-101 86 Stockholm (tel 24-46-60)
Switzerland
Australian Embassy, 29 Alpenstrasse, Berne (tel 43 01 43)
also in Geneva
Thailand
Australian Embassy, 37 South Sathorn Rd, Bangkok 12 (tel 287 2680)
UK
Australian High Commission, Australia House, The Strand, London WC2B 4LA (tel (01) 379 4334)
also in Edinburgh and Manchester
USA
Australian Embassy, 1601 Massachusetts Avenue NW, Washington DC, 20036 (tel (202) 797 3000)
also in Los Angeles, Chicago, Honolulu, New York and San Francisco.
West Germany
Australian Embassy, Godesberger Allee 107, 5300 Bonn 2 (tel 02221 376941-7)

Working in Australia

Officially, working in Australia is completely *verboten* on a regular tourist visa, but visitors do sometimes find jobs. There are no social security cards, national insurance cards or the like in Australia *yet*. The Great Barrier Reef resorts employ lots of short term and temporary staff and many visitors move from job to job and resort to resort although getting a foot in the door initially can be difficult. There tends to be a very high staff turnover at many resorts, partly because the staff is fairly footloose and partly because the work is very seasonal. Many resorts work on the NBO (next boat out) principle, sacking excess staff as soon as times go slack, taking more on when school holidays roll around.

MONEY

US dollars	US$1	=	A$1.35
New Zealand dollars	NZ$1	=	A$0.80
UK pounds sterling	UK£1	=	A$2.25
Singapore dollars	S$1	=	A$0.70
Hong Kong dollars	HK$1	=	A$0.17
Japanese yen	Y100	=	A$0.95
West German Deutsche marks	Dm 1	=	A$0.80
Dutch guilders	fl 1	=	A$0.70
Canadian dollars	C$1	=	A$1.10

The Australian dollar (A$) is divided into 100 cents (c). Unless otherwise indicated all dollar prices in this book are in Australian dollars. There are 1c, 2c, 5c, 10c, 20c, 50c, $1 and $2 coins. Notes are $5, $10, $20, $50 and $100.

Bankcard (the standard Australian/New Zealand credit card), Mastercard, Visa, American Express and Diners Club are widely accepted at the island resorts. At most of the resorts everything is (or can be) added to your bill and settled at the end. Magnetic, Hamilton and Thursday islands are the only ones with banks but some of the resorts have Commonwealth Savings Bank agencies and changing travellers' cheques at the resorts is no problem.

Costs

The cost of visiting Barrier Reef islands can vary enormously. At one extreme you can camp on national park islands for no more than a few dollars for a camping permit. You bring your own food, and on many islands your own water as well, and there's absolutely nothing to spend money on even if you wanted to. At the other extreme there are resorts like Bedarra where the daily cost per person is $400. In between there's everything from youth hostels where a bunk bed will cost you $10 to $15 a night or lower key resorts where the per person costs could be anything from $100 to $250 a night.

If you want to enjoy the reef islands without running through the national budget there are several alternatives. One is to stay on the mainland and day trip out. Cairns is a particularly good place for this as there are many reefs and cays easily accessible from the mainland and a great many trips operate out to them. In the Whitsundays, on the other hand, the reefs are further out but there are a variety of resort islands, many of which actively encourage day trippers.

The other way of getting to the islands on the cheap is to look for special deals and standby packages. Some of the resorts never discount their rates and you're unlikely to find anything at peak holiday times but when things are quiet, or during the off season, many resorts will offer standby rates. If you just happen to be at Airlie Beach, the jumping-off point for Whitsunday trips, at a quiet time you may find the travel agencies promoting all sorts of special standby deals at much lower rates than usual and often including transport out and back.

Tipping

Although with the increasing flow of overseas visitors tipping is becoming more common (especially for overseas visitors!) it is still not the norm in Australia. Australian workers are not paid a low wage which is then balanced up by their tips, as is the case in some countries. They're reasonably paid and tipping them is not necessary or even expected, particularly on the reef resorts.

TOURIST INFORMATION

There are a number of potential sources for information on the Great Barrier Reef.

Australian Tourist Commission

The Australian Tourist Commission is strictly an external operator. They'll tell you all about Australia, and the Great Barrier Reef, before you come to Australia. Within the country tourist promotion is handled by state or local tourist offices. Addresses of the ATC offices for literature requests are:

Australia
GPO Box 2721, Sydney, NSW 2001 (tel (02) 360 1111)
Canada
Suite 1730, 2 Bloor St West, Toronto, Ontario M4W 3E2 (tel (416) 925 9575)
Hong Kong
Suite 604-605, Sun Plaza, 28 Canton Rd, Tsimshatsui, Kowloon (tel (3) 311 1555)
Japan
8th floor, Sankaido Building, 9-13, Akasaka 1-chome, Minato-ku, Tokyo 107 (tel (03) 582 2191)
4th floor, Yuki Building, 3-3-9 Hiranomachi, Chuo-Ku, Osaka 541 (tel (06) 22 3601)
New Zealand
15th Floor, Quay Tower, 29 Customs St West, Auckland 1 (tel (09) 79 9594)
Singapore
Suite 1703, United Square, 101 Thomson Rd, Singapore 1130 (tel 255 4555)
UK
4th Floor, 20 Saville Row, London W1X 1AE (tel (01) 734 1965)
USA
Suite 2130, 150 North Michigan Ave, Chicago, IL 60601 (tel (312) 781 5150)
Suite 1200, 2121 Avenue of the Stars, Los Angeles, CA 90067 (tel (213) 552 1988)
31st floor, 489 Fifth Ave, New York, NY 10017 (tel (212) 687 6300)
West Germany
Neue Mainzer Strasse 22, D6000 Frankfurt-Main 1 (tel (069) 23 5071)

Queensland Government Travel Centres

The Great Barrier Reef is entirely within the state of Queensland and no effort is spared to promote the state's greatest tourist attraction. The Queensland Government Travel Centres are primarily booking offices rather than information centres but you can still find out a great deal about the reef and its resorts. There are offices of the QGTC in a number of overseas countries and also in each state:

International offices:

Canada
Queensland Tourist & Travel Corporation, Suite 1730, 2 Bloor St West, Toronto, Ontario M4W 3E2 (tel (416) 922 2305)

France
Queensland Tourist & Travel Corporation, 16 Rue Pierret, F-92200 Neuilly sur Seine (tel 474 76215)
Japan
Queensland Tourist & Travel Corporation, Suite 1303, Yurakucho Denki Building North Wing, 7-1 Yurakucho 1 Chome, Chiyoda-ku, Tokyo 100 (tel (3) 214 4931-2)
New Zealand
Queensland Tourist & Travel Corporation, 9th floor, Key Tower, 29 Customs St West, Auckland 1 (tel (9) 39 6421)
Singapore
Queensland Tourist & Travel Corporation, 101 Thompson Rd, No 07-04, United Square, Singapore 1130 (tel 253 2811)
UK
Queensland Tourist & Travel Corporation, Queensland House, 392/3 Strand, London WC2R OLZ (tel (01) 836 1333)
USA
Queensland Tourist & Travel Corporation, Suite 2130, 150 North Michigan Ave, Chicago, IL 60601
Queensland Tourist & Travel Corporation, 611 North Larchmont Blvd, Los Angeles, CA 90004 (tel (213) 465 8418)
Queensland Tourist & Travel Corporation, 9th floor, 645 Fifth Ave, New York, NY 10022 (tel (212) 308 5520)
West Germany
Queensland Tourist & Travel Corporation, Post Box 330743, 8000 Munich 33

State offices:

Australian Capital Territory
Garema Place, Canberra City 2601 (tel (062) 48 8411)
New South Wales
516 Hunter St, Newcastle 2300 (tel (049) 26 2800)
75 Castlereagh St, Sydney 2000 (tel (02) 232 1788)
Queensland
corner Adelaide & Edward Sts, Brisbane 4000 (tel (07) 833 5337)
South Australia
10 Grenfell St, Adelaide 5000 (tel (08) 212 2399)
Victoria
257 Collins St, Melbourne 3000 (tel (03) 654 3866)
Western Australia
55 St George's Terrace, Perth 6000 (tel (09) 325 1600)

Queensland National Parks & Wildlife Service

Most of the Great Barrier Reef islands are completely or mostly national park and the 'on site' management is handled by the Queensland National Parks & Wildlife Service (QNPWS). They have interesting brochures and publications on many of the islands or on wildlife and plantlife found on and around the islands. The QNPWS also handle permits if you want to camp on a national park island and a complete list of the relevant offices will be found in the Camping section.

Great Barrier Reef Marine Park Authority

If the QNPWS looks after the islands then it's the Great Barrier Reef Marine Park Authority (GBRMPA) which looks after the water around the islands. In actual fact the division is not that straightforward and there's some overlap, and a great deal of cooperation, between the two organisations. The GBRMPA's aim is to increase understanding of the reef and ensure that we use it in the most enjoyable and least harmful fashion.

Other Sources

There are a host of other organisations which can provide information about the Great Barrier Reef. Many towns have local tourist offices which provide a great deal of information about local tourist facilities and actively promote their islands. The town tourist offices in Bundaberg and Gladstone are good examples of these local offices.

The two national domestic airlines have a great interest in the Great Barrier Reef because they bring many of the visitors to the reef and they own or are linked with a number of the resorts along the reef. In particular Australian Airlines owns Great Keppel, Bedarra, Dunk and Lizard while Ansett owns or has links with Hamilton, Hayman, South Molle and Hook. Finally the resorts themselves can tell you about their own facilities and attractions.

Reef flat, One Tree Island (MN)

GENERAL INFORMATION
Post

Australia's postal services are relatively efficient but not too cheap. All the resorts sell postcards and stamps and will handle incoming and outgoing mail. Hamilton, Magnetic and Thursday Islands actually have post offices.

Telephone

The resort reef islands generally are on the main trunk dialling network and calls can be dialled directly. Phone numbers given in this book include the area code (for example 079 for the Whitsunday area). Drop that code when calling within the area.

To call an Australian number from overseas dial the international access code (011 in the USA, 010 in the UK), then the Australia code (61), then the area code minus the 0 (so the Whitsundays would be 79) and finally the number.

To call overseas from Australia dial 0011 for the international access code, then the country code (1 for the USA, 44 for the UK, etc) and then the local area code (dropping the initial 0 on UK codes) and the number.

During the off peak calling time you can phone the USA for $1.80 a minute, the UK for $1.50 a minute. Calls made from island resort hotels are not subject to the extremely heavy surcharges which hotels commonly add in some countries. You can dial international calls yourself from pay phones which are equipped for ISD (international standard dialling). They take 20c, 50c and (most important) $1 coins.

Electricity

Electricity in Australia is 240 volts, 60 cycle. The resort islands all have electricity, usually provided through a generator. The sockets are three pin with the two live pins in a position that you can usually fit US two-prong plugs if you twist the prongs to the required angle. Some US plugs now have one prong longer than the other which may cause difficulties so if you're packing a bunch of electrical gadgets a converter plug may be a good idea. Don't try plugging 120 volt appliances into 240 volts even if the plug fits!

If you plan to camp out on the uninhabited islands bring some candles or a lamp.

Time

Australian Eastern Time is 10 hours ahead of GMT so when it is 12 noon on the Barrier Reef Islands it is 2 am in London and 6 pm the previous day on the US west coast.

There are three possible variations from that time difference:

Daylight Saving – Northern Hemisphere

During the northern hemisphere summer when the US or European countries are on daylight saving time the times are an hour closer – 12 noon on the reef is 3 am in London and 7 pm the previous day on the US west coast.

Daylight Saving – Southern Hemisphere

In the southern hemisphere summer the east coast is 11 hours ahead of GMT – 12 noon on the reef is 1 am in London, 5 pm the previous day on the US west coast.

Permanent Daylight Saving

One or two reef resorts like to differentiate themselves from the rest of Australia by pretending it's summer all year round. They're permanently on daylight saving.

HEALTH

So long as you have not visited an infected country in the past 14 days (aircraft refuelling stops do not count) no vaccinations are required for entry to Australia. Medical care in Australia is first-class and only moderately expensive. A typical visit to the doctor costs around $25. Health insurance cover is available in Australia, but there is usually a waiting period after you sign up before any claims can be made. A health and accident insurance policy is a wise investment.

Most of the resorts will have some sort of medical advice or a nursing sister available but only Hamilton and Magnetic are big enough to have a doctor. Serious medical problems will require returning to the mainland.

Health Insurance

A travel insurance policy to cover theft, loss and medical problems is a wise idea. There are a wide variety of policies and your travel agent will have recommendations. Check the small print: some policies specifically exclude 'dangerous activities' such as scuba diving; you may prefer a policy which pays doctors or hospitals direct rather than you having to pay now and claim later; check if the policy covers ambulances or emergency flights home.

Medical Kit

It's always a good idea to travel with a basic medical kit even when your destination is a country like Australia where most first aid supplies are readily available. Some of the items that should be included are: Band-Aids, a sterilised gauze bandage, Elastoplast, cotton wool, a thermometer, tweezers, scissors, antibiotic cream and ointment, an antiseptic agent, burn cream, insect repellent and multi-vitamins.

Don't forget any medication you're already taking, paracetamol or aspirin (for pain and fever) and contraceptives if necessary.

Health Precautions

There are no particular health precautions necessary to visit the Great Barrier Reef. It's in the tropics but malaria, endemic in Papua New Guinea just to the north of Australia, is not present in Australia. Nor are you likely to come up against any food or upset stomach problems on the reef resorts. The two main things to be careful about are probably the sun and the coral.

Travellers from the Northern Hemisphere need to be aware of the intensity of the sun in Australia. In these latitudes the sun can be fierce, and even on overcast days it's quite easy to get badly sunburnt. Australia also has a high incidence of skin cancer, a fact directly connected to exposure to the sun.

Apart from the dangers of the sun, turning lobster pink on your first day out is no way to have fun so remember to limit your exposure. Wear a T-shirt or some sort of covering if you're going to be out in the sun for too long, a hat to protect your face and a good sun protection lotion. Hats, caps and suntan lotion are all readily available from resort shops.

Don't think that lazing on the beach is the only way to get sunburnt. Snorkelling, for example, is an ideal way to burn your back. If you're going to be snorkelling for a prolonged period wear a T-shirt.

If you take the time to acclimatise, drink sufficient liquids, and avoid excessive alcohol and strenuous activity when you first arrive you can avoid the other health problems (such as heat stroke and heat exhaustion) associated with hot climates.

Finally, if you're out reef walking remember that coral is sharp; a pair of old running shoes will protect your feet and are much easier to walk in than thongs.

Marine Dangers

For some people coral reefs conjure visions of hungry sharks, fierce moray eels, stinging jellyfish and other aquatic menaces. In actual fact the dangers are slight and in most cases it's simply a matter of avoiding touching or picking up things which are best left alone! The basic rules of reef safety are:

1. Don't walk on reefs or in the shallow water between reefs without wearing shoes with strong soles.
2. Don't eat fish you don't know about.
3. Don't pick up cone shells.
4. Don't swim in murky water, try to swim in bright sunlight.

Sharks Hungry sharks are the usual idea of an aquatic nasty but on the Great Barrier Reef there are no shortage of meals which are far tastier and more conveniently bite size than humans. Tiger sharks and whaler sharks are found on the reef but generally on drop-offs from the outer reef. Sharks are a negligible danger.

Jellyfish Australia has a very dangerous jellyfish, the box jellyfish or sea wasp. Fortunately the chances of meeting this creature on the reef or islands is remote. It is chiefly found around river mouths or in other muddy, shallow water and only during the summer months. It is possible that a box jellyfish could drift out from the mainland to one of the closer islands but most unlikely.

Vinegar neutralises stinging cells which may have adhered to the skin but not actually fired. Don't peel off adhering tentacles, this will cause more of the stinging cells to fire. Death from a box jellyfish sting is due to respiratory arrest so keeping the victim breathing, if necessary through artificial respiration, is most important. Medical help should be sought as quickly as possible. An antivenom is available.

Butterfly Cod & Stonefish These two fish are closely related and have a series of poisonous spines down their back. The butterfly cod, also known as the lionfish or firefish, is

1	Blue-lined surgeonfish *Acanthurus lineatus*
2	Blue tang *Paracanthurus hepatus*
3	Damselfish
4	Clown anemone fish *Amphiprion percula*
5	Boxfish (female) *Ostracion solorensis*
6	Boxfish (male) *Ostracion solorensis*
7	Diagonal-banded sweetlips
8	Stonefish *Synanceia horrida*
9	Saddled butterfly fish/coral fish *Chaetodon ephippium*
10	Black-backed butterfly fish/coral fish *Chaetodon melannotus*
11	Cleaner Wrasse *Labroides dimidiatus*
12	Long-snouted butterfly fish/coral fish *Forcipiger longirostris*
13	Blue-barred parrotfish *Scarus ghobban*
14	Clown triggerfish *Balistoides conspicillum*
15	Coral Cod *Cephalopholis miniatus*
16	Fairy basslet *Anthias pleurotaenia*
17	Butterfly cod/firefish *Pterois antennata*
18	Blue-girdled angelfish *Pomacanthus navarchus*
19	Semicircle angelfish *Pomacanthus semicirculatus*
20	Moorish Idol *Zanclus cornutus*
21	Flutefish/Trumpet fish *Aulostoma chinensis*
22	Squirrelfish *Myripristis vittatus*
23	Harlequin tuskfish *Choerodon fasciatus*
24	Weedy Scorpion fish *Rhinopias frondosa*

an incredibly beautiful and slow moving creature – it knows it's deadly and doesn't worry about possible enemies. Even brushing against the spines can be painful but a stab from them could be fatal. Fortunately it's hard to miss a butterfly cod so unless you stepped on one or deliberately hit one the danger is remote.

Stonefish are the ugly sibling of the beautiful butterfly cod. They lie on the bottom, where they merge into the background. When stepped on their 13 sharp dorsal spines pop up and inject a venom that causes intense pain and can cause death. Fortunately stonefish are usually found in shallow, muddy water, but they can also be found on rocky and coral bottoms.

Wearing shoes with strong soles is the best protection but if you are unlucky, bathing the wound in very hot water reduces the pain and the effects of the venom. An antivenom is available and medical attention should be sought as the after effects can be very long lasting.

Cone Shells Cone shells kill their prey by firing a poisonous barb and several of them are so poisonous that they have caused human deaths. Although the barb is fired from the pointed end of the shell it's possible to get stung from any angle. The geographer cone is particularly dangerous. Cone shells are very pretty but any Great Barrier Reef shell, and particularly the cones shells, should be handled with great caution.

Pressure immobilisation, as for snake bites, is the recommended treatment. The affected limb should be tightly bound with bandages (not a tourniquet) and tied to a splint or in some way immobilised.

Blue-Ringed Octopus The blue-ringed octopus, which is found in a smaller southern variety and a large tropical type, can inflict a potentially deadly bite with their beak. The pretty little blue-ring is the world's only deadly octopus. To be bitten by an octopus you must first pick it up so the easy answer is don't do so! Unwary people, especially curious children, occasionally pick up octopuses which have been stranded in rock pools by the tide. The blue-ringed octopus is easily identified by the bright blue circles which appear when it is threatened.

Pressure immobilisation is the preferred treatment and medical attention should be sought as quickly as possible. The poison can result in respiratory failure so keeping the victim breathing is most important.

Fish Poisoning Man-bites-fish can be just as dangerous as fish-bites-man. Ciguatera poison is a poison which seems to accumulate in certain types of fish due to the consumption of certain types of algae by grazing fish. The poison seems to concentrate the further up the food chain it goes so it isn't the original algae-eating fish which poses the danger, it's the fish which eats the fish which eats the algae-eating fish! The danger is remote but erratic and recovery, although usually complete, is very slow. Chinaman-fish, red bass, large rock cods and moray eels have all been implicated.

Other fish are poisonous all the time. Don't consider dining on pufferfish unless you're a Japanese *fugu* fan.

Stingrays Stepping on stingrays is also not a good idea. They lie on sandy bottoms and if you step on one their barbed tail can whip up into your leg and cause a nasty, poisoned wound. Furthermore sand tends to drift over them so they can become all but invisible while basking on the bottom. Fortunately although they may be invisible to you, you are certainly not invisible to them and stingrays will usually wake up and zoom away as you approach. If you're out walking on the sort of shallow sandy surface which rays like it's wise to shuffle along and make some noise. Bathing the affected area in hot water is the best treatment and medical attention should be sought to ensure the wound is properly cleaned.

Sea Snakes Sea snakes are deadly poisonous and they have the scary habit of being extremely curious. The last thing one wants is something potentially fatal winding itself around your arm in order to sneak a peek inside your diving mask! Fortunately their curiosity is usually friendly rather than malevolent and people unfortunate enough to get bitten by sea snakes are usually fishers

who have pulled them out of the water, that's enough to make any sea creature see red.

Other Stinging Things Don't step on spiny sea urchins, the spines are long and sharp, break off easily and once embedded in your flesh are very difficult to remove! All coral is poisonous and brushing against fire coral or the feathery stinging hydroid can give you a surprisingly painful sting and an itchy rash which takes a long time to heal. Anemones are also poisonous and putting your arm into one can give you a painful sting. Leave them to the clown fish.

Coral Cuts The most likely Great Barrier Reef marine injury is the simple coral cut. Coral is nasty, sharp stuff and brushing up against it is likely to cause a cut or abrasion. Since coral kills its prey with poison you're likely to get some of that poison in the wound and tiny grains of broken coral are also likely to lodge there. The result is a small cut can take a long, long time to heal and be very painful in the process. The answer is to wash any coral cuts very thoroughly with fresh water and then treat them liberally with mercurochrome or some other antiseptic.

An even better answer is not to get cut by coral in the first place. Wear shoes to protect your feet if you're walking over coral. If you're diving remember that wet suits don't just keep scuba divers warm, they also protect them if they brush up against coral. A coral cut is also a two way thing, in cutting yourself you've probably damaged the coral. If you're swimming through a coral garden try not to blunder along, bumping into things and breaking off fragile branching coral.

Other Marine Dangers If you go out of your way looking for trouble it's certainly possible to find it and lots of fish will bite if you put your fingers in their mouths. Lots of scuba divers find this out when they're hand feeding fish but fortunately a bite from most small fish is nothing more than a playful nip. A bite from a moray eel is said to be a much more serious affair but eventually every Barrier Reef scuba diver seems to get the opportunity to tickle a friendly moray eel under the chin and they never seem to bite anybody.

FILM & PHOTOGRAPHY

There are lots of photographic possibilities on the Great Barrier Reef but also a number of photographic challenges. Light on the islands or out on the reef can often be very tricky. That time proven rule for photography in tropical light applies to the Queensland coast – you should shoot early or late as the sun is often high overhead between around 10 am and 3 pm and photos taken at that time tend to be flat or washed out. At the best of times exposure settings can be critical. It's very easy to end up with over-exposed photos and you should beware of backlighting from bright sunlight and of reflected light. A polaroid filter can work wonders when photographing over the sea.

At the other extreme, lack of light can also be a problem. On rainforest islands like Dunk or Hinchinbrook it can be remarkably gloomy in the forests and you will need a high-speed film for good results. The contrast between dark and light can also pose difficulties. If your picture has both brightly lit and shadowed areas you must often choose to correctly expose only one or the other.

Film is available at the resort islands but is generally expensive. In major cities Kodachrome or Fujichrome 36 exposure slide film including processing can be bought from around $12 a reel. If you're simply taking snapshots and want to see the results quickly a number of the larger resorts offer fast turn around photo developing.

Underwater Photography

Of course the urge to take underwater photographs is going to come upon many Great Barrier Reef snorkellers and divers. In recent years underwater photography has become a much easier activity. At one time it required complex and expensive equipment whereas now there are a variety of reasonably priced and easy to use underwater cameras available. Very often it's possible to rent cameras,

including underwater video cameras, from diving operators on the reef.

As with basic cameras above surface level the best photos taken with the simplest underwater cameras are likely to be straight-forward snapshots. You are not going to get superb photographs of fish and marine life with a small, cheap camera but on the other hand photos of your fellow snorkellers or divers can often be terrific.

More than with other types of photography the results achieved underwater can improve dramatically with equipment expenditure, particularly on artificial lighting. As you descend natural colours are quickly absorbed, starting with the red end of the spectrum. You can see the same result with a picture or poster that has been left in bright sunlight for too long, soon the colours fade until everything looks blue. It's the same underwater, the deeper you go the more blue things look. Red has virtually disappeared by the time you're 10 metres down. The human brain fools us to some extent by automatically compensating for this colour change, but the camera doesn't lie. If you are at any depth your pictures will look cold and blue.

To put the colour back in you need a flash and to work effectively underwater it has to be a much more powerful and complicated flash than above water. Thus newcomers to serious underwater photography soon find that having bought a Nikonos camera they have to lay out as much money again for flash equipment to go with it. With the right experience and equipment the results can be superb. Generally the Nikonos cameras work best with 28 or 35 mm lenses, longer lens do not work so well underwater. Although objects appear closer underwater with these short focal lengths you have to get close to achieve good results. Patience and practice will eventually enable you to move in close to otherwise wary fish. Underwater photography opens up whole new fields of interest to divers and the results can often be startling. Flash photography can reveal colours which simply aren't there for the naked eye.

Shells

Invertebrate creatures which inhabit shells are all in the group *Mollusca* although not all molluscs have shells. The group is a huge one including creatures as diverse as common garden snails at one extreme and octopus at the other. The variety found on the Great Barrier Reef is also immense and falls into several categories. *Chitons* or coat-of-mail shells are a small and ancient group. The huge variety of *Gastropods* or univalves includes most of the shells of interest to collectors and interested observers including cowries, cone shells, volutes and strombs. The third category is the bivalves such as oysters, scallops and clams. Finally there are *Cephalopoda* which includes octopus, squid, the pearly nautilus and cuttlefish.

Limited shell collecting, which the Great Barrier Reef Marine Park Authority defines as collecting of not more than five examples of a particular species in any 28 day period, is only permitted in areas of the Great Barrier Reef zoned General Use A or B. Many of the areas around national park islands on the reef where resorts are located are zoned Marine National Park A or B, where collecting is not permitted.

Cowries Cowrie shells are noted for their gently rounded shape, their beautiful patterns and their glossy surface. They are a firm favourite amongst amateur shell collectors but living examples are mainly seen at night, when they come out in search of food.

Volutes Volute shells are also brightly coloured and vary considerably in size. Like cowries they mainly emerge at night when they hunt bivalves and other molluscs. During daylight hours they usually bury themselves in the sand in coral lagoons although volutes can sometimes be seen crawling across the sandy bottom on dull days. The largest of the Great Barrier Reef volutes is the huge baler or melon shell which can weigh up to two kg and reach 40 cm in length. It takes its name from its use by Aboriginals as a water baler.

Cones Cone shells are also beautiful but it's a dangerous beauty as the cone can shoot out a barbed dart known as a radular tooth. A potent venom is then forced down this hollow tooth and although it is usually used to kill the carnivorous shell's prey cone shells have caused human deaths. *Conus geographus* is the particularly dangerous cone shell but all cone shells should be treated with great caution. In the case of a severe sting death comes from respiratory failure.

Strombs Strombs have a strong foot which is used to close off the shell opening when the creature is inside. The spider shell is a particularly popular stromb with collectors. ∎

Moorish Idol

Moray Eel

Cod Hole, outer reef near Lizard Island

Potato Cod

Underwater photos taken without a flash (TW)

ISLAND DESCRIPTIONS

The Barrier Reef has a great selection of islands and they're extremely variable in what they are and what they have to offer. Don't let the catchword 'reef island' suck you in. Only a few of the islands along the coast are real coral cays on the reef. Most of the popular resort islands are actually continental islands and some are well south of the Great Barrier Reef. It's not necessarily important since many of them will still have fringing reefs and in any case a bigger continental island will have other attractions that a tiny, dot-on-the-map coral cay is simply too small for – like hills to climb, bushwalks, and secluded beaches where you can get away from your fellow island-lovers.

The islands vary considerably in their accessibility – Magnetic Island is a short trip by a regular commuter ferry, some other islands are also reasonably close to the mainland while Lady Elliot and Lizard are a long

way out and in most cases have to be flown to. If you want to actually stay on an island rather than just day trip from the mainland that too can vary widely in cost.

If you want to stay on the islands the choice is generally between resorts or camping. Most visitors at the resorts will be staying on all-inclusive package deals. Many of the islands are national parks and have camping sites, a handful (Great Keppel and Dunk for example) have both resorts and camping sites. Some islands have proper sites with toilets and fresh water on tap while, at the other extreme, on some islands you'll even have to bring drinking water with you.

Viewing the Reef

The cheapest way to get a good look at the reef is to do a day trip from somewhere like Cairns, where the reef is relatively close to the coast. Other options are to go to one of the islands on a package deal which includes boat and snorkelling trips or take a one or two day island trip and make reef trips from there independently. See the Getting Around chapter for complete details on the mainland jumping-off points.

Resort Types

Active or passive seems to be the main division between the islands. Some emphasise running you ragged from dawn to long after dusk – this can range from diving and other watersports activities at islands like Lizard or Heron to assiduous pursuit of the opposite sex at young people's resorts like Great Keppel or the Contiki Long Island resort. Other resorts are passive with the emphasis on fine food and wine and luxurious accommodation – Hayman and Bedarra are good examples of this type of island. Of course every island is a bit of both, the whole idea of an island vacation entails some lazing on the beach and navel contemplation. Similarly nobody is going to get this close to the reef without at least thinking about strapping on a mask and snorkel and having a closer look.

There are two important considerations about the resorts – how you pay and what happens with children. Most of the resorts are all-inclusive – the daily tariff covers your room, all meals and most activities. Drinks and powered watersport activities are the usual extras but at Bedarra 'all-inclusive' really means that, even drinks, whether you have mineral water or Moet & Chandon, are included. Some resorts, however, are room only – everything else costs extra. Hamilton and Hayman, where you can really run up an impressive bill, are in this category.

Attitudes to children are ambivalent. Some, like Bedarra, ban them completely, others, like Lizard, place a minimum age limit on them. Most of them welcome them with open arms particularly during school vacation time when there will be a much wider variety of children's activities and programmes on tap. Lindeman even has a children's camp well away from the main resort area! It's surprising how even islands like Great Keppel, heavily promoted for young singles, becomes a family resort come school holiday time.

So what categories do islands fit into:

Diving Specialists Heron, Lady Elliot & Lizard

Rainforest Islands Bedarra, Dunk & Hinchinbrook

Young People's Great Keppel & Contiki Whitsunday on Long Island

Coral Cays Green, Heron & Lady Elliot

Activities for Kids Great Keppel, Hayman, Lindeman & South Molle

Small Resorts Bedarra, Hinchinbrook & Orpheus

Big Resorts Dunk, Great Keppel, Hamilton & South Molle

Exclusive & Expensive Bedarra, Hayman, Lizard & Orpheus

Mass Market Great Keppel & South Molle

Cheap & Cheerful Lady Elliot, Magnetic & Fitzroy

Good Food Bedarra, Hayman & Hinchinbrook

Cheap If you Camp Dunk, Great Keppel, Hinchinbrook, Magnetic, Hook & numerous islands without resorts

Best Beaches Great Keppel & Lizard

Resort Accommodation

Although the resort accommodation varies quite widely most of them emphasise 'getting away from it all' by not having too many telephones, radios, TVs or other contact with the outside world. At some resorts there may be only one or two phones on the entire island and if the office is shut then so is the phone.

Otherwise the usual amenities of an Australian hotel/motel are generally available. This means almost without exception every room will have tea and coffee making equipment plus supplies of tea and coffee. Many rooms will have a fridge (to keep the beer cold) and laundry facilities including irons are usually available.

Costs & Bookings Accommodation costs at the resorts vary widely from resort to resort and season to season. Mid-winter school holidays (June-July) is usually the peak cost time. Daily costs at the 'all-inclusive' resorts typically run from $150 per person per day at lower key resorts like Great Keppel or South Molle right up to $400 per day at Bedarra. Non-inclusive costs can range from $85 for a cabin on Fitzroy (and fix your own meals) to $255 to $450 for a room at Hayman Island (and with meals your costs can soon head towards the Bedarra level). Of course most visitors to these resorts will be on some sort of package deal including airfares.

At a number of resorts standby deals are an interesting possibility. Heron, South Molle, Daydream, Hamilton and Hinchinbrook Islands are some of the places offering standby rates during off peak periods. These are usually available only from agents in the mainland jumping-off points (Gladstone for Heron, Airlie Beach/Shute Harbour for the Whitsunday Islands). There will be various restrictions such as when bookings can be made and how long they can be made for, but the bottom line is often half price or less and very often including transfers to and from the island. If you just happen to be up the coast and fancy a few days on an island these deals can be worth watching out for.

Similarly, when business is slack on the reef, special packages are often offered in the southern capitals, seven days on island X at $Y including airfare from Sydney might be the deal.

Any cheap deal is, of course, only going to be available at the quiet times of year. At the other extreme, school holidays once again, you have to book well in advance. When a chill June wind blows over Melbourne and the kids are on school vacation many Barrier Reef resorts will be posting 100% occupancy rates. If you plan to visit the reef at that time of year *book ahead*.

Other Accommodation Alternatives

If your credit cards aren't strong enough to support resort living there are a number of alternatives, apart from camping. Great Keppel and Magnetic islands have youth hostels or backpackers' accommodation, while several other islands have cabins or permanent tents. Magnetic has a wide variety of hotels, motels and other accommodation.

Camping

While staying on the Barrier Reef islands costs some people hundreds of dollars a day others have just as good a time for only a few dollars. They're camping and there is an amazing variety of camping possibilities along the reef. Many of the islands are national parks and with a permit from the QNPWS (Queensland National Parks & Wildlife Service) you are able to camp on a wide variety of islands at minimal cost. A few islands have resorts and campsites. At Great Keppel, for example, you can camp for $8 a night and wander along to the resort to get wrecked in the Wreck Bar disco, just like the resort guests.

Camping facilities vary widely – sites like Great Keppel, Dunk or Fitzroy are just like mainland commercial camping sites with running water, flush toilets, shops and supplies. Others may have minimal facilities – perhaps just pit toilets and fresh water. Others may have virtually nothing at all – bring a shovel for toilet use and water for drinking.

The QNPWS make a number of suggestions and requests to campers. They include:

• pets are not allowed in the national parks

• do not interfere with the natural surroundings – do not harm wildlife or cut down vegetation

• if you can bring it in you can take it out, do not leave or bury rubbish

• if possible use a fuel stove – if you must have a fire use fireplaces provided and take extreme care

• remember that water is scarce on the islands – in places it is only found seasonally. Always bring sufficient water for your needs and a surplus to cover any emergencies or delays.

Camping is not allowed at all national park islands but on those where it is a permit is

Divers and crown-of-thorns starfish (GBRMPA)

required. The chart below details the possible camping islands or island groups, facilities offered and which QNPWS office handles permit requests. In some groups, like the Whitsundays, there are a great number of possible camping areas. See the island chapters for more details.

Islands from south to north:

Camping Islands	T	D	QNPWS
Capricornia			
Lady Musgrave Island	*		Rockhampton/ Gladstone
North West Island	*		Rockhampton/ Gladstone
Masthead & Tryon Islands	*		Rockhampton/ Gladstone
Keppel Group	*		Yeppoon
Cumberland Group			Seaforth
Whitsunday Islands			
Molle Group	*		Conway
Henning & Hook Islands, Repulse Group			Conway
Whitsunday & Thomas Islands	*		Conway
Orpheus Island	*		Ingham
Hinchinbrook Island	*	*	Cardwell/ Ingham
Family Islands			Cardwell
Dunk Island	*	*	Cardwell
Lizard Island Group	*	*	Cairns

T – toilets, D – drinking water, QNPWS – office for bookings & information

Permits for camping on national park islands are classified as A, B or C and cost $2 per person for the simplest, most spartan camping area (up to a maximum of $5 per site), or $5 and $7 per site at the better equipped areas. The permits should be applied for at least six and at most 12 weeks in advance. Since there are limits on the maximum number of campers at most islands, at peak times of year it's possible an island can be booked right out.

Enclose a stamped addressed envelope when applying for a permit and give the group leader's name and address, boat number if you have your own boat, number in the party, expected date of arrival and proposed length of stay and desired site or alternatives. If you've left it too late to apply in writing it's worth phoning the relevant office as, if there is still space, it may be possible to get a permit number over the phone.

The relevant Queensland National Parks & Wildlife Service offices are:

QNPWS
5th to 7th floor
MLC Centre
239 George St, Brisbane, Qld 4000
(PO Box 190, North Quay, Qld 4002)
(tel (07) 227 4111)

QNPWS
Central Regional Centre
Royal Bank Building
194 Quay St
Rockhampton, Qld 4700
(PO Box 1395, Rockhampton, Qld 4700)
(tel (079) 27 6511)

QNPWS
Gladstone District Office
Roseberry St
Gladstone, Qld 4680
(PO Box 315, Gladstone, Qld 4680)
(tel (079) 76 1621)

QNPWS
Keppel Islands-Capricorn Coast
Rosslyn Bay Harbour
Yeppoon, Qld 4703
(PO Box 770, Yeppoon, Qld 4703)
(tel (079) 33 6608)

QNPWS
Mackay District Office
64 Victoria St
Mackay, Qld 4740
(PO Box 623, Mackay, Qld 4740)
(tel (079) 57 6292)

QNPWS
Cape Hillsborough
MS 895, Seaforth, Qld 4741
(tel (079) 59 0410)

QNPWS
Northern Regional Centre
Marlow St
Pallarenda, Townsville, Qld 4810
(PO Box 5391, Townsville Mail Centre, Qld 4810)
(tel (077) 74 1411)

QNPWS
Great Barrier Reef Wonderland Office
Flinders St East
Townsville, Qld 4810
(tel (077) 21 2399)

QNPWS
Whitsunday District Office
Airlie Beach, Qld 4802
(PO Box 332, Airlie Beach, Qld 4802)
(tel (079) 46 9430)

QNPWS
Hinchinbrook District Office
2 Herbert St
Ingham, Qld 4850
(PO Box 1293, Ingham, Qld 4850)
(tel (077) 76 1700)

QNPWS
Cardwell Office
Bruce Highway
Cardwell, Qld 4816
(PO Box 74, Cardwell, Qld 4816)
(tel (070) 66 8601)

QNPWS
Far Northern Region
41 Esplanade
Cairns, Qld 4870
(PO Box 2066, Cairns, Qld 4870)
(tel (070) 51 9811)

QNPWS
Mission Beach Office
Garners Beach Rd
Mission Beach, Qld 4854
(PO Box 89, Mission Beach, Qld 4854)
(tel (070) 68 7183)

A problem with many of the national park camping islands is getting out to them. It's no problem on resort islands like Great Keppel or Dunk where transport is regular and reasonably priced but if you don't have your own boat it's more problematic on some other islands. In some cases there are regular day trips which can get you out to the islands, in the Whitsundays you can often arrange to be dropped off and later picked up from one of the regular 'moseying around the islands' day trips. On other islands the only way to do it may be by chartering a boat, in which case you'll probably want to get a group of people together in order to share the costs. There are more details under the individual islands.

FOOD & DRINK

With the exception of Hamilton and Magnetic Island, where accommodation is room only and there are a wide variety of restaurants to sample, the food situation on the islands usually follows two opposite extremes. Either you bring everything yourself (if you're camping out on an island for example) or everything is included in the price (most resort islands quote all-inclusive tariffs which include all your meals).

Food

Don't plan to lose weight on a reef resort visit. They feed you well. Breakfast will include fruit, cereals and a cooked breakfast too if you can manage it. At most larger resorts lunch will be help-yourself buffet style and at dinner time there'll be a four course meal.

Seafood Of course there will be some emphasis on fresh seafood although, surprisingly, the fish may not come from around your island getaway. It's likely that your island is zoned as part of the marine park where commercial fishing is not allowed. So while you may be able to catch a fish yourself and ask the chef to cook it for you the resort can't go out and catch one for all their guests. Nevertheless there will be seafood and it will be fresh.

Some seafood specialities you may encounter include barramundi, one of

Australia's best eating fishes – it's found in rivers in northern Australia. The coral trout is probably the best eating fish on the reef, and also one of the prettiest. Other popular fish caught along the reef include tuna, sweetlips, bream (pronounced *brim*) and mangrove jack.

A great number of prawns are caught along the Queensland coast, many of which are frozen and exported although a fair number are served up fresh. You'll see the prawn trawlers anchored off some reef resorts as they usually trawl by night and sleep by day. Moreton Bay is in the south of the state near Brisbane, and Moreton Bay *bugs* (what an off-putting name) are a sort of miniature lobster or giant-size prawn. They rarely get over 15 cm long but whatever size they're delicious and often feature on Queensland menus.

So do mud crabs, also known as mangrove crabs. These monsters can grow to a couple of kg and are indeed fond of mud. They've got big bodies, big claws and are very tasty. Americans reckon they're similar to the Dungeness crab of the San Francisco area.

Fruit Fresh Queensland fruit will often feature on the menu come dessert time and in recent years it's become much more interesting as a great deal of attention has been turned to growing exotic tropical fruits in north Queensland. The exotic tropical fruits found in South-East Asia take a long time to establish but many Australians have come back from Indonesia or Thailand with a taste for rambutans, mangosteens, custard apples and other strange delicacies and they're starting to appear in Queensland fruit salads. It certainly makes a difference to the great Australian dessert, the pavlova, a concoction of meringue, whipped cream and fruit.

Drink Resort bars will have a wide variety of Australian wines, champagnes and beers. The winelists usually include a good selection of popular Australian wines by the bottle or the glass.

Beer is a chauvinistic subject in Queensland and as well as the familiar 'southern' brands like Swan, VB and Fosters you'll also find Cairns NQ, Fourex and the new, and very popular, Powers. Boutique beers have also caught on in a big way in Australia and there are also popular specialist brands like Cascade and Redback. A cold beer goes down well after a hot day on the reef.

BOOKS & MAPS
Guides
For the complete story on the Barrier Reef's creatures and creations, liberally illustrated with a great number of superb colour plates the number one book is undoubtedly the *Reader's Digest Book of the Great Barrier Reef* (Reader's Digest, Surry Hills, 1984). This is not, however, a book to take with you to the islands to casually leaf through while lying on the beach. It's a hefty volume, nearly as big as the reef itself. Recently an abbreviated version of this book has also been produced. If you want the full story make sure you get the original.

The *Reader's Digest Guide to the Coast of Queensland* (Reader's Digest, Surry Hills, 1986) follows the coast from the New South Wales border to the top of Cape York and Torres Strait. There are aerial photographs of many areas of interest and numerous asides on everything from mangroves and crocodiles to how aerial photographs are taken.

100 Magic Miles of the Great Barrier Reef – The Whitsunday Islands by David Colfelt (Windward Publications, Sydney, 1985) concentrates on the Whitsunday area. This large format paperback guide could be subtitled 'everything you could possibly want to know about the Whitsundays'. There are photographs and articles on the resorts; features on diving, sailing, fishing, and even camping; natural history; an exhaustive collection of aerial photographs and charts; and descriptions of boat anchorages all around the islands.

David and Carolyn Colfelt also produced *Colfelt's Barrier Reef Traveller* (Windward Publications, Woodhill Mountain, 1989) with a complete run down on the reef resorts and many fine photographs.

Cruising the Coral Coast by Alan Lucas

(Horwitz Grahame, Sydney, 1988) is the complete sailing guide to the Queensland coast and the Great Barrier Reef. There are innumerable charts and photographs and a great deal of interesting advice for cruising yachties.

Discover the Great Barrier Reef Marine Park by Lesley Murdoch (Bay Books, Kensington, 1989) is a simple and colourful book on the reef, its creatures, its islands and the Great Barrier Reef Marine Park Authority. Although now out of print, *Great Barrier Reef – A Traveller's Companion* is a very useful publication written by Ron Walker in 1980, and produced by the Australian Tourist Commission.

Description & History

The Missing Coast – Queensland Takes Shape by J C H Gill (Queensland Museum, South Brisbane, 1988) is a fascinating account of the European exploration of the Queensland coast starting with the early Portuguese, Spanish and Dutch visitors and continuing with Cook, Bligh, Flinders and a colourful cast of less famous visitors.

The Book of Australian Islands is edited by Geoffrey Dutton (Macmillan, South Melbourne, 1986) and contains a series of essays on islands all around the coast of Australia. Reef islands covered are the Torres Strait Islands, Raine Island, Lizard Island and Dunk Island.

See the Dunk Island section for information on E J Banfield's classic *The Confessions of a Beachcomber* and Michael Noonan's fascinating biography of Banfield, *A Different Drummer*. Other books on individual islands or groups are covered in the relevant chapters.

Maps

The *Great Barrier Reef* by Travelog Maps is a handy 1:2,200,00 map of the whole reef. This same map, or a close variant of it, seems to appear in a number of publications on the reef. Travelog also produce *Whitsunday Passage*, a 1:100,000 map of the Whitsunday Islands. This is the best general tourist map of the Whitsundays. Sunmaps, the Queens-

land Government mapping organisation, have *Australia's Whitsundays*, a 1:150,000 map, but the Travelog map is superior.

Discovering Coastal Queensland (University of Queensland Press, St Lucia, 1988) is subtitled 'A Complete Guide to the Queensland Coast' but its principal value is as a reasonably large scale atlas of the coast.

ACTIVITIES

The resort islands along the reef have the whole range of typical resort activities from tennis and squash to windsurfing and sailing. There are also some fine bushwalking opportunities on a number of islands but snorkelling, scuba diving, reef walking and sailing are some of the Great Barrier Reef's major attractions.

Snorkelling

If you can swim then you can also snorkel and this is simply one of the best places in the world for this activity. Some islands are much better than others for snorkelling, at some there's virtually none to speak of while at others there's a wonderland waiting just a few steps out from the beach. Everywhere there will be snorkelling and diving trips on offer, however. Trips out to the outer reef will always offer an opportunity to do some snorkelling and scuba diving trips will often take snorkellers along as well.

If you've never tried snorkelling before you'll soon pick it up and many resorts give brief free snorkelling lessons in their swimming pools. Every resort will have snorkelling equipment which you can borrow or rent. Of course if you've got your own that certainly makes life somewhat easier and you won't face the risk of finding that you've got an odd-shaped face which most masks won't fit.

There are three pieces of equipment for snorkelling, each of which is also used for scuba diving:

Mask First and most essential there's the mask, this is what lets you see underwater. The reason you can't see underwater normally is that your eyes won't focus in water.

Fish eyes were designed to focus underwater, ours weren't. The mask introduces an air space in front of your eyes so you can focus and see just as well as the fish.

Masks cost anything from $10 to hundreds of dollars and as with most things you get what you pay for. Any mask, however, no matter how cheap, should have a shatterproof lens. That's the one essential to check before you try a mask on. Next you must make sure it fits and this is highly dependent on the shape of your face. Some people find almost any mask fits easily, others find oval masks fit better, others square. If the mask doesn't fit well it will gradually fill with water and you'll have to stop periodically to clear the water out which can be annoying. To check if a mask fits well simply fit it to your face but without the strap around the back of your head. Breathe in through your nose and the suction should hold the mask on your face if the fit is good.

If you're shortsighted and serious about snorkelling or scuba diving you can get the mask lens ground to your optical prescription or, rather easier, get stick-on optical lens to attach to the inside of the mask lens. If you wear contact lens you can wear these with a mask although there is the risk of losing them if your mask is accidentally flooded. Actually the altered focal length of light underwater often compensates quite well for shortsightedness. I wear glasses all the time but never miss them when underwater.

Snorkel With your mask on you can now see fine underwater but every time you want to breathe you must raise your head out of the water. This will be the instant that fish you were quietly observing shoots for cover. A snorkel lets you breathe with your face down in the water. It's simply a curved tube with a mouthpiece which you grip in your teeth. The tube curves round beside your head and you breathe in and out through your mouth. When you dive underwater the snorkel tube fills with water which you expel, once back on the surface, by simply blowing out forcefully. The snorkel tube has to be long enough to reach above the surface of the water but should not be either too long or too wide. If it is too big then you have more water to expel when you come to the surface and it's not pleasant to find that first gulp of fresh air is mostly seawater! Also, each breath out leaves a snorkel full of used air. Normally, this only slightly dilutes the fresh air you breathe in but if the snorkel is too big you could breathe in too large a proportion of carbon dioxide.

Fins The third part of a snorkeller's equipment is not absolutely necessary. If they're there it's always nice to have fins but if not you can still snorkel fine without them. As with masks, fin selection is very much a matter of personal preference. What fits and suits one person another person simply cannot get along with. Fins either fit completely over your foot or have an open back with a strap around your heel. The latter generally offer more adjustment and are more comfortable. If you're serious about your underwater activities then you should really buy fins in conjunction with wet suit boots. These make the fins more comfortable and fit better and can also be used for walking across reefs.

Diving

Scuba diving has always been a big attraction along the Great Barrier Reef but in recent years it has become simply enormous. There are diving schools right up and down the coast and most resorts have dive shops and offer diving courses. The main consideration with scuba diving is that it requires knowledge and care. You can sling a mask and snorkel on and be a snorkeller in minutes. Adding an air tank on your back and diving in is asking for trouble. If you want to take up scuba diving you should first complete a good diving course which leads to an approved diving certificate.

Although learning to scuba dive requires some application it is not difficult to learn and it does not require any sort of superhuman strength or fitness. In fact one thing you quickly learn is that doing things with the minimum expenditure of energy is what diving is about. Your diving time is limited by your tank of air and the more gently you do things the longer that air is going to last. It's remarkable how much longer the same tank of air will last with an experienced diver compared to a beginner. Women often have an advantage over men in this area, they don't breathe so much air!

Diving Courses Full time diving courses last about a week and typically cost around $250 to $350. A good course will have classroom instruction and underwater experience in a pool, followed by some real dives in the sea. The best way of finding out if the course is good is to ask somebody else who has done it. Resorts, with a reputation to protect, usually ensure their dive school operators know what they're about. If you're a backpacker making your way up the Queensland coast there are many dive schools, often loosely associated with the popular backpackers' hostels. Word of mouth should let you know which ones are good. Of course you can also learn about diving before you leave home. Diving courses in your hometown are likely to be part time rather than full time. I did my diving course in Melbourne, two nights (half class, half pool practice) a week for six weeks, followed by a solid weekend of classes and diving in the sea.

What do you learn in a diving course? One thousand ways to kill yourself underwater was one succinct description. Actually it's the reverse of that, a diving course should teach you to anticipate possible problems and avoid them. Much of the course is designed to drum into you things which have to become second nature when you're underwater – always keep breathing, don't hold your breath as you ascend, how to adjust your buoyancy; all these soon become straightforward techniques. Of course you also spend some time learning how to grapple with those tricky decompression tables.

Certificates The end result of your diving course is not just a basic knowledge of scuba diving it's also a certificate to prove you know it. A certificate is like a driving licence. You can't walk into a rent-a-car agency and rent a car without a driving licence, nor can you go out on a diving trip without a diving certificate. Once you have a recognised certificate, however, you'll be welcomed by diving operators all over the world. Certificates in Australia are generally issued by PADI (Professional Association of Diving Instructors) or FAUI (Federation of Australian Underwater Instructors). PADI is the largest and best known internationally but either certificate is quite acceptable.

As well as successfully completing the course you must have a diving medical examination before your certificate can be issued. Certain medical conditions, such as asthma, do not go with diving.

Don't let having a certificate lull you into thinking you know everything. Like any activity experience is vitally important. As well as your diving certificate every diver has a log book in which they should record every dive they make. If a proposed dive is deep or difficult a good dive operator should check your log book to ensure your experience is sufficient. A high proportion of diving accidents happen to inexperienced divers 'getting out of their depth'.

Equipment Dive operators can rent out all diving gear but most divers prefer to have at least some of their own equipment. The usual minimum is mask, snorkel, fins and boots. These are items for which most divers have personal preferences and are happiest using their own equipment. They are also relatively light and compact to pack.

Other necessary scuba diving equipment includes:

Air Cylinders – don't bother bringing your own.

Buoyancy Vest – readily available but some divers prefer to have their own.

Depth Gauge & Tank Pressure Gauge –

readily available but again some divers like their own familiar equipment.

Regulator – many divers like to have their own regulator with which they are familiar and confident.

Weight Belt & Weights – there is absolutely no reason to bring lead weights with you to the reef!

Wetsuit – the waters of the Great Barrier Reef may be warm but a wet suit is still necessary for comfortable diving, particularly in the southern part of the reef. Having a properly fitting wetsuit is also important, gushes of cold water rushing down your back are never comfortable. On the other hand a wetsuit is relatively bulky to carry around and if you normally dive in colder waters your regular suit may be too thick for the reef.

Walking on the Reef

A popular alternative to snorkelling or diving is to simply walk over a stretch of reef at low tide. Strolling across the reef is always a thrill but there are a number of precautions to be taken, both for your own safety and for the reef's. Some stretches of reef can be walked on straight from the islands, other areas of the main barrier reef can be reached by aircraft or boat.

The essential rules of reef walking:

• Take care of the reef – walk gently, try to avoid breaking fragile coral, replace any rocks that you move (that could be somebody's home you've shifted) and don't be a collector.

• Wear strong soled shoes – an old pair of sturdy runners are ideal – coral cuts can be difficult to heal, urchin spines are difficult to remove and you certainly don't want to find out what happens when you step on a stonefish. Ankle and leg protection is also a good idea since you can easily cut yourself by brushing against coral.

• Wear a hat, a shirt and sun protection – it's easy to get sunburnt.

• Take care at all times – watch for the turn of the tides, you may only be centimetres above sea level and tides can flood in rapidly;

be careful what you pick up, cone shells and the blue-ringed octopus are both venomous.

Sailing

Sailing is a popular Great Barrier Reef activity whether it's cruising the length of the reef in your own yacht, taking a turn round the bay in a resort catamaran or chartering a bareboat for a week. Bareboat means you rent the fully equipped boat which you then provision and sail yourself. The vast majority of bareboat chartering on the Great Barrier Reef is in the Whitsundays, see that chapter for more details.

THINGS TO BRING

Most of the resorts are very casual and few rules are made although at some of the more expensive resorts there is some dressing up for dinner. Otherwise dressing up usually means a change from swim suit to shorts and T-shirt. Most resorts specify shirts for men, no bare feet or thongs at dinner time and the like. Hayman actually suggests (but doesn't expect) jackets and ties in their fancier restaurants. Mainly Great Barrier Reef resort wear is cool and casual. Apart from not needing to wear very much almost all the resorts have laundry facilities so you can always wash clothes if necessary.

Come prepared for the tropical sun, however. A T-shirt to slip over a swimsuit – even when swimming if you're planning to do a lot of snorkelling – is a good idea. A hat and sunglasses will also provide some relief from the sun. Don't forget good sun protection lotion as well.

Bring comfortable sandals or thongs for times when the sand is too hot for comfort and if you plan to do much walking then running shoes will be necessary. An old pair of running shoes are also essential for reef walking – walking on the reef barefoot is neither comfortable or safe.

Most of the year even in the evenings you're unlikely to need anything as warm as a long sleeve shirt. If you are visiting the reef in mid-winter (June to August) particularly further south, then a sweater or light jacket will probably be a good idea for the occasional chilly evening. If you're there in the middle of the summer rainy season be prepared for lots of rain. You might want an umbrella or even a waterproof poncho, particularly on wet rainforest islands like Hinchinbrook or Dunk.

THINGS TO BUY

Resort stores generally have toiletries, suntan lotion, insect repellent, magazines, books, film, souvenirs and the like. Although most of those essential but easily forgotten items are there they are also generally rather more expensive than on the mainland.

If you need a souvenir of the islands the resort T-shirts are probably the best buys. There's usually a boutique or at least a boutique section in the resort stores and they often have an excellent selection of summery clothes and swimgear. Surprisingly the prices are often not too outrageous and if you need a new swimsuit you may well find the choice is better than back home. Shells, shell jewellery and coral jewellery are sold at many resorts. With strict regulations about shell collecting you can be sure they have been properly collected but, nevertheless, shells are still best left in the sea.

Coral Cays

Coral cays are low islands, formed by the growth of a coral reef and the collection of debris from the reef. This entirely natural creation of new land is a fascinating story.

As a reef grows it eventually forms a reef flat which breaks the surface of the water at low tide. The coral cannot continue to grow above water level as coral has to be covered by water to survive although coral can survie a few hours out of water at low tide. Waves break off sticks of branching coral and storms may cause more widespread destruction. This coral debris collects on the reef flat and if the prevailing wave action piles up debris in a particular area of the reef flat, an island, continually above sea level, is gradually formed.

At this stage the island is a very fragile creation. A severe storm or cyclone can scatter the collected material across the flat and it may be years before regular wave action again collects it in one area. Gradually wave action grinds the debris down to create shingle and sand and eventually a sand cay forms. This is usually very unstable and shifts back and forth around the reef as weather conditions alter. There are over 200 totally unvegetated sand cays along the Great Barrier Reef.

Gradually the sand cay stabilises and once it is consistently above water level seabirds start to nest on it. Hardy plants now start to grow on the sand, some washed ashore, others transported by the birds either stuck to their

feathers or in their digestive tracts. This early and limited vegetation adds to the cay's stability and decaying vegetable matter and bird droppings start to change the sand into a richer soil, providing a suitable environment for a wider range of plant life. Even at this stage cays are not truly stable and a particularly severe cyclone can wipe them out. There are 65 vegetated sand cays along the Great Barrier Reef.

Cays are not uniformly distributed along the reef. Vegetated sand cays are only found in the south, particularly in the Capricorn-Bunker Groups, and in the north, starting with Green Island off Cairns. For over 600 km in the central section of the Great Barrier Reef there are no vegetated sand cays at all. The great tidal variation here may well be a factor – wave action at one tide level may move debris to one area, only for the action at another level to move it somewhere else. Cyclones in this region are also more severe than further north or further south and are therefore more likely to scatter whatever debris has built up.

Only in the south are vegetated shingle cays found; these require stronger but consistent ocean swells to move the larger coral debris. On the other hand low wooded islands are only found north of Cairns. On these a leeward sand cay and shingle ridges around the edge of the reef flat combine to create a central reef area where mangroves can grow. The Low Isles off Port Douglas are a good example of this pattern. All the Great Barrier Reef coral cays are comparatively young in the geological sense as it was only about 6000 years ago that sea level stabilised at about its present level and the development of cays could commence. ∎

Getting There & Away

Getting to the Barrier Reef islands may involve two moves – from overseas to Australia and then from within Australia to the various jumping-off points to the reef islands. You can fly directly from overseas to two major reef jumping-off points – Cairns and Townsville – but other places will require further travel within Australia.

To Australia

Basically getting to Australia means flying. Once upon a time the traditional transport between Europe and Australia was by ship but those days have ended. Infrequent and expensive cruise ships apart, there are no regular shipping services to Australia. It is, however, sometimes possible to hitch a ride on a yacht to or from Australia, you'll certainly see plenty of cruising yachts sailing through the Great Barrier Reef.

Australia is a long way from anywhere. Coming from Asia, Europe or North America there are lots of competing airlines and a wide variety of airfares but there's no way you can get around those great distances. If you want to fly to Australia at a particularly popular time of year (the middle of summer, ie Christmas time, is notoriously difficult) or on a particularly popular route (like Hong Kong/Sydney) then plan well ahead.

Australia has a large number of international gateways but if you're heading for the reef the most convenient ones will be Cairns or Townsville, right on the reef coast, followed by Brisbane, the capital of the state of Queensland, and then Sydney. Although Sydney is Australia's busiest gateway it makes a lot of sense to avoid arriving or departing there. Sydney's airport is stretched way beyond its capacity and flights are frequently delayed on arrival and departure. Furthermore the customs and immigration facilities are cramped, crowded and too small

for the current visitor flow so even after you've finally landed you may face further long delays. If you can organise your flights to avoid Sydney it's a wise idea.

Discount Tickets

Buying airline tickets these days is like shopping for a car, a stereo or a camera – five different travel agents will quote you five different prices. Rule number one if you're looking for a cheap ticket is to go to an agent not directly to the airline. The airline can only quote you the absolutely straight-up-and-down, by-the-rulebook regular fare. An agent, on the other hand, can offer all sorts of special deals particularly on competitive routes.

Ideally an airline would like to fly all their flights with every seat in use and every passenger paying the highest fare possible. Fortunately life usually isn't like that and airlines would rather have a half price passenger than an empty seat. Since the airline itself can't very well offer seats at two different prices what they do when faced with the problem of too many seats is let agents sell them at cut prices.

Of course what's available and what it costs depends on what time of year it is, what route you're flying and who you're flying with. If you want to go to Australia at the most popular time of year, on one of the very popular routes or via a route where there is little alternative competition you are likely to have to pay more. Similarly the dirt cheap fares are likely to be less conveniently scheduled, go by a less convenient route or be with a less popular airline.

FROM EUROPE

The cheapest tickets in London are from the numerous 'bucket shops' (discount ticket agencies) which advertise in magazines and papers like *Time Out* or *Australasian Express*. Pick up one or two of these publications and ring round a few bucket shops to

Harlequin tusk-fish (GBRMPA)

find the best deal. The magazine *Business Traveller* also has a great deal of good advice on airfare bargains. Most bucket shops are trustworthy and reliable but the occasional sharp operator appears – *Time Out* and *Business Traveller* give some useful advice on precautions to take.

Trailfinders (tel (01) 938-3366) at 46 Earls Court Rd, London W8 and STA Travel (tel (01) 581-1022) at 74 Old Brompton Rd, London SW7 and 117 Euston Rd, London NW1 are good reliable agents for cheap tickets.

The cheapest flights from London to the east coast are about £425 one-way or £650 return. Such prices are usually only available if you leave London in the low season, March to June. In September and mid-December fares go up about 30% while the rest of the year they're somewhere in between.

Many cheap tickets allow stopovers on the way to or from Australia. Rules regarding how many stopovers you can take, how long you can stay away, how far in advance you have to decide your return date and so on, vary from time to time and ticket to ticket, but recently most return tickets have allowed you to stay away for any period between 14 days and one year, with stopovers permitted anywhere along your route. As usual with heavily discounted tickets the less you pay the less you get in terms of convenience and popular airlines.

Regular by-the-book fares are around £650 one-way or from £1000 return but there are all sorts of ticketing variations and rules including advance purchase periods, seasonal variations in fare and so on.

FROM NORTH AMERICA

There are a variety of connections across the Pacific from Los Angeles, San Francisco and Vancouver to Australia including direct flights, flights via New Zealand, island hopping routes or more circuitous Pacific rim routes via nations in Asia. Qantas, Air

New Zealand, American, United and Continental all have USA/Australia flights, Qantas and Canadian Airlines International operate Canada/Australia.

One advantage of flying Qantas or Air New Zealand rather than Continental or United is that if your flight goes via Hawaii the west coast to Hawaii sector is not treated as a domestic flight as it is by the US airlines. This means that you don't have to pay for drinks and headsets because it is still an international sector. Furthermore when coming in through Hawaii from Australasia it's not unknown for passengers who take a long time clearing customs to be left behind by the US airline and have to take the next service!

To find good fares to Australia check the travel ads in the Sunday travel sections of papers like the *Los Angeles Times, San Francisco Chronicle-Examiner, New York Times* or *Toronto Globe & Mail*. The straightforward return excursion fare from the US west coast is around US$1000 to US$1500 depending on the season but plenty of deals are available. You can typically get a one-way ticket from US$500 west coast or US$550 east coast, returns from US$800 west coast or US$900 east coast. At peak seasons – particularly the Australian summer – seats will be harder to get and the price will probably be higher.

In the US good agents for discounted tickets are the two student travel operators Council Travel and STA, both of which have offices around the country. Canadian west coast fares out of Vancouver will be similar to the US west coast. From Toronto fares go from around C$1500 return.

FROM NEW ZEALAND

Air New Zealand and Qantas operate a network of trans-Tasman flights linking Auckland, Wellington and Christchurch in New Zealand with most major Australian gateway cities. You can fly directly between a lot of places in New Zealand and a lot of places in Australia including directly to the Barrier Reef gateways of Cairns and Townsville.

Fares vary depending on which cities you fly between and when you do it but from New Zealand to Sydney you're looking at NZ$600 to NZ$800 return. One way fares are not much cheaper than return but there is a lot of competition on this route – with United, Continental and British Airways all flying it as well as Qantas and Air New Zealand, so there is bound to be some good discounting going on.

FROM ASIA

Ticket discounting is widespread in Asia, particularly in Singapore, Hong Kong (currently the discounting capital), Bangkok and Penang. There are a lot of fly-by-nights in the Asian ticketing scene so a little care is required. Also the Asian routes have been particularly caught up in the capacity shortages on flights to Australia. Flights between Hong Kong and Australia are notoriously heavily booked while flights to or from Bangkok and Singapore are often part of the longer Europe-Australia route so they are also sometimes very full. Plan ahead.

Typical one-way fares to Australia from Asia include from Hong Kong for around HK$2750 (US$370) or from Singapore for around S$600 (US$300). These fares are to the east coast capitals although Brisbane and Cairns are sometimes a bit cheaper.

FROM AFRICA & SOUTH AMERICA

The flight possibilities from these continents are not so varied and you're much more likely to have to pay the full fare. There is only one direct flight between Africa and Australia and that is the Qantas Harare (Zimbabwe)/Perth/Sydney route. An alternative from East Africa is to fly from Nairobi to India and South-East Asia and connect from there to Australia.

Two routes now operate between South America and Australia. The long running Chile connection involves a Lan Chile flight Santiago/Easter Island/Tahiti from where you fly Qantas or another airline to Australia. Alternatively Aerolíneas Argentina now has a Buenos Aires/Auckland/Sydney route across the Antarctic. This is operated in conjunction with Qantas and eventually Qantas may also fly on this route.

ROUND-THE-WORLD-TICKETS

Round-the-world tickets have become very popular in the last few years and many of these will take you through Australia. The airline RTW (Round-the-World) tickets are often real bargains and since Australia is pretty much at the other side of the world from Europe or North America it can work out no more expensive or even cheaper to keep going in the same direction right round the world rather than U-turn when you return.

The official airline RTW tickets are put together, usually by a combination of two airlines, and permit you to fly anywhere you want on their route systems so long as you do not backtrack. Other restrictions are that you (usually) must book the first sector in advance and cancellation penalties then apply. There may be restrictions on how many stops you are permitted and usually the tickets are valid for from 90 days up to a year. RTW packages that include Australia are Air New Zealand with Cathay Pacific, Thai International or Singapore Airlines; Qantas with TWA, Pan Am, Delta or American Airlines; Continental with Cathay Pacific or Malaysian Airlines; Canadian Airlines International with Philippine Airlines, Alitalia or Cathay Pacific.

Typical prices for these South Pacific RTW tickets are £1400 to £1700 or US$2500 to US$3000. An alternative type of RTW ticket is one put together by a travel agent using a combination of discounted tickets. A UK agent like Trailfinders can put together interesting London to London RTW combinations including Australia for £850 to £1000.

CIRCLE PACIFIC TICKETS

Circle Pacific fares are a similar idea to RTW tickets which use a combination of airlines to circle the Pacific – combining Australia, New Zealand, North America and Asia. Examples would be Continental-Thai International, Qantas-Northwest Orient, Canadian Airlines International-Cathay Pacific and so on. As with RTW tickets there are advance purchase restrictions and limits to how many stopovers you can take. Typically fares range between US$1500 and US$2000. A possible Circle Pacific route would fly Los Angeles/Honolulu/Auckland/Sydney/Bangkok/Hong Kong/Los Angeles.

ARRIVING & DEPARTING
Arriving in Australia

Australia's dramatic increase in visitor arrivals has caused some severe bottlenecks at the entry points, particularly at Sydney where the airport is often operating at more than full capacity and delays on arrival or departure are frequent. Even when you're on the ground it can take ages to get through immigration and customs. One answer to this problem is to try not to arrive in Australia at Sydney, particularly if you are heading straight to the reef.

There is generally an airport bus service at the international airports and there are always taxis available.

Leaving Australia

When you finally go remember to keep $10 aside for the departure tax.

To Queensland & the Reef

Having arrived in Australia you then have to make your way to the jumping-off points from where you go out to the reef islands. There are five major coastal towns from where you transfer to the islands plus a number of lesser starting points. The major centres are, from south to north, Rockhampton, Mackay, Proserpine, Townsville and Cairns. You can fly to all of these centres and they can also be reached by car, bus or rail. In addition there is one island, Hamilton in the Whitsundays, with a large airstrip and flights from other major centres. Hamilton will eventually have direct international flights as well.

AIR

Australia's two major domestic airlines, Australian Airlines and Ansett, both connect the main coastal centres with other major cities in Australia and Ansett also has direct flights to Hamilton Island. You can usually book connecting flights from these arrival ports directly to many of the reef islands. See the following Getting Around chapter for information about transport from the coastal cities to the islands.

Addresses of Ansett and Australian Airlines in major Australian cities and at the reef entry point cities are:

Adelaide, South Australia
    Ansett, 150 North Terrace (tel (08) 212 1111)
    Australian Airlines, 144 North Terrace (tel (08) 217 3333)
Alice Springs, Northern Territory
    Ansett, corner Todd & Parsons Sts (tel (089) 52 4455)
    Australian Airlines, corner Todd & Parsons Sts (tel (089) 50 5222)
Brisbane, Queensland
    Ansett, corner Queen & George Sts (tel (07) 854 2222)
    Australian Airlines, 247 Adelaide St (tel (07) 223 3333)
Cairns, Queensland
    Ansett, 84 Lake St (tel (070) 51 3366)
    Australian Airlines, corner Shield & Lakes Sts (tel (070) 50 3777)
Canberra, Australian Capital Territory
    Ansett, 4 Mort St (tel (062) 45 1111)
    Australian Airlines, The Jolimont Tourist Centre, corner Northbourne Ave & Alinga St (tel (062) 68 3333)

Darwin, Northern Territory
    Ansett, Shop 14, Smith St Mall (tel (089) 80 3333)
    Australian Airlines, 16 Bennett St (tel (089) 68 3333)
Hobart, Tasmania
    Ansett, 178 Liverpool St (tel (002) 38 1111)
    Australian Airlines, 4 Liverpool St (tel (002) 38 3333)
Mackay, Queensland
    Ansett, 99 Victoria St (tel (079) 57 1555)
    Australian Airlines, 105-109 Victoria St (tel (079) 57 1444)
Melbourne, Victoria
    Ansett, corner Swanston & Franklin Sts (tel (03) 668 2222)
    Australian Airlines, 50 Franklin St (tel (03) 665 3333)
Perth, Western Australia
    Ansett, corner St George's Terrace & Irwin St (tel (09) 323 1111)
    Australian Airlines, 55 St George's Terrace (tel (09) 323 3333)
Proserpine, Queensland
    Ansett, 40 Main St (tel (079) 45 1133)
    Australian Airlines, Shute Harbour Rd, Airlie Beach (tel (079) 46 6273)
Rockhampton, Queensland
    Ansett, 137 East St (tel (079) 31 0755)
    Australian Airlines, 75 East St (tel (079) 31 0555)
Sydney, New South Wales
    Ansett, Oxford Square, corner Oxford & Riley Sts (tel (02) 268 1111)
    Australian Airlines, corner Hunter & Phillip Sts, Chifley Square (tel (02) 693 3333)
Townsville, Queensland
    Ansett, 350 Flinders Mall (tel (077) 81 6666)
    Australian Airlines, Townsville International Hotel, Flinders Mall (tel (077) 81 6222)

Airfares are identical on Ansett or Australian Airlines. Regular economy one-way fares to the coastal entry point cities from other major centres are:

One Way Airfares					
	Cairns	Mackay	Proserpine	Rockhampton	Townsville
Adelaide	382	337	345	315	358
Alice Springs	248	420	427	404	244
Brisbane	241	170	182	133	206
Canberra	320	281	290	255	291
Darwin	277	427	303	410	300
Hobart	403	366	373	347	379
Melbourne	358	317	325	294	332
Perth	412	484	491	468	427
Sydney	299	257	267	229	269

The fares above are the straightforward economy one-way fares but a variety of other fares are also available. You can pay more and fly business class or there are a variety of discount fares available. If you're travelling on a package deal to one of the island resorts you can get a 25% discount, except at certain times of year, so long as you stay at least seven days. Other discount deals in brief are:

Flexi Fare (Ansett) or Excursion 45 (Australian Airlines)

An advance purchase fare where you nominate the day of flight but the actual flight you will take is only revealed shortly before the date of departure. Various penalties and restrictions and a 45% discount on the round trip.

Apex

Book and pay 30 days in advance, stay away a week and get a 35% discount.

Standby

If there's a seat available at departure time you get a 20% discount on it.

Groups

Ten or more adults travelling together get a 15% discount.

Children

Up to age three they travel free on your knee, under 15 they travel at half fare.

Students

Secondary school students aged 15 to 18 get 50% discount, post secondary school students under 26 including overseas students can get a 25% discount.

There are also Airpasses available which allow 6000 km travel for $600 or 10,000 km for $950. Overseas visitors can get a See Australia ticket discount of 30% on the regular airfare with certain restrictions and there's a slight variation on the Airpass also available to overseas visitors. Overseas visitors can also use Qantas flights on certain domestic sectors.

BUS

Competition between Australia's bus lines has been fierce and there are a number of companies offering regular services right up the east coast all the way to Cairns. If you're going to be visiting a number of islands some of these services may well be useful to get from one coastal jumping-off point to another.

Because of the intense competition on the interstate routes the fares are quite variable. Approximate fares and travel times to Brisbane include from: Sydney $35 to $50, 15 to 16 hours; Melbourne $80 to $100, 20 to 25 hours; Adelaide $120 to $140, 26 to 32 hours. See the Getting Around chapter for information on bus travel up the coast.

TRAIN

You can also get to Brisbane by train. State booking office phone numbers are NSW (02) 217 8812, South Australia (08) 217 4455, Victoria (03) 620 0771 and Western Australia (09) 326 2222. The fare from Sydney is about $80 in economy, $120 in 1st class or $160 for a 1st class sleeping berth.

Sex & Fish

Nobody ever told reef fish those nice straightforward 'birds and the bees' stories – a high proportion of the fish you see around the Barrier Reef are able to change their sex at some time in their life! Some of them are *protandry* – they start as males then switch to become females – others are *protogyny* – they start as females and switch to become males. Some of these fish are *monandric*, that is they are all born one sex and only switch to the other sex later. Other species may be born either sex but some of them may later change sex.

The tiny blue and gold angelfish is an example of *protogyny*. These fish normally live in small groups of four to seven which control a territory of several square metres. The group usually consists of one larger dominant male with a 'harem' of female fish although there may sometimes be a smaller 'bachelor' male fish present. The dominant male guards the group's territory and warns off any intruding angelfish. At mating time the male mates with all the females in the group. If the dominant male dies the largest female changes sex and takes over. It appears to be the dominant male which prevents females from changing sex earlier. The male 'dominates' and harasses the larger females and somehow this affects their hormone balance and prevents them changing sex. As soon as the male is removed the largest and most aggressive female is able to switch sexes and start in on dominating her sisters!

The opposite situation can be observed in the familiar clown anemone fish. The small group which shelters around a protective anemone usually consists of a large adult female and a group of smaller males. The female mates with only one of the males and this mature male fish keeps all the other 'bachelor' anemone fish in line. If something happens to the female then the chief male switches sex and becomes the new female while the most dominant and aggressive of the other males takes over as the new chief male.

Scientists have postulated a number of reasons for this strange state of affairs. Life on the reef is dangerous and very much dog eat dog. If changing sex were not possible and the sole male or female in the group dies then the group cannot reproduce. As it is there's just a quick change of sex on the part of one fish and life continues as normal! Competition on the reef is fierce and by staking out their own small territory and defending it against intruders the small groups of fish ensure their own survival. ■

Clown fish (GBRMPA)

Getting Around

Having arrived in Queensland you then have to get out to your island which usually means getting to the appropriate mainland jumping-off point. There are very few direct connections from one reef island to another, you will almost always have to go back to the mainland and on to the next mainland departure point. Specific information on transport to each island is with the relevant chapter, an overview follows.

AIRLINES
Hamilton Island in the Whitsundays has an airport capable of taking Boeing 767s and similar size widebody jets. This is the one island you can fly directly to from a state capital city and Ansett has direct connections with major centres around Australia, mostly via Brisbane but including some direct flights to and from Sydney and Melbourne.

Other airlines useful for getting to the mainland jumping off points or out to the reef islands include:

Australian Regional Airlines
Australian Regional Airlines operates De Havilland Twin Otters to Brampton, Dunk and Lizard. Bookings are made through Australian Airlines.

Seair Pacific
Seair Pacific operates amphibious aircraft and Britten-Norman Islanders. Their services connect Cairns, Mackay, Proserpine, Townsville and Whitsunday (Shute Harbour) to Hayman, Hinchinbrook, Lindeman and Orpheus Islands. Lindeman has an airstrip but the other islands are serviced with the amphibious aircraft. Phone Whitsunday (tel (079) 46 9133) or Townsville (tel (077) 25 1470) for flight details.

Sunstate
Sunstate fly from Brisbane to Bundaberg and Gladstone, the jumping-off points for Lady Elliot and Heron Islands respectively. They operate flights out to Lady Elliot and also to Great Keppel from Rockhampton. For information on Sunstate contact Australian Airlines or phone (04) 860 4577 in Brisbane.

Sunbird
Sunbird Airlines fly from Cairns to Cooktown, Thursday Island and numerous other destinations in far north Queensland including many islands in the Torres Strait. Phone (070) 53 4899 in Cairns for details.

BUSES
A number of bus lines operate up and down the coast between Brisbane and Cairns. Travel times and approximate fares from Brisbane up the coast are:

Brisbane/Bundaberg	6 hrs	$45
Bundaberg/Rockhampton	3½ hrs	$45
Rockhampton/Mackay	3¾ hrs	$40
Mackay/Proserpine	1½ hrs	$25
Proserpine/Townsville	3 hrs	$40
Townsville/Cairns	4½ hrs	$40

TRAIN
There's a rail service from Brisbane up the coast to Cairns. The trains are slower than buses but the fares are about the same if you travel by economy class. The trains are almost all air-con and you can get sleeping berths on most trains for $17 a night in economy or $29 in 1st class.

DRIVING
The Bruce Highway, which runs 1728 km from Brisbane to Cairns, is a good well-surfaced road and driving along the Great Barrier Reef coast presents no problems or surprises. Unfortunately the road very rarely runs right on the coast and some of the towns which act as jumping-off points for the reef are actually some distance off the main road.

Rental cars are available from the major nationwide operators like Avis, Budget, Hertz and Thrifty at all the main centres as well as at tourist centres like Airlie Beach. You can rent cars on a one-way basis with the major operators. Usually there is no repositioning charge so long as a minimum rental period of three days applies.

BOATS
Boat services operate out to the reef islands and the reef itself from towns up and down the coast. High-speed catamarans have become the standard transport for most reef resort transfers.

DEPARTURE POINTS
Moving up the coast from south to north the main jumping-off points for the Great Barrier Reef islands are:

Bundaberg
Bundaberg is 378 km north of Brisbane by road and there are regular Sunstate flights Brisbane/Maryborough/Bundaberg/Gladstone. From Bundaberg day trips are made out to Lady Musgrave Island and there are flights to Lady Elliot, the southernmost of the Great Barrier Reef islands.

Gladstone
Gladstone is 547 km north of Brisbane and the same Sunstate flight from Brisbane to Bundaberg continues on to Gladstone. From Gladstone there are regular high-speed catamaran services and helicopters to Heron Island. Day trips are made on the same catamaran to adjoining Wistari Reef, and Gladstone is also a good base to set out on camping trips to other islands in the Southern Reef group.

Rockhampton/Yeppoon
Rocky is 651 km north of Brisbane and is connected by regular Ansett and Australian Airlines flights. From Rockhampton there are flights out to Great Keppel Island or you can transfer there by any of a variety of boats operating from Rosslyn Bay, just south of Yeppoon. Yeppoon is 40 km from Rockhampton, on the coast. Day trips are made from Rosslyn Bay to Great Keppel and to

reefs in the northern part of the Southern Reef group.

Mackay
Mackay is 988 km north of Brisbane and has regular Ansett and Australian Airlines flights. From here flights operate to Brampton, Lindeman and Hamilton Islands. There are also catamaran services from Mackay to Brampton both for resort guests and day trippers. Other day trips out of Mackay with Roylen Cruises (tel (079) 55 3066) go to Hamilton and to Credlin Reef with snorkelling and scuba diving facilities available. Longer five-day trips around the Whitsundays and out to the reef are also available.

Proserpine/Airlie Beach/Shute Harbour
Proserpine was the main airport for the Whitsundays before Hamilton Island's airport opened. Now people flying to the Whitsundays usually go directly to Hamilton Island and since Ansett has an interest in Hamilton Island's airport Australian Airlines has been rather left out in the cold. Proserpine is 1114 km north of Brisbane and it's another 25 km to Airlie Beach and 10 km from there to Shute Harbour right on the coast.

Airlie Beach is the 'dormitory suburb' for the Whitsundays and here you can find cheap accommodation, book day trips to the Whitsundays or the outer reef or enquire about standby accommodation deals at the Whitsunday resorts. Finally Shute Harbour is where the various transfer boats operate out to the Whitsunday resorts, where the day trip boats depart from and where the Whitsunday's burgeoning bareboat operators are based. Just before Shute Harbour is the Queensland National Parks & Wildlife Service office where you go for camping permits for the Whitsunday Islands. The small Whitsunday airstrip is also just before Shute Harbour and from here light aircraft and amphibious aircraft operate out to resorts and the reef.

Townsville

Townsville is 1379 km north of Brisbane and has Ansett and Australian Airlines flights as well as international connections. The town is the jumping-off point for Magnetic, Orpheus, Hinchinbrook and Dunk Islands and is also a Barrier Reef attraction in its own right because of the Great Barrier Reef Wonderland complex which is also one of the Magnetic Island ferry terminals. The complex includes a wraparound Omnimax theatre where a film on the Great Barrier Reef shows several times daily. The Great Barrier Reef Aquarium is one of the finest aquariums in Australia and includes a 38 metre long reef tank, a predator tank with a healthy selection of sharks as well as a variety of individual tanks and displays, a touch tank, a shop and other attractions. The Great Barrier Reef Marine Park Authority is also located in the complex and you will also find a Queensland National Parks & Wildlife Service office there.

Ferries shuttle across to Magnetic Island, which is virtually a suburb of Townsville, with great regularity. Seair Pacific operate amphibious aircraft services from Townsville to Orpheus and Hinchinbrook while Australian Regional Airlines fly Twin Otters from Townsville to Dunk Island. The connection between Orpheus and Hinchinbrook is one of the few places, apart from the Whitsundays, where you can fly directly from one Great Barrier Reef island to another. Guests going to Bedarra Island fly to Dunk and continue from there by launch.

Cardwell

The small town of Cardwell is 1543 km north of Brisbane and from here there are launch services across to the resort at the northern tip of Hinchinbrook as well as day trips to the island. Hikers intending to do the coastal walk on Hinchinbrook can arrange to be dropped off from Cardwell and picked up by a boat from Lucinda at the other end.

Mission Beach

Tully is 1587 km north of Brisbane and from here it's about 20 km to Mission Beach from where boats are available to Dunk Island and for day trips to the outer reef.

Cairns

Cairns, at the far north of Queensland, is the most popular visitors city in north Queensland. It's 1728 km from Brisbane and as well as direct Ansett and Australian Airlines flights it also has a variety of international connections including to New Zealand, the USA, Asia and Europe.

From Cairns Ansett has flights to Hamilton Island in the Whitsundays, Australian Regional has flights to Dunk and to Lizard Island, and Seair Pacific has flights to Hinchinbrook and Orpheus. Services also operate from Cairns to Thursday Island and other islands in the Torres Strait.

Cairns is also the centre for a great number of boating connections, day trips and scuba diving trips. Fitzroy and Green Islands are both reached from Cairns. Because the reef is closer to the mainland here Cairns is particularly popular for scuba trips. Boats also operate from Cairns on cruises to Cape York and Thursday Island.

Port Douglas

Port Douglas is 1780 km north of Brisbane and almost at the end of the main road along the coast. From here day trips operate out to the Low Isles and the outer reef.

Jellyfish

A variety of jellyfish are found in reef waters but fortunately most of them do not pose serious dangers. The Portuguese man-of-war, actually a hydrozoan colony rather than an individual jellyfish, is not common in Great Barrier Reef waters and although the large lion's mane jellyfish can cause injury the box jellyfish is Australia's real aquatic horror story. Fortunately the box jellyfish, sea wasp or *Chironex fleckeri* is not a danger on the Great Barrier Reef or reef islands. Box jellyfish are found only in northern Australia and only during the summer months and since they are usually found around muddy river mouths or in shallow water close to shore they do not pose a danger once you get away from the mainland. Magnetic Island, close enough to the mainland to present a danger, has netted swimming areas which exclude the jellyfish.

The 'box' name comes from the four-sided bell from which tentacles hang at each corner. The near transparent jellyfish can trail as many as 60 tentacles up to three metres (10 feet) long. It's only found north of the Tropic of Capricorn and lives on prawns which it captures in

Box jellyfish

shallow water, particularly near river or creek outlets. The prawns are captured by paralysing them and an adult sea wasp has enough poison to kill not just a vast number of prawns but alternatively three or four adult humans.

If you're so unfortunate as to get entangled in a box jellyfish's tentacles there are millions of little capsules some of which contain a sticky substance so they stick to you and others with stinging cells which inject the deadly venom into you. The immediate result is intense pain quickly followed by the effect of the poison which can kill you within three minutes by stopping the heart and breathing. The complex venom also destroys red blood cells and damages skin tissue.

To avoid them the first step is simply not to go where they are likely to appear. During the summer months avoid swimming in river mouths, particularly after rain or on overcast days. If you are in the water in a high risk area then wear a T-shirt and make sure you have someone with you in case of emergencies. Shallow, muddy water around river mouths is particularly dangerous. Seek local advice.

An antivenom serum is available from hospitals, doctors, ambulance depots and lifesaving clubs in the tropical areas. Pouring vinegar on undischarged venom cells will neutralise them, do not attempt to pull the tentacles off as this may cause more venom capsules to 'fire'. A container of vinegar is often readily available on popular swimming beaches where box jellyfish may be present. Finally be prepared to resuscitate the victim if he or she stops breathing.

While it is wise to be prepared to deal with box jellyfish it's highly unlikely to be necessary since, as noted above, they are found around river mouths on the coast, not out on the reef islands. Mysteriously when the summer ends the sea wasps do too. Even aquariums have been unable to keep sea wasps alive beyond the end of the summer. There are other jellyfish which can give you a painful sting but none approach the sea wasp for simple lethal danger. All of them are coastal and are more likely to appear when the water is warmer – late summer is the worst time. ∎

Southern Reef Islands

The Capricorn Marine Park, known as Capricornia or the Southern Reef Islands, is the southernmost part of the Great Barrier Reef. It begins north-east of Bundaberg with Lady Elliot Island from where a string of coral reefs and cays dot the ocean for about 140 km up to Tryon Island, east of Rockhampton. There are 300-plus cays on the whole Barrier Reef and many of the most accessible are in the Capricornia section. Although Capricornia is inshore from the main outer reef these are real coral reef islands, formed from reef debris, as opposed to the continental islands like Great Keppel, the Whitsundays or Hinchinbrook, which generally lie closer to the mainland and are the tops of submerged hills rather than coral islands. Cays are often surrounded by calm lagoons formed by the coral reefs which they top.

Several vegetated cays in the Capricornia section are open to visitors for camping or day trips and two of them even have resorts. They are excellent for reef walking, snorkelling and diving and just getting back to nature – though reaching them is generally more expensive than reaching islands nearer the coast.

Apart from Lady Elliot Island, isolated at the south end, the Capricornia islands fall into two main groups: the Bunker Group, which includes Lady Musgrave and the Fairfax and Hoskyn Islets; and further north the Capricorn Group, which includes Heron, Masthead, Wilson, Tryon and North West Island. Many of these cays are national parks. The Tropic of Capricorn runs through the Capricorn Group, passing very close to Heron Island.

Several of the islands are important breeding grounds for turtles including the endangered green turtle. Turtles arrive at night from late October to early February to lay their eggs, and the young emerge from mid-January to April. Sea birds also breed on the islands and at nesting time a number of the islands are home to massive numbers of shearwaters (mutton birds), terns and other birds. Humpback whales also pass through the waters of Capricornia on their annual migration from the Antarctic. Whale watching trips are run out of Bundaberg from mid-August to mid-October.

The Southern Reef Calendar

What with whales migrating north and south, turtles nesting, birds mating and hatching, there's plenty of activity year round on the islands of the Southern Reef section. January-February-March and May-June are usually the wettest months of the year. It can get surprisingly chilly on these islands during the winter months, you certainly need a good wet suit in June and July.

January – peak breeding season for Heron Island's reef herons. Turtle hatchlings have started to appear in late December and continue through to late April or early May.

February – shearwater (mutton bird) chicks start to hatch.

March – this is the end of the turtle nesting season, and migratory birds like the ruddy turnstones and eastern golden plover start to depart and head for the Arctic. Buff-banded rails and black noddy terns are nesting.

April – adult shearwaters start to leave the islands and soon after their abandoned chicks emerge from their burrows. Most of the noddy terns leave the islands.

May – the young shearwaters are busy teaching themselves to fly and by the end of the month should all have left the islands, in pursuit of their parents. The last of the baby turtles have made the dangerous trek down to the sea.

June – humpback whales start to pass through the Southern Reef Islands on their migration north from the Antarctic.

July – humpback whales are seen more regularly. This is the coldest month of the year with average water temperatures around 18 to 23°C

August – the cold winter water is starting to warm up.

September – black noddy terns start to return and nest while migratory birds from the northern hemisphere start to arrive. Mating turtles may be seen in the sea.

Whales

Cetaceans, the marine mammals which include dolphins, porpoises and whales, are found along the Great Barrier Reef. Some, like dolphins, live continuously in the reef waters, while others migrate through the reef or come to the reef to breed. In all there are about 80 species of cetaceans and over 50 of these are found in the waters of the Great Barrier Reef.

Whales can be divided into two groups. *Odontocetes* or toothed whales are predators which hunt fish and other creatures. Dolphins and killer whales are examples of this group and if you're out on a boat around the reef you will often see dolphins frolicking around, leaping the bow wave and engaging in other typical dolphin-like amusements. *Mysticetes* or baleen whales strain vast amounts of water through the hairy baleen plates in their mouth. This 'filter' strains out the tiny fish and krill (planktonic crustaceans) on which the whale lives. It's a curiosity that these largest of living creatures live by consuming such minute ones.

Eight species of baleen whale are seen in Australian waters and the most visible and spectacular of these are the great humpback whales which come north from the Antarctic to enjoy the warm waters of the Barrier Reef during the southern winter between July and October. The humpback's activities are a delight to watch and include spectacular 'blows' as the 10-metre-plus whale breathes out through its blowhole. As the whale starts to dive again it arches its back out of the water, hence the 'humpback' name. Most spectacular of all is a 'breach', when a 40 tonne, 15 metre long whale makes a stupendous splash as it leaps out of the water. Apart from their physical activities, which also includes swimming lazily on one side flapping a huge pectoral fin above the water,

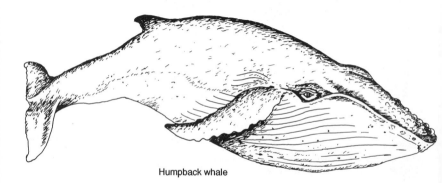

Humpback whale

humpbacks are also known for the complex 'songs' with which they communicate. They are the most vocal of the great whales.

Humpbacks breed while they are around the Great Barrier Reef. The gestation period is about a year and the newborn whales are around five metres in length and weigh about 1.5 tonnes. A mother whale provides her new baby with about 500 litres of milk a day and during the first weeks the whale calf puts on 50 to 100 kg of weight a day! They stick close to their mother for the 5000 km return trip to Antarctica and throughout their first year.

At one time whales were hunted off the Queensland coast and the whaling station at Tangalooma on Moreton Island took over 7000 whales in the 10 years prior to its closure in 1962. By that time humpback whales had almost disappeared from the coast. As many as 10,000 whales were estimated to visit the Barrier Reef Waters each year prior to whaling, as few as 200 when whaling finally stopped. They are now protected and their numbers are slowly recovering, today there are thought to be about 600 whales around the Great Barrier Reef during the winter months. Whale watching as they migrate through the waters of the Southern Reef islands is becoming a major tourist attraction. ■

Humpback whale (GBRMPA)

October – the humpback whales which have given birth to their calves while in the warm waters of the Great Barrier Reef can now be seen heading south back to the Antarctic for the summer. The shearwaters return to the island to nest and the jaunty little silvereyes which are resident on the islands year-round start to nest.

November – the female turtles start to come ashore to lay their eggs while the shearwaters clean out and repair their burrows. Black noddies' eggs start to appear in their precarious and shoddily built nests. This is usually the month when corals spawn, the exact date is related to the lunar month and may be in December.

December – the birdlife will be noisy and active as black noddy tern chicks start to hatch and shearwaters lay their eggs. Turtles continue to lay their eggs while the first turtle hatchlings start to appear and head for the sea.

Camping

On the four national park islands where camping is allowed (Lady Musgrave, Masthead, Tryon and North West) campers must be totally self-sufficient. There are no reliable water supplies and all garbage should be taken when you leave. The number of campers is limited so it's advisable to apply well ahead for your camping permit. You can book six months ahead for these islands instead of the usual six to 12 weeks for other Queensland national parks. The busiest times are December and January, school holiday periods, and May and November when the diving is at its best. For permits and info contact the Queensland National Parks & Wildlife Service on Roseberry St in Gladstone (tel (079) 76 0766). The postal address is PO Box 315, Gladstone, Queensland 4680.

When and if you receive your permit you'll also receive info on any rules such as restrictions on the use of generators, and on how not to harm the wildlife. Turtles nest on these islands between October and February and care should be taken not to disturb them. Camping should be avoided on the foredunes, and fires should not be built with island wood whether it has grown there or arrived as driftwood.

A variety of seabirds nest on the Capricornia cays, particularly between October and May, and campers should take great care not to disturb or harm the birds.

Some birds, especially the black-naped terns, are easily disturbed and may abandon their nests which can result in the loss of their eggs or chicks to scavenging gulls. Mutton birds dig burrows which can collapse under the weight of unwary walkers, with dire results for any bird in the burrow at the time. Also, their long wings make it difficult for mutton birds to make sudden changes in direction when coming in to land, so don't get in their way and don't camp on their 'runways' used for take-offs and landings. Feeding seagulls can disturb the islands' ecological balance as gulls often wreak havoc on their less aggressive neighbours.

Co-existing with the cays' birdlife can have a more mundane side. The noddies play a vital role in the cay's life cycle by fertilising the soil with their droppings. Camping under pisonia trees during the nesting season can result in your tent getting a healthy dose of droppings as well!

Getting There & Away

Access to the Capricornia Islands is from Bundaberg, Gladstone or Rosslyn Bay near Rockhampton. Regular transport services to the islands are covered below under the individual islands.

It's also possible to charter boats for day trips or drop-offs to the islands. For example the *Katarei-Too* (tel (079) 72 5922) in Gladstone will do island drop offs for $75 per person for a minimum of eight people or will do overnight charters for $800 a day. The *Aristocat* (tel (079) 72 5326) also does charters and drop-offs to North West, Masthead or Tryon.

The *Marlin I* in Gladstone is also available for charter for camping drop-offs or pickups. It charges $900 per day for up to 10 people. Contact Lee and Wayne Thompson at PO Box 406, Gladstone, Qld 4680 for details or phone (079) 78 1938. Departures are from O'Connell Wharf in Gladstone.

The *Robert Poulsen* operates to North West Island for $140 return trip per person for 14 people or more. Ring P&0 Marine Division (tel (079) 72 5166) for details. For groups of 12 people, the *Reef Explorer* (tel (079) 78 1977) can be chartered for around $110 per person per day.

Another possibility is the Keppel Barge Service (tel (079) 33 6721) at Rosslyn Bay. Barges from Gladstone, which will carry around 40 people, cost about $2000 to $3000.

Operators tend to come and go, and boats frequently change hands, but Gladstone Promotion & Development (tel (079) 72 4000), 100 Goondoon St, Gladstone, Qld 4680 has an up-to-date list of charter operators registered with them.

Lady Elliot Island

Area: 0.42 square km
Type: coral cay
High point: 3 metres
Maximum visitor population: 120
Per person daily cost: $140

In brief: Lady Elliot is the only cay on the whole Great Barrier Reef with an airstrip. It's a simple, no-frills place, popular for diving.

The Island

Right at the southern end of the marine park and the Great Barrier Reef, Lady Elliot Island is very popular with divers and has been the scene for numerous shipwrecks. Indeed the island has such an attraction for wayward ships that it has been dubbed Queensland's 'Shipwreck Island'.

The island was the starting point for Australia's bêche-de-mer industry in the last century. Early explorer Matthew Flinders was shipwrecked on Wreck Reef (not Wreck Island in the Capricorn Group) 170 km from Lady Elliot in 1803. As a result of the survivors' period on the reef, an early trader in this region, James Aickin, went there looking for this Chinese delicacy. He failed to find them on the reef in commercially viable quantities but did find them on Lady

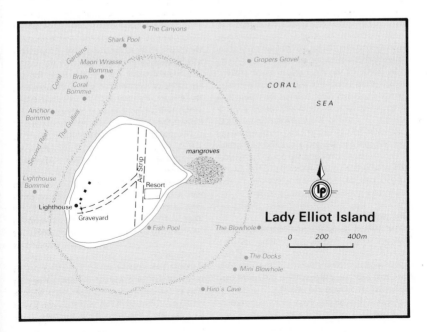

Lady Elliot Island

Elliot Island. In the following years, collecting bêche-de-mer became an important activity right up the coast. If Aickin's bêche-de-mer island was indeed Lady Elliot he didn't bother to name it or chart its position. The island had to wait another 13 years for a name, which was given it by Captain Thomas Stewart of the ship *Lady Elliot* in 1816. The *Lady Elliot* was en route from Calcutta to Sydney but on her return voyage, heading for Batavia (now Jakarta) in the Dutch East Indies, the ship was wrecked with the loss of all its crew on a reef off Hinchinbrook. The reef also bears the ship's name.

Later, in the 1860s, the island was exploited for its guano deposits. Coupled with overgrazing from goats the island has never totally recovered from this Victorian era rape. Since the airstrip was built in 1969 the vegetation has recovered amazingly, as a comparison with photographs of the island earlier this century or even at the time the airstrip was built will show, but it's still rather bare compared to some other densely vegetated Capricornia islands. The small stand of pisonia trees in the resort area is the only one to be found on the island. The picturesque lighthouse dates from 1873 but has now been converted to automatic operation.

In 1843 Professor Joseph Beete Jukes, naturalist on HMS *Fly* which was surveying the Great Barrier Reef, visited the island and made some interesting notes on its natural history. W Saville-Kent, another naturalist, visited the island in 1892 and commented on the rich marine life and also on the destruction of the tree cover and the scarcity of birds and turtles due to the activities of the guano miners and the lighthouse operators. Fortunately the wildlife is returning today.

Shipwrecks

Ships started ploughing into the island at an early stage in Australia's history and the activity has still not come to a halt. There have been numerous wrecks in the '70s and '80s and bits and pieces of various ships can be found all around the island.

Lady Elliot shipwrecks probably started with the 620 ton cargo ship *Bolton Abbey* which sank off the island in 1815. Its remains were only recently located. The cargo steamer *Port St John*, which ran aground here in 1938, was one of the largest ships the island claimed.

The year 1975 was a bad year for island wrecks when the groundings included the 18 metre *Vansittart*, involved in a turtle-farming project in the Torres Straits, which managed to get off the reef a few hours later and continued north the next day. The 15 metre cutter *Tahuna* was not so lucky when it struck the reef and was later washed up on to the beach.

Five years later 1980 was another bad year with the schooner *Thisby*, crippled by a cyclone, washed ashore early in the year. The heavy timbers from this old boat were used to construct the resort's *Thisby* bar and it's easy to identify the chunks of its wreckage around the eastern point. The island's most famous, and probably most expensive, wreck followed six weeks later for the leading boat in the Brisbane to Gladstone Yacht Race. The 19 metre *Apollo I*, designed by America's Cup designer Ben Lexcen and skippered by a Sydney millionaire who had made his mint through one-armed bandit gambling machines, ploughed straight into the island in a 20 knot wind. They'd been led astray by the lights of a catamaran which also went on to the reef, but managed to extricate itself. The yacht's bow forms a servery from the resort's bar into the dining room.

More wrecks followed including, in April 1989, the Fremantle yacht *Tenggara II*, (tenggara is Indonesian for 'south-east'). She hit the reef during bad weather in the middle of the night and was washed right up on the reef and eventually abandoned. These days wrecked yachties are supposed to clear up the mess they make as bits and pieces of boat soon end up spread right across the reef flat.

Information

Reservations can be made through Australian Airlines or Sunstate Airlines. You can phone for resort reservations on toll free (008) 07 2200 or write to the Lady Elliot Resort, Mail Bag No 6, Bundaberg, Qld

Top Left: Wreck, Lady Elliot Island (TW)
Top Right: Lady Elliot lighthouse (TW)
Middle Left: Sea star (TW)
Bottom: Wreck, Lady Elliot Island (TW)

4670. There is no telephone on the island but the administration number on the mainland is (071) 71 5867. The island resort has a shop with general supplies.

Lady Elliot – First Island of the Great Barrier Reef by Anthony Walsh (Boolarong Books, Brisbane, 1987) is an interesting little book about the island and its often fascinating history. It's available at the resort shop.

Around the Island
You can stroll gently right round the island in less than an hour but there are plenty of distractions. The coarse sand of the beach is composed of pounded coral and sand and the glints of rainbow colours hint at the coral reef around you. You don't even have to get more than your feet wet to start exploring the reef as a low tide reef walk will provide plenty of interest. Fish, crabs, octopus, eels and cowry shells are all waiting for the keen observer and blue-spotted rays or wobbegong sharks, lying motionless on the sandy bottom, can also be seen. At low tide look for parrot fish which often come in large schools in to surprisingly shallow water near the shore.

The island is also a bird sanctuary and a popular stopping place for migrating species. Look for the bright blue wings of sacred kingfishers, or eastern reef herons and white-faced herons searching the shallows for fish. Turtles nest on the island in the summer and their offspring hatch out and make for the sea in the autumn.

The Lighthouse
A temporary lighthouse was built on the island in 1866 but a storm blew it down six years later. A sturdier replacement, one of the state's first steel-frame lighthouses, was completed in 1873. It was converted to automatic operation in 1988 but it's an accoutrement which seems to have done remarkably little to warn sailors of the dangers of the Great Barrier Reef's first island. The lighthouse keepers' cottages, beside the lighthouse, are now used as staff accommodation for the resort.

Just inland from the lighthouse is a tiny fenced-in graveyard with two graves. One is to Miss Phoebe Phillips, a lighthouse keeper's rather reclusive 30-year old daughter who died on the island from pneumonia, in 1896. The other is Susannah McKee's, a lighthouse keeper's wife. The loneliness of island life led to her committing suicide by drowning in 1907.

Diving
The island has glass bottom boats, friendly fish come up to be fed in the coral pools and there's good snorkelling. As the island does not suffer from heavy boat traffic or strong currents the underwater visibility is usually extremely good and the coral is excellent. In the 'fish pond', a favourite snorkelling locale, butterfly fish and sergeant-majors will gather round snorkellers to snatch bits of bread. Many other fish can be seen in the coral around this pool, just a few steps from the shore on the resort side.

A real advantage of the island for scuba divers is that there is superb diving straight off the beach. The coral gardens area on the opposite side of the island from the resort offers wonderful diving right along the western side of the island. Divers walk round there, pulling little trolley carts containing their gear. From the edge of the reef you can fin out to attractions like the Canyons, Shark Pool, Maori Wrasse Bommie, Brain Coral Bommie and the Gullies. Sharks may indeed be seen in the shark pool, where they gather before moving out at the change of tide. Huge (and harmless) manta rays are often seen serenely winging past and turtles are regularly spotted around the reef.

Around the Anchor Bommie, also on the western side of the island, a number of old anchors can be seen. It's thought they belonged to the guano ships which used to anchor here during the time when the island was mined for guano. When a sudden wind shift put the guano boats in danger of being blown onto the reef they would sometimes have to cut their anchors in order to escape. Off the lighthouse at the south-west corner of the island the Lighthouse Bommies are another shore dive attraction.

Dives off the eastern side of the island

have to be made from a boat and the winds have to be co-operative in order to dive here. Hiro's Cave, the Mini Blowholes and the Docks are popular dives here but the Blowhole is probably Lady Elliot's premier dive. You enter the blowhole at about 14 metres depth and follow it down and around to emerge horizontally on the reef drop-off at 23 metres.

The island rises up from water 40 metres deep. The resort has good diving facilities and you can take certificate courses which start on Mondays, last five days and cost $395. All equipment is available for hire and dive costs for shore dives are $15 per dive for the first two dives a day, additional dives are $10. A boat dive or night dive costs $30. They're diving crazy on this island so it's often possible to do more than two dives a day. Because you have to fly out of the island there are restrictions on when you can make your last dive before departure.

Accommodation

The small resort (tel (079) 71 6077 for the mainland contact, there is no phone on the island) was just a campsite for divers until the extensive 1985 update. It's still a very straightforward place with two styles of accommodation. Costs include all meals, and children three to 14 pay 50% of the adult rate.

The solid looking safari-style tents are basically permanently erected. Toilet and shower facilities are shared and costs are $90 per night for two or three adults sharing, $80 per night for four. There's a $30 supplement to take a tent as a single.

The 'Reef Units' are simple motel-type rooms with a common verandah area out front and attached bathrooms. Nightly costs are $150 single, $120 per person for two or three people, $110 per person for four.

The island's maximum visitor population, if every room had a family in it with two kids in the bunk beds, would be about 150 but 120 or 130 would be a more accurate 'maximum' figure. There's no swimming pool or heavily organised entertainment but something usually goes on in the evening and there is a ping pong table and a video recorder. Basically, however, this is a place to get away from civilisation and concentrate on the diving.

Food

There's a dining room where the food is as simple and straightforward as the accommodation. Lady Elliot is not going to win any Great Barrier Reef cuisine awards! Never mind, diving gives you a phenomenal appetite and since many of the resort guests are here for the diving there are unlikely to be many complaints as any shortfalls in culinary quality are overshadowed by healthy quantities!

The adjoining Thisby bar takes its name from the 1980 wreck of the *Thisby*. There are large chunks of *Thisby* wreckage along the north-east beach and the bar's sturdy top is made from timbers from the ship. There's a reasonably priced winelist.

Getting There & Away

This is the only coral cay on the reef with an airstrip. You can fly there from Bundaberg with Sunstate Airlines (tel (071) 72 2322) at 188 Bourbong St, Bundaberg. Flight time for the 80 km trip from Bundaberg is 35 minutes and the cost is $140 round trip. There is a 10 kg baggage weight limit which is only rigidly enforced if the flight has weight problems. If so Sunstate can store your excess gear at Bundaberg airport. You don't need fancy clothes at Lady Elliot. A day trip from Bundaberg costs $170. While you're at Bundaberg airport say hi to Commanche, the airport cat!

Anchorages for visiting yachts at Lady Elliot are difficult and very poor unless the wind is being very co-operative. Getting supplies out to the island is not easy, a barge comes out from the mainland once a month bringing non-perishable supplies. It's parked over the reef at the change of tide and the supplies are manhandled ashore at low tide. All fresh food has to come out by light aircraft.

The Bunker Group

The Bunker Group starts with Lady Musgrave Island, only about 40 km north of Lady Elliot. If the visibility is good it's possible to see them as you fly to or from Lady Elliot. The group takes its name from Captain Ebenezer Bunker, a legendary whaler, who sailed through the group aboard his ship the *Albion* in 1803. He also appears to have spotted Lady Elliot but named only the group. Flinders had seen at least one of the group from afar in 1802 and it's possible that Cook may have sighted North West Island back in 1770.

LADY MUSGRAVE ISLAND

The tiny 0.15 square km Lady Musgrave cay is an uninhabited national park about 100 km north-east of Bundaberg. The island sits at the western end of a huge lagoon measuring five km from end to end and occupying 12 square km. It's the southernmost of the Bunker Group, but seems like only a stone's throw south of the Fairfax and Hoskyn Islets. The island was charted in 1843 and its name comes from Queensland governor Sir Anthony Musgrave's American wife Jeannie.

The perfect lagoon is one of the very few along the entire Barrier Reef where ships can safely enter; a fact which is taken advantage of by many visiting yachties. It's said that the lagoon entrance was artificially created when the island was exploited for its guano deposits, late in the last century or early in this one.

In the early 1900s goats were released on the island, part of a British Admiralty plan to provide a food source for shipwrecked sailors! Whether any unfortunate seamen did manage to run down a surefooted goat and butcher it for survival rations is unknown but what is more certain is that the goats totally overran the island and stripped it bare of vegetation. Not until 1971 were the goats

Lady Musgrave Island (BTDB)

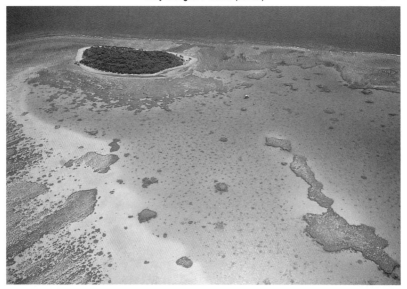

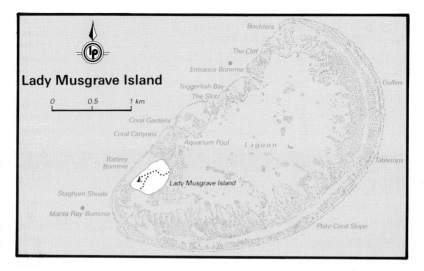

cleared off and since then the vegetation has recovered remarkably. The depredations of guano miners must have been much less severe than on Lady Elliot for Lady Musgrave's vegetation, particularly the pisonia trees, is much denser.

In the typical fashion of the southern reef cays the tangled central pisonia growth is surrounded by hardy casuarinas and pandanus. It takes about half an hour to walk right around the island and there is also a trail leading across from the usual landing place to the camping site and the western end of the island. The island is an important nesting ground for mutton birds and white-capped noddies while green and loggerhead turtles also come here to lay their eggs.

Despite an automatic light beacon which was installed on the island in 1974, Lady Musgrave has also had its share of collisions with passing ships. In 1985 the 35,000 ton bulk carrier *TNT Alltrans* went aground on the reef but was floated off a day later, having suffered fairly extensive damage to its bottom although fortunately not losing fuel or cargo.

Diving

Lady Musgrave offers some excellent diving opportunities which are regularly enjoyed by day-trip visitors. The lagoon offers excellent snorkelling and some good shallower scuba dives for beginners. The fish have become so used to being fed that they virtually mob divers and snorkellers and it's an idea to wear gloves if you're going to be handing out goodies.

Diving outside the reef is usually on the northern side of the lagoon both because it is much quicker to reach from the lagoon anchorage and also because this side is sheltered from the prevailing winds and currents. Dives along this face of the reef are usually around 12 metres depth with the exception of two popular dives at opposite ends of the reef. Manta Ray Bommie at the western corner is about 17 metres deep and yes, there are indeed frequent sightings of manta rays here.

Just outside the lagoon entrance the Entrance Bommie is a superb dive with a maximum depth of just over 20 metres. The bommie has a swim through and a number of

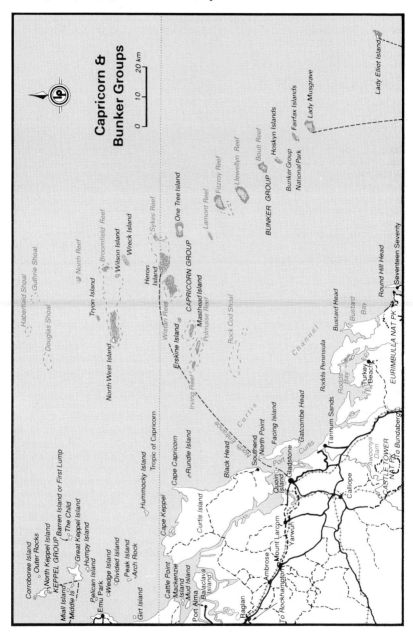

resident fish, including two elderly and surprisingly large lionfish, which regularly come out to greet divers. The only catch with this dive is that it can only be made at the turn of the tide, due to the rapid currents sweeping in or out of the lagoon entrance at other times. A dive, if you've come out to the cay with the *Lady Musgrave*, costs $30 including a full tank and all gear.

Camping

With a national parks permit you can camp on the island but there are no facilities apart from some surprisingly luxurious bush toilets. Campers – a maximum of 50 at any one time – must be totally self-sufficient in drinking water and firewood or fuel. The enormous amount of fallen pisonia wood around the island must be very tempting but, no doubt, it would soon be gone if campers were allowed to burn it. Generators cannot be run on the island between 9 pm and 7 am.

The large centipedes on the island, which usually appear after dark on rainy days, are harmless but if you're unlucky enough to get a bird tick they should be removed. These tiny ticks, carried by noddies, will cause itching, but are not a serious problem unless you have a reaction to them. The easiest way to avoid them is not to camp under the pisonia trees where noddies nest.

Getting There & Away

You can reach the island by the fast catamaran *Lady Musgrave* from Bundaberg. It's operated by Lady Musgrave Barrier Reef Cruises (tel (071) 52 9011) at 1 Quay St in Bundaberg. The cost is $75 which includes lunch, snorkel gear and a glass bottom boat ride. The trip takes 2½ hours each way and you have about four hours on the island. The boat leaves from Burnett Heads wharf on the coast near Bundaberg at 8.45 am on Tuesdays, Thursdays, Saturdays and Sundays and you return at 5.45 pm. You can also use this service for a camping drop-off and pick-up at a cost of $120. A connecting bus service is also operated from Bundaberg and Baraga, it costs $5 total for morning pick-up and evening drop-off. Cruises to Lady Musgrave

are supposed to be operating from Round Head as well.

Lady Musgrave is one of the few cays on the Barrier Reef where visiting yachts can safely anchor within the lagoon. At most cays the water within the reef is too shallow or there is no suitable entrance. Anchoring outside a cay's reef is seldom practicable.

OTHER BUNKER GROUP ISLANDS

The Fairfax Islets are two tiny cays north of Lady Musgrave Islet. These cays were, unfortunately, devastated by practice bombing during WW II, grazing by goats and guano mining. They are no longer open to visitors. Slightly north again are the Hoskyn Islets, also national parks and the most unspoiled of the group. They have been open to day visitors but may not be at present. The western of the two Hoskyn Islets is almost completely vegetated by pandanus apart from a few pisonia. The Hoskyn and Fairfax Islets are the southernmost recorded nesting ground for gannets which come here from September to January.

North again are the Boult, Llewellyn and Fitzroy Reefs before you reach the Capricorn Group. The Fitzroy Reef, 30 km north-west of Lady Musgrave, is another coral lagoon where visiting yachts can safely enter and anchor. It's rather like the lagoon at Lady Musgrave, but without an island in the lagoon. Boult Reef has an enclosed lagoon and a very conspicuous trawler wreck, perched on the eastern edge of the reef. Llewellyn has a deep and extensive enclosed lagoon.

The Capricorn Group

North of the Bunker Group and straddling the Tropic of Capricorn are the islands and reefs of the Capricorn Group. These islands include Masthead, North West and Tryon, all popular camping islands, and Heron Island with its resort, probably the most popular diver's island on the whole Great Barrier Reef.

HERON ISLAND
Area: 0.17 square km
Type: coral cay
High point: 3 metres
Maximum visitor population: 250
Per person daily cost: $190
In brief: very small cay right on the reef, popular for divers, national park, a great deal to see and do at this fascinating island.

The Island
Heron is a real coral cay and the Tropic of Capricorn virtually runs through the island. The tiny 0.17 square km island rises only three metres above sea level although it's quite densely vegetated with *pisonia* trees that can reach 15 metres high. Although the tiny island is less than a km in length it's surrounded by 24 square km of reef where keen divers will find a vast variety of marine life. The island takes its name from the distinctive reef herons seen here. The resort covers the north-eastern third of the island but although the rest is national park and includes a marine research station you cannot camp here.

The island has had a long, varied and interesting history. HMS *Fly*, which did so

Heron Island (TW)

much of the surveying of the Southern Reef Islands, anchored off Heron Island in 1843 and Professor Joseph Beet Jukes, the expedition's naturalist, noted the island's many reef herons and named it in their honour. In 1910 and several times in subsequent years ornithologists visited the island to study its bird life but in 1925 a lease

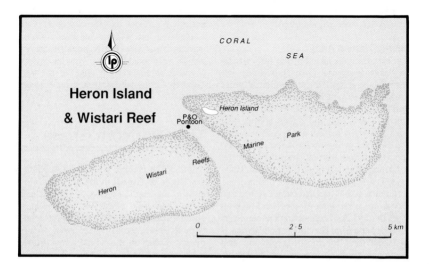

was granted to establish a turtle soup factory on Heron Island. The initial company failed two years later without commencing operations but another company took over the lease. By 1930 turtles were already becoming so scarce that this company also ceased operations and no more has been heard about large scale turtle operations.

In 1932 Captain Christian Poulson commenced work on converting the turtle soup canning factory into a small resort. The Poulson family was to play a major part in the development of Heron Island as a resort. After WW II Captain Poulson started flights to Heron from Brisbane. He purchased three ex-RAAF Catalina flying boats and cobbled them together to make one usable 28 seater aircraft, landings were made either within the shallow Heron lagoon or between Heron and Wistari Reefs. Unfortunately, in 1947 Christian Poulson drowned while returning to the resort from a boat moored offshore. The resort was taken over by P&O in 1973.

Information

The resort phone number is (079) 78 1488; there are a couple of pay phones by reception. Write to Heron Island Resort, via Gladstone, Qld 4680. Reservations can be made through P&O Resorts (tel (07) 268 8224), 482 Kingsford Smith Drive, Brisbane, Qld 4007. The Queensland National Parks & Wildlife Service has an information centre (tel (079) 72 5690) on the island.

Heron Island time is one hour behind Australian eastern standard time. Don't ask me why.

Books The resort shop and the diving shop both have an interesting selection of books on the Barrier Reef for sale. The National

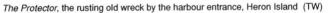

The Protector, the rusting old wreck by the harbour entrance, Heron Island (TW)

Parks information centre has a varied little library of titles but they're only out for perusal when there's a parks ranger on duty in the centre. *Discover Heron Island* by Neville Coleman (Sea Australia Resource Centre, Rochedale South, Qld, 1988) is an interesting little book on the island, principally devoted to brief descriptions of the island and its surrounding reef's flora and fauna.

An interesting series of $1 booklets are also available from the resort shop. Look for *Reef Walking, Sea Turtles of Heron Island* and *The Birds of Heron Island*.

Activities

Heron is a diver's island and night-time activities take second place although there is a bar, disco, tennis courts, games nights and other activities. If you have to have a TV the resort does have one, it's in the departure lounge. Guided reef-walks and nature walks around the cay led by the resort staff or the Marine Park rangers are popular daytime activities and there are also lectures on the reef and its management by scientists from the island's research station. Fishing trips are another everyday activity at Heron.

Around the Island

Heron's a fascinating island to wander around and you can walk right around the beach or take the stroll through the dense pisonia forest in the centre of the island. There's usually an island walk and a reef walk organised every day. Like other cays in the Southern Reef group Heron follows a very similar pattern. A fine sand beach encircles the island with patches of beach rock. Beyond the high-water mark you first find the hardier she-oaks and pandanus trees, able to withstand the wind and salt spray. Further inland are the stately pisonia trees with their cool canopy of light green leaves. And everywhere there's the noise and odour of the island's huge bird population.

Keep to the walking tracks when you're exploring the island, straying from the tracks can easily lead to stepping on a shearwater's burrow, with possibly dire results to any

occupant and to yourself. The main walking track wanders from the resort through the centre of the island to Shark Bay at the eastern end. Here you will often see gummy sharks or small rays basking on the sandy bottom of the bay.

Heron's harbour is a controversial subject. Like many other cays, getting boats in is a problem and in Heron's case it was solved by dredging a harbour and building a jetty. Unfortunately silt from the harbour has affected the coral in places but the harbour is also causing changes to the water flow right across the reef. Normally as the tide drops water spills off the reef in all directions, now there's a natural drain for it to run out and this is sucking the sand off the northern edge of the island, near the resort area. Don't mess with nature!

The rusting old wreck beside the harbour entrance is the *Protector*. Launched in England in 1884 she was originally built for the South Australian Navy, when Australia was still composed of a number of separate colonies. She saw service during the Boxer Rebellion, and as the *Sidney* was to be used by the US Army in WW II in New Guinea, but following a collision with a tug was abandoned on Facing Island near Gladstone. In 1943 she was towed out to Heron Island to make a breakwater, long before the harbour entrance existed, and has been there ever since. The *Protector* is a picturesque part of Heron to some eyes, an ugly, rusting eyesore to others. A number of birds nest on the *Protector* including the shy black-naped terns which have abandoned the island itself.

Heron Island Research Centre

Originally established in 1951 the research station is now run by the University of Queensland. The station conducts work on numerous projects connected with the islands and reef and has laboratories, workshops, aquarium facilities, a library, boats and diving equipment together with accommodation facilities. Apart from researchers actually working on projects at the station there are often conventions and other academic gatherings plus visits by groups of secondary and tertiary students. Visits to the station can be arranged although the level of activity fluctuates considerably through the year.

Diving & Snorkelling

Heron Island, which is a national park, is famed for its superb scuba diving and each October or November the Heron Island Underwater Festival includes a host of diving seminars, lectures and other activities. Spear fishing is banned and the reef here is fortunate to have escaped attacks by the crown-of-thorns starfish which have caused so much damage further north. Although diving is so popular there are also glass bottom boats for the less energetic and even walking (carefully) across the reef flats at low tide will provide lots of interest.

It's only a few steps out to the reef for snorkellers and there are regular excursions with the resort's dive boat, good diving sites are found only 15 minutes from the resort. All diving is from boats, however; there is no shore diving at Heron. For non-divers the resort also has glass bottom boats and a semi-submersible.

As at other islands in the Southern Reef group diving at Heron has the natural safety net that the reef drop-offs all tend to end by 20 to 30 metres depth. There are some superb spots starting with the famed dive right outside the harbour entrance known as The Bommie. It's not just 'the bommie' but a whole series of huge bommies going step by step down the reef slope from around 10 to 18 metres depth. The Bommie is particularly well known for Harry and Fang, Heron's two 'tame' moray eels which live in the bommies and regularly come out to meet divers. Just east of the bommies is a large anchor; there's no history to it, the anchor was simply put there to add some interest!

Round the north side of the reef Gorgonia Hole with its dramatic drop-off, the Coral Grotto at 10 metres, Hole in the Wall at 15 to 18 metres, Coral Cascades at the same depth and Tenements I and Tenements II are other popular dives. There are more dives along

the north-east edge of Wistari Reef at six to 24 metres depth. When you've finally exhausted all the diving possibilities around Heron and Wistari there are also 'Adventure Diving' trips to other islands and reefs in the area.

Two dives a day are usually possible, sometimes a night dive too, although these are often heavily booked. Day dives cost $9 for a tank and airfill plus $15 for the boat per dive. All equipment can be hired from Heron's comprehensively equipped dive shop. June is a good month for diving at Heron because your airfills and boat charges are free! Heron is a popular place to learn diving. Six day certificate diving courses cost $280.

Accommodation

Accommodation on Heron Island consists of lodges or suites and all prices are inclusive of all meals. The 26 Lodge rooms are basically simple little bunkrooms with beds for three or four and share toilet and bathroom facilities. There's nothing special about them but most people staying here will be worrying about the diving, not the creature comforts. Daily cost in a Lodge room is $100 per person but, although you can book a single bed, sole use of a Lodge room is not available. If the resort is uncrowded you may get a room to yourself, if it's busy you may find yourself making some new friends.

In the other rooms costs are per person but you can take a room by yourself for a $37.50 surcharge. These 'suites' are motel-like with bathrooms, verandahs, fridge and tea-coffee making equipment. There are 38 Reef Suites at $155 per person, 40 Heron Suites at $170 per person and four Point Suites and one Beach House at $180 per person. The suites are all comfortable, modern, well equipped and have all the mod cons you could ask for although Heron makes a point of not having telephones or TVs. Children from three to 14 years of age pay 50% of the adult rate, under three they stay free.

Out of season there are often special deals to Heron Island which can reduce the cost of

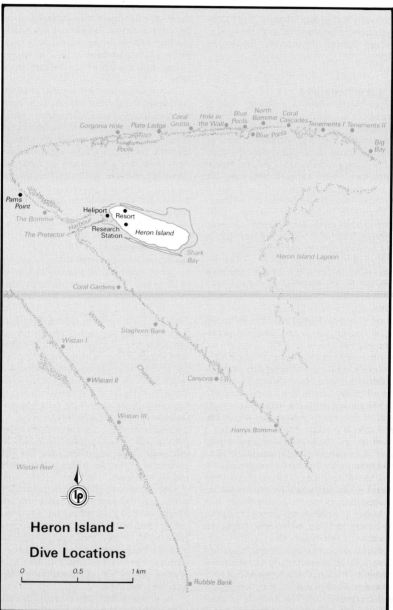

Gorgonia Hole
Plate Ledge
Coral Grotto
Hole in the Wall
Blue Pools
North Bommie
Coral Cascades
Tenements I
Tenements II
Big Bay
Pools
Blue Pools

Pams Point
The Bommie
Heliport
Resort
Research Station
Heron Island
Harbour
The Protector
Shark Bay
Heron Island Lagoon

Coral Gardens

Wistari
Staghorn Bank

Wistari I

Wistari II
Channel
Canyons

Wistari III
Harrys Bommie

Wistari Reef

Heron Island –

Dive Locations

0   0.5   1 km

Rubble Bank

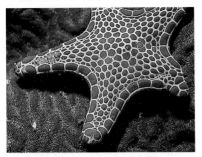

Sea star on brain coral (MN)

a diving holiday. If you're in Gladstone it's worth enquiring about standby rates at the resort. Gladstone Travel World (tel (079) 72 2288), Leisure Travel International (tel (079) 72 2577) and Sunstate Airlines (tel (079) 72 3488) can all offer standby rates if rooms are available. Standby helicopter and catamaran transfers are also available.

Food

There's just one place to eat at Heron, breakfast and lunch are buffet style while at dinner time you order from a menu. On day one you're assigned a table and although nobody makes a fuss about it you're supposed to stick to that table throughout your stay – Heron is not an island for romantic tête-à-têtes and let's face it, a lot of the conversation is diving talk! Never mind, your meal companions tend to change from day to day as people come and go. And the food really is pretty good. Of course the diving-honed appetites tend to be decidedly healthy ones but even if you haven't been burning up the energy metres below the surface you still won't be disappointed.

At dinner time the menu would typically have a soup, followed by a choice of a couple of starters, three main courses (one of them seafood), then a couple of desserts. Plus serve-yourself salads, fruit salad, cheese and biscuits and coffee. Nobody goes hungry and generally there's praise for the quality as well as the quantity!

The drinks list includes beers at around

$2.50, wine by the glass for $1.80 and by the bottle for around $15 to $25.

Getting There & Away

Off shore, 72 km east of Gladstone or about 100 km from Rockhampton, Heron Island is a real reef island. Due to its distance from the mainland it's one of the more expensive islands to get out to.

Air The sexy way of getting to Heron is by helicopter, the catch is it costs you $173 one-way or $290 return but in about 30 minutes you're whisked out to Heron with spectacular views over Polmaise Reef, Masthead and Erskine Islands and finally Wistari Reef as you go. A quick circuit of Heron Island, on arrival or departure, completes the trip. If you're going out to Heron by chopper phone Gladstone (079) 78 1777 the day before to check departure time.

Reef, Heron Island (MN)

Turtles

The Great Barrier Reef is a very important habitat for sea turtles and they are often seen around many of the reef islands. They nest on a number of islands including Heron, Lady Elliot and the other islands of the Southern Reef groups but most particularly Raine Island in the far north where thousands of turtles have been seen on one night.

There are three types of turtles found on the reef – loggerhead, hawksbill and green turtles. Three other types are found near the mainland or further out, beyond the outer edge of the reef. Remarkably little is known about the life cycle of turtles. Mature turtles are a common sight along the reef and turtles breed here but after hatching out the baby turtles simply disappear, not being seen again in reef waters until they have grown to about 40 cm in length. It is thought that young turtles drift with ocean currents but although turtles bred in captivity may mature in less than 10 years, in the wild this may take up to 50 years.

At one time turtles were harvested for food or, in the case of the hawksbill turtle, for its shell. Turtles take a long time to reach maturity and a very high proportion of them die along the way so commercial exploitation can have disastrous effects. Today they are protected except for Aboriginals and Torres Strait Islanders from native communities who may only take them for their own consumption. Nevertheless their survival is still threatened by commercial development (loss of the beaches where they lay their eggs) and by prawn trawlers which accidentally catch them and drown them in their nets.

Turtles in the Capricornia Islands

The islands of the Southern Reef group are important breeding sites for turtles and visitors regularly see them on Lady Elliot and Heron Islands during the November to March nesting season. The turtles come ashore at night, crawl laboriously up the beach, dig a hole with their flippers and bury a clutch of eggs which typically range in number from 50 for a flatback to 120 for a loggerhead or green turtle. The loggerhead and green turtles' eggs look like ping pong balls while the flatbacks are slightly larger. It's a wonderful sight as these creatures, so ungainly and awkward on land, return to their element and glide effortlessly away. The turtles seem totally unaware of onlookers and it's possible to see them almost anywhere around the circumference of the island. Occasionally a late high tide will see them returning to the sea after dawn and they've even been known to appear in the resort!

Sea turtles return several times each season to lay more eggs. A green turtle will come back up to eight times at 13 days intervals but they then take a rest of several years before nesting again. The warmth of the sand incubates the eggs which typically take eight or nine weeks to hatch although in the cooler sand of the early part of the season, or if there is a wet spell, the period may stretch to 12 weeks. Curiously the eggs are not sex determined when they are laid. The heat of the sand determines the turtle's sex – warm sand produces more females, cooler sand more males.

The eggs hatch at night and the tiny turtles make a dash for the relative safety of the sea; waiting crabs or seagulls can easily pick them off in those dangerous first moments. The lighter sky over the horizon guides them on this important first voyage and guests at the Lady Elliot and Heron resorts are warned not to leave more lights on than necessary as this can distract them. Each year some turtles are lured to their death by the lighthouse on Lady Elliot. Life is still far from safe for a baby turtle once it reaches the sea and for the males that short sprint down the beach is likely to be their only taste of life on dry land. Females will probably not put flipper to land again until they come back to nest.

Important nesting sites for green turtles are North West, Hoskyn and Wreck Islands. The most important logger-head islands are Erskine, Masthead, Tryon and Wreck Islands. It's possible to camp on North West during the nesting season but Heron and Lady Elliot, with their resorts, are the islands where most visitors see turtles. On Heron there are typically 50 green turtles nesting every night during the peak season and over 1000 turtles have nested there in one summer. North West can have several thousand in a good season and as many as 400 may make it ashore in a single night. Loggerheads are much rarer on Heron with typically less than 100 visitors in a season and rarely more than six on any one night. Wreck Island will get over 1000 loggerheads in a good season. Hawksbills also visit the Capricorn waters, but don't nest there. ■

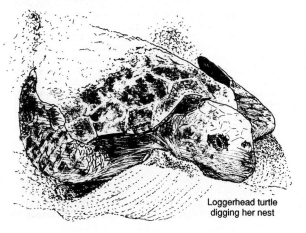

Loggerhead turtle
digging her nest

Flying Mishaps

Flying to Heron Island has had a slightly dramatic history although, fortunately, only once have regular fare paying passengers come to grief. Perhaps its a spin off from those lousy landers the island's mutton birds, whose arrival attempts are often more crashdown than touchdown. Back in WW II an air force Avro Anson aircraft on a training flight made slightly too low a pass over the island, clipping the tops of the pisonia trees and crashing on the island, killing four of the five crew.

The Poulson's services to the island with Catalina flying boats passed without mishap but helicopter flights to Heron have had a few problems over the years. In 1969 a helicopter crashed on take-off from Gladstone, seriously injuring one passenger. Three years later a helicopter took off from the resort to investigate a distress flare but crashed killing the pilot, the resort manager and a resort employee.

Only a year later there were three helicopter mishaps in the space of two months during 1973. First a chopper made an emergency landing at sea near Polmaise Reef. A second helicopter dropped its passengers off on Masthead Island then returned to the stricken helicopter only to puncture a float on landing and sink, fortunately without harm to the passengers. The third incident again took place near Polmaise Reef. The undamaged helicopter was towed to near Masthead Island where the passengers were transferred to a boat but when the tow continued the helicopter turned over and sank!

Sea The *Reef Adventurer* high-speed catamaran will take you out to the island from Gladstone in less than two hours for $65 ($130 return). The crossing can be rather choppy. Anchorages for visiting yachts are very restricted and day visitors to Heron are not welcome in any case.

WISTARI REEF

Wistari Reef is the large reef right next to Heron and although day visitors are not permitted on Heron they can visit Wistari and study Heron with binoculars, only a km or so away. P&O, which operates the resort on Heron, has a pontoon just off Wistari Reef and run a reef trip from Gladstone on the *Reef Adventurer* catamaran which continues on to Heron with resort guests.

The Wistari Reef trips operate on Monday, Wednesday, Friday, Saturday, Sunday and public holidays, departing Gladstone at 8 am and returning at 6 pm. The trip costs $75

including lunch and there are glass bottom boat trips and snorkelling gear is provided or you can study the reef from the pontoon's own underwater observatory. Bookings can be made through P&O Resorts (tel (07) 268 8224) or through Gladstone Travel World (tel (079) 78 1138) at 124 Goondoon St, Gladstone.

ONE TREE ISLAND

South-east of Heron Island this island is another National Park island and, like Heron Island, it has a marine research station, operated in this case by Sydney University. No visitors are permitted on this desolate island and it has rather more than one tree! The island was originally named by officers on HMS *Fly* during its 1843 visit and they noted a sea eagle's nest on the island which is still there today. North of One Tree and east of Heron is Sykes Reef with its very small lagoon.

Exposed reef crest, edge of One Tree Island lagoon (MN)

MASTHEAD & ERSKINE ISLANDS

Masthead Island was named by officers on HMS *Beagle* when it sailed by in 1839. It's an uninhabited national park island slightly south-west of Heron Island. Camping is permitted, with limits of 30 people in the summer bird-nesting season and 60 people in winter, but there are no facilities and campers have to be completely self-sufficient. It's also a 'silent' island, no radios or generators are permitted. The island has a dense central forest of pisonia trees, one of the largest stands of this interesting tree in the Capricornia Islands. Masthead is an important nesting ground for green turtles. Wedge-tailed shearwaters and black noddies and a number of other birds also nest here.

Transport to Masthead is charter boat only. See the Getting There & Away section at the start of this chapter for information on charter boats from Gladstone.

Erskine Island is just north of Masthead and only day visits are permitted. Even these are discouraged from October to March because of the many birds which nest here.

You see both these islands from the *Reef Adventurer*, en route to Wistari Reef or Heron Island, and get superb views of them from the helicopter. Irving Reef, west of Polmaise, usually has sufficient water cover for boats to sail right over it.

WILSON ISLAND

North of Heron Island, Wilson is a national park and a popular day trip for Heron guests looking for a break from diving. They spend a pleasant day there swimming off the island's excellent beaches and enjoying a barbecue lunch. There's superb snorkelling around Wilson Island which does not have the extensive surrounding reef area found on most other Capricornia islands. Not everybody enjoys the visitors, it's said the island's roseate terns abandoned the island when regular visitors started to turn up.

P&O Resorts (tel (07) 268 8224) has a new resort of tents erected on platforms. The cost is $85 per day including all meals. The *Reef Adventurer* will drop you off for $130 return.

Top: Snorkelling on the reef (BTDB)
Middle: Nudibranch (GBRMPA)
Bottom: Studying the reef (GBRMPA)

WRECK ISLAND

Just to the north-west of Wilson Island, Wreck Island is a Preservation Zone and no access is permitted. The island is a major rookery for loggerhead turtles and roseate terns and has had an interesting history. One of the first shipwrecks in the Southern Reef Islands, that of the *America* in 1831, probably took place here. The 391 ton *America* was built in Quebec in 1827 and was bound from Sydney to Batavia (modern day Jakarta) when she ran hard on to a reef. It's been suggested that the island might have been Lady Elliot but in 1843 Captain Blackwood of HMS *Fly* reported the remains of a wreck on the Wreck Island reef and found inscriptions on trees stating 'The America, June 1831' and also from the ship *Nelson*, which played a follow up part in the *America* saga. The island was named by Captain Blackwood after the wreckage he noted there. More recently hand-hewn ballast stone has been found on the reef flat.

The survivors from the *America* eventually made their way to Moreton Bay, a fraught journey taking a month or more. The wreckage was sold at auction and later that year the *Caledonia* sailed north to retrieve whatever could be scavenged from the reef. The unfortunate *Caledonia* arrived too late, the whaler *Nelson* had already done a salvage job on the wreckage and sailed on to Sydney in late 1831.

Matters were to turn distinctly worse for the unfortunate *Caledonia* for when it arrived at Moreton Bay a convict escape took place and the ship was hijacked, along with the ship's master, Captain Browning, who was taken along since none of the prisoners could navigate. The *Caledonia* eventually ended up in Tonga, over two months later, where the ship was scuttled. By this time only two or three of the original 15 escapees were still with the ship. Browning eventually escaped and was rescued by the barque *Oldham* but none of the convicts was brought back to Australia.

NORTH REEF

North of Wilson and Wreck Islands is tiny North Reef Island where a lighthouse was completed in 1878. It was noted at the time that the island 'is composed of nothing but dead coral, which shifts more or less during heavy gales, its total extent not exceeding 200 yards by 80'. Over the years the island certainly has shifted. The lighthouse started off right in the middle but gradually moved along the island until it hung right off one end, at which point the island about turned and moved back until the lighthouse is once more in the middle! Sensibly the lighthouse was bedded right into the solid rock, beneath the moving coral debris which formed the island.

Today the lighthouse is an automatic one but it didn't save the 3879 ton steamship *Cooma* which was wrecked on the eastern side of the reef in 1927. It's visible at low water and the reef offers great diving. Broomfield Reef with its high sandbank is about midway between North Reef, to the north, and Wilson and Wreck Islands to the south.

NORTH WEST ISLAND

At 0.9 square km, North West Island is the biggest cay on the Great Barrier Reef. Guano was mined on the island from 1894 to 1900 and at times there were over 100 people living and working here. Over 4000 tons of guano had been exported from the island when guano mining ceased, most of it went to New Zealand. A picket fence encloses the tiny grave of Dorothea Sundvall, daughter of the guano ship *Limari's* captain. She was born at sea in 1899, died a few days later and was buried on the island at the north-western end. There are said to be other graves on the island including two Japanese divers but any markers have now disappeared.

Turtles were also killed and processed into turtle soup on the island, this activity continued intermittently right up until 1928. A few bits and pieces of rusting equipment remain from the turtle soup days and the island is infested with cats and chickens from that period. Today turtles, now fully protected, have returned to North West which is the most important nesting site for green turtles in the Capricornia Group.

The island is all national park and you can camp there independently with a permit but there are also day-trips from Rosslyn Bay near Rockhampton and several commercial enterprises have made noises about setting up camping ventures on the island.

Camping

There's a limit of 150 people camping on the island and it's often fully booked at holiday periods. There are pit toilets and the hut on the island (the *Tanby Hilton*) may have some water although campers are advised to take their own. A track runs across the island from the hut. One of the possible commercial camping ventures has suggested a $40 a day deal which would include food and hire of all camping gear. There would be a maximum 15 people at the site and it would be open to the general public only outside school holidays.

Getting There & Away

Day trips are on the *Capricorn Reefseeker*, a fast catamaran which leaves Rosslyn Bay at 9 am usually four days a week, calling at Great Keppel Island to pick up more passengers on the way. The $70 fare includes lunch, a glass bottom boat ride, snorkelling and transport to/from accommodation in Rockhampton or on the coast. For info contact Great Keppel Island Tourist Services (tel (079) 27 2948 or 33 6744) at 168 Denison St, Rockhampton or at Rosslyn Bay harbour.

You may also be able to use the *Capricorn Reefseeker* for camping drop-offs. Alternatively the Keppel Barge Service (tel (079) 33 6721) from Rosslyn Bay does North West drop-offs three Saturdays a month for $125 a head return (minimum 10 people). Another way of reaching North West Island is by helicopter from Great Keppel Island.

TRYON ISLAND

Immediately north of North West Island this minute (only about 10 hectares or a tenth of a square km) national park island is a typical cay that has had little disturbance from humans although it may have been briefly exploited for guano. There is much birdlife on the island including shy black-naped and bridled terns. Wedge-tailed shearwaters also nest here as do green turtles. The north-facing beach on Tryon has many cordia trees with their bright orange flowers while despite the island's tiny size there is a small stand of pisonia trees in the centre.

You can camp here but there's a limit of 30 campers and you must be totally self-sufficient, there are not even pit toilets. Like Masthead Island this is a 'silent' island where generators and other noisemakers are not permitted. There doesn't appear to be any regular access service to the island – inquire at Gladstone or Rosslyn Bay.

SWAINS REEF

Offshore from the Capricornia area, on the main outer reef, the Swains Reef area is claimed to have some of the best fishing on the whole Great Barrier Reef. Coral trout, red emperors and Spanish mackerel are all common here.

SOUTHERN REEF FLORA & FAUNA

The islands of the Capricornia group generally support a similar plant and birdlife. Resident animal life is minimal; feral cats are found on North West but otherwise the regular visits by turtles to lay their eggs are about all there is. The birdlife, on the other hand, is limited in its scope but amazingly prolific in its number. 'Far too prolific' a visitor to Heron Island, kept awake by the constant night time caterwauling of mutton birds, might feel.

Pandanus & She-Oaks

The cays of the Southern Reef all develop basically similar vegetation patterns. Once the island has stabilised sufficiently for trees to grow it is pandanus palms and she-oaks which grow at the outer fringe since they are best able to withstand high winds and a salty environment.

Pandanus palms are instantly recognisable both by their leaf forms and their stilt-like roots which continually extend additional roots to ensure their stability. The pandanus fruit looks very much like a pineapple and with careful preparation are a food source in traditional Aboriginal society.

The she-oaks or casuarinas have leaves very much like a pine tree and the sea breezes whispering through these needles make a quite distinctive sound. The oak appellation comes from a supposed similarity of their wood, not from the most un-oak-like way they look. The bush-like tournefortia trees with their soft leaves are also able to withstand saltwater, and silvereyes and land-rails both like the tree's fruit.

Pisonia Grandis

The most characteristic tree of the Southern Reef cays is the central stands of pisonia. Closer to the sea the hardy casuarina, pandanus, scaevola and argusia are able to withstand salt spray and wind but if the cay is large enough then pisonia, with its dinstinctive wide, light-green leaves and soft wood grows in the centre of the island. On the larger cays the central canopy may be almost continuous and the tallest trees can reach 20 to 30 metres in height.

The leaves may thin out and turn yellow during the dry season from September to December but pisonias have adapted very well to the strictures of life on small coral cays. They have remarkable powers of regeneration and are able to produce new trees from fallen trunks and even, in good conditions, from a dropped branch. This is a useful ability when the occasional severe tropical storm may wreak havoc across a low lying island.

In summer pisonias produce great numbers of very sticky seed clusters which stick to birds' feathers and are carried to other islands. Not all birds simply get roped in as free transport, the seeds are so sticky that if a bird

The spikey flowers and the seed cone of the she-oak

Top Left: Buff breasted rail (GBRMPA)
Top Right: Silvereye (GBRMPA)
Middle Left: Masked boobies (GBRMPA)
Bottom: Brown boobies (GBRMPA)

inadvertently collects too many they can actually stick the bird's wings together and great numbers of birds die this way every year. The Queensland National Parks & Wildlife Service warns that, sad sight though this is, it's not possible to save birds in this predicament and you should not try.

Noddies

One of the most common of the Capricornia seabirds is the white-capped or black noddy. They nest in the pisonia trees in great numbers on many of the cays between October and March. December is the peak nesting season and the Capricornia cays are one of the most important nesting sites for these birds in the south-west Pacific. At the height of the nesting season Heron Island may have as many as 100,000 noddies on the island. Their smell pervades the island and their droppings drop so regularly that at this time of year you're strongly advised to wear a wide brimmed hat while walking the island foot trails. The birds remain on the island throughout the year.

When mating season approaches, noddies go through an elaborate mating ritual. The female bird sits in the tree where the nest will be built while the male carefully selects an appropriate leaf to use for building the nest. Having checked the leaf from every perspective he reverently hands it to his potential mate who disdainfully discards it. This process is repeated until a pile of discarded leaves litters the ground. Finally he hands her the right leaf, and she defecates on it! This leaf then forms the keystone of the nest, constructed from the previously discarded leaves cemented together with droppings.

The ritual far exceeds the quality of the resulting nest, however. No way about it, noddies build a shoddy nest. Into the shallow depression on this grotty little nest a single egg is laid and incubated for an average 35 days. That is if the egg doesn't simply fall out of the nest. If that happens they just start all over. Unfortunately chicks are also prone to falling out of the noddies' slipshod nest and in that case they, too, are simply abandoned. A storm during nesting time can wreak havoc upon a noddy colony.

Once the chicks are old enough to leave the nest they wander round in groups known as creches. During the day their parents venture far out to sea hunting small fish which swim close to the surface. When they return at night they call to their offspring, which recognise their parents' call and break away from the creche to be fed on regurgitated stomach contents. Soon the young birds also start to leave the islands each morning, at first returning earlier than their parents, which continue to feed them.

Noddy droppings are a vital element in fertilising a cay's soil and helps to account for the often surprising lush vegetation found on small cays. It is the countless thousands of years of bird droppings which build up the high phosphate guano deposits for which many coral cays have been exploited.

Wedge-tailed Shearwaters or Mutton Birds

While the noddies nest in trees mutton birds or wedge-tailed shearwaters live in burrows in the sand. Many noddies stay on the islands year round but shearwaters are only seen (and more definitely heard) during the mating and nesting season. From their winter homes the male shearwaters return to the Southern Reef Islands regular as clockwork in early October. They return to exactly the same burrow as in previous years and clean things up in preparation for the arrival of their mates.

Shearwaters mate for life and when their companion, unseen for the past year, turns up all hell breaks loose. From dawn to dusk they shriek, wail, groan and howl to each other. The whole colony seems to get together on this and the noise builds up to an absolute crescendo then suddenly ceases. But just as island visitors at this time of year heave a sigh of relief and decide they can finally get to sleep a single groan will recommence the whole symphony. You soon get used to it. It's said that sailors became convinced that certain islands were haunted. All night long this horrible, almost human-like noise would be heard, but come dawn the island would be found empty. The shearwaters had set out just before dawn to spend the day fishing.

Mutton birds have a wingspan disproportionately large compared to their body size. This makes for easy flying but difficult take offs and landings. On the islands the birds have well defined 'runways' where they line up to make their pre-dawn departure. When coming in to land, once they're committed on their final approach they have great difficulty in making changes of direction and have been known to collide with trees, buildings or casual strollers if they get it wrong! The mutton bird nest are usually in the outer fringe of an island's central pisonia growth while the 'runways' lead through the fringing vegetation towards the beach.

Apart from the tiring noise, island visitors should also take care to keep away from their nesting area. The nesting burrows are liable to collapse under a walker's weight and the unfortunate birds may be killed. The single egg is incubated for about 50 days and the chick is fed so energetically that it may eventually grow to be bigger than its parents! Then the parents abandon their offspring and fly off, leaving their well fed chick to survive on its body fat, learn to fly and follow its parents. It's been suggested that shearwaters' lousy take off and landing abilities is not unrelated to the fact that their parents leave them to learn this vital skill by trial and error!

Silvereyes

The tiny olive green silvereyes, named for the whitish-silver ring around their eyes, are one of the cheekiest of the islands' birds. At Lady Elliot and Heron Islands they've learnt to exploit the advantages of a handy resort and can often be seen inspecting the food offerings. At Heron they even learned to lift the lid of sugarbowls by concerted group efforts, forcing a changeover to sugar sachets! These tiny birds are continuous residents, they don't come and go from the islands and are not identical to their slightly smaller mainland cousins. This interesting small captive population has been studied on Heron for over 20 years. Unlike their island neighbours the noddies, whose nest is nothing if not jerry built, the silvereyes build a nest which is a model of craftsmanship. The neat little cup shaped nest is constructed of pandanus leaves, bound together with spider webs!

Other Birds

Other birds found on the Capricornia cays include silver gulls which are very common and usually nest in the late summer. Gulls often harass other birds and will peck open their eggs if left unattended and even kill their chicks. Visitors to the cays should not encourage these notorious scavengers.

A variety of terns are found on the island. Bridled terns have a white eyebrow line but are otherwise mostly brown. They nest from October to March and their nests are scattered indiscriminately across the island, their eggs often hidden in grass or fringe vegetation. When alarmed, bridled terns make a noise like a dog's bark. Elegant black-naped terns are also found on some of the islands and visitors should take care not to disturb these nervous birds. On Heron Island they've taken such a dislike to human contact that they've all moved off the island and now nest on the harbour breakwater, the rusting old Protector. Roseate terns are also notoriously shy and are generally only found on islands where human visits are few.

Heron Island's elegant reef herons gave their name to the island although they are more correctly known as eastern reef egrets. They can be seen stalking imperiously along the water's edge at low tide, or hanging around at the top of the beach. The grey and white varieties are simply a colour variation.

Banded land-rails are found on several of the Capricornia islands. The hen-like birds are able to fly but prefer to stay on the ground. They've adapted well to human contact and can be seen scrounging around the resort at Heron. Bar-shouldered doves are also often seen with the rails. Sooty oystercatchers have totally sooty-black plumage, contrasting nicely with their red eyes, bright orange/red bill and pink legs. Oysters are a principal part of their diet. They distract would be predators from their young by putting on an elaborate act which can include pretending they have broken a wing or even rolling on the ground as if they are on the point of death.

Ruddy turnstones do just that, they wander along the waters edge flipping over stones, shells or bits of weed to see if there's anything interesting underneath. These birds breed in the Arctic and migrate here for the Australian summer months from September to April. Many of the young birds also spend their first winter in Australia before attempting the long migration flight for the first time.

Although the bird populations are essentially the same from island to island there are often unusual sightings. Since the mid-80s Lady Elliot has even had a handful of rare red-tailed tropic birds nesting on the island. Raine Island, far to the north, is the only other known nesting site on the east coast of Australia for this bird.

Hermit Crabs
The Capricornia islands have two species of terrestrial hermit crabs. During daytime these crabs hide away in vegetation or coral rubble, emerging after sunset to

Hermit crab (GBRMPA)

search for food (scraps left by island visitors on the beach are quite acceptable) and top up the 'shell water' they keep in their shells. Once a year, over several nights after the full moon in January, the crabs mate by the water's edge. Male crabs attract females by making a quacking noise, it can actually be heard if it's a very quiet night. Apart from visits to the sea to replenish the water in their shells this is the only time in their adult life that these hermit crabs return to the sea.

Their eggs, however, are washed out by the outgoing tide and once they have hatched out the young crabs go through six moulting stages over the next eight months, before making their way back to land, finding a suitable shell and taking up the dry land phase of their life. These hermit crabs always prefer turban shells but if you pick one up don't turn it upside down as the water in the crab's shell may drain out endangering its life until it can fill it up again. Don't put it in the ocean either, they can drown. ∎

Great Keppel

Area: 14 square km
Type: continental
High point: 175 metres
Maximum visitor population: 400-plus at the resort
Per person daily cost: approximately $200
Resort operator: Australian Airlines
In brief: This relatively large island is heavily promoted to a younger group but it's also popular for families during school holidays and it has a youth hostel and campsite. The island has superb beaches and is popular for day trips

The Island

Owned by Australian Airlines, the Great Keppel resort has been heavily promoted as a young people's escape – 'get wrecked on Great Keppel', 'after a holiday on Great Keppel you'll really need a holiday' and so on. The resort certainly attracts a young crowd at certain times of the year but at other times it's also a popular family resort. Plus the island has a range of budget accommodation, separate from the resort area, including a youth hostel and a campsite. And it's very popular for day trippers with a variety of boats shuttling out from Rosslyn Bay on the coast. What Great Keppel most definitely is not is sophisticated; don't come here looking for fancy accommodation, fine food or high class entertainment, you won't find it.

The island was named by Captain Cook when he sailed by in May 1770 after Rear Admiral Augustus Keppel. Cook did a great deal of naming as he cruised the east coast of Australia and often with a keen eye to the honoured individual's later importance. Keppel eventually became the First Lord of the Admiralty. The first European known to visit the island was a naturalist named McGillivray of the ship *Rattlesnake* in 1847. At that time Aboriginals lived on the island which they named Wapparaburra, thought to mean 'resting place'. The campsite on the island today is named Wapparaburra.

First settled by Europeans in 1906 the early settlers were a disreputable bunch who poisoned the flour of the island Aboriginals with strychnine after some of their sheep were killed. From the 1920s through the 1940s the Leeke family grazed sheep on the island and gave their name to Leeke's Beach and Leeke's Creek. You can still see their old homestead which has been restored and is a popular walk destination from the resort. The island resort opened in 1967 but other people still live on the island. The Svendsen family at the northern end are professional fishers.

Although it's not on the reef, Great Keppel is a fine island, big enough that you won't see all of it in an afternoon but small enough to explore over a few days. Its 14 square km is fringed by 28 km of very fine beach. Great Keppel is only 13 km off the coast and there's a wide variety of air and sea transport out to the island so getting there is easy and reasonably priced. Together with the good choice of cheaper places to stay it's an unbeatable combination for budget travellers.

Information

The resort phone number is (079) 39 1744 and the address is Great Keppel Island Resort, PO Box 108, Rockhampton, Qld 4700.

There are ISD pay phones in the resort but the rooms don't have phones. The resort reception has Commonwealth Savings Bank facilities. The resort Island Shop has clothes, sunscreen protection, toiletries, newspapers and magazines, postcards and stamps and maps of the island.

Zoning Most of the waters around Great Keppel are zoned General Use A or B but the area directly off Fisherman's Beach is all Marine National Park A which allows limited line fishing but prohibits shell or coral collecting. The waters around Middle Island are zoned the more restrictive Marine National Park B.

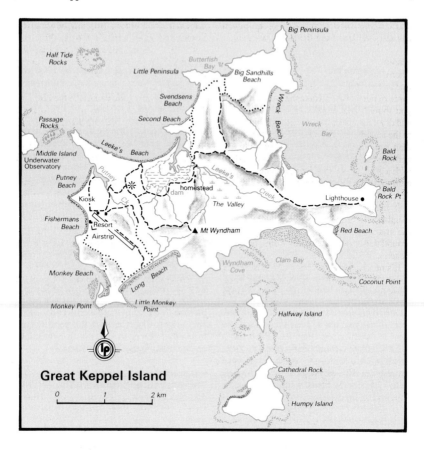

Great Keppel Island

0   1   2 km

Beaches & Snorkelling

It only takes a short stroll from the main resort area to find your own deserted stretch of white-sand beach. These are amongst the best beaches on any of the resort islands and it's remarkable how many of Great Keppel's noted 'ragers' make no effort to try any of them apart from Fisherman's Beach, the one right in front of the resort, and nearby Putney Beach. Small Shelving Beach is only a few minutes' walk from the resort or further afield Long Beach and Leeke's Beach are also pleasant. Some beaches, like Red Beach near the lighthouse, are only accessible by boat.

The water around the island is clear, warm and beautiful and there is good coral at many points, especially at Shelving Beach and Monkey Beach. Further out there's more good coral between Great Keppel and Humpy Island to the south, particularly around Halfway Island.

The resort hires out water sports equipment through Keppel Kuatics on the beach. Snorkelling equipment is free to resort guest, non-residents can rent it at $6 for half a day and $10 for a full day. Snorkelling equipment can also be hired from the hostel warden.

Walks

There are a number of fine bushwalking tracks but don't underestimate the island, some of the walks can take the whole day and you should bring water as it can be very hot and dry. During its farming period some parts of the island were treated with somewhat less than good care and in a few places ugly garbage dumps and other eyesores could do with a good clean up. The goats you may see around the island are a legacy of the farming days.

It takes about 20 minutes to walk the length of the airstrip to Long Beach and you can make a circuit of it by walking back around the coast via Monkey Point, Monkey Beach and Shelving Beach.

It's nearly three km to the old homestead, count on about an hour each way. The walk starts from near the Shell House and climbs up to a lookout before dropping down to the homestead near Leeke's Creek. You can make this a partial round trip by taking the turning down to Leeke's Beach and walking along the beach and over the headland to Putney Beach.

The more energetic can make the climb to Mt Wyndham, at 175 metres the highest point on the island. The trail branches off the homestead route and the summit is clearly visible from the resort, rising up to the east of the airstrip. It takes about 1½ hours from the resort to the top.

There are two longer walks which continue on beyond the homestead. It's nearly eight km to the lighthouse, climbing up to the ridge line beyond the homestead and Leeke's Creek and following the ridge to its 170 metre high point and down to Bald Rock Point and the lighthouse. The walk takes 2½ hours each way so allow the whole day for this outing. At the top of the ridge you can turn north-west instead of south-east and

Great Keppel Island sunset (TW)

walk down to Big Sandhills Beach on Butterfish Bay.

Diving

The Great Barrier Reef is a long way out at this latitude but there's good diving much closer to Great Keppel and you can go diving with Haven Diving (tel (079) 39 4217), just beyond the Wapparaburra Kiosk. They have a five-day Monday to Friday diving course for $195 – all inclusive except for a medical certificate. Free introductory sessions are offered on Wednesday afternoons at 2 pm.

Certified divers are catered for on the *Saracen* (tel (079) 39 1646), a 26-foot catamaran, which does daily dive trips from Rosslyn Bay, picking up at Great Keppel Island on the way. You can do an introductory dive from the *Saracen* if you're not already qualified.

The Tropic Diva (tel (079) 39 4431) runs snorkelling, fishing and diving trips to various locations around the islands. A day costs $25 for non-divers, $35 for divers or $55 with all diving gear and two air fills. They'll drop you on Great Keppel at the end of the day if you wish. You can arrange transport to the harbour through Rockhampton Diving (tel (079) 28 0433) or Yeppoon Backpackers Hostel.

If you do want to get out to the reef *Capricorn Reefseeker* departs from Rosslyn Bay at 9 am four days a week and stops by Great Keppel on its way out to North West Island. At the reef you can snorkel, view the coral through a glass bottomed boat or scuba dive. It's operated by Great Keppel Island Tourist Services (tel (079) 27 2948 & 33 6744).

Close to Great Keppel itself Man & Wife Island and Bald Rock are two popular diving attractions. The water off the southern end of Halfway Island and the shallow Middle Island Reef between Putney Point and Middle Island also has good coral and sea snakes. Parker's Bommie, off the southeastern tip of Great Keppel is claimed to offer the best diving around the island, so long as the weather is calm. The bombora rises almost to the surface from water about 20 metres deep and is surrounded by a great variety of sea ferns, sponges, coral and a great number of fish. See the following Other Keppel Bay Islands section for more information on diving in the area.

Fishing & Sailing

You can rent windsurfers and small sailing craft off the beach and from Fishermans Beach, in front of the Shell House, you can be taken for an hour's sail for $6 or to Humpy Island for $20. Two-hour sailing cruises on a 27-foot yacht leave from near Keppel Kuatics at 10.30 am and 2 pm.

Keppel Isles Yacht Charters (tel (079) 33 6577) has vessels for hire from $140 a day. Several other vessels are available for longer diving, fishing or cruising trips – ask at Rockhampton tourist office or Rosslyn Bay harbour. One possibility is Keppel Island Cruises (tel (079) 39 1825).

Other Activities

The Great Keppel resort is heavy on entertainment — a resident rock band, lots of planned activities, guaranteed exhaustion! People who come for that usually reckon it's a lot of fun and the resort makes some provision for day-trippers with a pool, bar, outdoor table and umbrellas outside the main resort area.

On dry land the resort has squash courts, tennis courts, a small golf course, a playground and a couple of swimming pools. Resort guests are also kept busy with archery, aerobics, volleyball and other organised activities. They don't want you to get bored.

On the beach two places hire out water sports equipment – Keppel Kuatics on Fishermans Beach is run by the resort, or there's the Beach Shed on Putney Beach. Both have snorkelling gear, jet skis, windsurfers, catamarans, motor boats, fuel, tackle and bait. Non-powered equipment like aqua bikes, catamarans, sailboards, paddle skis and snorkelling gear is free to guests but it's also available, for a charge, to non-residents. The Beach Shed has slightly cheaper rates.

Keppel Kuatics motor boats are $12 per hour or $35 for six hours. There are limits on how far you can take a motor boat, generally only as far as Leeke's Beach in the north and Long Beach in the south. You might be able to talk your way into an $18 ride to Humpy Island and back with Keppel Kuatics if they're not busy. You can also take a para-flight with Keppel Kuatics for $18, you're only up for about seven minutes but that must be long enough as it's so popular that you need to book on arrival if you're not staying on the island overnight. Waterskiing ($7) is another popular activity.

Hour-long horse rides organised by the resort head off to the homestead several times a day at a price of $15 for non-resort guests – book at the resort. If you've got money to burn you can even take helicopter trips from Keppel, including out to the Great Barrier Reef. Check with Logan Aviation (tel (079) 39 1454).

During school holidays the Keppel Kids Klub can keep kids occupied all day long. Finally, like almost every resort up the coast, Great Keppel has a lorikeet feeding table where the colourful birds appear for their 4 to 4.30 pm feed every day. Possums can appear around the resort any time.

Accommodation

The Australian Airlines Great Keppel resort is so well known that it's easy to forget there are some excellent budget priced alternatives. At the resort the great majority of visitors will be on some sort of all inclusive package but Great Keppel also has a camp-site, a youth hostel and other alternatives so it's one of the limited number of resort islands where backpackers can stay at a reasonable cost.

The Resort Australian Airlines has a variety of package tours to Great Keppel. Depending where you start from seven days there will cost you around $1400 to $2000 twin-share including airfare; in the high season it's about $80 more. The price includes accommodation, food and all the facilities. Daily costs are officially $172 single or $280 double for the 'garden units', $202 single or $334 double for the 'beachfront units'. If you stay

seven nights or more the daily cost drops to $129/210 for single/double garden units and $151/250 for beachfront units.

There are over 150 units, fan cooled and with tea/coffee making and fridges. They're plain and straightforward older motel-type units, just like you'll find in hundreds of country towns all over Australia. The beachfront and garden units are essentially the same, only the location differs. There are also family garden units which have a couple of bunk beds in a screened off area. The rooms have a verandah out front and there are laundry facilities in each block. Surprisingly, despite Great Keppel's rock-on-till-all-hours image, noise doesn't seem to be a real problem – the disco and other centres of disturbance are kept down at one end of the grounds. Ventilation can, if the wind's blowing the wrong way, be more of a problem; the room design doesn't encourage breezes to blow through.

The Hostel The *Great Keppel Youth Hostel* (tel (079) 27 5288) has room for 55 people and costs $9 a night in the dorms, or $10 in the rooms. Despite a recent clean-up and paint job it's still rather shabby but that doesn't stop it being very popular and often booked out for weeks ahead. It has two large dorms, two rooms for four, and one room with seven beds, two kitchens, a new laundry and a barbecue area. You can book the island hostel through the Rockhampton YHA but if you want to be certain of a bed it's wise to book well ahead through the YHA headquarters in Brisbane. The hostel is a short walk behind the Wapparaburra Kiosk.

The Campsite Great Keppel offers several camping possibilities. At the *Wapparaburra Haven Tourist Park* (tel (079) 39 1907) you can camp on a sandy, shaded area close to the beach for $8 per person with your own equipment. There are also pre-erected tents, complete with mattresses, which cost $12 per person or $15 at peak periods. They're known as the *Keppel Tent Village* and each tent takes four people. The Tent Village has some under-cover cooking and washing-up facilities but there's no fridge or kitchen gear although it is planned to make improvements in this area.

There are also cabins at the Wapparaburra complex – they cost $75 for two people, $15 for each additional person. The cabins sleep six and have full kitchen facilities, laundry and bedding but share bathrooms with the other Wapparaburra inhabitants. By mainland standards the cabins aren't cheap but for the islands they're a bargain.

Right next door to Wapparaburra Haven is *Keppel Kamp-Out* (tel (079) 39 2131) (or you can book toll free on tel (008) 03 0711) an almost identical tent village, in outward appearance, to Wapparaburra's. However the concept (and price) is different. It's geared to the 18 to 35 age bracket with organised activities and the cost of $65 per person includes twin share tent accommodation, three meals (wine with dinner) and all activities such as water sports, parties and video nights. The tents are large, the gardens are lovely and the staff are friendly.

Other Camping Other possibilities used to include camping at designated spots around the island but this is no longer allowed. You can camp on some of the islands near Great Keppel – North Keppel, Pumpkin, Miall, Middle, Humpy and Halfway Islands – see under Other Keppel Bay Islands.

Food

The Resort Most resort visitors will be on all-inclusive deals which includes breakfast, lunch and dinner at the *Admiral Keppel Restaurant*. Breakfast and lunch are buffet style, dinner is from a limited menu. The food is very much Aussie pub food; there's nothing wrong with it but unless counter meals are your idea of great dining it quickly gets tedious. There's an earlier kids dinner followed by organised activities so parents can get the children out of their hair.

Other Possibilities There's no alternative restaurant at the resort but if you just need a snack or if you're camping, staying at the hostel or just day-tripping there are several other places you can get something to eat. At the resort the *Keppel Kafe* offers burgers from $2.60, meat pies, and other snacks. If you're not staying at the resort you can still get the lunchtime smorgasbord for $15 and on weekends, when the number of day-trippers is much greater, there's a $6 barbecue.

Half-way between the resort and the kiosk, along the path, the *Shell House* has a good shell collection and sells excellent homemade scones and rock cakes. A Devonshire tea costs $2.60. The owner is an interesting character who's lived on Keppel for many years and worked as a chef in the resort's early days. He's happy to chat about the island's history and his tropical garden offers a pleasant break from the sun.

The *Wapparaburra Kiosk* has a small dining area where evening meals are offered from $7.50 to $15. A camper's platter – a salad, meat patty and pineapple plus a bread roll – costs $7. Sometimes there are pasta nights with a smorgasbord of pasta and salads – all you can eat for $8.

Cooking for Yourself If you want to cook your own food on the island it's best to bring a few basic supplies from the mainland. The Wapparaburra Kiosk at the campsite has basic supplies including fruit, vegetables, groceries and dairy food but variety is limited and prices are, of course, higher on the island. It's open from 8 am to 9 pm daily and it does a roaring trade – it's unusual not to have to queue there.

Entertainment

Night-time entertainment is a big deal at Great Keppel and getting wrecked in the Wreck Bar with a live band or disco is a popular activity. The resort doesn't particularly encourage campers and hostellers to join in its nightly merrymaking but so long as you pay the $5 cover charge for the nightly rage you won't be turned away.

The Sunset Lounge and the Sand Bar are alternative places for a drink at the resort.

Getting There & Away

Air Sunstate Airlines flies at least twice daily

between Rockhampton and Great Keppel. The 50-km flight costs $42 one-way and there are usually connections with Australian Airlines flights up and down the coast. Book through Australian, they can be reached via the resort on (079) 39 1744.

Sea Ferries for Great Keppel leave from Rosslyn Bay on the Capricorn Coast. At least four craft make the crossing daily, and some do more than one trip. A price war between the various operators dropped the cost to absurd levels in recent years but typically it costs about $15 return plus another $5 for the connecting bus from Rockhampton. You can book the ferries through your accommodation or agents in Rockhampton or the Capricorn Coast. The youth hostel in Rockhampton often has special bargain deals.

Cheapest are two slow boats, the *Seafari* and the *Denison Star*, both taking about 45 minutes from Rosslyn Bay to Great Keppel. Both have connecting buses which will pick you up and return you to accommodation in Rockhampton. The *Seafari* people will also pick up and drop off along the coast between Yeppoon and Emu Park. Both vessels leave around 9 am and return from the island between 3.30 and 5 pm. The *Denison Star* also makes one or two other return trips between these times, with the last departure from Rosslyn Bay usually at 4 pm. The *Seafari* is operated by Great Keppel Island Tourist Services (tel (079) 27 2948 & 33 6744) at 168 Denison St, Rockhampton. For *Denison Star* info and bookings, phone (079) 27 6996.

More expensive options are the *Aquajet* and the *Victory*, also operated by Great Keppel Island Tourist Services. The *Victory* leaves daily about 9 am and takes 20 minutes: for $23 you get the ride to Great Keppel and back and an optional free cruise from the island, with boomnetting. This popular activity consists of being soaked by riding alongside the boat in a net strung outboard on booms. For a further $6 you can visit the Middle Island observatory. After all this you

then have three hours on Great Keppel before the *Victory* heads back at 3.30 pm. Lunch is available for $8. The *Aquajet* is a fast launch which makes two or three return trips daily and takes 15 minutes one-way. The return fare of $15 also entitles you to the daily 10 am to 12.30 pm cruise on the *Victory*; this cruise is free to resort guests. There are free pick-ups from Rockhampton and the Capricorn Coast timed to coincide with the *Victory*.

The *Saracen* dive boat (tel (079) 39 1646) also acts as a ferry between Rosslyn Bay harbour and Great Keppel. It costs $15 return and leaves Rosslyn Bay at 8 am, Great Keppel at 4 pm daily. The *Golden Phoenix* catamaran (tel (079) 39 1154) does a $35 day cruise four times a week which takes in Great Keppel and the Middle Island observatory. You get lunch and you can snorkel, windsurf and jet-ski for free.

Rosslyn Bay, departure point for the Great Keppel services, is south of Yeppoon. You can get there on the ferry operators' connecting buses, by bus from Rocky to Yeppoon and then by taxi or with your own vehicle. There's a daily $5 car parking charge at Rossyln Bay; alternatively you can leave your car at the Kempsea Car Park (tel (079) 33 6670) at Scenic Highway, Yeppoon, for $40 per week.

If you come to Great Keppel with your own boat the anchorages around the island are reasonable although rather unprotected. Svendsen's Beach is a popular anchorage. The island is also a good place to pick up a ride on a yacht heading north to the Whitsundays or beyond; check the notice-board at the Wapparaburra Kiosk.

Other Keppel Bay Islands

Great Keppel is only the biggest of the 18 continental islands dotted around Keppel Bay, all within 20 km of the coast. The other islands in the Keppel group are all virtually undeveloped. Part of the reason for this is lack of water – only Great Keppel has a

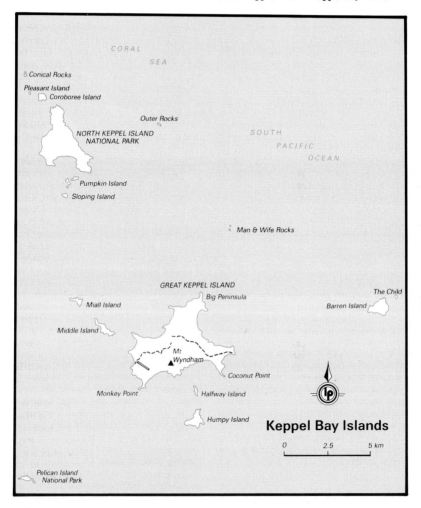

Keppel Bay Islands

CORAL SEA

Conical Rocks
Pleasant Island
Coroboree Island

Outer Rocks

NORTH KEPPEL ISLAND
NATIONAL PARK

SOUTH PACIFIC OCEAN

Pumpkin Island
Sloping Island

Man & Wife Rocks

GREAT KEPPEL ISLAND
Big Peninsula

The Child
Miall Island
Barren Island

Middle Island

Mt Wyndham

Coconut Point

Monkey Point
Halfway Island

Humpy Island

0   2.5   5 km

Pelican Island
National Park

permanent water supply from wells. You may get to visit Middle Island, with its underwater observatory, or Halfway or Humpy Islands if you're staying on Great Keppel.

Some of the islands are national parks where you can maroon yourself for a few days' self-sufficient camping, while Pumpkin Island is privately-owned and has a few cabins where you can get away from it all in slightly more comfort. Most of the islands have clean white beaches and several, notably Halfway, have fringing coral reefs which are excellent for snorkelling or diving.

Camping

To camp on a national park island you need to take all your own supplies including water

Emperor angelfish (GBRMPA)

– on North Keppel and Humpy Islands water is only available for washing, and on most others there's none at all. You also need a camping permit, and since the numbers of campers are limited, these can be hard to come by for some islands. You can get info and permits from the national parks office at 194 Quay St in Rockhampton (tel (079) 27 6511) or the ranger base at Rosslyn Bay harbour (tel (079) 33 6608), PO Box 770, Yeppoon, Qld 4703.

Diving

There are a number of good diving spots around the Keppel Bay Islands. Visibility is generally clear, it's usually at its best in the June-July-August winter months. Large manta rays are often seen in these waters and sea snakes are quite common around the reefs. The olive sea snakes are inquisitive creatures and often give divers a scare by peering into their face masks or winding around their legs. Sea snakes are poisonous but harmless as long as you don't annoy them.

Although there is some good diving around Great Keppel itself the water tends to be clearer and deeper around the outer islands where manta rays, turtles and other larger species are seen more frequently. Barren Island and The Child are a particularly popular diving locale.

Getting There & Away

Water taxis (tel (079) 33 6350) from Rosslyn Bay harbour cost $18 per person (minimum two) one-way to any of the Keppel Bay islands. They'll also take you from Great Keppel to the other islands. The *Ariake* or the *Saracen* are popular boats. You can bareboat charter a six-berth boat from Yeppoon for $140 a day, phone (079) 33 6577 for details.

For transport to North West Island and the Capricorn Group islands on the Barrier Reef beyond Keppel Bay, see the Southern Reef Islands section.

BARREN ISLAND & THE CHILD

Rising sheer from the water Barren Island is indeed rather barren but here, on the outer edge of Keppel Bay, the water is generally clear and there is a great variety of marine life. The Child is a smaller rock thrusting up from the sea just north of Barren Island. The narrow channel separating the two islands has a steeply sided gully which offers fascinating diving.

NORTH KEPPEL ISLAND

The second largest of the group and one of the most northerly, six square km North Keppel is a national park. The most popular camping spot is Considine Beach on the north-west coast, where there are toilets and well water for washing but not drinking. The camping limit is 150 people at one time. South of Considine Beach are a collection of shacks which you can rent for $230 a week. Contact Brian Hooper Real Estate (tel 079) 39 6581) in Yeppoon but note that there are very few facilities and no water. Take insect repellant for North Keppel as the mosquitoes and other six-legged wildlife can be fierce.

PUMPKIN ISLAND

Just south of North Keppel, tiny Pumpkin Island has beaches, reefs, mangroves and some fine views. Three cabins here accommodate five people each at a cost of $60 per day for the whole cabin. There's water and solar electricity. Each cabin has a cooking area with stove and fridge, a bathroom with shower, one double bed and three single beds. Bedding is provided but take all your own food and drinks other than water. Phone (079) 39 2431 for info and bookings. You may be able to get discounts through Yeppoon Backpackers Hostel. A water taxi costs about $70 return for two people.

MIALL & MIDDLE ISLANDS

These two small islands just north-west of Great Keppel are national parks with no facilities and tight limits on the numbers of people who can camp there at one time – eight on Middle, six on Miall.

Just off Middle Island is the underwater observatory (tel (079) 39 3139) which is visited by cruises from Rosslyn Bay and from Great Keppel, you can easily see the observatory from the resort. A confiscated Taiwanese fishing junk was sunk next to the observatory to provide a haven for fish and there's usually plenty to see.

Boats shuttle across from the beach near the resort, usually every hour from 11.15 am daily. A visit to the observatory costs $6 including the boat trip. Tickets can be bought from the Wapparaburra Kiosk or right on the boat. Tours on the *Victory* catamaran from Rosslyn Bay also take in the observatory.

HALFWAY ISLAND

Just south of Great Keppel, little Halfway Island is a national park with a good reef, no facilities and a camping limit of six.

HUMPY ISLAND

A short way south of Halfway Island, Humpy has little shade as its vegetation bears the brunt of the south-east winds. Like Halfway, it's a national park and a popular snorkelling ground. There's a camping limit of 30, toilets and water for washing but not drinking.

OTHER ISLANDS

Further south are Pelican, Divided and Peak Islands. Camping is not permitted on Peak Island during the turtle season while Pelican and Divided Islands are very rocky. There are limited anchorages and few beaches on these three islands. None of them have any facilities. Wedge and Hummocky Islands are privately owned.

Duke Islands

Half way north between Yeppoon and Mackay many of the Duke Islands are privately owned. Few people stop here and even most yachties skip the group altogether (the anchorages are not very good) and head for the Percy Isles instead. Other problems with the Duke Islands is that access to Stanage Bay, the most obvious jumping-off point for private boats, is by a long stretch of dirt road. The Shoalwater Bay Military Training Area is a further restriction on access and the islands also suffer from seven metre tides. Wild Duck Island has an airstrip but attempts to set up a resort there have been so unsuccessful that it is known locally as Lame Duck Island.

Percy Isles

The Percy Isles – Middle Percy, North East and South Percy – are also difficult to reach without your own boat but since Middle Percy is about half way between the Keppels and the Whitsundays it's a popular rest stop for yachties.

Surrounded by sandy bays the island is a good anchorage with washing and shower facilities for visitors.

Andy Martin lives on the island and lets people stay in his A-frame building on the west side; you can contact him by writing care of Mackay Post Office, Qld 4740. Pine Islet, just to the west of Middle Percy, had a manned lighthouse until 1987 when it was converted to automatic operation.

Sea Snakes

Divers and snorkellers often see sea snakes which are found in many places along the Great Barrier Reef. Sea snakes are a marine adaptation of normal land snakes. They have evolved paddle like tails to propel them through the water and a means of sealing their nostrils when they are submerged. They generally come to the surface to breathe every 20 to 30 minutes. The different hunting technique required underwater has also resulted in the development of extremely potent venom. On land a snake can bite its victim and then follow its scent until it dies. Following disabled prey is not so easy underwater and there is always some other predator ready to jump in and grab an easy meal. So sea snakes have developed a venom which guarantees instant death!

Fortunately for divers sea snakes are retiring creatures and most unlikely to pose any danger to humans unless they are molested. They do not like to be netted or hooked on fishing lines, fishermen note! The olive sea snake has given more than a few people momentary cause for concern as they are extremely curious and seem to have a deep interest in scuba divers. Having a highly venomous creature stare in your face mask or wrap itself around your limbs is likely to make you nervous, even if you know its intentions are friendly! ■

Sex & Coral

Coral's sex life may be infrequent (it only happens once a year) but when it does it's certainly spectacular. Some coral polyps are all male or all female while other colonies' polyps are hermaphrodite, that is they are both male and female. In a few types of coral these polyps can produce their own young which are released at various times over the year. In most cases, however, an hermaphrodite polyp's sperm cannot fertilise its own eggs or other eggs from the same colony.

Although the mass spawning which creates new coral only takes place once a year the build up to the big night lasts for six months or more. During that time the polyps ripen their eggs which are initially white but then change to pink, red, orange and other bright colours. At the same time the male testes form in the polyps and develop the sperm.

The big night comes in late spring or early summer beginning a night or two after a full moon and building to a crescendo on the fourth, fifth and sixth nights. At this time the water temperature is right and tidal variation is at a minimum. Within the coral the eggs and sperm are formed into bundles and a half hour before spawning time the bundles are 'set', that is they are held ready at the mouth of the polyp, clearly visible through the thin tissue. Then all over the reef these tiny bundles are released and float towards the surface.

The remarkable thing is all over the reef this spawning takes place at the same time. Different colonies release their egg and sperm bundles, single sex polyps eject their sperm or their eggs, everything floats up. The egg and sperm bundles, big enough to be seen with the naked eye, are a spectacular sight. It's been described as looking like a fireworks display or an upside down snowstorm and since the event can be so accurately predicted divers are often able to witness it.

Once at the surface the bundles break up and the sperm swim off to find eggs of the same coral type. Obviously corals of the same type have to spawn at the same time in order for sperm from one colony to reach eggs from another but on the reef all the corals spawn at once. It's obviously far from easy for an individual sperm to find the right egg when the water is swarming with them but scientists think that by all spawning at once they reduce the risk of being consumed by the many marine creatures that would prey on them. By spawning soon after the full moon the reduced tidal variation means there is more time for fertilisation to take place before waves and currents sweep them away.

Once fertilisation has taken place the egg cells begin to divide and within a day have become swimming coral larvae known as *planulae*. These are swept along by the sea but after a few days the planulae sink to the bottom and if the right spot is found the tiny larva becomes a coral polyp and a new coral colony is begun. ∎

Brampton & the Cumberland Islands

The Cumberland Islands, sometimes referred to as the southern Whitsundays, lie immediately to the south of the Whitsundays. Indeed the line which separates the Cumberlands from the Whitsundays is really an arbitrary one, the islands are similar in appearance and they continue straight from one group to the next. The islands are all national parks except for Keswick, St Bees and part of tiny Farrier Island, just to the west of Goldsmith Island. Two of the islands, Newry and Brampton Islands, have resorts and with a National Parks permit you can camp on a number of the islands.

The local Ngaro Aboriginal people once visited the islands, paddling flimsy bark canoes out from the mainland. Aboriginal middens have been found on Brampton and other islands. The group was named after the Duke of Cumberland, brother of King George III, by Captain Cook when he sailed through in 1770. His mind must have been far away in the Lake District of northern England on that day as he named a number of the islands in the group after towns in the Lake District of England.

Around the turn of the century Europeans began to settle some of the islands and use them for grazing. Apart from the resort islands Farrier, Keswick and St Bees still have residents.

Newry Island Group

The Newry Island Group comprises half a dozen islands, three of which you can camp on. Rabbit Island to the west is the largest of the group and has a campsite at its south-east tip. Next to it is Newry Island itself, with the small resort at the north-east corner. Outer Newry Island flanks Newry Island to the east and also has a campsite. Immediately south of the three larger islands, between them and the mainland, are smaller Stone, Acacia,

Mausoleum and Rocky Islands. The islands are close enough to the mainland that box jellyfish may be found in the summer months, swimmers should beware.

The continental islands are rocky and wild-looking but Rabbit Island has a series of sandy beaches along its eastern side. Five of the islands – the three larger ones (Rabbit, Newry and Outer Newry) and two of the smaller islands (Acacia and Mausoleum) – are national park. These national park islands have grassy open forests and isolated small patches of rainforest. The towering hoop pines, Mackay cedars, tulip oaks, mountain ash, blue gums, ironbarks and bloodwoods are the main trees.

The islands have many possums and echidnas while koalas, which were introduced here, have thrived. Observant walkers may also see the holes scratched by bandicoots and the large mounds scraped together

by scrub fowl in order to incubate their eggs. Patches of seagrass around the island are grazed by gentle dugongs but you would have to be very lucky to spot one. Between November and January green turtles come up on the beaches of Rabbit Island to lay their eggs.

Camping
Rabbit Island has the main national park campsite with barbecues, tables and toilets. Although there is a water tank here, water may be in short supply during the summer months. The site on Outer Newry's western beach also has toilets, tables and water. The resort on Newry, which has camp sites as well, will boat you over to Rabbit or Outer Newry Islands. Camping permits for the national park sites are obtained from the Queensland National Parks & Wildlife Service (tel (079) 57 6292), 64 Victoria St, Mackay. The postal address is QNPWS,

Mackay District Office, PO Box 623, Mackay, Qld 4740.

NEWRY ISLAND
Area: 0.45 square km
Type: continental
Maximum visitor population: 120
Per person daily cost: approximately $60
In brief: small continental island with simple cabins and camping

The Island
There are day trips from Victor Creek to pleasant Newry Island, a little known island very close to the coast. There's good swimming, bushwalks and plenty of koalas but this is certainly not a big bucks tourist resort, most of the visitors are local cane cockies and fishermen or visitors from Mackay.

Information
The resort phone number is (079) 59 0214,

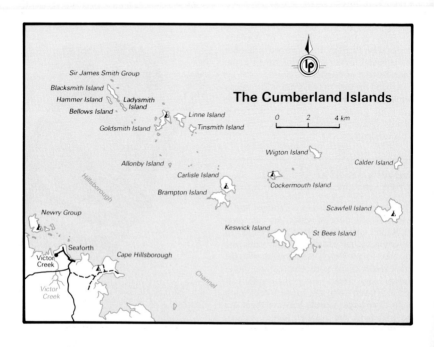

The Cumberland Islands

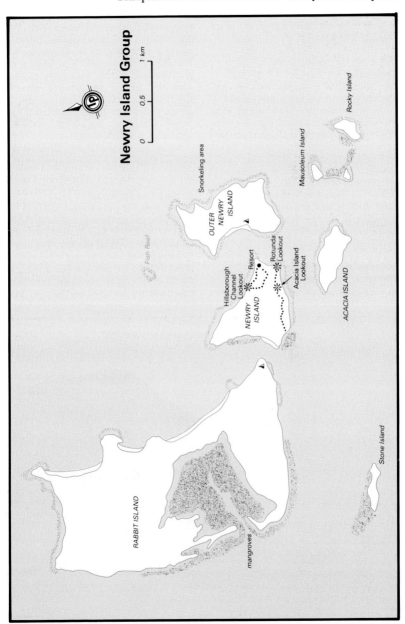

Newry Island Group

0   0.5   1 km

Fish Reef

Snorkeling area

OUTER NEWRY ISLAND

Hillsborough Channel Lookout

Resort

NEWRY ISLAND

Rotunda Lookout

Acacia Island Lookout

ACACIA ISLAND

Mausoleum Island

Rocky Island

RABBIT ISLAND

mangroves

Stone Island

or write to Newry Island Resort, PO Box 3, Seaforth, Qld 4741.

Activities

The island has a superb walk through patches of rainforest to a picnic site at Fish Point on the other side of the island, overlooking the Rabbit Island camping area. You may see koalas along the way and they have been known to swim between Newry and nearby Rabbit and Outer Newry Islands. The walk starts at the Rotunda lookout and it's about two km. Unfortunately the island beaches are not very good. Fishing and oystering are the main activities on Newry. There's some water skiing but no night life.

Accommodation & Food

The small resort accommodates only 30 people and has a licensed bar. The basic units are spartan bunkhouse style in a stone cabin and cost $15 a night per person. Self-contained units cost $60 for two people and $20 for each extra person. The units have showers and toilets, tea/coffee making equipment and a fridge. Some of the units have cooking facilities. There are also 20 camping sites at the resort which cost $7 per person. Camping is not allowed on Newry apart from at the resort site.

Meals are also available at the resort and cost around $9.

Getting There & Away

Newry Island is close to the mainland just north of Seaforth. The resort picks up people from Victor Creek, near Seaforth, a coastal holiday town north of Mackay. The cost is $10 return and you can ring the resort on (079) 59 0214 for pick ups. For an extra $5 the resort will collect you at the Leap Hotel near the Seaforth road-Bruce Highway junc-

View of Carlisle Island from Brampton Island (TW)

tion. The resort also operates day trips on certain days. There's not even a jetty at Newry so you have to get your feet wet when landing on the beach.

Brampton Island

Area: 4.6 square km
Type: continental
High point: 219 metres
Maximum visitor population: 240
Per person daily cost: approximately $200
In brief: although it's not actually part of the Whitsunday Group, Brampton is very similar to those islands. The resort is run by Australian Airlines.

The Island
Mountainous Brampton Island is a national park and wildlife sanctuary with lush forests surrounded by coral reefs. It is part of the Cumberland Group and is connected to nearby Carlisle Island by a sand bar which you can walk across at low tide. You can also walk out to tiny Pelican Island at low tide. In all essentials Brampton is just like the islands of the Whitsundays, just to the north. Although Cook named some of the other islands in the Cumberland Group it was not until 1879 that Brampton and neighbouring Carlisle were surveyed and named.

Starting before the turn of the century Brampton was used by the Queensland government as a nursery for palm trees. Nuts from the Dutch East Indies were germinated here before they were replanted on other islands, hence the island's particularly fine stand of this tropical island staple! Sisal hemp, planted on Carlisle with the intention of producing rope, has become a pest.

The Busuttin family who had been raising sheep on St Bees and Keswick, two other islands in the Cumberland Group, moved north to Brampton in 1916. After an unsuccessful attempt to breed chinchilla rabbits they turned to raising goats and breeding horses for the British Army in India.

A resort was established on the island in 1933, soon after Lindeman's, and the massive fig tree beside the older freshwater swimming pool dates from that year. At that time you could have a three week holiday on Brampton Island, including steamer fare from Sydney, for the princely sum of £27. Guests making the 10 minute flight or 45 minutes high speed catamaran trip out to Brampton from Mackay might pause to think that in those days it was a six hour boat crossing on the old *Woy Woy*, whose wheel now hangs in the resort's Nautilus Lounge. Guests could indulge themselves in turtle and dugong hunting and other activities which would definitely be frowned on these days.

Since the war the farming activity has departed and the sheep and cattle replaced with more and more guests. The Busuttin family sold the resort in 1959 and it eventually ended up with the Roylen group, who still operate the boat service between Mackay and Brampton. In 1962 the tramway connecting the all-tide wharf to the resort was built. Hayman already had such a system but the Hayman tramway was removed during that island's recent renovation. In 1985 Brampton was taken over by Australian Airlines who have made extensive alterations and additions. Apart from the resort area the island is all national park.

Information
The resort phone number is (079) 51 4499, the address is Brampton Island Resort, Brampton Island, Qld 4740. There are pay telephones by the main resort complex. The resort shop has a very limited supply of books including *Island that we Knew* by Valda Busuttin Winsor which relates her family's involvement with Brampton. There's also a good aerial photograph map of the island.

Zoning The waters around Brampton and neighbouring Carlisle Island are mainly zoned General Use B but the waters actually between the two islands are zoned Marine National Park A and B. Neither Marine

National Park zoning allows shell or coral collecting.

Activities

Brampton has swimming pools, tennis courts, a small golf course, a games room and a TV lounge. Children are well catered for during school vacations. Day visitors to the island are welcome and can use some of the guest facilities but they don't come over in such numbers that they over-run the resort. Yachties can get showers and water. Entertainment is in the resort's ground floor

Cumberland Lounge most nights. Captain Tom's disco is well away from the accommodation area, beside the golf course.

Walks

Trails lead from the resort to quiet bays on the other sides of the island or to the lookout at the island's high point. The circuit walk is one of the best on any resort island and takes you through great stands of Moreton Bay ash and poplar, gum forests, giant grass trees, past coral beach and offers sweeping panoramas. There are basically two walks, the seven

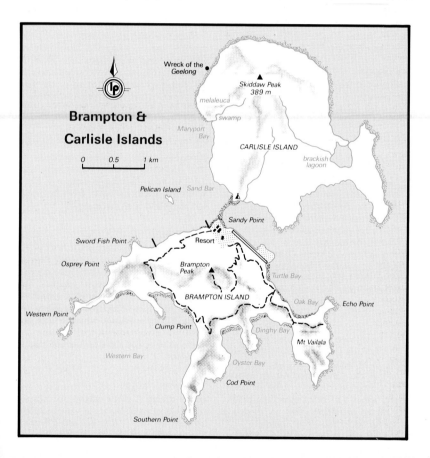

Brampton & Carlisle Islands

km long island circuit, with a spur leading off to Dinghy Bay and Oak Bay, and the two km ascent to the top of 219 metre Brampton Peak. Both walks start from near the resort golf course, by the airstrip parking apron.

Apart from the resort's resident emu a variety of other wildlife can be seen on the island. Scrubfowl (and their huge nesting mounds), sand goannas, grey kangaroos and koalas can all be found here. Fruit bats roost in trees near Turtle Bay.

Island Circuit The track climbs up on the slopes of Brampton Peak, overlooking the airstrip and follows alongside the airstrip until it descends down towards the shoreline right at the airstrip's end where it meets the vehicle track beside the the runway. There's a picnic area here at Turtle Bay and for a few steps the route is on the beach before climbing back up above the shoreline and turning south. A spur track branches off and descends to Dinghy Bay and Oak Bay continuing towards the end of Echo Point.

The main track here runs well above Dinghy Bay and Oyster Bay with superb views across the grassy slopes, punctuated with black boys, to the twin bays with their sandy beaches and clearly delineated inlets from the sea. The grassy areas of Brampton are probably a result of the goats which were once grazed here. Finally the track climbs up an open grassy slope to Far Point from where there are great views in both directions, north-east over Oyster and Dinghy Bays and west over Western Bay.

Far Point is the half way mark on the circuit track and from here the track soon descends into dense vegetation in which it remains for the rest of the track. The walk descends steeply to Western Bay, crosses a short stretch of beach and then follows round to a second strip of beach beside Clump Point, where there is a picnic area. Soon after this the walk crosses a vehicle track again then climbs up and over a ridge line before reaching the vehicle track again, between the resort and the deepwater jetty.

If you follow this track round counter-clockwise instead of clockwise it's easy to miss some of the signs which are more aligned to clockwise walking. In a couple of places the walk follows 4WD vehicle tracks then suddenly diverges off them. It's easy to miss these turnings if you aren't alert. The full circuit is about seven km and takes about three hours.

Brampton Peak The start of the walk to the island's highest point is also near the resort golf course. It follows the island ciruit route for just a couple of hundred metres before turning sharply off at a well signposted junction. From here the path switchbacks gently uphill to the lookout point which gives wonderful views over the resort area, Carlisle Island and the north-west. From near the top an alternative spur runs a short distance to another lookout with views over the south-west corner of the island.

This pleasant and gentle stroll takes about two hours round trip at an easy pace and the views from the top are well worth the effort.

Beaches, Snorkelling & Diving
Although there are beaches scattered right round the island – Dinghy Bay and Oyster Bay look particularly pleasant – Sandy Point right in front of the resort is just fine. There's good snorkelling at low tide over the coral in the narrow channel between Brampton and Carlisle Islands, again right in front of the resort, and there's a glass bottom boat of course. When conditions are suitable snorkelling trips are made to the wreck of the SS *Geelong*, round on the north-west side of Carlisle.

Brampton is not a divers island but the trips out of Mackay via Brampton to the outer reef stop at Brampton to drop-off day trippers and pick up Brampton guests. It's about 40 km from Brampton to the reef and day trips cost $40 including lunch. At the reef there's a pontoon with underwater observatory and a semi-submersible. Diving facilities are offered on these trips.

Accommodation
The resort is at Sandy Point at the north central corner of the island, looking across

the narrow strait to larger Carlisle Island. Since the Australian Airlines takeover in 1985 Brampton has been extensively updated. Accommodation is in the 'Blue Lagoon Units', which have attached bathrooms, tea/coffee making equipment, fridges and radios. The attractive units are in compact two storey blocks, most rooms with their own verandah or balcony. Some of them are right by the beach.

Daily costs are $180 per person and for a week's stay the price is $162 per day. Cheaper standby rates are also sometimes available. All meals are included and use of all non-powered equipment including golf, tennis, windsurfing, catamarans and the like. There's an additional charge for water-skiing and other activities requiring power.

Food
Breakfast, lunch and dinner are provided in the resort's upstairs Carlisle Restaurant area. Breakfast and lunch are serve-yourself buffet style, dinner is from a menu. The food at Brampton is not going to send any gastronomes into fits of rapture, it's uniformly bland and probably falls a step behind other similar resorts like Dunk. Once a week there's that Great Barrier Reef essential, a seafood smorgasbord night.

For those who cannot last from one meal to the next or for day visitors there's a small snack bar in the main resort complex. It does drinks, ice creams and light snacks.

Getting There & Away
Air It's only 35 km from Mackay to the island's airstrip and Australian Regional Airlines will fly you over in just 10 minutes at a one-way fare of $59.

Sea The *Spirit of Roylen* (tel (079) 55 3066) makes the 40 minute run to Brampton from Mackay harbour every day but the crossing can be rough in heavy seas. Return fare is $40. Some days the same boat goes on to Hamilton Island and Credlin Reef. You can day trip to Brampton from Mackay for $40.

Other Cumberland Islands

There are 70-odd islands in the Cumberland group and apart from the Newry Island Group covered separately it is also possible to camp on Carlisle, Cockermouth, Goldsmith and Scawfell Islands. See the following Whitsunday section for information on permit applications.

Getting There & Away
Roylens will do drop-offs to some of the Cumberland Islands on their services from Mackay to the Whitsundays. Call them on (079) 55 3066 for details. The *Elizabeth II* also does island tours. Tourism Mackay (tel (079) 52 2677) Nebo Rd, Mackay, or the Queensland Travel Centre (tel (079) 57 2292) have information on boat and plane charters out of Mackay. Fredrickson's Aerial Services (tel (079) 57 5701) is one air service that has seaplane charters from Mackay.

CARLISLE ISLAND
Carlisle is just a stone's throw from Brampton Island with its busy resort. Campers can sit on the beach and watch the resort activities separated only by the narrow channel between the two islands. Indeed at low tide a sand bar emerges between the island and you can walk across between them. With an area of just over five square km and Skiddaw Peak soaring to 389 metres it is both larger than its near neighbour and also looks down on it.

The island is covered in dense eucalypt forest and there are no walking tracks. Patches of rainforest are found in the gullies while there is a melaleuca (paperbark) swamp at the western end of the island which lies below sea level. There's a good area of rainforest behind the swamp. The small brackish lagoon at the eastern end of the island attracts pelicans, herons and other waterbirds.

SS Geelong
In 1888 the 431 ton iron steamship SS

Geelong (originally named the *Thomas Powell*) sheltered behind Carlisle during a severe storm. After sheltering there for more than a day a sudden shift of wind forced the captain to run the ship on to the beach. In getting a rope ashore two members of the crew were swept off and drowned but no passengers were lost. It was impossible to salvage the ship which began to break up within a matter of weeks. The bow of the ship still lies on the beach with trees growing through it today and a section of hull with brick ballast can also be seen. At low tide snorkellers can find another 13 metres of the keel in just five metres of water.

Camping

There are sites for 15 people at Southern Bay, directly across from the Brampton Island resort. The site is completely undeveloped, there are no facilities and there is no water. The national parks office warns that you cannot get water from Brampton; no doubt you could stroll over and buy a cold beer at low tide, however!

Getting There & Away

You can get to Carlisle Island via Brampton, the resort will transfer you across if the request is made in advance. Alternatively you can simply wait for low tide and walk across.

SCAWFELL ISLAND

Lying about 115 km north-west of Middle Percy, 50 km north-east of Mackay, and 12 km directly east of Brampton, Scawfell has a safe anchorage in Refuge Bay on its northern side. The 11 square km island is the largest in the group and is a popular resting place for yachts sailing between the Percy and Whitsunday Islands. Refuge Bay has a beach and a camping site but there are no facilities and water is only available during the wetter summer months. The island's coastline ends in granite cliffs while large patches of rainforest can be found on the steep mountain slopes.

ST BEES & KESWICK ISLANDS

St Bees and Keswick are separated by a narrow channel. Both are privately owned; St Bees was once a sheep property owned by the Busuttin family, original owners of the Brampton Island resort. Off to the west of Keswick is Singapore rock, named after the *Singapore* which was wrecked on it while en route from Shanghai to Sydney in 1877. The lighthouse steamer *Llewellyn* also went down somewhere near St Bees in 1919, while in 1943 the Dutch ship *Cremer*, being used to transport troops between New Guinea and Australia, ran into the island itself and was totally wrecked.

COCKERMOUTH ISLAND

Cockermouth Island has a good anchorage and sandy beach on its western side and campsites on the north-western beach but there are no facilities or fresh water. The hilly island is mainly covered with open grassland.

GOLDSMITH & FARRIER ISLANDS

North-west of Cockermouth in the Sir James Smith Group there is a good anchorage and campsite on the north-western side of Goldsmith Island. The island has excellent beaches backed by pandanus and she-oaks while inland there is open woodland with brush box, wattles and grasstrees. The campsite has toilets, barbecue fireplaces and tables – unlike Carlisle, Cockermouth and Scawfell which have no facilities at all – but there is no fresh water.

Tiny Farrier Island is immediately to the west of Goldsmith and there are a number of privately owned cabins on the south-east shore.

THE REPULSE ISLANDS

Well to the west of the Sir James Smith Group is South Repulse Island with a campground on the western beach. The site has similar facilities to Goldsmith but again there is no water. East and North Repulse Islands are just to the north.

THOMAS ISLAND

About 15 km north of Goldsmith Island is Thomas Island with its dense coverage of pine trees and several fine beaches.

Crustaceans – Crabs, Shrimps, Prawns & Lobsters

Crustaceans – the hard-shelled creatures which include crabs, shrimps and lobsters – are one of the most varied groups found on the Great Barrier Reef. Crabs scuttling across rocks or island beaches may be a quite familiar sight but many of the marine crustaceans are nocturnal creatures and thus rarely seen. For many reef visitors the most commonly seen crustaceans are the ones which decorate their plates at mealtime.

Barnacles and a variety of other small creatures are also members of the crustacean family but it is the *decapods* – crabs, shrimps, prawns and lobsters – which are the best known. They are characterised by their hard outer covering known as an exoskeleton. Since this cannot grow, crustaceans must shed their skin from time to time and then go through a rapid period of growth before the newly exposed skin hardens. *Decapods* have five pairs of legs with nippers or large claws called *chelae* on the front legs. They vary in size from minute shrimps, best seen under a microscope, to large spiny lobsters. Not only humans are aware how tasty crustaceans can be and therefore they tend to be wary, nocturnal creatures despite their often formidable looking armour and weaponry.

Shrimps, the smallest of this group, are amazingly diverse with even quite small reefs harbouring several hundred different species. Many of these small shrimps live symbiotically with other creatures. There are a variety of cleaner shrimps which offer a cleaning service to larger fish. Some shelter on coral or amongst the spines of sea urchins. Prawns, so important to commercial fishers along the coast, are found in shallow tropical waters but are not common on the reefs.

The *panulirid lobsters* are the largest crustaceans found on the reef. These spiny lobsters are confusingly known by a host of names including rock lobsters, crays and, most commonly, crayfish. Although they are tasty creatures they are difficult to catch since they will not enter traps, like the cold water lobsters found further south.

The Great Barrier Reef region is home to a great variety of crabs including varieties found on the beaches and rocks, in the tidal region and further out to sea. Hermit crabs, which shelter in abandoned gastropod shells in order to protect their soft abdomens, are a common and amusing sight. Children love to stage hermit crab races with the dry land varieties but there are others found in the water. Whereas other crustaceans shed their hard skins as they grow, hermit crabs simply switch shells. When their current abode becomes too small a hermit crab will carefully inspect a variety of new residences before quickly abandoning one and moving in to another. Sometimes a hermit crab will try to move into a shell which is simply too big, and after discovering the huge

Hermit crab

effort needed to move it around will change to a less grand mansion. Nor does the shell necessarily have to be empty before the move, if necessary a hermit crab will drag a resident mollusc out of its shell like a landlord evicting a tenant late with the rent.

Ghost or sand crabs are often seen on sandy beaches where they scavenge food washed up on the beach. They're a great danger to vulnerable newly hatched turtles on beaches where turtles lay their eggs. Ghost crabs scuttle across the sand at surprising speed and live in long burrows, up to a metre underground. Fiddler crabs are another shore based crab.

An enormous and fascinating variety of crabs is found on the reefs. Sponge crabs have tiny claws on their back legs which they use to clutch a sponge and hold it umbrella-like above themselves as disguise. The long legged and slow moving spider crabs rely on camouflage and disguise to evade their enemies. This group includes the decorator crab which covers itself in bits of debris and vegetation in order to blend into the background.

Swimming crabs and rock crabs are the most common crabs found on the reef. The swimming crabs include the Queensland gourmet's delight, *Scylla serrata*, the mud crab which is found in mangroves. Brightly coloured *Xanthidae* or rock crabs are very common around branching coral on the reef. Some varieties are even supposed to protect coral from the crown-of-thorns starfish by nipping the starfish's feet! ■

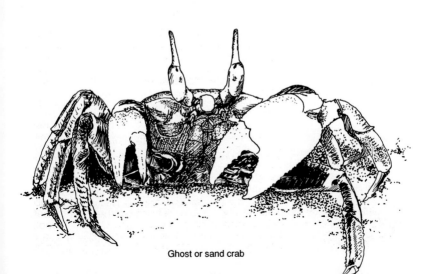

Ghost or sand crab

Whitsunday Islands

The 70-odd islands of the Whitsunday group are probably the best known and most developed of the Barrier Reef islands. The group was named by Captain Cook who sailed through here on 3 July 1770. The islands are scattered on both sides of the Whitsunday Passage, within 50 km of Shute Harbour, the jumping-off point for the many cruises through the group.

The actual Barrier Reef is at least 60 km out from Shute Harbour; Hook Reef is the nearest part of the reef. Many of the Whitsunday islands are National Parks. The large block of mainland national park opposite them, stretching from Airlie Beach south to Conway, is known as the Conway Range National Park. All the islands of the group are high continental islands and on most of them the beaches are not that special. There are large tidal variations in the Whitsundays and when the tide is way out, exposing large mudflats in front of some of the islands, it's time to head for the resort swimming pool.

Curiously the Whitsundays are misnamed – Captain Cook didn't really sail through them on Whitsunday. When he got back to England his meticulously kept log was a day out because he had not allowed for crossing the international date line! As he sailed through the Whitsundays and on further north, Cook was also unaware of the existence of the Barrier Reef, although he realised there was something to the east of his ship making the water unusually calm. It wasn't until he ran aground on Endeavour Reef, near Cooktown, that he finally found out about the Great Barrier Reef.

Information

Airlie Beach is the mainland centre for the Whitsundays and there are plenty of shops, banks, travel agents and tour operators. You can find all about cruises, trips, standby rates at resorts and so on in Airlie Beach. There is also a wide variety of accommodation at Airlie Beach and many visitors stay here and make day trips out to the islands. Shute Harbour, 10 km down the road from Airlie Beach, is the actual departure point for boats going out to the islands and the reef. There are booking offices here as well.

All but five of the Whitsunday Islands are national parks; in all over 95% of the island land area is park. The Whitsunday District Office of the Queensland National Parks & Wildlife Service is at Airlie Beach. The Conway National Park District Office, where you go for campsite bookings and other information, is on Shute Harbour Rd, between Airlie Beach and Shute Harbour.

Further Reading The Queensland National Parks & Wildlife Service has useful park guide and camping guide leaflets, both titled *Whitsunday Islands National Parks* as well as separate leaflets on *South Molle Island* and *Lindeman Island*.

The Travelog *Whitsunday Passage* map is the best tourist map of the islands. *100 Magic Miles of the Reef – The Whitsundays* is a comprehensive guide to the Whitsundays with charts and aerial photographs. See the introductory books and maps section for more information.

Zoning Most of the waters around the Whitsundays are zoned General Use A and B with some important exceptions around the islands. In those areas Marine National Park A and B zoning applies. The main difference for the visitor is that although both zones are 'look but don't take', Zone A permits limited fishing whereas Zone B permits no fishing at all.

Zone A applies to the waters around Long Island, the Molle Islands, Lindeman Island, Hamilton Island, Cid Harbour, Henning Island, between Whitsunday and Haslewood Islands, Nara Inlet and Saba Bay on Hook Island and the area around Hayman Island, Black and Langford Islands and across from there to Hook Island.

The more restrictive Zone B applies to Butterfly Bay and the other bays at the north of Hook Island, to Border Island and to Lupton Island and the east side of Haslewood Island.

The outer reef off from the Whitsundays is a also a mix of zones. The main reefs visited from the islands are Marine National Park A (Bait and Hook Reefs) and B (Hardy Reef).

Islands & Wildlife

The Whitsunday Islands are essentially drowned mountains with peaks rising clear of the sea. The islands were initially formed by volcanic eruption, the unmistakable shape of Pentecost Island is the remains of the plug of rock from a volcano cone. The sea level was about 100 metres lower during the last ice age, 18,000 years ago, and the Whitsundays would have been hills beyond which a plain stretched out to the coastal limestone hills which are today the Great Barrier Reef. As the polar ice caps melted about 10,000 years ago the sea rose and the Whitsunday Hills became the Whitsunday Islands.

Although the Whitsundays are not reef islands many of them have fine fringing reef systems. The great range between low and high tide in the Whitsundays creates fast flowing currents between the islands and in turn the nutrients carried by these currents feed a healthy variety of corals. Closer to the shore there are crabs, oysters, snails and worms and a variety of birds of prey which patrol the coastal strip.

Inland there are vine forests and the distinctive hoop pines found on most of the Whitsunday islands. Eucalypts and acacias predominate on the drier slopes while the grasstree or 'black boy' is a familiar understorey sight. There are not as many animals on the islands as on the adjacent mainland but on some islands goannas and bush-tailed possums have learnt to raid campers' provisions. Rock wallabies are found on Whitsunday Island and the unusual

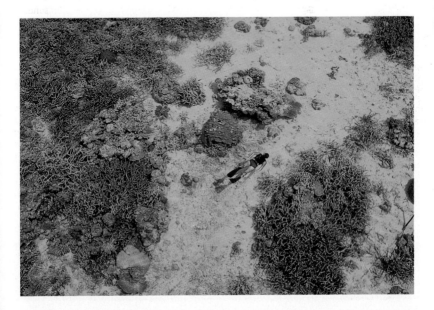

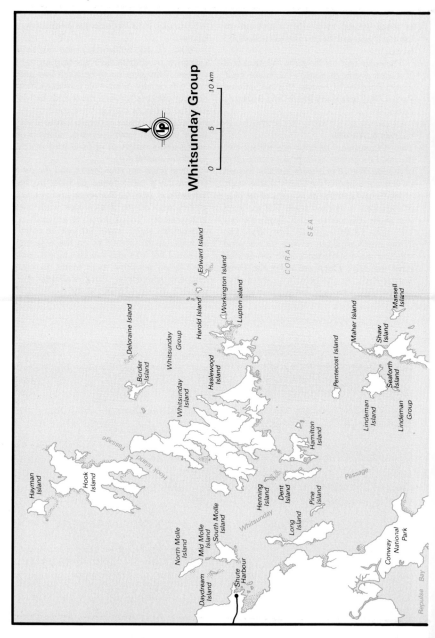

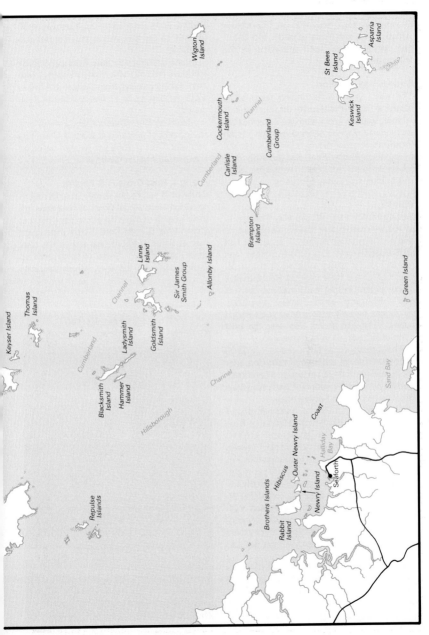

Proserpine rock wallaby on Gloucester Island. There are plenty of birds, 156 different species have been recorded in the Whitsundays.

Snorkelling & Diving
The water in the Whitsundays tends to be clearer at the northern end of the outer islands – Hook, Border, Deloraine and Langford are particularly popular snorkelling and diving locations. Regular diving trips are made out to the outer Barrier Reef. See the individual island sections for more details on good snorkelling and diving locations.

Boating
Sailing through the Whitsunday Passage in 1770 Cook wrote that 'the whole passage is one continued safe harbour'. In actual fact stiff breezes and fast flowing tides can produce some tricky conditions for small craft but with a little care the Whitsundays offers superb sailing and bareboat charters have become enormously popular. 'Bareboat' doesn't refer to what you wear on board, it simply means you rent the boat without skipper, crew or provisions.

The operators usually require a $500 bond, payable on arrival and refunded after the boat is returned in undamaged condition. Bedding is usually supplied and provisions can also be provided if you wish.

There are a number of bareboat charter companies at Airlie Beach. Mandalay Boat Charters (tel (079) 46 6298 or toll free (008) 07 5123) have Hood 23 yachts (seven metres) which can take up to four people. For one to three nights the cost is $150 per night, dropping to $130 per night for seven nights. Australian Bareboat Charters (tel (079) 46 9381 or toll free (008) 07 5000) start with Holland 25s at $160 to $210 per day depending on the season. They go up to larger yachts costing as much as $650 to $769 per day and they also have motor cruisers.

Cumberland Charter Yachts (tel (079) 46 7500 or toll free (008) 07 5101) has a variety of boats. For shorter three or four day charters (smaller boats) or five to nine day charters (bigger ones) the costs vary from $360 to $648 a day in the high season, $300 to $540 in the low. Motor cruisers are also available.

Other operators include Tropical Sailing Holidays (tel (02) 419 7544 in Sydney) who have yachts ranging from 32 feet at $230 to $285 per day, up to 41 feet at $360 to $460 per day.

Mandalay Boat Charters have a week long sailing school operated at sea in a Columbia 34 yacht. Cost is $600 per person, based on five participants on the boat.

Island & Reef Cruises & Flights
Cruises If you're not simply transferring to an island there are all types of boat trips out to the islands of the Whitsundays and beyond them to the Barrier Reef. Many trips originate at Shute Harbour, the end of the road from Airlie Beach. Some of these pick up from islands on the way, others originate

Walking on the reef (TW)

from the islands, particularly Hamilton and South Molle.

You can divide the trips into several categories. First of all there are the straightforward go-see-the-islands cruises. You go to resort island A, have an hour or two there to sample the beach, pool and bar then carry on to do the same at island B. Somewhere along the line you usually get a barbecue lunch thrown in. An excursion to the underwater observatory at Hook Island is often part of the picture. Typical prices for these cruises are $35 to $50. They're great if you want to make an on-the-spot assessment of the resort swimming pools.

A variation on these resort island trips is one that just takes you out to one island and leaves you there for the day. A day on Long Island, for example, costs just $19 if you're dropped off at Palm Bay. Whitsunday Connections, the South Molle boat operator, has a host of cruises around the Whitsundays including a South Molle day trip for $20.

Category two is the nowhere-in-particular trips, usually in smaller boats although Whitsunday Connections has these sort of trips as well. You usually stay away from the resort islands, perhaps try a beach here, a bit of snorkelling there, maybe some fishing somewhere else. Many of the boats operating these trips are yachts. A day on the former America's cup contender *Gretel* is yours for $38 for example.

There are also outer reef trips where you power out to the outer reef for a spot of walking on the reef itself and perhaps a bit of snorkelling too. The high speed catamarans used for these trips get you out there in no time at all. Beware of seasickness, the trips can often be surprisingly bumpy. Out on the reef the major operators all have their own pontoons with glass bottom boats, semi-submersibles, snorkelling equipment and diving facilities all waiting for you. These outer reef trips are generally more expensive (you're looking at $75 with lunch) but getting out to the reef is really an other worldly experience that, if you can afford it, should not be missed.

Finally there are all sorts of do-your-own-

thing odds and ends. You can get yourself dropped off on an island to camp or you can charter a bareboat yacht and sail yourself. Some typical Whitsunday boat trips include:

Emma Peel Three day trips on this schooner overnight at Nara Inlet on Hook Island and at Hamilton Island. All meals are included, a number of resort islands are visited and the cost is $170. Phone (079) 46 7376 for bookings.

Fantasea Budget priced outer Great Barrier Reef cruises on the high speed catamaran *Quick Cat II* cost $49 but bring your own lunch. Phone (079) 46 9569 for bookings.

Nari The twin-keeled Nari operates sailing cruises which may go to a variety of points around the group including Nara Inlet on Hook Island, a variety of locations on Whitsunday Island and numerous other places. Phone (079) 46 6224 for details, cost is $32 and lunch is included

Roylen Cruises Operating out of Mackay this operator takes you to Brampton to the south of the Whitsundays ($25), to Credlin Reef beyond Brampton ($80 including lunch), to Hamilton ($40) or to Lindeman ($60 including lunch). Phone (079) 55 3066 for bookings.

Trinity This trimaran does day trips to Hannah's Point on North Molle Island for $28 including lunch. Phone (079) 46 6255 for bookings.

Tri Tingira This large sailing catamaran departs from Airlie Beach on day cruises to Langford Reef, south of Hayman Island, and Stonehaven on the western side of nearby Hook Island. Scuba dives are also possible at Langford. Phone (079) 46 6848, cost is $32, lunch is extra.

Whitsunday Connections This major operator has a variety of trips including South Molle day trips ($20), South Molle and Hook Island ($38), those two and Whitehaven Beach as well ($50) or right out to the Great Barrier Reef ($55 or $70 with lunch). Phone (079) 46 6900 or toll free (008) 07 5127 for bookings.

Whitsunday Wanderer This older vessel does day trips to Nara Inlet and Black Island (Bali Ha'i) near Hayman where you ride the Yellow Submarine semi-submersible to view the fringing reef. Phone (079) 46 6224 for bookings, cost is $30 and lunch is extra.

Flights Scenic flights over the Whitsundays can run from $30 in a variety of aircraft including an old Tiger Moth biplane. From there the costs go up towards the sky. For $120 Seair Pacific (tel (079) 46 9133 will fly you out to Hardy Lagoon on the reef in their amphibious aircraft, there they have a glass bottom boat anchored and you get a couple of hours of coral viewing, reef walking and snorkelling before flying back. Seair Pacific have a host of other flights to the islands including picnic drop-offs on remote beaches.

Helijet (tel (079) 46 9144) have similar, but more expensive, deals. They'll give you a 15 minute panorama of the Whitsundays for $70 or take you out to the outer reef for a spell of snorkelling and semi-sub coral viewing for a mere $215!

Camping on the Islands

Accommodation on the resort islands is generally expensive but you can camp on a number of the national park islands with a permit from the Queensland National Parks & Wildlife Service office. All the National Park camping sites on the islands are category C which means the permit cost is just $2 per person per night. The office is located opposite the National Park campsite, about a km before Shute Harbour, and can provide more detailed information about your alternatives. It's open 8 am to 5 pm, Monday to Friday – contact The Ranger (tel (079) 46 9430), Conway Range National Park, Shute Harbour, Qld 4802.

Only a few islands have water supplies, on the others you'll have to bring your own. Those with water are North Molle (two campsites, one with showers) and Whitsunday Island where there are a couple of sites on Cid Harbour. There's a commercial site by the Hook Island underwater observatory resort. At the National Park sites you have to specify your island and how long you intend to stay when applying for a permit.

You can get out to your island with one of the day cruise boats (generally the sail-around ones rather than the island resort boats) or by water taxi. Some typical camping transport possibilities include the trimaran *Tri Tingira* which will drop and collect you at Stonehaven on Hook Island for $47. The *Nari* goes to Nara Inlet on Hook Island and a variety of places on Whitsunday Island. They'll drop you and collect you for $45 and give you lunch on the way.

The *Paladin* also costs $45 and will take you to Sawmill Beach on Whitsunday, Macona Inlet on Hook or to North Molle. By

taking them on successive days you can visit all three. Phone (079) 46 6848, the cost is $45. The *Trinity* will take you to North Molle for $36 return.

If you've got camping gear give it a try – Robinson Crusoeing on your very own island can be a lot of fun. If you haven't got your own equipment it can all be hired in Airlie Beach – try Airlie Camping & Gas Centre (tel (079) 46 6145) at shop 2/398 Shute Harbour Rd, Airlie Beach. An Esky would be handy to keep the wine cool! The booking offices in Airlie Beach are helpful and can advise on which boats are best to go where.

Island Camping

island	location	No of sites	water
Main Islands			
Henning Island	Geographer's Beach	3	no
Hook Island	Curlew Beach	10	no
North Molle	Hannah Point	5	yes
	Cockatoo Beach	10	yes
Shute Harbour	Shute Island	5	no
Whitsunday Island	Whitehaven Beach	20	no
	Scrub Hen Beach	10	no
	Dugong Beach	15	yes
	Sawmill Beach	5	yes
	Joe's Beach	4	no
Northern Islands			
Armit Island	NW point	5	no
Gloucester Island	Bona Bay	10	no
Grassy Island		2	no
Saddleback Island	NW beach	5	no
Southern Islands			
Shaw Island	Neck Bay	3	no
South Repulse Island	Western Beach	3	no
Thomas Island	Sea Eagle Beach	10	no

Getting There & Away

Air Although Proserpine was for many years the main gateway to the Whitsundays the opening of the airstrip on Hamilton Island allowed Ansett to fly wide-body jets right on to the islands. Many visitors to the Whitsundays now fly directly to Hamilton and transfer from there to their island, never setting foot on the mainland at all. The Ansett phone number for their Hamilton Island office is (079) 46 9390 or toll free (008) 17

7572. At Airlie Beach they're at Whitsunday Travel (tel (079) 46 6255).

Australian Airlines can only get you to Proserpine, 36 km from Shute Harbour. Their Airlie Beach office (tel (079) 46 6273 or toll free (008) 17 7245) is on Shute Harbour Rd.

Land About half the bus services up and down the Bruce Highway with the major bus companies detour into Airlie Beach and most continue right down to Shute Harbour. It's about 18 hours from Brisbane, two hours from Mackay, four hours from Townsville or nine hours from Cairns. See the Getting There & Away chapter for more information about bus travel to the Whitsunday region.

Otherwise, Sampsons (tel (079) 45 2377) have regular services Proserpine – Airlie Beach – Shute Harbour. It's $6 from Proserpine to Airlie Beach, $2.50 from Airlie Beach to Shute Harbour. The main bus stop in town is at the western end of the main street, opposite the post office.

If you drive to Shute Harbour the daily parking charge in the car park is $3. It's often full and you may have to park further back towards Airlie Beach. Commercial parking services offer outside car parking for $5 a day, undercover parking for $8 a day.

Boat Check the noticeboard at the Sailing Club at the end of Airlie Beach Esplanade for possible rides or crewing opportunities on passing yachts.

Getting Around
Air Lindeman and Hamilton are the only Whitsunday Islands with airstrips (an international airport in Hamilton's case). There are regular scheduled flights between Proserpine and Lindeman with Seair Pacific (tel (079) 46 9133) and they also use their amphibious aircraft for regular flights to and from Hayman Island. Additionally they will operate charters to just about anywhere at

just about anytime. Helijet (tel (079) 49 9144) will fly you there by helicopter if you really want to arrive in style, most of the resorts have helicopter landing pads.

Sea Transfers to the resorts are usually made from Shute Harbour or Hamilton Island. Some of the resorts have their own boats to ferry their guests back and forth – they range from the luxurious Hayman launches to the big Hamilton catamarans. The water taxis provide much the same service and can also be chartered for individual trips. See the individual island sections for details of regular transfers and the cruises section for information on cruises through the Whitsundays.

Hamilton Island

Area: 6 square km
Type: continental
High point: 230 metres
Maximum visitor population: over 1000
Per person daily cost: approximately $200
In brief: Hamilton is the Gold Coast of the reef islands – it's a town rather than a resort and by far the biggest along the Great Barrier Reef. There's a variety of accommodation possibilities and numerous restaurants and places to eat.

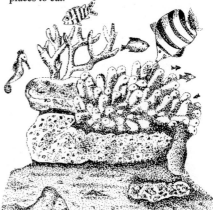

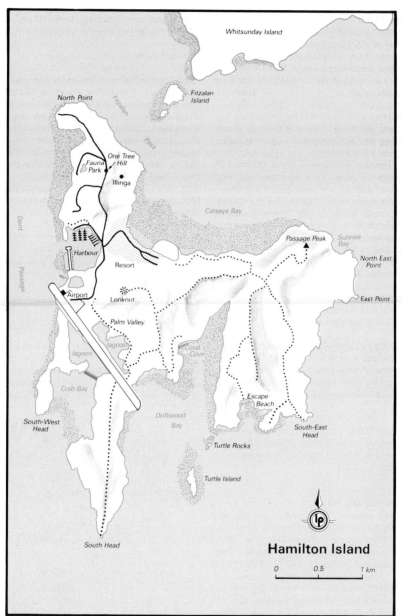

Whitsunday Island

Fitzalan Island

North Point

Fitzalan Pass

One Tree Hill

Fauna Park

Illinga

Catseye Bay

Passage Peak

Sunrise Bay

North East Point

Dent Passage

Harbour

Resort

East Point

Airport

Lookout

Palm Valley

lagoon

Coral Cove

lagoon

Crab Bay

Driftwood Bay

Escape Beach

South-East Head

South-West Head

Turtle Rocks

Turtle Island

South Head

Hamilton Island

0   0.5   1 km

The Island

Hamilton Island is certainly the most ambitious resort development along the Great Barrier Reef – not only does it have the largest freshwater swimming pool in Australia and a 400-boat marina but also its own international airport. There's an extensive (and expensive) range of entertainment possibilities including reef trips, helicopter joy rides, game fishing, parasailing, scuba diving and almost anything else you might care to think of.

Hamilton is fairly hilly, rising to 230 metres at Passage Peak. The resort includes a fauna reserve, restaurants, shopping facilities, tennis and squash courts, gymnasium and sauna and as well as the resort accommodation there are also condominiums and even some private houses, including one recently sold by George Harrison. Hamilton's airport is now one of the most important arrival points for guests bound for other Whitsunday Islands as well as Hamilton Island itself.

How It Happened

Hamilton is the creation of Gold Coast entrepreneur Keith Williams, backed with lots of other investors including Ansett Airlines who operate all the large-aircraft flights into Hamilton. Keith Williams took a lease on the island for deer farming and later managed the not inconsiderable feat of converting the farming lease to a tourism one! Of course all sorts of amazing feats were commonplace in Queensland in those pre-89 National Party days. Work started on his mega-resort in 1982, parts of the resort were in operation in '84 and by the end of '86 the show was up and running although there will continue to be more development in years to come.

Remarkably, even for Queensland, the conservationists kept surprisingly quiet while hilltops were levelled, harbours

Anemone fish (MN)

dredged out, artificial beaches created, runways laid and a 15 storey and two 13 storey apartment blocks were erected. The old 'no higher than a palm tree' adage was certainly ignored here where the buildings serve as useful yachting landmarks all over the Whitsundays. 'Controversial' is a word which has been tagged on to Hamilton but like it or hate it you've got to be impressed with the sheer energy with which it has been created.

Information

The phone number for the resort is (079) 46 9999, fax number is (079) 46 9425 and the address is Hamilton Island Resort, Private Mail Bag, Hamilton Island Post Office, Qld 4803. Reservations can be made directly by a toll free call to (008) 07 5110. The *Hamiltonian* is a regular publicity and information paper produced for the resort. It's notable for the amazing number of times Keith Williams' photo can appear in each issue!

The development at Hamilton is so big it's really a small town, not just a large resort. The main areas of Hamilton straddle a narrow neck of land where the resort (resortside) clusters on the east side, the marina and shops (harbourside) on the other. Most of the services on Hamilton Island – shops, restaurants, boat hire and so on – are operated independently of the resort. Nevertheless you can charge most things to your room account and pay for it all at the end.

You can even get married on Hamilton, the tiny island church has become yet another piece of the island's marketing. They'll put on a full wedding for $950, you can even rent Keith Williams' Rolls-Royce. Packaged Japanese Wedding Blessings are especially popular!

There are countless 'events' throughout the year at Hamilton including the annual Hamilton Island Race Week in April when the yachting fraternity heads to Hamilton en masse. There's even talk of a Hamilton Island motor racing circuit around the airport!

Medical Centre There's a medical centre with a resident doctor. It's open Monday to Saturday from 10 am to 12 noon and from 4 to 6 pm.

Shops Hamilton has a complete range of shops including a small supermarket, a newsagency, a National Bank branch, a post office, photo service, pharmacy, fish shop, delicatessen, ice cream parlour, hairdresser and beauty salon, boutiques, gift shops, even a TAB if you miss the opportunity of betting on the horse races.

Activities

The resort has spas, saunas, tennis courts, pools, squash courts, a recreation room, a gym and other sporting facilities. From Catseye Beach, the main resort beach, you can hire sailboard, catamarans, jet skis and other equipment. Parasailing is very popular at Hamilton ($35) and you can go waterskiing ($15 for 10 minutes).

The children are attended to as well, the Kids' Club handles children up to eight years of age from 9 am to 5 pm. Baby sitters can be arranged in the evening.

Walks

Hamilton is quite a large island and despite the size of the development there is a lot of relatively untouched land on the east side, dominated by 230 metre Passage Peak.

Passage Peak Walk This is the best walk on the island. A trail leads around the shoreline of Catseye Bay climbing gently at first, then becoming progressively steeper to the rocky summit of Passage Peak. From the top there are superb views back over the resort, across to Whitsunday Island or south to dramatic Pentecost Island, Lindeman Island and other islands of the southern Whitsundays.

Hamilton was not so comprehensively overgrazed as South Molle or some of the other islands in the Whitsundays and the vegetation is typical, with hoop pines and black boys. Apart from Hamilton's large bird and lizard population you may see some of the handsome goats, relics of the island's grazing days.

Other Walks Most of the other island walks are along bulldozed trails, more suitable for four-wheel drive or trail bikes rather than walkers. As the resort is further developed it's probable the walks will be improved – or turned into roads. You can get to the other walks either by starting out along the Passage Peak trail from the resort or by taking the route round by the airport.

Either way you can get to the Resort Lookout, on top of the flattened off hill where the airport navigation equipment is mounted. Technically you have to ask permission before venturing up here, call the operator on 9 and ask for the airport safety officer. You must also get permission to walk around the end of the runway to reach the part of the island beyond the airport.

The trail round by the resort side of the airport, not crossing the runway, passes by the small palm group known as Palm Valley and then winds up and then down to Coral Cove on Driftwood Bay. There's a pleasant sweep of beach here although, as with Catseye Bay, the water is very shallow. You can also reach Coral Cove from the resort side of the island, or follow the trail to Escape

Beach, an even more secluded sandy beach about 45 minutes' to an hour's walk from the resort. You catch tantalising glimpses of Coral Cove from the Escape Beach track.

Fauna Park & Wildlife
At the northern end of the island there's a fauna park (admission $5, children $2) with koalas, kangaroos and other wildlife. The brief period of deer grazing has left a few for the fauna park. While walking on the island trails you may well also bump into goats.

Hamilton also has plenty of birdlife including numerous raucous cockatoos, which have realised that tourists are always good for a free hand-out. You can often see them congregating on the verandahs of the Allamanda Lodge hotel rooms in the late afternoon. An oceanarium is planned for the harbour side but a couple of unfortunate dolphins are already held prisoner in a pool in the main resort complex.

Cruises
A variety of short trips and day cruises operate from Hamilton including Great Barrier Reef trips. The resort even has a 'war canoe' for short jaunts across to Coral Art on Dent Island, adventure cruises and sunset cruises as well as a high speed catamaran which makes regular trips to the five km stretch of Whitehaven Beach on Whitsunday Island ($20), to the Great Barrier Reef ($75) and to other islands in the Whitsundays ($35). The 20 metre yacht *Siska* also operates $25 half-day trips and $50 day trips from the resort. Children's fares are all half the adult cost.

Longer cruises, game fishing trips and, if you like your cruising well above sea level, helicopter reef flights are also operated. If you need to get away from the madding crowd you can zap out to the

Sulphur-crested cockatoo

reef at a steady 40 knots on Keith Williams' *Awesome*. Half-day trips to Whitehaven Beach cost $105, longer trips to the outer reef are $195. If that isn't fancy enough you can charter a number of other boats from Hamilton or take a cruise on the 35 metre *Achilles II*, but think about $2000 a day.

Diving
H20 Sportz by the harbour is the Hamilton Island dive shop and has all diving gear for hire from $35 a day. One day diving trips typically cost from $60. They go to Langford Reef, Butterfly or Manta Ray bays at the north of Whitsunday Island or you can go on the regular trips out to Hardy Reef. Diving trips seem to fill up fast at Hamilton so book early. A full five day certificate diving course costs $325.

Boats
Dinghies with small outboard motors can be hired at the marina and cost $30 for a half day. You can take them across to Dent Island, Henning Island or along one part of Whitsunday Island but basically you're restricted to the waters of Dent Passage. Fishing is popular and they will supply you with lines, hooks and bait. Or you can just laze on a beach or visit Coral Art on Dent Island.

The Charter Base at harbourside has a fleet of larger boats including Oceanic 42-foot yachts and Targa Cat 40-foot power cruisers, both available with or without crew. A range of power boats and game fishing craft are also chartered.

Main resort area, Hamilton Island (TW)

Dent Island
Adjacent to Hamilton Island, Dent Island shelters Dent Passage. At the north end of the island you can visit Coral Art run by Bill and Leen Wallace, an elderly couple who first settled on Hamilton Island in 1952. They have lived on Dent for many years, sell coral art and other bric-a-brac. They're a friendly pair and despite the proximity of Hamilton aren't overwhelmed by visitors and are often happy to have a chat.

Hamilton's golf course is being built on Dent Island.

Motorcycle Museum
Across the road from Hamilton's chocolate box little church is the Motorcycle Museum. It's a strange location for one but there's an extensive collection of beautifully restored British motorcycles of the '30s and '50s including better-than-new-looking Vincents, Scotts, Ariels, AJS, Matchless, Nortons, Triumphs and BSAs. A smattering of more recent Italian, Eastern European and modern Japanese motorcycles round out the collection. The racing motorcycles include a whole line of them raced by ex-world champion Barry Sheene. The museum, a reminder that Keith Williams founded his fortune in the motorcycle business, is open 2 to 5 pm daily and admission is free.

Accommodation
Hamilton has a variety of hotel rooms, apartments, lodges, bures and other buildings. The Hamilton Towers hotel is 20 storeys but the resort accommodation is generally in lower blocks. The resort is on a neck of land with the accommodation facing a beach partially made of imported sand while the marina and shopping facilities are on the other side of the neck.

Flanking the main resort complex with its reception area, restaurants, bars, shops and pools are 60 hotel rooms in the two storey *Bougainvillaea Lodge* and 60 more in the three storey *Allamanda Lodge*. Behind the resort complex are 51 individual *Bures*. The Bures and Allamanda Lodge rooms cost $200 a night, the Bougainvillea Lodge rooms

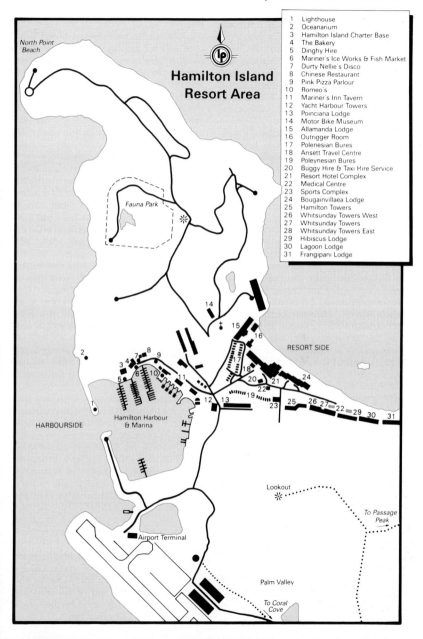

Hamilton Island Resort Area

North Point Beach

1 Lighthouse
2 Oceanarium
3 Hamilton Island Charter Base
4 The Bakery
5 Dinghy Hire
6 Mariner's Ice Works & Fish Market
7 Durty Nellie's Disco
8 Chinese Restaurant
9 Pink Pizza Parlour
10 Romeo's
11 Mariner's Inn Tavern
12 Yacht Harbour Towers
13 Poinciana Lodge
14 Motor Bike Museum
15 Allamanda Lodge
16 Outrigger Room
17 Polenesian Bures
18 Ansett Travel Centre
19 Poleynesian Bures
20 Buggy Hire & Taxi Hire Service
21 Resort Hotel Complex
22 Medical Centre
23 Sports Complex
24 Bougainvillaea Lodge
25 Hamilton Towers
26 Whitsunday Towers West
27 Whitsunday Towers
28 Whitsunday Towers East
29 Hibiscus Lodge
30 Lagoon Lodge
31 Frangipani Lodge

Fauna Park

RESORT SIDE

HARBOURSIDE

Hamilton Harbour & Marina

Lookout

To Passage Peak

Airport Terminal

Palm Valley

To Coral Cove

are $240 a night, single or double. The rooms have air-conditioning and ceiling fans.

The large 20 storey *Hamilton Tower* opened in early 1990 with 386 rooms and suites. They range from 18 junior rooms at $160 a night, 350 standard rooms at $260 a night and 18 suites from $650 a night up to $1350 for the two 'Presidential' suites, complete with private pool.

Next there are the two 13 storey *Whitsunday Towers*, each with 84 single bedroom apartments. These take four people at $265 a night. Then there are 60 two bedroom apartments in the *Hibiscus, Lagoon* and *Frangipani* lodges. These take five people and cost $350 a night. The apartments are modern, comfortable and equipped with complete kitchens with cooking utensils, plates, dishes, cups, cutlery and so on. Each apartment has a dining and sitting area and a large balcony. There's even a washing machine and clothes drier in the two bedroom apartments. The apartment blocks have small swimming pools and spa or you can use the large pool in the main resort complex.

Standby rates are often available if the resort is not full. It's worth enquiring if you're on the mainland as these reduced rates also include transfers between Shute Harbour and Hamilton Island.

If you really need room and cost is no obstacle then the *Yacht Harbour Tower* has self-contained penthouses accommodating eight at $1500 a night. Each four bedroom apartment occupies a whole floor. Or you could rent *Illalangi*, a private villa, costing around $5000 a night. You can even buy your own Hamilton condo and rent it out when you're not in residence, Hamilton Island even has a real estate agency. Of course Keith Williams has his own home on the island, topping the bluff beyond the resort area. Ex-Beatle George Harrison also built a *pied-à-terre* on Hamilton, although it's said he never actually found time to stay in it and it was sold in late '89.

A 'Mediterranean Resort' is also on the drawing boards for the north-western peninsula of the island with a 'village' of apartments around a harbour.

Food

Accommodation on Hamilton Island is all room only but there's a wide choice of places to eat or there's a supermarket and shops and you can prepare your own food in the apartments. The restaurants and shops are generally independently run so if you don't like the food or service complain to the operator, not the resort. Although they are individual entities you can still charge all meals at island restaurants to your room and settle the total bill on departure.

The *Dolphin Room* in the main resort complex serves breakfast and dinner beside the dolphin pool. The *James Cook Bar* is adjacent to this restaurant, and weekdays there's a 5.30 to 6.30 pm happy hour. Next to the bar is the *Coffee Shop* serving light meals, snacks and drinks from 7 am to 12 midnight or later. You can also get drinks, snacks and lunch or an early dinner at the *Beach Bar & Grill* overlooking the swimming pool and beach. There's also a bar (with swim-up facilities of course) on the pool island. The final option in the main resort area is the *Outrigger Room* which is open for dinner only and is an expensive seafood specialist.

There are a variety of other dining possibilities down at the harbourside village. Working your way round the harbourside from the Charter Base at the far end, first there's the *Bakery* with good fresh bread and other baked products and good value sandwiches. They even turn out a fairly unique variant on the great Aussie meat pie – crocodile pies for $4. Next up there's the *Ice Works & Fish Market* with a variety of seafood including excellent fish & chips for $4.50. They also do fine seafood salads – prawns, crab, lobster, Moreton Bay Bugs and the like – for around $8 to $14. You can take food away or sit at the tables out front, looking out over the Marina. This is a fine place to eat.

Also on this side of the Marina is the Chinese restaurant with a typical Chinese menu upstairs and a takeaway counter, also upstairs but at the end of the building. Nothing to write home about but good, straightforward Chinese dishes.

Turn the Marina corner, by the 'picnic tables in a sailing craft' creation – and you come to the General Store on one side of the road and the Italian duo on the harbour side. Both have open air dining and the *Pink Pizza Parlour*, with its verandah right on the Marina, is a fine place to dine and the pizzas are really quite good – around $13 to $18 for large ones. Right next door is *Romeo's* with typical Italian dishes at $12 to $16 for pastas either as starters or main courses, $18 to $24 for main courses.

The harbourside also has a public bar – the *Barefoot Bar* – and the *Mariner's Inn* with bar, dining area and snack bar. Sandwiches and snacks can also be found at the *Mariners Delicatessen* and an ice cream to finish with at the *Ice Cream Parlour*.

Entertainment
In the evening there are the bars in the resort and harbourside. The *James Cook Bar* has a pianist in the evenings or you can head to *Durty Nellie's Disco* at harbourside with a bar and from 10 pm a disco. Various other night time activities include the inevitable weekly Polynesian floor show.

Getting There & Away
Air The Hamilton Island airport has become the main arrival centre for the Whitsundays and will eventually take international flights. This is one place where Australia's twin operators don't neatly split things up, Ansett has an exclusive on the trunk routes to or from Hamilton, Australian Airlines don't fly here.

There's an Ansett/Qantas office in the resort which is open 8 am to 5 pm (phone extension 8247/8) or you can call the Whitsunday office on (008) 17 7572. Ansett have connections with all the state capitals including direct flights to Brisbane ($246), Cairns ($182), Melbourne ($436), Sydney ($359) and Townsville ($230). Return fares are double the one-way fares, though advance purchase Apex fares are about ⅔ of the normal return fare. One of the most interesting connections is the Perth – Alice Springs – Cairns – Hamilton Island route,

allowing you to combine central Australia with the Barrier Reef.

There are also shorter flights between Hamilton and Mackay ($105), Proserpine ($60), Shute Harbour Airstrip ($55) or Lindeman Island ($45).

Boat From Hamilton boat connections operate to the other islands and to Shute Harbour on the mainland. Since Ansett is also involved in Hayman Island and South Molle Island the Hamilton Island airport is, of course, used as the main arrival or departure point for those islands. The Hamilton Island catamaran or other launch takes 35 to 50 minutes to cross to Shute Harbour on the mainland and costs $15, children half fare. Departures from Shute Harbour are at 9 am and 5.15 pm daily, from Hamilton Island at 7.30 am and 4.30 pm daily. Whitsunday Water Taxis (tel (079) 46 9499) also has an airport service that meets flights into Hamilton and transfers passengers to other islands such as Lindeman Island and South Molle. The cost is from around $11 for these regular services, and at other times the taxis can be hired for a minimum of $55 (for one to five people). Other launch and water taxi fares include Hayman Island ($26) and Long Island ($26).

There are excellent anchorages for visiting yachts at the Hamilton Island marina and, unlike many Barrier Reef Resorts, visiting yachties are actively encouraged. The catch is the daily cost: $50 for yachts up to 12 metres, $60 for 18 metres, etc! Hamilton is also an important base for bareboat or crewed yacht charters around the Whitsundays.

Getting Around
On arrival and departure there's a free bus service between the airport and the resort. The launch from Shute Harbour or other islands docks beside the airport terminal.

Hamilton is big, no question about it. You can have a room where getting to a restaurant for a meal is a major trek. There are a couple of alternatives to fast walking. One is the island taxi service, radio-controlled minibuses which shuttle around the island

and charge per person rates – generally around $1 to $2 depending where you're going to and from.

The other, and much more expensive, alternative are the rent-a-buggies. They're small golf course buggies which can be rented for $15 an hour or $45 a day. For the limited distances involved they're pretty good for Hamilton although some of the steep hills are too much for them and neither the taxis or the buggies are allowed to go down the unsurfaced roads, like the track round the airport to Coral Cove. Buggies can be rented from the office near reception or from the Charter Base at harbourside.

Island bus tours are operated daily and cost $10.

Long Island

Area: 12 square km
Type: continental
High point: 272 metres
Maximum visitor population: 349 at Contiki, 75 at Palm Bay
Per person daily cost: $150 at Contiki, $60 to $100 at Palm Bay
In brief: Long Island is a long, narrow island close to the coast with two active resorts. One is a Contiki resort aimed at the young and energetic. The other is a small, low key, budget family resort.

The Island

Long Island is the closest of the resort islands to Shute Harbour, a channel only half a km wide separates it from the mainland although some of the swiftest and trickiest currents in the Whitsundays run through this deep stretch of water. The island is about 11 km long but no more than 1½ km wide anywhere. There are three resorts on the island, although one of them has been open and shut over the years and may be about to go through major changes.

The island was originally named Port Molle by Lieutenant Charles Jeffreys in 1815. Jeffreys was en route to Sri Lanka at the time and lucky Colonel Molle had his name bestowed on a number of other islands in the Whitsundays. Although North, South and Mid Molle still bear the colonel's name West Molle is now more often referred to as Daydream Island and Port Molle was given its current name by Matthew Flinders.

For many years the island was the most popular anchorage in the Whitsundays for ships travelling along the coast but all the Molle islands were frequented by Aborigines and there were a number of often violent clashes between them and the intruders. In the late 19th century timber was cut on the island and taken to the sawmill operating at that time at Cid Harbour on Whitsunday Island. Later there was a banana plantation on Long Island and it was the base for a mail boat which ran regularly around the Whitsundays.

Resorts on Long Island have had a chequered history with the first ones opening at Palm Bay and Happy Bay in the 1930s. The Happy Bay resort, which even gave its name to the bay, survived right up to 1983 when it changed hands and became Whitsunday 100, an attempt to make another 'get wrecked' Keppel style resort. Despite catchy slogans it only lasted three years and was then totally redeveloped by the tour operator Contiki.

Further south it was a cyclone rather than economics which wiped out Palm Bay but it's back in operation as a low key and low budget resort aimed at backpackers and families. The island's third resort at Paradise Bay, right at the south of the island, has been periodically opened and closed in recent years and there are plans on the drawing board for a major rebuilding.

Information

The Contiki resort is at the northern end of the island. The resort phone number is (079) 49 9400 or toll free (008) 07 5125 and the address is Contiki Whitsunday Resort, Long Island, via Shute Harbour, Qld 4802.

The Palm Beach Resort is about a third of the way down the island. The phone number is (079) 46 9233 and the address is Palm Bay

Resort, Private Mail Bag 28, Mackay, Qld 4740.

Down at the south of the island is the Paradise Bay Resort; contact the Whitsunday Travel Centre (tel (079) 46 6255) for details or phone the resort on (018) 77 7595.

Activities

The Contiki resort has a swimming pool, gym, games room, tennis courts, windsurfers, catamarans and all the other typical Barrier Reef resort equipment. Like the other youth-oriented resorts the emphasis is heavily on activities, there's something happening constantly. They continue after dark and the disco booms on until very late at night.

Facilities are rather more limited at the simpler Palm Bay resort but Palm Bay guests can enjoy the entertainment at the Contiki resort. Stumbling back along the bush track after the disco would probably be fun! The Paradise Bay resort also has windsurfers and catamarans but you can't walk to the other resorts from there.

Walks

Long Island has 13 km of walking track although the bottom half of the island has no tracks and pretty much untouched. Starting from the Contiki resort there's a three km trail which loops around the northern end of the island with some good views out to Dent, Hamilton and the other islands to the east. At the northern end of the loop a short spur runs off to an old banyan tree.

Another trail starts near the tennis courts and runs south to Palm Bay, just over two km away. A short distance along this trail is a junction where trails run west to Humpy Point lookout and east to a 1.5 km round-the-hill circuit. Further on short spurs run off to Fish Bay and Pandanus Bay, at a point where the island is only 100 metres wide. Finally there are glimpses of the Palm Bay Resort and yachts moored off it, before the trail drops down into the resort area.

Again the island is only 100 or so metres wide at this point and the trail picks up again from near the tents, on the eastern side of the island and continues four km south to Sandy Bay, there's an alternative route over the first km or so with some good views to the east. Sandy Bay is a disappointment as a final destination, at least when the tide is in.

Beaches

The mainland (western) beaches tend to be sandy, the eastern beaches are rocky and face the prevailing winds. They're not bad beaches for the Whitsundays although Long Island suffers even more than most of the islands with the extreme tidal variations. When the water's out at Happy Bay it's way out and you might as well head for the pool if you want a swim. November to March it's probably an idea to head for the pool anyway as Long Island is close enough to the mainland for box jellyfish (marine stingers, sea wasps) to be a potential danger. In fact there have been no fatal incidents in the Whitsundays but nobody wants to be the first.

Cutting the channel through the reef and dredging out Palm Bay has made it a good yacht mooring and allows swimming at all tides but the altered flow pattern has also washed most of the sand off the beach. Don't meddle with nature!

Wildlife

Long Island has some interesting native and introduced wildlife. Just behind the Hideaway Units at the northern end of the Contiki Resort you can see numerous fruit bats hanging in the trees. At sunset hundreds of them flap over the resort, heading for the mainland and a night's gorging.

If you wander the island's bush trails you may come across wallabies and some very healthy looking goats. Goannas are another island inhabitant and there are numerous species of birds, including some very regal looking peacocks around the Palm Bay Resort. Long Island's scrub fowl are very numerous and remarkably unfussed about humans. There are some spectacularly large incubation mounds around the island, including one beside the Palm Bay to Sandy Bay tracks which is so enormous there's even a bench beside it so you can sit down to admire it.

Shipwrecks

Unidentified shipwrecks around Australia have a strange tendency to be end up as 'Spanish galleons' and Long Island's galleon was discovered in the 1970s. Of course it was a Spaniard who discovered Torres Straits, at the northern end of the Barrier Reef, and gave it his name. Later other Spanish sailing ships may have used the straits when sailing to or from the Spanish colony at Manila in the Philippines but there's certainly no evidence that they went further south down the Barrier Reef. It's believed now that the Happy Bay wreck was of the *Valetta* which went down in 1825, although another source identifies it as the *Louisa*.

A more recent and more easily found wreck is the Taiwanese fishing junk just offshore at the northern end of Happy Bay, in clear view of the Contiki resort.

Accommodation & Food

Happy Bay Behind the long sweep of sand at Happy Bay is the new *Contiki Whitsunday Resort*, operated by the Contiki company which specialises in travel for 18 to 35 year olds. Their resort here is also packaged for that age group and although they don't check birth certificates it's not a place for children or those old enough to appreciate peace and quiet in the early hours of the morning!

The resort has two styles of accommodation. Most of the more expensive rooms are in two storey blocks with standard motel-style rooms with attached bathrooms, a ceiling fan and a balcony. There are facilities for tea and coffee making, music, no TVs (although you can rent one for $8) and, just to be different from so many other resorts, the rooms don't have fridges but do have telephones. Per person costs in the double rooms are $125 a night, standby deals are sometimes available. Costs in these rooms at Contiki include all meals, entertainment and use of all the non-powered equipment. There's an extra charge for dinghies, jet-skis and other equipment that burns fuel.

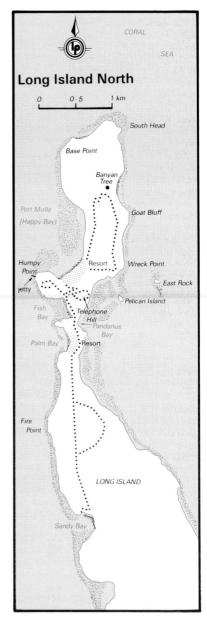

Long Island North

The alternative is the Contiki Lodges, four person bunk rooms at $25 per person for the first night and $15 for each subsequent night. The lodge accommodation allows you to use all the resort facilities but doesn't provide meals. The lodge 'kitchens' have no facilities apart from fridges so you'll have to take meals at the resort restaurant or snack bar. Most Whitsunday backpackers prefer the Hook Island Resort where they can fix their own food.

All meals are in the poolside restaurant and are serve-yourself buffet style. It's the pub food regulars, no surprises at all in that department – simple, well prepared food but nothing to get excited about. House wine is $5 a half litre or $8 a litre, or by the bottle it's $10 to $18 with the exception of a couple of $28 specials. At first the house wine was supplied free with meals – perhaps they were shocked to discover the consumption requirements of their 18 to 35 year olds. By the glass wine is $1.20, beer is $2.80 a can. Meals are $8 for breakfast, $14 for lunch (poor value) and $18 for dinner. The snack bar has sandwiches, pies and similar snack meals.

Palm Bay You can actually walk from the Contiki resort to *Palm Bay Island Resort* (tel (079) 46 9233) about two km south. The island is very narrow at this point and the resort has a sandy beach on the west (mainland) side and a stony one on the other. The resort is very simple with 12 individual cabins along the sandy sweep of Palm Bay and regimented lines of pre-erected 'tents' on the other side. In the middle is the lounge, reception and dining area, the swimming pool and other facilities.

The cabins have recently been modernised to include attached bathrooms and now cost $84/90 for singles/doubles without meals. The tents are fancy affairs with raised floors, electric lighting, beds, tables and chairs and they cost $26/30 for singles/doubles. You have to provide your own bedding and towels in the tent units. Palm Bay is also part of the Backpackers network and backpackers pay $12 per night if sharing the tents, which can accommodate up to four people.

At Palm Bay you have a choice of fixing your own food or an additional $28 per person per day covers breakfast, lunch and dinner – they're straightforward 'home style' meals. If you opt to fix your own there are cooking facilities in each of the cabins and a communal kitchen area for the tent occupants. The resort shop has supplies although, of course, you will find it cheaper to bring your own food over from the mainland. Dinner at Palm Bay is $13.

Paradise Bay The isolated resort at the south end of the island has cabins sleeping four to six at $45 to $55, backpackers huts for four at $10 per person and a camping area at $6 per person. There's a store with limited supplies.

Getting There & Away
Boats operate to Long Island from Hamilton for $26 or from Shute Harbour for $11. Fares are cheaper if you're booked into the resorts. It's a quick trip, just 20 minutes or so, from either jumping-off point. It's only two km between the Happy Bay and Palm Bay resorts and you can walk between them in just 15 to 20 minutes.

The Happy Bay pier is round at the southern end of the bay, some distance from the resort. A wooden walkway runs over the rocks round the edge of the bay to the resort and guests are shuttled back and forth by little electric vehicles towing a string of trailers like a toy train.

Palm Bay and Happy Bay are popular anchorages for yachties. It's the nearest safe anchorage to Shute Harbour so people chartering bareboats and leaving late in the day often head here as the conclusion of their first short day's sailing. A channel has been cut through the reef at Palm Bay and there's an anchorage right up by the beach. Nightly mooring cost is $30 at Palm Bay, $35 at Happy Bay.

Paradise Bay is reached by a daily launch from Shute Harbour which costs $20 return.

Shute Harbour (QTTC)

Daydream Island

Area: 10 hectares
Type: continental
High point: 51 metres
In brief: The smallest of the Whitsunday resorts is undergoing a major rebuild in 1990.

The Island

Also known as West Molle this small island is only a couple of hundred metres across at its widest point. It's about two km long and has some tree cover and a good white coral sand beach at its northern end. The island has suffered from severe water shortages but later had one of the most delightful swimming pools on the resort islands – a long convoluted affair with a bar-island in the middle. It's said the island took its name from a cruising yacht which was a regular visitor before WW II.

In 1989 the resort was closed down for a huge $70 million rebuild to take place. The old resort was at the southern end of the island; it's new replacement will include a mini-marina on the island's eastern side. It's expected to re-open in 1991.

Information

The resort phone number is (079) 46 9200, write to Daydream Island Resort, via Shute Harbour, Qld 4802.

South Molle

Area: 4 square km
Type: continental
High point: 198 metres
Maximum visitor population: 400
Per person daily cost: $175
In brief: An active resort owned by Ansett Airlines, not particularly sophisticated but a good place for children as they're well catered for. Most of the island is national park and although it suffered from overgrazing during its pastoral days there are some fine short walks.

The Island

Largest of the Molle group of islands, South Molle is virtually joined to Mid Molle and

North Molle Islands. You can walk across to Mid Molle anytime and West Molle (Daydream) is seemingly only arm's reach away.

South Molle has long stretches of sandy or coral beach and is criss-crossed by a network of walking tracks. The island has a somewhat central position in the Whitsundays and from the highest point, Mt Jeffreys, there are superb views across all the surrounding islands. There are several other excellent viewpoints, particularly Spion Kop and Balancing Rock.

The island was named in 1815 after Colonel George Molle, Lieutenant Governor of the colony of NSW from 1814. Later the Whitsundays were the scene for violent altercations between the new arrivals and the area's Aborigines. In 1864 the schooner *Eva* was driven ashore on the island but another ship saved the crew.

In 1927 Henry George Lamond settled on the island and lived here with his wife and three children for the next 10 years. He was the author of a number of books on horses and outback living. If you make the climb up to Lamond Hill there's a memorial to Hal Lamond, his son.

From 1934 E M Bauer also lived on the island and the bay in front of the resort is named after him. Bauer and his wife can claim credit for making the first tentative moves towards today's South Molle resort as they used to serve 'teas' to the infrequent visitors who dropped by.

Information

The resort phone number is (079) 46 9433, fax number (079) 46 9580. Write to South Molle Island Resort, via Shute Harbour, Qld 4802. There's a gift shop with newspapers, cards, clothing, souvenirs, toiletries and the like. A coffee shop sells snacks, ice creams and drinks. There's also a hairdresser. You can change travellers' cheques and foreign currency at reception where there is also a Westpac Savings Bank agency and mail is handled.

View from South Molle Island (TW)

The Queensland National Parks & Wildlife Service have a *South Molle Island* leaflet.

Activities

The South Molle resort is owned by Ansett and at times it feels like one of those flights where there's a constant effort to keep you from getting bored – the meals follow the movies follow the drinks follow the movie and oops it's time to land again. There's a constant buzz of activity, all neatly detailed in a daily activities list. Even the wildlife gets called in to play their part – at 9 am the fish appear by the pier for their daily feeding and at 3 pm the lorikeets fly in for their feed by the tennis courts!

Children get special attention here – you can check them in to a pre-school nursery or a school-age activities centre and pretty much forget about them for the day. Actually a lot of the kids seem happy to forget about their parents too and get on with serious play time. The resort promotes itself as 'the holiday with no hidden extras' and most activities are free.

Sporting Activities

There's a compact nine-hole golf course right behind the resort, watch out for wayward balls from visiting beginners. There are a couple of tennis courts, a squash court and a small gymnasium. The activities organisers lay on plenty of competitions and games from cricket matches to golf tournaments, archery contests, even touch football – the resort band seems to be the resident team! Shock, horror, there's a video games room full of buzz-zap-kerwang noises.

Watersports

There are surf skis, catamarans, windsurfers, waterbikes and a bunch of other watersport equipment – all free. Windsurfing and sailing lessons are provided free every morning. Powered equipment – dinghies, waterskiing, parasailing, jet skis, watersled rides, all that sort of thing, does have a charge. The resort has one swimming pool with a tiny kiddies pool beside it. The pool – a straightforward rectangle, deep at one end, shallower at the

other, betrays the resort's age. There's a sauna and spa of similar age.

Diving

The resort has a PADI dive school which offers a short resort course for beginners ($55) or longer courses leading to PADI accreditation as a scuba diver, consisting of an advanced three day course ($240) and a five to six day open water course ($325). Equipment can be rented for $30 a day with one tank plus $4 for each additional tank. The usual dive is on the day trip to Hardy Reef, see below. That gives you about three hours at the reef, time for a couple of good dives.

Beaches & Snorkelling

The Whitsundays are not noted for their out-of-this-world beaches and the beach right in front of the South Molle resort is OK but only at high tide. When the tide is right out there's an unattractive mud-flat which can actually get quite smelly at times. Those beachfront units aren't such an attractive proposition on those occasions.

If you continue round to the west of the resort – either a scramble across the rocks or a one km stroll on a bush track – you find yourself at Paddle Bay. The beach here is quite pleasant, less crowded than the resort beach and if you swim out over the rocky patch up towards the end of the beach – close to the spit leading to Mid-Molle – you'll find some good coral including some interesting bommies.

There's not much else by the way of worthwhile beaches around the island. Oyster Bay is rocky, Pine Bay right at the south of the island is very shallow and faces the prevailing winds head on. Also down at the south end of the island Sandy Bay faces across to Shute Harbour and has some good coral although it's really stony rather than sandy.

Free snorkelling lessons are provided in the pool most days of the week and snorkelling equipment is also available for free use.

Walks

Over much of the central and southern part of the island the bush is quite sparse due to overgrazing in the years prior to the island

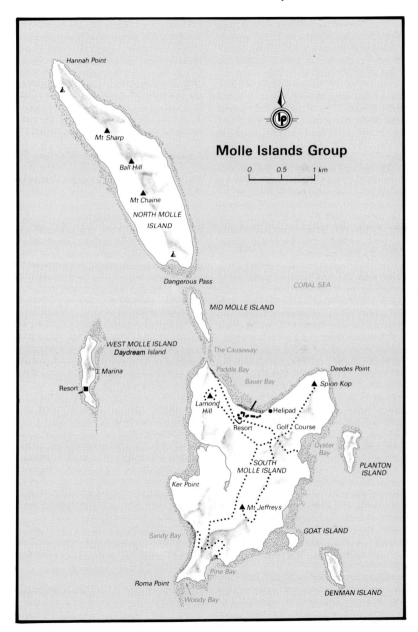

Molle Islands Group

0   0.5   1 km

Hannah Point

Mt Sharp

Ball Hill

Mt Chaine

NORTH MOLLE
ISLAND

Dangerous Pass

CORAL SEA

MID MOLLE ISLAND

WEST MOLLE ISLAND
Daydream Island

The Causeway

Paddle Bay

Bauer Bay

Deedes Point

Spion Kop

Marina

Resort

Lamond
Hill

Helipad

Resort

Golf Course

Oyster
Bay

PLANTON
ISLAND

SOUTH
MOLLE ISLAND

Ker Point

Mt Jeffreys

GOAT ISLAND

Sandy Bay

Roma Point

Pine Bay

Woody Bay

DENMAN ISLAND

becoming a National Park, but there are still many fine walks. The remaining forest cover is mainly at the north end of the island, around the resort. The middle part of the island is predominantly rolling grassland, punctuated by exclamation marks of black boys, those bullrush-like plants so often found in Central Australia. At the extreme south of the island there's again some very limited remnants of the earlier forest cover including a patch of hoop pines above Pine Bay.

The walks are easy to follow and very well signposted. Most of them start from up behind the resort golf course. You start by zig-zagging up the hill with the various trails diverting off again and again. If you've got tiny children they've even got baby-carrier backpacks available free. The walks include (distances from the starting point):

Spion Kop The three km walk to the top of Spion Kop is probably the finest walk on the island. The trail winds along the ridge with fine views down to Planton Island and Denman Island on the east side of the island and across to Hamilton, below you on the west side you can see Bauer Bay, the resort and North Molle. Leaving the grasslands the trail climbs onto a forested hillside, dips down briefly onto a saddle and then climbs up again to the rocky outcrop of Spion Kop at the extreme north point. You can clamber up through the hoop pines to the top of Spion Kop from where there are superb views in all directions, including back down on the resort.

Oyster Bay & Mt Jeffreys Turn south at the junction where the Spion Kop route heads north and after a couple of hundred metres you come to the point where the Oyster Bay trail diverges off and winds its ways down to the rock bay on the east coast. Oyster Bay is two km from the resort. Just south of Oyster Bay is Turtle Bay.

The Mt Jeffreys trail continues south, with the trail to the south diverging off it. The Mt Jeffreys trail continues along the east coast, generally through grassland with little origi-

nal forest cover. There are fine views of the Whitsundays, particularly Hamilton Island with its tell-tale skyscraper buildings. Finally the trail winds around to the top of Mt Jeffreys, a bare, grass-covered peak with superb 360° views. From the top you can see across the Molle group, north to Hayman, Hook and Whitsunday Islands, south-east to Hamilton, south to Long Island and west to the mainland with Shute Harbour easily identified by its cluster of yachts and boats. It's 3.5 km from the resort to the top of Mt Jeffreys.

Sandy Bay & Pine Bay These two bays are at the southern end of the island, 4.7 km from the resort. The trail runs through the centre of the island, through forest bush for the first half and then through rolling grassland with black boys. The trail curves around the west side of Mt Jeffreys and you can cross down from the Mt Jeffreys trail to this southern trail quite easily. There are some fine views of Long Island and the other islands south of South Molle before you get to the trail junction from where it is 500 metres to either bay.

The trail to Pine Bay winds down through a stand of hoop pines. The bay has a wide beach, sloping very gently into the sea and facing directly south so that the prevailing northerly breezes carry a wide assortment of flotsam and jetsam ashore. Apart from the traditional driftwood there's an amazing assortment of that modern addition – driftplastic. It's a convincing reminder of how indestructible our modern components and containers are! Strolling across this beach one day I even found, washed ashore, an attachment for the particular brand of vacuum cleaner we have at home!

The alternative trail leads down to Sandy Bay which is more stony than sandy but does have some pretty reasonable coral off shore. Right down at the end of the island there's Woody Bay. This southern tip of the island is the only remaining forest cover apart from that around the resort and north end.

Balancing Rock, Lamond Hill & Paddle Bay These trails lead off to the west and north-west of the resort. It's only 1.3 km to

Balancing Rock where there is indeed a balancing rock which looks remarkably precarious, and some truly superb views. You can see across to Daydream, across the central area of South Molle and to Mt Jeffreys, and over the resort to Spion Kop. The resort itself seems to be right at your feet.

You can continue on from Balancing Rock to Lamond Hill which is 3.5 km from the resort. It's a gently rounded hill, not so spectacular as Balancing Rock, but the views are equally fine. Just below the summit there's a memorial to Hal Lamond, son of the original European settler on the island who was killed in action in WW II.

Descend the km back down to the main trail and you can continue on to Paddle Bay, 1½ km from the resort, or loop back to the resort. Paddle Bay is just before the sand spit across to Mid-Molle and there's some good coral just off shore here.

Wildlife

Well there are a couple of more-or-less tame wallabies that hang around the golf course, a lot of very noisy and very tame lorikeets that will eat out of your hand at lorikeet feeding time (3 pm) and some very well trained fish that turn up for the 9 am feeding time off the pier. Some of the larger fish seem to turn up to feed on the smaller fish, rather than the resort hand-outs.

Other bird life is prolific; apart from the scavenging currawongs, those cheeky, large black and white birds that hang around the swimming pool looking for unattended plates to clean off. You'll see and hear all manner of birds around the resort or while walking the trail. You may come across a shy curlew standing by a path and you'll certainly hear their 'weee-loo' call across the golf course at night.

Look for quieter wildlife too, the bright red spiders that sometimes build their intricate webs right across the trails. Or the busy green ants which make their neat little shelters by gluing together groups of leaves on trees. You might see them constructing these homes, pulling the leaves together with a 'human chain' of ants and then gluing the leaf edges together with the aid of aphids, which they squeeze the adhesive out of. You'll see these homes in use in the trees or, when the leaves die and drop off, lying on the ground.

And of course there are cane toads, not so visible perhaps but come cane toad racing night in the bar (didn't I say this was middle-Australia?) there are plenty to be found. Cleverly, cane toad hunting is part of the children's activities earlier that evening, with the aid of torches they soon round up 10 or 20 on the golf course!

Accommodation

This is a plain middle-Australian resort with no pretensions and no special appeal. The rooms are very straightforward, mostly ordinary motel rooms from the '60s. They come in three categories and as with most of the reef resorts costs include all meals.

Cheapest at $115 per person per day are the Polynesian Units. These provide similar amenities to the Beachcomber Units, with a few Pacific touches, but are on the hillside further away from the resort.

The Beachcomber Units cost $130 per person. These are individual cabins, each with a double and a single bed and a verandah. Some of them are pleasantly isolated, looking out on the beach and in many ways these are the nicest rooms here.

Most of the accommodation is the middle priced Reef Units which cost $130. These are

South Molle Island resort area (TW)

side by side rooms, some facing the sea, some facing the golf course. They have paper-thin walls although the beds are (thankfully) commendably quiet. Each unit has a verandah and a bedroom alcove reached by sliding glass doors. The 'family' Reef Units have a second bedroom area separated by a sliding panel. If you've got kids, that separation is pleasant, although, since most of the light comes from the front doors it does make it rather dark in the back. The ventilation is not too good and the rooms are air-con, which I dislike on breezy islands. Basically they're plain, unpretentious and comfortable although they make South Molle look like what it is, a resort of 20 years ago.

Finally there are the Whitsunday Units at $150, a double-storey block right on the beach in the centre of the resort. The extra cost buys you the central location, tiles instead of carpet on the floor and somewhat more luxurious fittings.

Rooms have a fridge, radio, phone (with STD and ISD direct dialling) and TV. Family rooms have two TVs, which means there are two more TVs in one of these rooms than you'll find in total in some resorts. There are two videos shown each day. If life without the box is totally impossible you can even rent a video recorder and the gift shop has a small library of video tapes! A large coin-operated laundry provides plenty of opportunity for keeping clothes clean and there is a dry cleaning service through the gift shop. There's an ironing board and iron in the rooms as well, so there's no excuse for not being neat!

South Molle often has standby rates, available from Airlie Beach/Shute Harbour, that usually include the return boat trip to the resort

Food

The South Molle food story is equally middle-Australia – good quality pub food (when things are going well) is probably the best way to describe it. You start with a breakfast buffet, continue with a lunchtime buffet and finish with dinner offering the pub food regulars – steak, chicken, fish. You certainly won't starve but it's straightforward in the extreme and sometimes the standard can drop below reasonable standard pub food.

There are some alternatives – most nights there's a poolside barbecue as an alternative to the usual restaurant dinner and on Fridays there's South Molle's Island Night feast with an extensive spread of mostly serve-yourself food. The catch is that South Molle welcomes visitors to the island for this occasion so island guests may well find themselves at the back of a long queue. Fortunately most things don't run out although if you're in the late dining group you may well find yourself finishing your meal in total darkness as the show begins.

South Molle also has its *Coral Room* restaurant as an alternative to the normal dining area. They credit house guests $10 against the price of a meal here – which probably gives a pretty accurate picture of the regular food! Starters are $8 to $12, main courses $12 to $18 (or much more), desserts from the trolley $3. It's competent but unexciting food but don't condemn South Molle's eating possibilities out of hand as bland and unadventurous. This is basically a family resort and kids are well taken care of. While adults are having their dinner in peace the kids can be enjoying themselves at their own dinner, with games to follow until 8.30 pm. And if a couple of parent-less kids stumble dishevelled into the Coral Room at 8.25 there's no fuss made, they just whisk a couple of extra desserts onto the table. Even tiny children can be fed earlier (parents do the feeding) and then left in nursery care while the parents eat in peace. Regular babysitting is also available.

Getting There & Away

Hamilton, with its Ansett airport, serves as the main arrival port for South Molle. You can transfer from Hamilton either by helicopter or, more normally, by boat. The boat transfer costs $26 and takes about 20 minutes. From Shute Harbour the boat transfer costs $25 and also takes about 20 minutes.

Hayman Island

Area: 4 square km
Type: continental
High point: 250 metres
Maximum visitor population: 400
Per person daily cost: $400
In brief: Hayman is one of the most luxurious and expensive resorts on the Great Barrier Reef. The island is close to good scuba diving at the north of Hook Island and also closer to the outer reef than most other Whitsunday Islands.

The Island

Hayman Island is one of the oldest Barrier Reef resort islands as it was first established in 1950. The most northerly resort island of the Whitsunday group, the resort is fronted by a wide, shallow reef which emerges from the water at low tide. After a total rebuild which took nearly two years Hayman reopened in 1987 as one of the most luxurious resorts on the Great Barrier Reef.

The island was named in 1866 after Thomas Hayman, navigator of the naval ship HMS *Salamander* which spent many years in this area. In 1904 the sawmill in Cid Harbour was replaced by one on Hook Island, operated by Thomas Abell who at the same time leased Hayman Island for cattle grazing. In 1907 he sold out, handing over the lease and all the goats he had introduced for the sum of £30. In 1935 the island lease changed hands again, this time to the Hallam Brothers who set up a fishing resort.

Australian aviation pioneer Reginald Ansett took over 12 years later when he bought Bert Hallam's 1000 goats at £10 a head. The fishing resort, with its solitary coconut palm planted by that well known fishing enthusiast, novelist Zane Grey, was closed in 1948 but it was not until 1950 that the Hayman Resort opened. It lasted right through to 1985 before closing for its recent spectacular rebuild.

Information

The resort phone number is (079) 46 9100 and the address is Hayman Island, Qld 4801.

Hayman's shops are as exclusive as everything else about this resort. There are boutiques, a jewellery shop, a newsagency, and a hairdresser. The Club Lounge has a billiard table and also a library.

Resort Rebuilds

The '80s has been a time of amazing construction activity on the reef resort islands – new resorts have been built (Hamilton being the biggest example) while older ones have been rebuilt, upgraded or expanded. Hayman is probably the most ambitious example of the rebuild and upgrade programme.

Hayman opened in the 1950s and was one of the most luxurious island resorts at the time. For a while they were keen on calling it 'Royal Hayman' because Princess Margaret or some other lower-grade royalty had dropped by once. In the early '80s it was recognised that the resort was no longer in the forefront but throwing $260 million at it has certainly pushed it back towards the top.

What do you get for that sort of money? Well you get 214 rooms, six restaurants, seven bars, a hectare of swimming pools, a collection of antiques and arts, an 1840 Herron-Smith billiard table in the Billiard Room, a $3 million luxury launch (the *Sea Goddess I*) to whisk you over from the airport on Hamilton, a desalination plant that produces 600,000 litres of water a day and a fully automatic powerhouse with five generators. And that still left $7 million over to plant 900 coconut palms and over 600,000 other plants. There's even a traditional Japanese garden as a setting for the oriental restaurant and the main entrance is flanked by 20 stately nine-metre high date palms, transplanted from a convent in Swan Hill, Victoria. There's a resident landscaping staff of 15 to tend these gardens.

They're very proud of how much they spent on their renovation; a great deal of their publicity material is devoted to telling you how much the furnishings cost, how much the carpets are worth, how much they spent

White-lined cod (GBRMPA)

Barramundi cod (GBRMPA)

on the chandeliers in La Fontaine restaurant. Hayman definitely is sophisticated but in some ways it almost turns its back on the outdoors, the reef, the sun, sea and sand, all of which this is supposed to be about. There almost seems to be an attempt to deny that it's all out there, to shut the doors, turn the air-con up high and to pretend you're in some big city with limousines lined up outside.

There's plenty of club-room style furniture and furnishings but the rooms themselves are just modern international hotel style – this is a sophisticated resort, the Barrier Reef comes second. Recently the operators have been trying to tone down Hayman's image a little, emphasising that it's not really as ritzy as their initial marketing campaign tried to make out! They've even been offering standby rates to help fill their empty rooms.

Activities
Parasailing, waterskiing, windsurfing and sailing are also on the agenda while on dry land there's a sports centre with indoor tennis courts and a fully equipped gym. Since Hayman is a room-only resort everything costs extra.

Surprisingly, children are well catered for here, at least during school vacation time. In fact the daytime children's activities are one of the few things at Hayman which don't get added on to your bill. Activities are organised for the kids in the morning, afternoon and early evening, and the kids definitely enjoy

them. Despite the cost there are often a lot of kids here during the children's high seasons (ie school holidays).

Walks
There are a number of bushwalks around the island including an eight km circuit, two km across to Blue Pearl Bay or 3.5 km to Dolphin Point at the northern tip of the island. It's less than a km from the resort up to the Whitsunday Passage lookout overlooking Arkhurst Island. To get to the start of the walks follow the road round past the harbour and through the rather messy maintenance and power station site. Don't take the road that runs off up the hill to the water storage tanks but continue right to the end and take the path up by the quarried out water storage area.

All the other trails diverge off the round-the-island track. First there's the turn down to Blue Pearl Bay and then the turn-off to Whitsunday Lookout. The track continues rising gently through wooded grassland to the Blue Dolphin turn-off and then climbs through grassland studded with black boys to the turn off to Cook's Lookout. It's a short climb from the main track to the superb views from this point, the resort lies right at your feet and you can clearly see the reef and across to Langford's sweeping spit. There's a small shelter here and a water storage tank so there may be drinking water if there's been recent rain.

The round-the-island track continues from

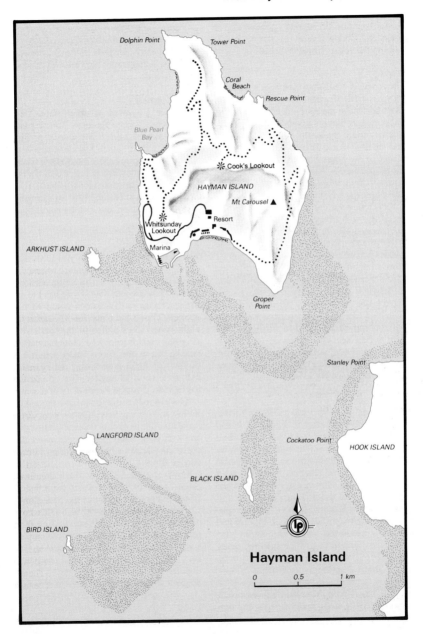

Dolphin Point

Tower Point

Coral Beach

Rescue Point

Blue Pearl Bay

Cook's Lookout

HAYMAN ISLAND

Mt Carousel ▲

Whitsunday Lookout

Resort

ARKHUST ISLAND

Marina

Groper Point

Stanley Point

LANGFORD ISLAND

Cockatoo Point

HOOK ISLAND

BLACK ISLAND

BIRD ISLAND

Hayman Island

0   0.5   1 km

the lookout turn-off round to the east side of the island, taking several turns down before turning the corner towards the resort.

Diving

Hayman has a full-time dive boat where you can get diving instruction in Japanese as well as English. The island is indeed well situated for diving as there is good diving at several points around the north of Hayman Island and nearby Hook Island. Hayman is also closer to the outer Barrier Reef than other, more southerly Whitsunday resorts. It's about 30 km north-east of Hayman to Hardy and Black Reef. Bait Reef in particular offers a spectacular variety of diving possibilities including wall dives, shallow lagoon dives and some superb drift dives.

Hayman's dive shop is located at the marina and offers a variety of diving courses from straightforward snorkelling instruction ($15) to scuba certificate courses ($485) and underwater photography courses ($205). Diving trips are made on the *Reef Goddess* dive boat and range in cost from a one tank half day trip off the island for $65 to full day trips to Bait Reef with two tanks for $115. A full range of equipment is available for hire including underwater cameras and even underwater video equipment.

Boats

Hayman is great for local sailing with that wide expanse of water to Langford Island with its long sand spit and Black Island (Bali Ha'i) as two convenient points to sail to. Water funnels through the narrow strait between Hook and Hayman and if the wind is low you can almost get sucked into the strait. If you sail around Black Island cut well back towards Hayman to avoid the current.

You may see turtles around Langford and Black – where the Yellow Submarine also circulates. Stingrays like the shallow, sandy reef flat in front of the resort. You'll often see them shooting away in front of your boat.

The resort rents Maricats ($20 an hour), and has free Lasers, paddleboards and dinghies.

Further afield there are cruises to neighbouring islands, gamefishing trips or you can take an underwater peek in the Yellow Submarine which operates between Hayman and Hook Islands.

Other Islands

There are a number of small, uninhabited islands very close to Hayman. You can walk out to Arkhurst Island at low tide, or from Langford Island, which has some fine coral around it, you can walk across to Bird Island. Black Island (they like to call it Bali Ha'i) is between Hayman and Hook Island. Years ago Maureen and I camped out for three days on Langford Island and had the whole place to ourselves.

Accommodation

This is not a resort to visit if you're worried about your mortgage payments, was how one magazine report summed up Hayman Island. The old adage about how if you have to ask the price you can't afford it could also be applied. This is the place for $300-plus per night rooms, $10 coffee-orange juice & a croissant breakfasts or $10 hamburgers for a snack, where the resort shop sells $150 bikinis (or $100 monokinis) and where a babysitter costs $8 an hour. No, don't come to Hayman if you're worried about the cost.

The 214 rooms and suites have air-conditioning and ceiling fans together with all the usual luxuries including toiletries, hairdryers and bathrobes. Each room has its own video player and there's a library of video films to choose from.

Costs start at $255 for the Palm Court rooms, some of them recycled from the old resort and not as elegant as the newer ones. Costs continue up to $400 to $475 for the newer Beachfront, West Wing and East Wing rooms. And finally launch through the stratosphere for the $700 to $800 West Wing and East Wing suites. All prices are for singles or doubles and room only. Oh, there is a penthouse if you really feel the need to spend up.

Food

With half a dozen dining possibilities to

choose from the resort intends to make the food as important as the accommodation. There's the *Coffee House* open 6.30 am to 9 pm for snacks, light meals, drinks and so on. They have the best food deal at Hayman (the $3 open sandwich) as well as the worst ($10 for a coffee, juice and croissants or pastry continental breakfast). A three course set dinner costs $25. In the morning the *West Lanai* also provides breakfast in the open air and snacks at other times of day.

La Fontaine is the main restaurant with, as the name indicates, French cuisine as its speciality – together with a Louis XIV style dining room with a central fountain, carpets specially woven in China from Australian wool and Waterford Crystal chandeliers. It's open only in the evenings and 'jacket and tie are preferred'. This is a long way from the resorts which only stipulate that you wear shoes, not thongs!

Two other restaurants open only in the evenings. The Asian restaurant offers oriental and Asian cuisine in a Japanese-style restaurant set in a formal Japanese garden. Starters are $14 to $16, main courses $20 to $30, desserts $8 to $10, the wine list mainly $20 to $30. Count on over $150 for two. *La Trattoria* is a more casual Italian bistro where you can dine al fresco. It's slightly cheaper with starters at $12 to $14, pastas and pizzas at $11 to $15, main courses at $18 to $22, desserts at $5 to $8. Dinner for two is still going to cost well over $100. Afterwards you can recover from all that culinary extravagance in the wood-panelled luxury of the English Club Lounge.

Other dining possibilities include the poolside *Planters Restaurant* and barbecues are featured in the Lanai.

Entertainment
Hayman's big bucks approach to life enables it to attract big name performers for its Entertainment Centre. Live music also features at the Club Lounge, in La Fontaine Restaurant and poolside.

Getting There & Away
Air Seair Pacific have amphibious aircraft services between Hayman and the Whitsunday airstrip at Shute Harbour.

Sea Hayman guests generally arrive at Hamilton Island and are then transferred to the island on the luxury cruisers *Sun Goddess* or *Sun Paradise*. Guests are also collected from Shute Harbour but even the transfers to the island are not like those at other resorts, en route to Hayman you complete registration formalities and sip champagne on the way.

Hook Island

Area: 53 square km
Type: continental
High point: 454 metres
In brief: Hook has a number of excellent beaches, some of the best diving sites around the Whitsunday Islands, some very popular yacht anchorages and a small and very low-key resort and camping site which is popular with backpackers. It also has the Hook Island Underwater Observatory, at the same site as the resort.

Nara & Macona Inlets
The bottom half of Hook Island is indented by two very long and narrow fjord-like bays, running a good five km into the island. The beautiful Nara Inlet is a very popular deep-water anchorage for visiting yachties and you can often see a crowd of them far up the inlet. Caves with Aboriginal wall paintings have been found in Nara Inlet and there's a boardwalk to one of the caves.

Macona Inlet runs nearly as far into the island and has a National Park camping site.

Underwater Observatory
Underwater observatories have become a little old fashioned with the advent of semi-submersible tourist submarines and the high-speed catamarans, which whisk visitors out to the real outer reef in a fraction of the time it used to take to get there. Nevertheless the Hook Island Underwater Observatory is still a popular Whitsunday attraction and a

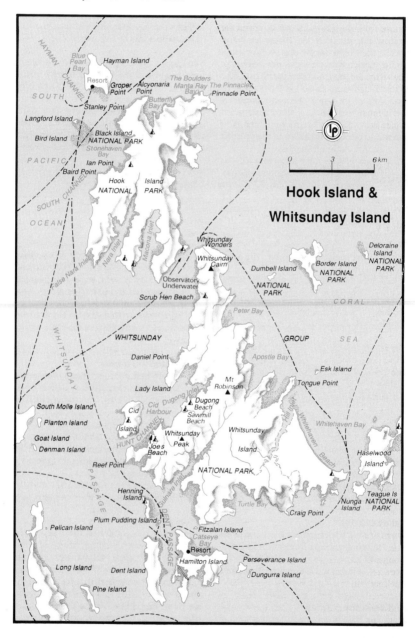

Hook Island &

Whitsunday Island

number of the cruises stop here to admire the underwater scenery from 10 metres below the surface and to sample the pleasant beach at the adjacent resort. The observatory is open from 10 am to 2 pm daily and admission is $8.50 (children half price). The observatory is close to the south-eastern corner of Hook Island, by the narrow channel which separates Hook Island from Whitsunday Island.

Hook Island Resort

Just round the headland from the observatory is the sandy sweep of Yuengee Beach, named after the Aboriginal tribe who once frequented the Whitsundays. It's a pleasant little beach with good swimming and snorkelling although you should take care not to swim too far out into the strait. At times the current whips through between Hook and Whitsunday Islands so swiftly that you can see the whitecaps on otherwise calm days.

The resort is popular with backpackers and has no fancy facilities or entertainment. A volleyball net on the beach and paddle skis are about all the equipment there is on offer. The resort has a small dive shop and offers resort courses and complete five day certificate courses. There's good diving right off the beach if conditions are good although the fast current through the narrow passage by the resort can stir the water up. Videos on reef topics are sometimes shown in the resort lounge area at night.

Walks

A short walk from the resort site leads to the observatory and round to Back Beach, another gentler track leads straight to the beach. From here you can follow a trail up and over the promontory from the sheltered straits side to Pebble Beach on the ocean side. If you continued through the resort alongside the passage there are fine views over to Whitsunday Island from Bluff Lookout at the tip of the promontory. From there you could rock hop around the headland to Pebble Beach and come back on the trail.

Wildlife

Hook Island has a wide variety of wildlife and impressively large goannas are often seen around the resort. Campers are warned not to leave food in their tents as 'the goannas may chew through to it'!

Northern Diving Spots

Hook Island offers some of the best diving and snorkelling locations in the Whitsundays. They're mainly at the northern end of the island where they enjoy protection from the prevailing northerly winds and are also on the outer edge of the Whitsundays. Alcyonaria Point, Butterfly Bay, The Boulders, Manta Ray Bay and Pinnacle Point are amongst the most popular spots for diving and snorkelling trips.

Manta Ray Bay is particularly popular with good snorkelling near the beach and a huge variety of small fish. There are also some good diving spots on the western side of the island, particularly Stonehaven and around Langford and Black Islands, between Hook and Hayman Islands.

Accommodation & Food

Hook Island Resort The resort adjacent to the underwater observatory has cabins and a campsite. Staying in the cabins costs either $15 per person in bunkrooms accommodating up to eight people or $40 for a double. Bedding is provided but you have to supply your own towel. There are camping areas at both ends of the beach and the cost is $7.50 per person. Toilets and showers by the resort buildings are shared by the cabins and campers.

There is only a radio telephone at the resort. Bookings are handled by the South Molle Travel Centre (tel (079) 46 6900 or (008) 07 5127) at 43 Shute Harbour Rd in Airlie Beach or by any of the Airlie Beach and Shute Harbour booking agents.

The resort has a small gift shop, a restaurant and a bar. The food varies from sandwiches and pies to quite good pub-style meals or you can use the barbecues or kitchen area provided. The resort has basic food supplies available or you can bring your own over from the mainland. A kit of cooking utensils can be borrowed from the resort on payment of a $10 refundable deposit.

Other Camping The observatory doesn't attract big crowds of day trippers and in any case their visits are fleeting but if you want to get right away from signs of civilisation there are other camping areas on the island. Curlew Beach in Macona Inlet is a pleasant National Park camping site with limited facilities. Butterfly Bay on the west side of the island has no facilities but there is water at some times of the year. You can also camp at Stonehaven and Butterfly Bay East although there are no facilities or water.

Getting There & Away

Normally a boat runs out to the resort around 8.15 am and returns around 10 am. The return fare is $20. If there aren't sufficient resort visitors then one of the cruise boats is used instead, dropping off resort visitors when it pauses to visit the observatory.

Lindeman Island

Area: 8 square km
Type: continental
High point: 210 metres
Maximum visitor population: 300
Per person daily cost: $150
In brief: Lindeman has recently had a major renovation and is now pleasantly modern. It's a low key, family style resort just far enough away from the centre of Whitsunday activity to avoid the day tripper crowds of some of the more central resorts. Children are well catered for.

Lindeman Island

The Island

Lindeman was the oldest of the Barrier Reef resorts, first established back in 1929, but in 1988 it reopened after a major redevelopment which has brought it right up to date. It's a very pleasant middle-of-the-road type of resort, falling neatly between the sophisticated up-market ambience of Hayman and the mass market pub-food atmosphere of South Molle. It's also pleasantly mid-sized and since Lindeman is slightly further away from the Shute Harbour and Hamilton transit points you don't have to cope with the comings and goings of so many day-trip boats.

The island is a National Park and has 20 km of walking trails. There are seven beaches dotted around the island and there are also a number of islands close to Lindeman itself. Seaforth, with its fine beaches on both sides of the island, is straight in front of the resort and is a popular excursion. You can also be dropped off at Shaw Island if you'd like to escape from the resort for the day.

Like a number of the island resorts Lindeman does its best to take care of the kids during school holidays and there are children's activities, children's evening meal times and, best of all, even a children's camp in Adventure Valley behind Plantation Beach. The kids can go off for an overnight stay at the permanent campsite and their parents can really go on holiday!

Like other Whitsunday islands Lindeman has had an earlier history of sheep and goat grazing. Angus Nicholson took over the grazing lease in 1923 and later opened the first resort. Goats still survive from those early days and you may spot them while bushwalking. The scrub fowls tend to be more elusive.

Information

Phone number of the resort is (079) 46 9333, fax number (079) 46 9598 and the address is Lindeman Island Resort, Lindeman Island, Qld 4741. Bookings can be made within Australia by phoning (008) 77 7322 toll free.

The resort shop has clothes, beachwear, toiletries, newspapers and magazines, post-

cards and those other necessities. The
Queensland National Parks & Wildlife
Service produces a *Lindeman Island* leaflet.

Activities

The resort has a pool, playground, tennis and
squash courts and probably the best golf
course to be found on the reef islands. On the
beach the Beach Hut has runabouts, sailboards, catamarans, jet skis, paddle skis and
snorkelling gear. All the unpowered equipment is free to resort guests.

Parasailing, waterskiing, fishing trips and
yacht cruises are other resort activities. If you
want to get away from the resort you can be
dropped off (and picked up) on Seaforth
Island for $5 or Shaw Island for $12.

Walks

Most of Lindeman Island is a National Park
and the QNPWS *Lindeman Island* leaflet has
information on the island's vegetation and
where you might find it. Apart from birds the
island is also noted for its many butterflies,
particularly the impressive Blue Tiger which
is very common from October to May. They
are often seen in shady gullies on hot days.

All walks on the island start from the air

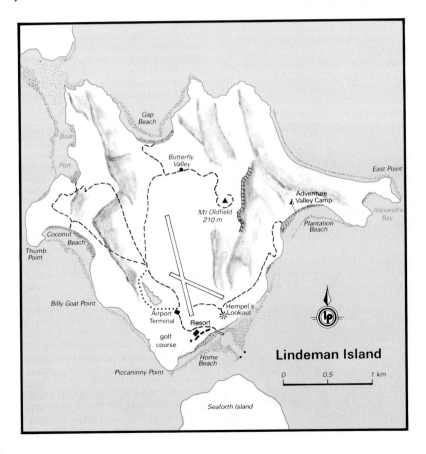

terminal and the favourite one is the four km climb to the top of 210 metre Mt Oldfield. From near the north end of the airstrip the path climbs gently through scrub and forest, passing through Butterfly Valley, before emerging into clearer land around the summit. The path circles right round the peak and to the east there is a sheer cliff face, looking down on the kid's camp in Adventure Valley and the eastern side of the island. From the summit there are superb views of the whole island and across to other islands in the group. To the north you can see the unmistakable shape of Pentecost and off to the north-east Hamilton with its airport runway.

Starting off in the same direction from the air terminal you can take the six km loop walk which drops down to Coconut Beach and Boat Port with the remains of an old pier. A trail branches off the Mt Oldfield path and descends to Gap Beach on the northern side of the island.

Lindeman Island resort (TW)

Another trail crosses the airstrip from the terminal and passes Hempel's Lookout before dropping down to the water's edge, crossing a small gully and continuing on to the long sweep of Plantation Beach. You can cross the headland at the far end of the beach and go down to Alexandra Bay. Watch for the many small stingrays basking on the shallow sandy bottom off Plantation Beach.

Finally shorter strolls loop around the dam lake sometimes known as Loch Nicholson, after the farmer who established the first resort here. At the end of the golf course there are fine views from Piccaninny Point.

Diving

Lindeman is not the best island for scuba divers. Since it's further from the centre of Whitsunday activity and fairly small there aren't diving trips every day. If you *must* go diving you should check ahead to see if there will be a diving trip during your stay on the island. Nevertheless there's a diving school on the island and a variety of dive courses are offered. Some local diving is done around Lindeman and longer diving trips are made to other islands in the Whitsundays.

Accommodation

The 1988 revamp of Lindeman Island was a thorough one taking a full year to complete. Some of the older Whitsunday units were retained and refurbished during the resort's renovation. Those up the hill behind the resort are fairly typical of the sort of country-motel-style units built in the '60s.

On the level land by the beach the new resort with its pool, dining and entertainment areas is flanked by 104 Whitsunday Waterfront and new Seaforth units, all looking out over the beach and water. These rooms have fan and air-conditioning, telephones, TV (with videos shown every day) and a small refrigerator. Each room is fronted by a small balcony.

The full board daily cost is $193 single or $314 double in the Whitsunday units, $253 single or $396 double in the Seaforth units. There is a laundry room in each block.

Food

Most meals are in the *Islander Restaurant* with a buffet breakfast, smorgasbord lunch and a dinner chosen from a limited menu. The food is surprisingly good, indeed it's some of the best food found at the reef resorts, particularly their desserts which are decidedly too tempting. The restaurant is a pleasant, airy place but if couples don't want to share a table, or if you want one of the window tables around the edge, you should book a table ahead of time.

Other eating possibilities are the *Coffee Shop*, just above the pool, where you can get light meals and snacks all day. Alternatively there's *Nicolson's* restaurant above the Islander with an extensive menu and a full wine list.

Entertainment

Lindeman isn't a mega-resort with all sorts of activity but there is usually live music in the Lobby Bar in the evening and after 10 pm the all purpose building up by the airstrip becomes *Juliet's Nightclub*. It's far enough from the main resort area that the noise isn't annoying to guests wanting a good night's sleep. During the day the 'nightclub' building becomes the golf course clubhouse – except when aircraft arrive or depart when it's the airport terminal!

Getting There & Away

Air Much of Lindeman Island is a high plateau and it's topped by a grass airstrip. Reef World Airlines flies here from Mackay

Plantation Beach, Lindeman Island (TW)

($51), Whitsunday (Shute Harbour) ($42) and Proserpine ($42). Flights from Townsville ($136) go via Whitsunday.

Sea There are launch connections from the airport at Hamilton Island or from Shute Harbour.

Other Islands

Apart from the main resort islands there are a great many other islands in the Whitsundays. The largest of all, Whitsunday Island, is unpopulated apart from campers, visiting yachties and the many day trippers who come to magnificent Whitehaven Beach. Other islands range from popular camping get-aways and good anchorages for cruising yachties, to isolated dots on the map which hardly see a visitor from one year to the next.

BORDER ISLAND

To the east of Whitsunday Island there's good snorkelling and diving at the entrance to Cataran Bay on Border Island. It's a good area for camping but there are no facilities and there's no water. Border Island is a popular destination for many cruise trips.

HASLEWOOD ISLAND

To the east of Whitsunday Island there are good diving possibilities at White Bay on Haslewood Island. You can camp at Chalkie's Beach or at Windy Bay. Across from Windy Bay is Lupton Island.

HENNING ISLAND

Immediately north of Dent Island and to the south-west of Whitsunday, Henning Island has a fine campsite on Geographer's Beach. There's sheltered camping in the forest behind the beach and good views from the grassy hill to the east but there's no water available. The anchorage off the beach is poor so you're unlikely to be disturbed by too many day visitors. North Spit also has a camping area although once again no water is available.

NORTH MOLLE

The narrow Unsafe Passage, which is actually quite safe for most vessels seen in the Whitsundays, separates North Molle from Mid Molle and South Molle Islands. It's one of the closer islands to Shute Harbour and has two popular National Park campsites. The coral beach at Hannah Point, at the north of the island, is popular with day visitors.

Camping

There are small campsites at Hannah Point at the northern end of the island and Cockatoo Beach at the southern end. Both sites have seasonal water available and the Cockatoo Beach site also has showers.

PENTECOST ISLAND

The unmistakable shape of Pentecost Island rises almost sheer from the sea between Lindeman and Hamilton Islands. It's easily spotted from aircraft approaching or departing Hamilton Island airport. The island was named by Captain Cook and has a 208 metre high cliff face shaped remarkably like an Indian head.

SHUTE HARBOUR ISLANDS

There are several small islands right in Shute Harbour with good coral for snorkelling. Shute Island has a small campsite and a sandy beach but there is no water and no facilities. Repair and Tancred islands are even closer in and Tancred has some camping possibilities but so close to the activity at Shute Harbour these are not places to get away from it all.

WHITSUNDAY & CID ISLANDS

The largest of the Whitsunday islands, Whitsunday covers 109 square km and rises to 438 metres at Whitsunday Peak. There is no resort development on the island but Whitehaven Beach on the north-east coast is the longest and finest beach in the Whitsunday group and it's a popular destination for many cruises.

Right at the northern tip of the island Whitsunday Wonders is a popular diving spot with excellent snorkelling near the shore.

Whitehaven Beach

The Whitsunday's best known beach stretches for six km so there's enough for everybody. Off the southern end of the beach there's good snorkelling around the coral bommies.

Cid Harbour

The story that the US fleet assembled here before the Battle of the Coral Sea is considerably exaggerated but this deep harbour, sheltered by Cid Island, is a popular spot for day trip cruises and has several good camping areas. There's a walking track between Dugong Beach and Sawmill Beach.

Sawmill Beach takes its name from the sawmill James Whitnall set up there in 1888. For the next 13 years hoop pine timber from the island was cut at the mill but today it's the sandy beach, good anchorages and the coral off the headland at the south end of the beach which attract visitors.

Camping

Whitsunday has a number of popular camping spots and, because many cruise boats go to Whitsunday, they're easy to get to. The Scrub Hen Beach site at the northwest end of Whitsunday, close to the passage between Whitsunday and Hook Islands, is mainly used by organised camping groups.

The camping area on Whitehaven Beach is at the southern end of the beach but there's no water and open fires are not permitted. There are marked areas for day visitors, individual campers and organised camping groups.

There are three camping areas along Cid Harbour. Dugong Beach is a large site with water, showers, toilets and other facilities including gas barbecues. There's a good sandy beach and an interesting rainforest area behind it. A one km walking track leads from Dugong Beach through coastal rainforest to Sawmill Beach where a creek has water for part of the year. This smaller campsite also has good facilities including showers and toilets.

At the southern end of Cid Harbour is Joe's Beach. This is a good campsite with a fine beach and snorkelling but no water supply.

Cid Island itself has camping at Homestead Bay on the west side but there's no water and no facilities.

NORTHERN ISLANDS

Gloucester Island to the north-west of the Whitsunday group, has a campsite with limited facilities at Bona Bay. Other small sites can be found on Armit, Saddleback and Grassy Islands.

SOUTHERN ISLANDS

Neck Bay on Shaw Island, close to Lindeman, has a small undeveloped campsite with no facilities. You can also camp at Burning Point. Western Beach on South Repulse Island, immediately south of Cape Conway, is similarly spartan.

Thomas Island is south of Shaw Island. There is good snorkelling off sandy Sea Eagle Beach to the south-east. There is a larger camping area here with some facilities although there is no water. Naked Lady Beach to the north-west also has good anchorages and a campsite.

THE OUTER REEF

Cruise boats operate out to the Great Barrier Reef from the Whitsundays every day. It's a 30 to 60 km trip but the modern high-speed catamarans get you out there very fast. A typical day trip costs around $75 and while you are anchored at the reef there's time for some snorkelling, a peek beneath the surface in a glass bottom boat or in the semi-submersible 'submarines' which have become *de rigeur* on Barrier Reef trips or, if you arrange it in advance, a couple of scuba dives. Lunch is usually included in the cost.

If you're prone to sea-sickness some people find they get very sick indeed on these trips. The catamarans are very fast and on a choppy day they seem to give a lot of people very severe and very high-speed sea-sickness. On one trip I was on, one unfortunate women got so sick she had to charter a floatplane to come out from the mainland to fly her back. If you do get seasick it's wise to take some sort of anti-seasickness medication before you depart.

Bait Reef, Hook-Hardy Reef and Black Reef are the most popular reefs for Whitsunday trips. Furthest to the west, Bait Reef is a smaller oval-shaped reef offering some superb diving opportunities. Diving trips from Hayman Island often go here to explore diving locales like the Stepping Stones, Anemoneville, Gary's Lagoon, Manta Ray Drop-off and Gorgonia Hill.

The Hook and Hardy Reefs are particularly popular for Whitsunday day trips and there's a regular flotilla of pontoons, glass bottom boats and semi-submersibles parked out here. Popular diving spots are the Canyons, the Pinnacles (good for snorkelling), the Pontoon (lots of fish come here to be fed by divers and snorkellers), the Beach (also good for snorkelling) and Shark Alley (aptly named!). Black Reef, further east, also offers good diving including a variety of caves and canyons at the Cathedral and many turtles at the spot known as Turtle St.

Brittle Stars & Feather Stars

Brittle stars and feather stars are two more examples of the incredible variety of forms which *echinoderms* manage to assume. It's hard to imagine that starfish, sea cucumbers and sea urchins are closely related to the tentacled brittle stars and the plant-like feather stars.

The starfish or sea star is the clearest example of the five-armed echinoderm body plan and the brittle stars, part of the *ophiuroid* group, are very similar. A small circular body contains the main organs, unlike starfish where each arm has a full complement of organs and can reproduce itself if cut off. The brittle star's arms are constructed of segmented sections of 'skeleton', rather like the vertebrae in a mammal's backbone. It's the arms which give the brittle star its name as they are indeed very brittle and will break off if the creature is mishandled.

Feather stars or *crinoids* are the most primitive of the echinoderm group and look much more like a plant than an animal. At one time crinoids were the dominant form of sealife but feather stars are the only species in the family still found. Although feather stars can move around they usually stay firmly attached in one place, holding on to the coral, rock or some other suitable anchor with their *cirri* while the arms wave in the water, their numerous *pinnules* giving them their characteristic feather-like appearance.

The number of arms varies from as few as five to as many as 200 but they radiate from five areas around the feather star's central body, maintaining the echinoderm's five part pattern. In some feather stars there are no cirri in which case the creature simply hangs on with some of its arms. Feather stars like to anchor themselves in areas of consistently flowing currents, where they can feed on the passing plankton. ■

Feather star

Octopus & Squid

It scarcely seems credible that *cephalopods*, the tentacled octopus and squid, should be related to oysters, clams, cowries and cone shells, yet all are molluscs. The eight-tentacled octopus usually shelters in a cavity or cave in the coral, coming out to grab unwary fish or crustaceans which it kills with an often venomous bite from its beak-like jaws. The common Barrier Reef octopus spans about 60 cm across its tentacles but the only variety which is dangerous to humans is the tiny blue ringed octopus. This pretty little octopus is instantly identifiable by the bright blue rings which appear all over its head and legs when it is disturbed. Although it only grows to about 15 cm across its bite can cause death from respiratory arrest.

Squid are rather like a longer, streamlined version of an octopus. Like an octopus they move by a form of jet propulsion, squirting out the water which is taken over their gills. They can move at remarkable speed and catch their prey, usually small fish and crustaceans, by shooting out two long tentacles. Like octopus they are also masters of disguise, able to change their colour by squeezing or flattening out cells which contain coloured material.

Blue ringed octopus

Cuttlefish are like a larger squid and along with speed and the ability to change colour they are also able to perform a type of animal smokescreen trick. When threatened they turn a dark colour then shoot out a blob of dark ink which takes a cuttlefish-like shape. The real cuttlefish then rapidly turns a lighter colour and shoots away, leaving the predator to grab at its ghost! The familiar cuttlebone found washed up on beaches is a cuttlefish's internal skeleton. It is made up of thin layers and by filling the space between layers with gas the cuttlefish uses it as a flotation device.

Octopus and squid have evolved from earlier *cephalopods* which had shells. The chambered nautilus is the best known and most spectacular survivor of these creatures. The large brown and white nautilus shell is divided into chambers and the tentacled creature can vary its buoyancy by changing the amount of gas and liquid in individual chambers. ∎

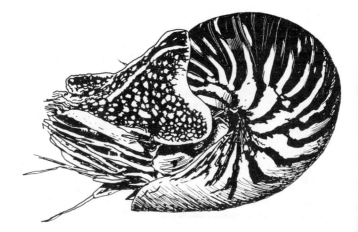

Magnetic Island

Area: 52 square km
Type: continental
High point: 497 metres
In Brief: Magnetic Island is very close to
Townsville and has lots of accommodation,
generally moderately priced and including a
number of popular backpackers' hostels.
With its good beaches and bushwalks this
predominantly National Park island is a
popular travellers' centre.

The Island
Magnetic is one of the most popular reef
islands for backpacking travellers because
it's so cheap and convenient to get to and has
such a great selection of cheap places to stay.
In general the population is around 2500 but
at peak times the number of people on the
island can balloon up to 7000. It's also big
enough and varied enough to offer plenty of
things to do and see, including some really
fine bushwalks.

Only eight km offshore from Townsville
(a 20 to 30-minute trip on the high speed
catamaran ferries), Magnetic Island is almost
a suburb of Townsville and a popular day trip
from that city. The island was given its name
by Captain Cook, who thought his ship's
compass went funny when he sailed by in
1770. Nobody else has thought so since! The
island is often rough, rugged and rocky but
it has some fine beaches, lots of bird life,
excellent bushwalking tracks, a koala sanctuary and an aquarium. It's dominated by 497
metre Mt Cook.

There are several small resort towns along
the coast and a variety of accommodation
possibilities. Since the island is a real year
round place it has a quite different atmosphere to the purely resort islands along the
reef. This is one of the larger islands and
about 70% of the island is national park;
much of the wildlife is extraordinarily fearless.

Aboriginals certainly lived on the island,
which they could easily reach from the mainland, but the first European settlement was
established by timber cutters at Nelly Bay in
the early 1870s. They soon left the island and
in 1887 Harry Butler and his family settled
at Picnic Bay. They soon started to put up
visitors from the mainland and thus the Magnetic Island tourist business was born. The
Butler story is recounted in *The Real Magnetic* by Jessie Macqueen, another early
resident of the island.

The arrival of Robert Hayles in 1899, who
built a hotel at Picnic Bay, really put Magnetic on the map as he also started a ferry
service with an ex-Sydney Harbour ferry *The
Bee*. The Hayles operation was the main
force in Magnetic Island tourism right up to
the late 1980s.

Orientation
Magnetic Island is roughly triangular in
shape with Picnic Bay, the first stop for the
ferries from Townsville, at the bottom
(southern) corner of the triangle. All the
development is along the eastern side of the
island and there's a road running through a
string of small towns from Picnic Bay to
Horseshoe Bay along that coast. A rough
track runs along the uninteresting west coast
but along the north coast it's a walking track
only. Picnic Bay is the main town on the
island and has shops, bicycle, motorcycle
and Moke rental agencies and other amenities but there are places to stay in each of the
small centres.

Information
There's a tourist information office at the end
of the pier in Picnic Bay. They have a variety
of brochures and will book tours, accommodation, rent-a-vehicles and anything else you
might require. Along the waterfront Esplanade (also known as The Mall) in Picnic Bay
there are several other travel agents handling
Magnetic travel possibilities. There are lots
of brochures turned out by the Magnetic
Island travel operators and you can also stock

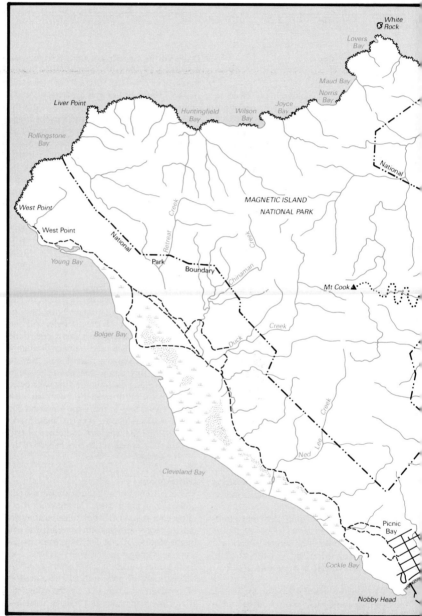

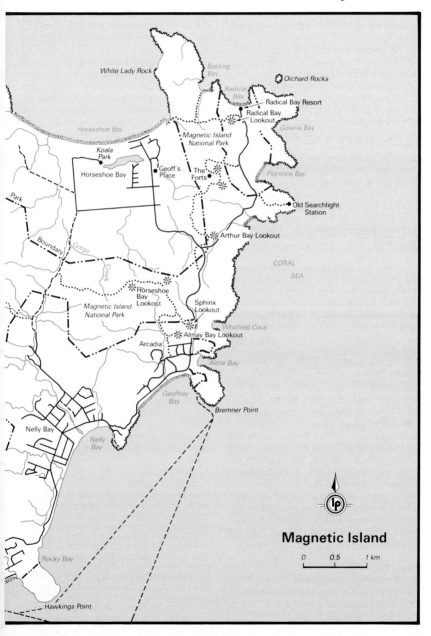

Magnetic Island

up on them at the ferry terminals in Townsville.

The Queensland National Parks & Wildlife Service have an office in Picnic Bay. They have information on the various walks along the island's 22 km of walking tracks.

Discovering Magnetic Island by James G Porter (Kullari Publications, Tully, Qld, 1983) has information on the island's history, shipwrecks, wildlife, climbing Mt Cook and other fields of interest.

There's a National Bank branch in Picnic Bay Mall (The Esplanade). Other banks only have agents on Magnetic Island.

Zoning Geoffrey Bay, Arcadia and Five Beach Bay on the north coast of the island are zoned Marine Park B and fishing is not permitted.

Warning Box jellyfish (marine stingers, sea wasps) are found in the waters around Magnetic Island between October and April. There is a netted swimming area at Picnic Bay and on weekends Alma Bay is patrolled and the waters netted but otherwise swimming is not recommended during the danger months.

Picnic Bay

Many travellers stay in Picnic Bay because it's convenient for the ferry, has a good selection of shops and places to eat and has a number of good places to stay. There's a lookout above the town and just to the west of Picnic Bay is Cockle Bay with the wreck of the *City of Adelaide*. The 1112 ton ship was being towed to Picnic Bay to be used for a breakwater when she went aground in 1916; she's remained there ever since. Heading around the coast from Picnic Bay you soon come to Rocky Bay where a short, steep walk leads down to a beautiful and secluded beach.

Nelly Bay

Next round the coast is Nelly Bay with Shark World. With the magnificent Great Barrier Reef Wonderland Aquarium in nearby Townsville it's hard to justify the $5 entry

charge but the sharks get their daily feed at 2 pm and there are tanks with tropical fish and various displays.

There's a good stretch of beach running north from the aquarium with shade, barbecue areas, a reef at low tide and catamarans for hire. At the far end of Nelly Bay there are some pioneer graves but the most controversial issue to hit Magnetic Island in many years is also found here. The fierce arguments over the huge Magnetic Quay development with marina, hotel, shopping centre and other amenities have pretty well torn the island apart and the issue is still not completely settled although construction has commenced. It's expected to take until 1991 or 1992 to complete, barring further interruptions.

Arcadia

Round the headland from Nelly Bay, and what will be the Magnetic Quay hotel, you come to Geoffrey Bay with another pleasant stretch of beach. Then there's Arcadia with the popular Arcadia Resort with its hotel, a swimming pool which is open to the public, live bands at the weekend, toad races on Wednesday nights and other scenes of Magnetic Island debauchery on some evenings. The second ferry stop is also at Arcadia.

Just round the headland from Arcadia is the very pleasant Alma Bay beach and beside the road just back from the beach is the small Arcadia Pottery Gallery, open most days with pottery from more than 30 potters.

Cane Toad Racing

Various places in Queensland feature cane toad racing and the Arcadia Resort is a popular place to witness this strange rite of northern Australian life. Long ago somebody had the clever idea of bringing cane toads from Hawaii to eat a bug which was causing problems for the sugar cane farmers. Unfortunately, in their new abode cane toads had no interest whatsoever in eating the bugs they were so fond of in Hawaii, instead they just concentrated on breeding like, well, rabbits and soon became a plague across a vast sweep of tropical northern Australia.

Nobody has built a toad-proof fence across Queensland yet but Queenslanders get their own back on the pest by racing them. Travelling cartoonist Tony Jenkins commented once that 'there is no indignity to which a third world chicken cannot be subjected'. He could truthfully add to that 'or a Queensland cane toad'. To race cane toads, you first catch a dozen or so of the obnoxiously ugly critters and paint a dash of colour on each one's back so you can tell one from the other. Then you auction them off to the clamouring spectators – 'who'll give me $25 for the commie frog', bellowed a Magnetic Island auctioneer as the bidding for the red toad rose to a crescendo.

Toads auctioned, the audience is then arrayed around the outside of the circle and the toads released in the centre. Like good racing toads, they hop off in all directions but as they near the outer circle and the screams of encouragement rise to pain level, it dawns on the fast frogs that something is waiting outside the circle and suddenly they all seem to stall, just a hop from victory. Finally one of them (not the green Irish toad which sat a hair's-breadth from the line for an eternity) hops over and its lucky 'owner' scoops the pool, several hundred dollars if the auctioneer has done his stuff.

Of course in northern Queensland sexism is still alive and well, so should the winning owner be a woman she's likely to be invited to 'kiss the toad' before collecting her winnings. Nor do children get off lightly, on another island we visited when toad racing evening rolled around the business of procuring the toads was neatly handled by organising a toad-hunting competition for the kids. Four teams of children rounded up 16 good racers in less than half an hour!

Radical Bay & the Forts

After Arcadia the road runs back from the coast until you reach the junction to the Radical Bay road. There's a choice of routes here. You can take the road which runs down to the Radical Bay resort with tracks leading off to Arthur Bay and Florence Bay or you can take the track via the forts. On the Radical Bay road there's also a track leading off to the old searchlight station on a headland between Arthur and Florence Bays. There are fine views from up here and the bays are also pleasant and secluded.

Alternatively you can take the track to the forts, starting from right at the Horseshoe Bay-Radical Bay junction. You can drive most of the way down to the forts but it's also a pleasant stroll and the views from the WW II forts are very fine. The forts comprise a command post and signal station, gun sites and an ammunition store. As an alternative to backtracking to the road junction you can continue downhill from the forts and rejoin the Radical Bay road just before the resort. From the resort you can walk across the headland to Balding Bay and Horseshoe Bay.

Horseshoe Bay

Whether you continue along the road from the Radical Bay junction or walk across from Radical Bay you eventually end up at Horseshoe Bay, the end of the road and the other end of the island from Picnic Bay. Here there are more shops and accommodation possibilities, a long stretch of beach, a lagoon bird sanctuary and a koala park, a long drive off the main road.

At the fine beach there are rentals for boats, surfboards and those big plastic water tricycles. You can also walk from here to Maud Bay, round to the west, or down the beach and across the headland to Radical Bay. Along the Radical Bay track another trail branches off down to pretty little Balding Bay, a popular place for skinny-dipping.

Bushwalks

The National Parks produce a walks leaflet for Magnetic Islands' excellent bushwalking tracks. Possible walks include:

1 Nelly Bay-Arcadia		5km	1½hrs
2 Picnic Bay-West Point		8km	2hrs
3 Horseshoe Bay road			
	-Arthur Bay	2km	½hr
	-Florence Bay	2km	½hr
	-The Forts	2km	1½hrs
4 Horseshoe Bay			
	-Balding Bay	3km	¾hr
	-Radical Bay	4km	¾hr
5 Mt Cook ascent		8km	all day

Except for the long Mt Cook ascent none of the walks require special preparation. You can string several walks together to make an excellent day's outing. Starting from Nelly Bay walk directly inland along Mandalay Ave and follow the signpost to Horseshoe Bay Lookout from where the trail drops down and around to Arcadia. This walk is about six kms and takes 1½ hours.

Towards the end of the track there's a choice of routes. Take the longer track via the Sphinx Lookout which brings you on to the Horseshoe Bay road beyond Arcadia. You've then only got a short walk to the Radical Bay junction from where you can walk to the Forts and on down to the Radical Bay resort. From here it's up and over to Horseshoe Bay, via Balding Bay if you wish. You've then walked almost the entire length of the island and from Horseshoe Bay you can take the bus back to the other end.

If you want to make the Mt Cook ascent a compass and adequate water supply should be carried. There is no marked trail but it's fairly easy to follow a ridge line from the saddle on the Nelly Bay-Arcadia track. The summit is heavily wooded and the view is actually better from Arua Peak (350 metres) before you reach the top. The big rock slab there offers fine views in all directions. From Arua Peak it's two peaks further west to the summit of Mt Cook itself, marked by a rock cairn. After heavy rain there's a waterfall on Peterson Creek.

You can also hike along the west coast from Picnic Bay to Young Bay and West Point.

Wildlife

The island has a great deal of native Australian wildlife. Possums are probably the creatures most often seen by visitors, these noted freeloaders specialise in making nightly courtesy calls at a number of island restaurants. Koalas, rock wallabies and wombats are also seen around the island as are rock-pythons and dangerous, but inactive, death adders. The koalas were introduced to the island in the 1920s and the prolific possums were also probably an introduced species.

The bush stone curlew or southern stone plover is the bird you will hear, if not see, most often on Magnetic Island. All night long the relatively fearless birds' haunting 'weeloo' call can be heard wailing around the island. The island has much other bird life including noisy sulphur-crested cockatoos and rainbow lorikeets.

Diving

There are a number of dive operators in Townsville but Sportsmans Dive Service in Townsville does five-day diving courses for $275 at Geoff's Place. Phone (077) 72 3244 in Townsville or (077) 78 5727 on Magnetic Island. The course includes accommodation at Geoff's Place and ocean dives around Magnetic Island plus either at Orpheus Island or on the outer Barrier Reef.

Magnetic Diving (tel (077) 78 5799) offers accommodation at Foresthaven and certificate diving courses at similar prices. They have dives around Magnetic Island for $40 including equipment.

Cruises

The 16 metre catamaran *Worripa* does $25 day trips from Horseshoe Bay on Magnetic including a beach barbecue. Phone Jayne on (077) 78 5937, the trips operate Tuesday to Sunday. MV *Orpheus* also operates a beach and bay cruise out of Picnic Bay each day for $39 including lunch. Phone (077) 21 3666 for details.

Rainbow lorikeet

Radical Bay, Magnetic Island (TW)

You can sail to Magnetic Island on the America's Cup yacht *Southern Cross*. Phone (077) 72 4688 for details of the $25 cruises to the island which operate every day except Saturdays and Mondays from the Plume St Jetty in Townsville.

Other Attractions & Activities

The Koala Park (tel (077) 78 5260) at Horseshoe Bay is open 9 am to 5 pm daily and also has wombats, wallabies and other Australian wildlife.

You can ride horses or camels at Bluey's Horseshoe Ranch, phone (077) 78 5109 for details. Sunset Lodge (tel (077) 78 5772) also has horse riding at $10 to $20 for one to two hour sessions.

Accommodation

Magnetic Island's great popularity with travellers is due in part to the wide choice of very popular backpackers' hostels. You'll find them in Picnic Bay, Nelly Bay, Arcadia and Horseshoe Bay. On top of that there are hotels, resorts and a great many holiday flats. Despite this diversity of accommodation it can still get booked out at certain times of year so if you're coming during a busy season it's wise to phone ahead and book if necessary.

Accommodation – Backpackers' Hostels

Most of the backpackers' places offer special deals inclusive of transport over and back and a certain number of nights accommodation. These can be good value and are easy to check out in Townsville. The Magnetic Island hostel scene is very competitive with hostel minibuses often meeting ferries at Picnic Bay.

Picnic Bay Only a minute's walk from the ferry pier at Picnic Bay is the garishly painted *Backpackers Headquarters* (tel (077) 78 5110) at 32 Picnic St. Accommodation in the bunkrooms costs from $9 a night (plus a $10 key deposit) and they have a $26 deal for two nights accommodation and the return ferry

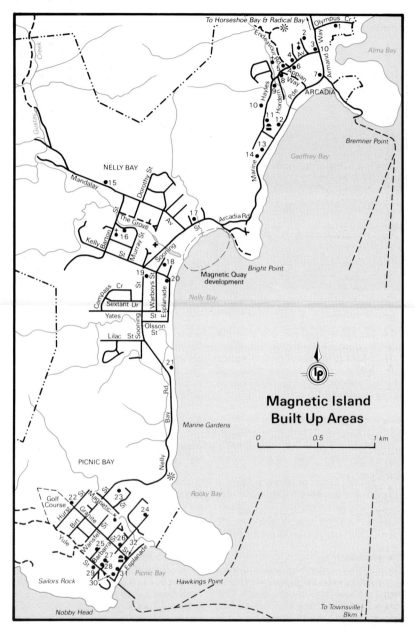

Magnetic Island
Built Up Areas

1	Alma Den Beach Resort
2	Foresthaven
3	Alla Capri
4	Magnetic Retreat
5	Magnetic North Holiday Units
6	Magnetic Reef
7	Tradewinds Arcadia Resort
8	Dandaloo Holiday Units
9	Loyang Holiday Units
10	Wongalee Holiday Flats
11	Tonkin Bakery & Banister's Seafoods
12	Centaur House
13	Arcadia Beach Holiday Apartments
14	Island View Apartments
15	Latitude 19 Resort
16	Camp Magnetic
17	Anchorage Holiday Flats
18	Mexican Munchies
19	Possums
20	Surfside Palms Holiday Units
21	Shark World
22	Queensland National Parks & Wildlife Service
23	Magnetic Island Recreation Camp
24	Magnetic Island Hostel
25	Ti Tree Lodge Flats
26	Picnic Bay Holiday Flats
27	Tropical Palms Inn
28	Backpackers Headquarters
29	Magnetic Island Holiday Units
30	Picnic Bay Hotel
31	Crusoe's
32	Maggies

non-members it's $9.50 on the first night and $6 on subsequent nights. There's a kitchen and the hostel is open all day but the office is closed from 10 am to 5 pm. To get there walk along The Esplanade away from town to Granite St, then straight up to the top and turn right. The local bus will take you there free. There's a tennis court and bicycles and snorkelling gear for hire.

Nelly Bay As you round the bend into Nelly Bay the first place you see is *Shark World* (tel (077) 78 5187) with a variety of backpackers' accommodation. It costs $5 a night to camp, $7 for a bed in a marquee or $10 for a bed in an A-frame cabin or a Camp-O-Tel, a cross between a cabin and a tent with beds or bunks.

Camp Magnetic (tel (077) 78 5151) is the Uniting Church Camp on Mango Parkway, a few blocks back from the coastal road in Nelly Bay. They can take 36 in dorms and charge $6. There are cooking facilities and a pool but it's pretty basic accommodation.

A backpackers' accommodation centre is planned for the Magnetic Quay development.

Arcadia In Arcadia the very popular *Centaur House* (tel (077) 78 5668) is at 27 Marine Parade, opposite the beach. The atmosphere in this homely place is relaxed, there's a pleasant garden and a bed in the clean and spacious dorms costs $10. Guests have free use of snorkelling gear and windsurfers.

Also in Arcadia is *Foresthaven* (tel (077) 78 5153) at 11 Cook Rd. It has a lovely bush setting and units with kitchens and dorm beds at $10 each. The smaller rooms can be taken as doubles in which case you can look upon them as low priced holiday flats. Excellent barbecues are put on regularly in the large courtyard. Koalas, wallabies and many tropical birds are often seen just a short walk away.

Horseshoe Bay *Geoff's Place* (tel (077) 78 5577) is at the end of the line coming from Picnic Bay but continues to be very popular with young travellers. There are extensive

trip. It's a friendly, busy place with laundry facilities, TV room and a very cramped kitchen.

At the end of Picnic St at No 80 is *Magnetic Island Hostel* (tel (077) 78 5755). This is a very pleasant hostel in a fairly new building on a quiet street but still conveniently close to the shops and restaurants. There are two flats, each with a fully equipped kitchen. The rooms have three beds each at $8 per person plus $1 extra for sheets.

A little further out from the centre, about a 15-minute walk from the pier, is the *Magnetic Island Recreation Camp* (tel (077) 78 5280) with space for 36. It's an associate YHA hostel and is popular despite the ban on alcohol! The price for members is $6, for grounds where you can camp for $5 per person, take a bed in a marquee for $7 or there are A-frame cabins at $10 per person or $24 as a double. There's a $5 linen deposit, returned when you hand back the sheets. They have a bunch of special transport and accommodation deals combining the ferry trip from Townsville, a pick up from Picnic Bay and accommodation.

The dining area does breakfast for $3 or dinners for $4 to $7. There's also a bar although you can only buy drinks if you've also eaten there. If you want to fix your own meals there's a kitchen and if you're fed up with the world there's a TV lounge. Geoff's Place also has a swimming pool and lots of often noisy entertainment although it has to stop at 11 pm to keep the neighbours happy:

Boat Races

I thought toad racing was the height of Magnetic Island Aussie kulcha until I happened to stay at Geoff's Place on boat race night. The rules are quite simple, six contestants line up straddling a bench, hands on head, an unopened can of beer in front of them. At the 'go' signal the first one opens the can, drinks it and places it upside down on his or her head to show it's empty. The next in line then opens their can and drinks. This continues down the line until the last one finishes and stands on the bench. The members of the winning team get a free night's accommodation in another backpackers' hostel along the coast. The members of the team which comes in last get thrown in the swimming pool.

Accommodation – Hotels & Holiday Flats

Magnetic Island has a wide variety of accommodation possibilities apart from the backpackers' places but it's holiday flats that predominate. They're indicative of the quiet, family holiday nature of the island and vary from larger commercial operations with a full time office and daily room service to small operations which you may only find out about by word of mouth.

Most of the holiday flats quote weekly rates although it's always worth asking if you want to stay for a shorter period. Prices vary with the season and with demand – even in the season you may find bargains if there just happens to be a room vacant. The flats usually have cooking facilities and fridges but check whether you have to supply bedding, towels and the like. At most places everything is supplied but there are some exceptions. Most of the Magnetic Island holiday flats have a swimming pool, barbecues and other facilities. They're essentially like a modern motel except better equipped and you're left to fend for yourself rather more.

Single-bedroom flats are typically in the $200 to $300 per week bracket, two-bedroom flats are in the $250 to $400 range. Check with the Queensland Government Travel Centre for a full list of flats.

Despite the predominance of holiday flats there are also a few conventional hotel/motel places, the larger Latitude 19 and Arcadia Resorts and under construction there's the big Magnetic Quay complex.

Picnic Bay Right by the pier on The Esplanade in Picnic Bay the *Picnic Bay Hotel* (tel (077) 78 5166) is also known as the Magnetic Island Hotel. Rooms are $35 to $45 for twins, all with bathrooms, fan, tea/coffee making equipment and refrigerators. There's also a laundry and pool and the hotel was going through some renovations and upgrading in early 1990.

At 34 Picnic St, right behind the hotel and right next door to the Backpackers Headquarters is the new *Tropical Palms Inn* (tel (077) 78 5076. Units with air-con, fans, TV and a kitchenette are $55 for two. Round the corner at 16 Yule St the *Magnetic Island Holiday Units* (tel (077) 78 5246) has eight one and two bedroom units accommodating two to five people. The rooms are fully equipped right down to kitchen and laundry facilities and there's a pool and barbecue. Double rooms cost $65 to $75.

One of the cheapest holiday flats around is *Ti Tree Lodge Flats* (tel (077) 78 5499) at 18 Barbarra St in Picnic Bay. There are just a couple of flats with room for two to five people and one cottage which accommodates six. Everything is supplied and rooms have attached bathrooms, fan, TV, radio, cooking facilities and a fridge. There's also a barbecue and laundry. Daily costs are $40 to $50 for two.

Picnic Bay Holiday Flat (tel (077) 78 5161) is on the corner of Granite St and The Esplanade.

Nelly Bay The *Latitude 19 Resort* (tel (077) 78 5200) is on Mandalay Ave and is the biggest resort on the island. Or at least it will be until the Magnetic Quay development in Nelly Bay is completed. There are 73 units and 16 suites, all with air-con, fans, telephone, TV, radio, tea/coffee making equipment and refrigerator. There's a swimming pool, tennis court and laundry facilities. Room costs are from $80 to $100 for the units but there are often cheaper standby deals available.

Nelly Bay has lots of holiday flats. *Camlachie Holiday Units* (tel (077) 78 5499) is on the waterfront at 122 Sooning St and has just two units with room for four to six people each. Everything is supplied and rooms have fans, TV, radio and cooking facilities. There's a barbecue and laundry and costs are $50 a night for a double.

The *Anchorage Holiday Flats* on Sooning St are a new development of two bedroom units with kitchen and laundry facilities. The units accommodate two to four people, there's a swimming pool, barbecues and nightly costs from $60. The position is going to be rather spoilt when the Magnetic Quay development pops up in front of it. *Surfside Palms Holiday Units* (tel (077) 78 5855) is on The Esplanade on the corner of Kelly St.

At 13 The Esplanade the *Island Palms Resort* (tel (077) 78 5571) is one of the larger Magnetic Island developments with 12 two bedroom units which accommodate four to six people. Everything is supplied and the rooms have air-conditioning, TV, cooking facilities and fridges. There's also a barbecue, swimming pool, spa, half tennis court and laundry facilities. Costs are from $90 a day for two people.

Arcadia The *Tradewinds Arcadia Resort* (tel (077) 78 5177) has rooms with attached bathroom, air-con and fan, television, telephone, radio, tea/coffee making equipment and refrigerators. The resort also has a laundry and guest pool as well as the public swimming pool near the bar and restaurant area. Double rooms are $68 or $78 poolside.

There are a number of holiday flats along Hayles Ave. Starting from the Alma Bay end of the street *Magnetic Retreat* (tel (077) 78 5357) is at No 17 on the corner with Rheuben Terrace. There are modern one and two bedroom units, all fully equipped, a swimming pool, barbecues and prices from $65 to $75 for doubles.

Almost across the road at No 32-34 is *Magnetic Reef* (tel (077) 78 5449) also with comfortable, modern and fully equipped two bedroom units. Again there's a pool, barbecues and other facilities. The *Magnetic North Holiday Units* (tel (077) 78 5647) is at 2 Endeavour St, on the corner with Hayles Ave. Once again the two bedroom units are modern and well equipped and there's a pool and barbecue. Nightly costs are from $75 for two people.

Dandaloo Holiday Units (tel (077) 78 5174) is at 40 Hayles Ave and has eight one-bedroom units which accommodate four people. The rooms have attached bathrooms, fan, TV, cooking facilities and fridge and there is also a barbecue, laundry and swimming pool plus a playground. Costs are from $50 for two. A few steps further down this popular street the *Loyang Holiday Units* (tel (077) 78 5158) at 44 Hayles Ave has four fully self-contained units which accommodate up to four.

Wongalee Holiday Flats (tel (077) 78 5361) is at 17 McCabe Crescent, a little further along Hayles Ave. There are four two and three bedroom units which accommodate two to six people. As usual there's a barbecue, laundry and swimming pool and nightly costs are from $40 for two.

The *Island View Apartments* (tel (077) 78 5387) at 40 Marine Parade have air-con two bedroom units for $55 to $75. There's a pool and barbecue facilities.

Alma Bay Just beyond Arcadia the *Alma Den Beach Resort* (tel (077) 78 5163) has 15 units for two and three larger suites. Everything is supplied and rooms have fans, TV, radio, cooking facilities and fridges. There's a pool, barbecue and laundry and costs are from $65 for two.

Radical Bay Between Arcadia and Horseshoe Bay you come to the turn-off which takes you along a winding and sometimes bumpy road to Radical Bay. This is one of the nicest beaches on the island but the *Radical Bay Resort* (tel (077) 78 5294) is rundown and in need of a complete revamp. There are bungalows with one double and one single room for $60 and villas with a double, a single and a fold down single bed for $75. The rooms have a TV, radio, fridge and tea/coffee making equipment and there's a pool and laundry facilities. Despite the resort's run down appearance – a major rebuild has been planned for some time – the food here is surprisingly good. Main courses are $9.50 to $12, lighter meals from $3.50.

Horseshoe Bay The *Coolawin Holiday Flats* (tel (077) 78 5117) at 13 Pacific Drive have seven one or two-bedroom flats which accommodate two to four. The rooms have TV, cooking facilities and a fridge plus there's a pool, barbecue and laundry. Costs are from $50 for a double.

Also on the waterfront, *Weemalah* (tel (077) 78 5223) is at 1 Pacific Drive and has six units which accommodate up to five. Again everything is supplied including TV, video, radio, cooking facilities and fridge. There's a barbecue, pool and laundry and costs are from $55 for two.

Food

Picnic Bay All the Picnic Bay eating possibilities are along the waterfront Esplanade. Right in front of the jetty the *Picnic Bay Pub* is the counter meal part of the Magnetic Island Hotel. Meals are $5.50 to $10 and there are cheaper snacks. The hotel also has a restaurant section.

Heading along The Esplanade from the hotel you first come to *Fork 'n View* with an amazing burger selection from $2.20 to $4.

Crusoe's (tel (077) 78 5480) is a straightforward little restaurant with a great reputation and evening meals from $5.50 to $12. They do breakfast, lunch, dinner and takeaways including good pies.

Joan's Coffee Lounge is another light meal possibility on The Esplanade or there's the *Magnetic Island Chinese Restaurant* in the Picnic Bay Arcade. Down at the end of The Esplanade is *Maggies* with meals from $6 and sandwiches. It's open seven days a week and for dinner from 6.30 pm Tuesday to Sunday.

Nelly Bay *Mexican Munchies* (tel (077) 78 3658) at 37 Warboy St in Nelly Bay runs the Mexican gamut from enchiladas to tacos and is open from 6 pm Saturday to Thursday. Nearby there's *Possums* for snacks and takeaways in the small shopping centre on Sooning St.

Arcadia The *Arcadia Resort* has a number of dining possibilities including a poolside snack bar. The usual steak, chicken and so on counter meals are in the $7.50 to $12 range and are served from 11.30 am to 2 pm daily and from 5.30 to 7.30 pm except Sundays. The more expensive *Skippers Restaurant* has main courses at $15 to $17.

Alla Capri (tel (077) 78 5448) at 5-7 Hayles Ave is just behind the Arcadia Resort. They have pizzas and pastas from $7 to $9 and a pleasant indoor/outdoor eating area with visiting possums to provide entertainment. Other main course dishes are around $10 to $14, pizzas are $8 to $11 and there's house wine by the half litre and litre. The food is only average but there's big quantities if not high quality and it's a pleasant place for a late night drink. It's open from 6.30 pm but closed on Wednesdays.

There's a small shopping centre at the corner of Hayles Ave and Bright St in Arcadia. On the Hayles Ave side of the junction *Tonkin Bakery* (the *Bakehouse*) has bakery products and is good for an early morning coffee and croissants. Next door is *Banister's Seafoods* which is basically a fish & chips place with an open dining area outside. It's open 9 am to 8 pm, the food is excellent and they have a BYO licence so you can bring a bottle of wine or cans of beer from the Arcadia Resort's bottle shop. Calamari, chips and salad cost $9.

Horseshoe Bay On the waterfront at the bay you can get takeaways or snacks at *The Bounty* or *The Chook House*. In the evening *Geoff's Place* is the only place for a meal in Horseshoe Bay, main courses are $4 to $7.

Getting There & Away
There are two ferry operators from Townsville across Cleveland Bay to the island. Their high speed catamarans start from the Ross Creek terminals just a couple of hundred metres apart and take about 20 to 25 minutes to the island. The fierce competition has kept prices down and the service quality up. A standard ticket costs $6 one-way ($5 for students, $3 for children) or $10 return ($8, $5). There are lots of special deals including bus travel and lunch on the island or family fares. The backpackers' hostels also have special transport and accommodation deals.

Westmark (tel (077) 21 1913) depart from the Great Barrier Reef Wonderland complex and have about 10 services daily between Townsville and Picnic Bay. Last regular departure to the island is 5.45 pm, from the island it's 6.15 pm. On Fridays there's also a 9.30 pm boat to the island, 10 pm return. On Saturdays the late trip is 11.30 pm to the island, 12 midnight return.

Magnetic Marine (tel 077) 72 7122) depart from the terminal at 168-192 Flinders St East, between the town centre and the Great Barrier Wonderland. Their catamarans also stop at the Breakwater Terminal on Sir Leslie Thiess Drive, near the casino down Ross Creek towards the sea. They also have about 10 services daily and some of them continue beyond Picnic Bay to Arcadia. Their last departure from Townsville is at 6.50 pm weekdays, 6.15 pm Saturdays, 6.45 pm Sundays. From the island it's at 7.25 pm, 6.50 pm and 7.25 pm respectively. They have no late night services.

Magnetic Marine have a budget ferry service to the island which operates four or five times daily and costs $6 return. This older, slower ferry is sometimes cancelled if the weather is bad. The catamarans are usually not affected.

Magnetic Marine have a barge service taking cars over to Arcadia. Monday to Friday it operates three times a day, Saturday and Sunday only twice. Phone (077) 71 6737 for details of this service. Costs are $60 return for a car including passengers, $12 return for a motorcycle plus $4 return for each rider and passenger. You need to book ahead at peak periods. If your visit to the Magnetic Island is a short one it's probably not worth the expense of taking a car over.

Getting Around
Bus The Magnetic Island Bus Service (tel (077) 78 5130) operates up and down the island between Picnic Bay and Horseshoe Bay 10 to 15 times a day. Additional services only operate Picnic Bay/Arcadia and Arcadia/Horseshoe Bay. Three time a day there are services from Arcadia to Radical Bay and twice a day from Horseshoe Bay to the Koala Park. If you've got a ferry to catch it takes about 45 minutes all the way from Horseshoe Bay to Picnic Bay, 30 minutes from Arcadia to Picnic Bay.

You can either get tickets from place to place or a full day pass for $5.

Taxi Taxis meet arriving ferries at Picnic Bay. Phone (077) 78 5484 to book a taxi.

Bicycle Hire Magnetic Island would be an ideal size for biking around if only the bikes available were a bit better, unfortunately most of them are old clunkers. You can rent bikes in Picnic Bay from various places along The Esplanade such as Magnetic Sports or from a number of the resorts and backpackers' places. Typically bikes costs from about $5 a half day or $5 to $8 a day. Tandems are also available.

Motorcycle Hire The scooters are much better. Road Runner (tel (077) 78 5222) is at

Shop 2, Picnic Bay Arcade on the Picnic Bay waterfront. Including insurance and a crash helmet the cost for one day is $22 if you're over 25 years of age, $25 if you're 21 to 25, $28 if you're under 21. Short two hour rentals, half day rentals or longer period rentals are also available. Petrol is included in the hire. No motorcycle licence is required for these small 50 cc scooters, just a valid car drivers licence. You certainly don't need anything larger to explore Magnetic with.

Various other places also hire scooters including Magnetic Island Leisure Hire (tel (077) 78 5544) at the TAB office on the Picnic Bay Esplanade.

Moke Rental Mokes are the open, doorless utility vehicles based on a British Mini and you soon get the impression that 90% of the vehicles on the island are Mokes. At times there seems to be nothing else. There are several Moke hire places on the island and a number of the accommodation centres also have a Moke or two to rent out. By far the biggest, however, is Magnetic Island Rent-A-Moke (tel (077) 78 5377) at Picnic Bay with over 100 Mokes, the world's largest fleet of Mokes. They have a free phone at the Townsville ferry terminals so you can call ahead to book one.

Daily charge is $25 if you're over 25 years of age, $27 if you're 21 to 25. Plus there's a 20c per km distance charge but cheaper rates are available for long-term rentals. All petrol and insurance is included but beware they

Magnetic Mokes (TW)

don't try and slap on an overnight insurance charge if you take the car late one day for a short rental period. Mokes cannot be taken up the dirt road on the western coast of the island.

Other Moke agents include Holiday Moke Hire (tel (077) 78 5703 in the TAB office on the Picnic Bay Esplanade.

The hassle with Mokes is that there is no safe place to leave things but this isn't much of a problem on Magnetic Island, where you can't go far enough from home base to need very much! Small Mazda 121s, Suzuki jeeps and Daihatsu minivans can also be rented at slightly higher costs.

Hitching Another cheap and easy alternative is to hitch around. Plenty of people do it – just start walking, and if you don't get a lift you end up in the next town before long.

Tours Agencies along The Esplanade at Picnic Bay book reef and island tours out of Magnetic. See the following Orpheus Island chapter for details of day trips to Orpheus or the Around Magnetic section for reef and sailing trips.

Around Magnetic Island

There are various trips out from Townsville to outer reefs and to the Palm Islands north of Magnetic. These trips usually stop at Magnetic on their way out from Townsville. See the Orpheus Island chapter for details of the Westmark day trip to Orpheus. Other possibilities include:

KELSO REEF
Pure Pleasure Cruises (tel (077) 21 3555) have day trips on their 30 metre wavepiercer catamaran to Kelso Reef, east of the Palm Island group. Cost is $85 (children four to 14 years $42) and includes lunch, glass bottom boat viewing and snorkelling equipment. Scuba divers can dive while out at the reef.

WRECK OF THE YONGALA

The 3664 ton Adelaide Steamship Company vessel *Yongala* went down off Townsville in 1911 during a cyclone. She went down with all 121 of her crew and passengers and for years her disappearance was a complete mystery. During WW II the ship's location was discovered and the first diver went down to the *Yongala* in 1947. The 90 metre long wreck lies intact on the sea bottom in 30 metres of water and has become a haven for a huge variety of marine life and is one of the best dives in Australia.

A number of Townsville dive operators run trips to the *Yongala*. Pro-Dive (tel (077) 21 1760) in the Great Barrier Reef Wonderland do day trips, usually on Thursdays, to the wreck for $115 plus equipment hire. A morning and afternoon dive is made. The MV *Hero*, operated by Coral Sea Wilderness Expeditions (tel (077) 72 3119), is a dive boat which makes trips to the *Yongala* as well as the outer reef.

Sharks

Sharks are not a problem for divers on the Great Barrier Reef, there's simply too much else for them to eat. Nevertheless a variety of sharks can be found around the reef and if you are lucky you might spot one. Usually they are either shy and timid and disappear at first sight or, more often, they simply ignore divers as a harmless intruder.

Sharks are a primitive form of fish with a cartilaginous skeleton. Primitive or not they are superbly practical creatures with a sleek and highly streamlined shape. The white-tipped reef shark is a small, unaggressive, territorial shark rarely more than 1½ metres long and often seen over areas of coral or off reef edges. Black-tipped reef sharks are also timid, shallow water dwellers. Even more retiring is the tessellated wobbegong which is sometimes found in reef pools and lies still, relying on its camouflage, rather than trying to escape. On the other hand the whaler shark can be threatening and very aggressive towards divers and should be treated with caution.

Whale sharks are sometimes seen off the outer reef and can reach over 15 metres in length. They are the largest fish in the sea but feed on plankton and tiny fish and are harmless. If, however, you spot a five metre tiger shark, a rare possibility on the reef, it's time to get out of the water. ■

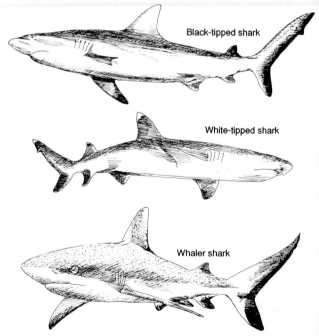

Black-tipped shark

White-tipped shark

Whaler shark

Symbiotic Relationships

A number of species on the reef engage in interesting symbiotic relationships, where two unrelated species get together in some activity for their mutual good.

The best recorded and, to the casual onlooker, most visible of these relationships is probably that of the anemone fish and the anemone. The brightly coloured anemone fish are a type of damselfish which have become acclimatised to living amongst the stinging tentacles of anemones. The bright orange clown anemone with its white vertical stripes edged with black is one of the most instantly recognisable fishes on the reef. A typical group of anemone fish will consist of several males and one larger female fish. They spend their entire life around the anemone, emerging briefly to feed then diving back into the protective tentacles at the first sign of danger. Anemone fish are not naturally immune to the anemone's sting, it is thought they gradually acquire immunity by repeatedly brushing themselves against the tentacles. Possibly they coat themselves with a layer of the anemone's mucus and the anemone does not sting the fish, just as its tentacles avoid stinging one another.

The relationship between anemone fish and the anemone is probably somewhat one sided. The anemone fish may attract other fish within the anemone's grasp but an anemone can live without the anemone fish, the anemone fish are never seen without a protective anemone nearby.

A more equal relationship is that between the goby fish and the alpheid shrimp. Two gobies and two shrimps share a burrow into which they retreat when danger threatens. The shrimp is the burrow builder while the gobies act as lookouts. The shrimps appear to have poor sight so while they are outside they always keep close to the fish, literally 'in touch' by means of their long antenna. When a threat appears the gobies' movements are instantly signalled to the shrimps and the foursome quickly head for the safety of their burrow.

Cleaner fish are another interesting reef relationship. The small cleaner wrasse performs a service job on larger fish. They set themselves up at 'cleaner stations' and wait for customers. The cleaners perform a small 'dance' to indicate they're ready for action and then zip around the larger fish nibbling off fungal growth, dead scales, parasites and the like. They will actually swim right into the mouth of larger fish to clean their teeth! Obviously this must be a tempting opportunity to get a quick free meal but cleaner fish are not threatened while they're at work.

The cleaner stations are an important part of reef life; some fish will regularly travel considerable distances for a clean and brush up and experimental removal of the cleaner fish from a section of reef has resulted in an increase in diseased and unhealthy fish and a fall in the general fish population. Certain varieties of shrimps also act as fish cleaners but in nature every situation presents an opportunity for some other creature and the reef also has false cleaners. These tiny fish masquerade as cleaners and then quickly take a bite out of the deceived larger fish. They've been known to take a nip at swimmers!

Even coral, that basic building block of the Great Barrier Reef takes part in a symbiotic relationship. Within the cells of coral polyps are tiny single cell plants known as *zoocanthellae*. Like other plants they utilise sunlight to create energy and they also consume carbon dioxide produced by the coral. Their presence enables coral to grow much faster. ■

Orpheus & the Palm Islands

Orpheus is one of the islands of the Palm Island group, south of Hinchinbrook. The group consists of 10 main islands, all except two of which are Aboriginal reservations where you must have permission to visit. Orpheus and Pelorus are the only islands of the Palm group which are not part of the reserve. Orpheus is National Park while Pelorus, immediately to its north, is crown land.

ORPHEUS

Area: 14 square km
Type: continental
High point: 172 metres
Maximum visitor population: 74
Per person daily cost: $300
In brief: Orpheus is a relatively large island with excellent fringing reef and a small and fairly exclusive resort. Children under 12 are not permitted.

The Island

Orpheus is long (about 11 km from end to end), narrow (less than a km wide) and heavily forested. The island, second largest in the Palm group, is a national park and there is much birdlife, some fine beaches and some of the best fringing reef to be found on any of the Great Barrier Reef islands. The resort is quiet, secluded and fairly expensive.

Traces of the island's original Aboriginal visitors can still be seen, there is a shell midden near the Marine Research Station. The island was named by Lieutenant G E Richards on the HMS *Paluma* in 1887. He named the island after HMS *Orpheus*, the largest warship in Australia when it was

Yankee Bay, Orpheus Island (TW)

177

wrecked in New Zealand in 1863 with the loss of 188 lives.

Later sheep were run on the island and there are traces of stone sheep pens and the remains of an old stone homestead above Pioneer Bay. The wild goats which roam the island are the descendants of animals released here to provide food for possible shipwreck survivors. It's estimated there are now as many as 4000 goats on the island and controlling their numbers is proving very difficult.

At one time oysters were also gathered here commercially and at Yankee Bay cement pilings mark the position of an old WW II submarine degaussing or demagnetising station. This process was intended to stop them detonating magnetic mines.

Information

The resort phone number is (077) 77 7377 and the address is Orpheus Island Resort, Private Mail Bag, Townsville, Qld 4816. There is only one phone line to the island and it is only available during office hours. The Queensland National Parks & Wildlife Service produce a visitor information leaflet on the island.

Zoning Most of the water around the island is zoned Marine National Park B – 'look but don't touch'. From the top of Hazard Bay to the southern tip is zoned A which allows limited line fishing. Collecting shells or coral is not permitted.

Beaches & Snorkelling

Orpheus has some of the finest fringing reef to be found around any island along the reef and also has some very pleasant sandy beaches. Guests at the resort can take out an outboard dinghy and find their own private beach for the day. Turtles are often seen around the island and you may spot schools of dolphins, particularly off the southern end of the island.

Hazard Bay, in front of the resort, is very shallow at low tide with much of it actually drying. At high tide the extreme tidal varia-

tions here make it a pleasant place for a swim but at low tide the most interesting activity is wading through the shallow water looking for the stingrays which bask quietly on the sandy bottom.

A little south of the resort there's better low tide swimming at Mangrove Bay or at Yankee Bay where the beaches are very attractive and there's some fine coral for snorkelling or diving. The day trip catamaran from Townsville comes in to the Yankee Bay jetty. At the southern end of the island is South Beach, looking across the narrow channel separating Orpheus from Fantome Island.

A short walk across the top of the island from the resort takes you to Picnic Bay on the seaward side. There's no beach here, just stones and boulders leading into the water, but there's a very pleasant shady tree and some fine snorkelling just off shore.

North of the resort Pioneer Bay has a fine beach but again the water is shallow at low tide. As at Hazard Bay you can often see stingrays on the bottom here. About 100 metres back from the beach there's the remains of what was clearly once a quite substantial stone cottage. Further out in Pioneer Bay and around the headland from Little Pioneer Bay round to Hazard Bay there are some excellent coral and good bommies. Cattle Bay at the northern end of the island has good snorkelling.

Diving

Orpheus' fine fringing reef offer some excellent diving opportunities. Apart from around Orpheus itself there are also good stretches of reef off Fantome Island to the south and Pelorus Island to the north. Local reef dives with the island's dive centre cost $20 for the boat trip plus $40 for the usual regulator, buoyancy compensator, wet suit plus one air tank. The centre offers a one day introductory scuba course for $100 or a full five day course leading to PADI certification for $425. Trips to the outer barrier reef can also be arranged from Orpheus.

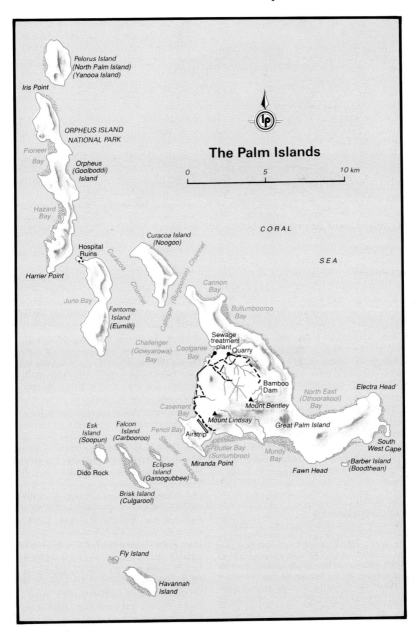

Pelorus Island
(North Palm Island)
(Yanooa Island)

Iris Point

ORPHEUS ISLAND
NATIONAL PARK

Pioneer
Bay

Orpheus
(Goolboddi)
Island

Hazard
Bay

Hospital
Ruins

Harrier Point

Juno Bay

Fantome
Island
(Eumilli)

Curacoa Island
(Noogoo)

Curacoa
Channel

Calliope (Bulgoomini) Channel

CORAL

SEA

Cannon
Bay

Bullumbooroo
Bay

Challenger
(Gowyarowa)
Bay

Coolgaree
Bay

Sewage
treatment
plant
Quarry

Bamboo
Dam

▲
Mount Bentley

North East
(Dthoorakool)
Bay

Electra Head

Casement
Bay

▲
Mount Lindsay

Great Palm Island

South
West Cape

Esk
Island
(Soopun)

Falcon
Island
(Carbooroo)

Dido Rock

Eclipse
Island
(Garoogubbee)

Pencil Bay

Steamer Passage

Airstrip

Butler Bay
(Surrumbroo)

Miranda Point

Mundy
Bay

Fawn Head

Barber Island
(Boodthean)

Brisk Island
(Culgarool)

The Palm Islands

0   5   10 km

Fly Island

Havannah
Island

Mangroves, Orpheus Island (TW)

Walks, Vegetation & Wildlife

There aren't many walks on Orpheus although the open, grassy areas scattered around the island offer fine views if you can get to them. From Orpheus you can see across to the coast, 20 km west, and to Curacoa, Fantome and Great Palm Islands to the south. A short walk leads from the villas, above the resort, to Penny's Bay and Horseshoe Bay on the eastern side of the island. Orpheus is only a few hundred metres wide at this point. From here you can walk north towards Fig Tree Bay and up to Fig Tree Hill.

A Dog's Gravestone

Close to the top you can find the gravestone of a small fox terrier named Mr Nicholson, a visitor from a yacht who died in 1966 from, so it is said, the effects of cane toad consumption. The ugly toads are poisonous and can kill whatever eats them. Apart from cane toads Mr Nicholson also liked to chew on shoes and his owners left the last shoe he had been working on by his grave. In the years since then a collection of shoes has grown around the grave, it's said to be lucky to leave an old shoe here!

A more interesting walk winds through a forested area from the southern end of the Hazard Bay beach across the island to Picnic Bay. This is a popular snorkelling spot and the shady tree behind the beach would indeed be a good spot for a picnic.

Although there are no permanently flowing streams on Orpheus the greener vegetation clearly shows where water flows after rain. At the north end of Hazard Bay a jumble of rocks tumbling down the hillside marks an impressive, though usually dry, waterfall. The vegetation in the open woodland is typically Moreton Bay ash and acacias while the rainforest found in the gullies and around sheltered bays includes fig trees. The best rainforest patch is on the western side of Iris Point at the northern end of the island. Interestingly some of the open grassland areas are natural features, they did not appear as a result of human activity on the island.

Orpheus' most visible wildlife is introduced – goats and cane toads have done a fairly comprehensive job of taking the island over. Around the resort at night, bandicoots (small rat-sized marsupials) make a shy appearance and echidnas (spiny anteaters) can also be seen. There are a variety of harmless snakes and small skinks and geckos. The birdlife is prolific and includes herons, pheasant, sunbirds, scrub fowl and some very impressive ospreys.

Activities
The resort has a tennis court, swimming pool, catamarans, windsurfers and a small fleet of outboard-powered dinghies. All this equipment, including the dinghies, are free for the use of guests. Although this is a low-key resort where organised activities are not the norm, the morning trip to dump the resort's food scraps for a regular crowd of freeloading fish is always worth watching.

Marine Research Station
At Little Pioneer Bay, north of the resort, the James Cook University Marine Research Station specialises in breeding and raising giant clams and other Barrier Reef clams. Clams raised here are being transplanted to Pacific island reefs where overgathering has wiped them out. The clams grow surprisingly fast and it's hoped that the station will also raise them commercially as a food supply. In the station you can see the clams in the large water tanks (including the 'stud clams' used

Orpheus Island International Airport (TW)

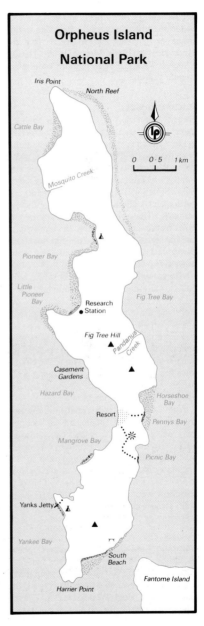

for breeding) while other clams are raised out in the shallow waters of the bay. The station manager can tell you where to find the Aboriginal shell midden near the station. Phone (077) 77 7336 to enquire about visiting the station.

Accommodation

Resort The resort is low-key but sophisticated – the staff manage to combine black tie waiters in the evening with first name terms with the guests. The original Orpheus resort dates from the 1940s but in 1981 it was totally rebuilt in a very Mediterranean style by two Italian Australians. The resort has subsequently changed hands but the flavour remains. The prolific bougainvilleas and other tropical flowers add to the atmosphere and the stylish square rooms are a definite cut above the typical square boxes found at so many other Great Barrier Reef resorts.

Along the beach there are 23 studio units and two slightly larger bungalows. They're tastefully furnished with a verandah area out front and air-conditioning and ceiling fans. There's piped music, a fridge and tea/coffee making equipment but no telephone or television in the rooms. The studios are $350 for one person or $280 each for two. The bungalows are only available as doubles at $320 per person. Tariffs include all meals and use of all the resort equipment.

Above the main resort, up the hill towards the island's central saddle, are six delightfully designed and furnished two bedroom villas. Architect Marco Romoli of Florence was responsible for the villas and it was originally intended that they would be sold at something like $350,000 each. This plan somehow went awry and they're now available at $380 per person per night for a minimum of two people.

Camping Applications to camp on Orpheus should be made to the Queensland National Parks & Wildlife Service office at Ingham, information is available from the office at the Great Barrier Reef Wonderland in Townsville. See the Facts for the Visitor chapter for

addresses and more details. The Orpheus campsites are category C.

There are campsites at Yankee Bay and Pioneer Bay. Both sites have toilet facilities and a picnic area but there is no regular freshwater supply and a fuel stove should be used. It's easy to get to the Yankee Bay site on the day trip boat from Townsville, getting to the Pioneer Bay site can be more difficult. Yankee Bay offers better low tide swimming and snorkelling but if you want to get away from it all that won't be so easy until the day trippers leave.

Food

Breakfast at the resort is served as a mixture of serve-yourself buffet style and from the menu while lunch and dinner are both from the menu. Orpheus is an island that prides itself on its food although at times they simply try too hard with dishes a little too complex and heavy for island tastes. There's a bar and a fairly straightforward wine list with most wines around $25 to $30. The open dining area looks right out on the beach and the sunsets can be particularly spectacular.

For between meal snacks the lounge area has coffee, tea and a fridge with cold water or juice and something interesting with which to wreck any diet. If you're planning on taking a dinghy to find your own island beach they will pack a picnic hamper for you.

Getting There & Away

Orpheus is 80 km north of Townsville and about 20 km off-shore from Lucinda Point near Ingham. The Great Barrier Reef is only about 20 to 25 km west of the island. Hinchinbrook, with its high peaks, is only a little to the north and is very visible from Orpheus.

Air Most resort guests arrive by seaplane and Seair Pacific fly more or less to order from Townsville to Orpheus. The flight takes about 40 minutes, depending on the aircraft, and costs $91 one-way. The amphibious aircraft lands in the bay right in front of the resort and ties up at a float about four metres square bearing a sign announcing that it is 'Orpheus Island International Airport'!

Seair Pacific also fly Cairns/Hinchinbrook/Orpheus, the Hinchinbrook/Orpheus flight is one of the very few direct transfers you can make from one Great Barrier Reef island to another. The Cairns/Orpheus fare is $128.

Occasionally Seair Pacific are unable to provide flights to Orpheus in which case guests fly from the nearby Great Palm Island airstrip. The resort is building a helicopter landing pad.

Sea Few guests come to the resort by sea although it is only a little over 20 km from Lucinda Point. You can get out to Orpheus from Dungeness, near Lucinda, by water taxi. Westmark (tel (077) 21 1913) operate day trips to Orpheus from Townsville and Magnetic Island. The Westmark catamaran departs Townsville at 8.30 am, stops at Picnic Bay on Magnetic Island at 9 am and returns at 5 pm. Visitors are on the island from around 11 am to 2.30 pm and the resort will collect guests from Yankee Bay if they want to come this way.

The Westmark jetty at Yankee Bay on Orpheus is surrounded by good coral for snorkellers and there's a fine stretch of beach here. There's a glass bottom boat and scuba divers can arrange a dive. Camping drop-offs at Yankee Bay can also be made, picking up on a subsequent trip. The day trip costs $75 for adults, $65 for students and $40 for children aged four to 14 years. Lunch is included in the fare.

Although you have to anchor a long way out from shore visiting yachties often pause at Hazard Bay in front of the resort. At one time the resort had a reputation for being less than welcoming to cruising yachts but that no longer appears to be the case. There is also good anchorage at Pioneer Bay but care should be taken to anchor well clear of the Marine Research Station's reef research areas in the bay. Prawn trawlers working this stretch of coast often anchor during the daytime in these bays.

Other Palm Islands

Orpheus is the second largest of the Palm Island group but apart from Orpheus and nearby Pelorus all the other islands are Aboriginal reserves and permission must be obtained from the Department of Aboriginal & Islander Advancement in Townsville before you can land on them. The Aboriginal islands include Brisk, Curacao, Eclipse, Esk, Falcon, Fantome, Havannah and Great Palm Islands.

GREAT PALM ISLAND
The largest island in the Palm Island group, this island was named by Captain Cook who actually stopped and landed there. Even at that time it was inhabited by an Aboriginal tribe. An Aboriginal mission was established here in 1918 and the population at Casement Bay is about 1300. Great Palm Island has an airstrip.

FANTOME ISLAND
Immediately south of Orpheus Island and separated from it only by a narrow channel, Fantome Island had a leper colony until a fire destroyed all the buildings in 1974 and the inhabitants were shifted to Palm Island. The remains of the buildings are on the low saddle near the northern tip of the island.

Rattlesnake & Herald Islands

Flights heading out of Townsville to Orpheus, Hinchinbrook or Dunk Island usually fly right over these two adjacent islands north of Magnetic Island. The Westmark day cruise from Townsville to Orpheus may sail between them. These islands and Acheron Island to the north are used for RAAF target practise and boats must keep away when that is going on.

Bivalves & Clams

Bivalves, which include oysters and scallops, have a two-half shell which can be closed by powerful muscles. Some bivalves embed themselves in rocks and others can swim but most live in mud or sand. Great Barrier Reef bivalve shells are generally much more colourful than their cousins from the colder waters found further south.

Clams are a common sight on reef flats. The family name is *Tridacnidae* and the colourful *Tridacna maxima* or boring clam is the most familiar example on the Great Barrier Reef. They gradually grind away coral boulders until they are completely embedded. All bivalves are covered by a flap of skin known as the mantle. The edge of the mantle meets the edge of the shell and creates the shell by adding layer after layer of calcium carbonate along its edge. Only the fleshy shape of the open mantle is visible but this comes in many different colours and makes a fascinating sight for reef walkers. When disturbed they quickly slam shut.

Found in the far north of the Great Barrier Reef *Tridacna gigas*, the giant clam, is the largest bivalve in the world. They can reach over a metre in length and weigh over 200 kg. Stories abound of divers inadvertently putting their foot into the shell opening and being unable to

Giant clam

escape when the huge clam clamps shut. As divers and snorkellers will soon realise this is obviously just a story, for the clams shut slowly and none too tightly. Their adductor muscles are certainly strong, however, and persuading a closed clam to reopen is not easy. They can also squirt water out as they close and if the water is shallow a giant clam can slam shut with sufficient force to give an onlooker a shower.

Clams are a popular delicacy in parts of Asia and the Pacific and the adductor muscle of the giant clam has a reputation as a powerful aphrodisiac. As a result many Pacific reefs have been stripped bare of their clams. At Orpheus Island the Marine Research Station is breeding and raising clams, initially with the intention to repopulate overfished reefs but also with a view to commercially farming them. Dried adductor muscles are worth over US$100 a kg in parts of Asia.

Despite tales of their great age research shows that they actually just grow fast. A giant clam can reach half a metre in length in less than seven years and a 50 year old clam has reached a venerable age. The clams start out as microscopic swimming larvae then settle down as minute clams only 0.2 mm long. By six months of age artificially reared clams reach about 1.5 cm in length and can be transferred to the sea in protective cages. ■

Vietnam's Barrier Reef Island

Half way through 1989 one of Australia's Great Barrier Reef Islands floated off to Vietnam and can now be found in the Saigon River. The original concept behind the island was impeccable – scuba divers like the Great Barrier Reef so why not build a floating five star hotel and park it right beside a great reef?

Unfortunately things didn't work out so smoothly. For a start there were ecological fears that a 200 room, 12,000 ton hotel could cause considerable harm to the reef if something went wrong. Those concerns were eventually ironed out and the hotel was built in Singapore, utilising offshore oil rig technology. Of course there were cost and time overruns and it was eventually completed more than six months behind schedule and $4 million over the $22 million contract price. Further delays ensued when a cyclone arrived the day before its scheduled opening but the first guests finally arrived at the *Four Seasons Barrier Reef* mid-March 1988.

Unfortunately things continued to go somewhat less than smoothly. The floating swimming pool to be moored beside the hotel sprung a leak. Fantasy Island – a complex complete with bar, theatrette and palm trees and also moored beside the floating hotel – went one better and sank 10 days after being put in place. It's now Fantasy Reef. Then there were complaints about the hotel itself. And worst of all the reef it was anchored on wasn't that superb after all, it had been heavily worked over by crown of thorns starfish in 1982-83. Add some staff unhappiness, falling occupancy rates and before you know it the owners (Barrier Reef Holdings) were trying to kick out the operators (Four Seasons Hotels) and the whole mess looked like ending up in court.

While it was still an Australian island the hotel had been at the John Brewer Reef, about 70 km north of Townsville, out to the east of Great Palm Island. When the end finally came the floating hotel was floated off to Vietnam, where there is a hotel shortage, and is now 'quayside at Hero Square' in the centre of Ho Chi Minh City (Saigon). The *Saigon Floating Hotel* claims to be 'one of Asia's top hotels' and still has a Down Under Discotheque. ■

Hinchinbrook

Area: 393 square km
Type: continental
High point: 1121 metres
Maximum visitor population: 60
Per person daily cost: $200
In brief: This huge rainforest island is Australia's largest island national park and has a small resort at its northern tip. The three or four day coastal walk along the island's eastern side is the finest walk on any Great Barrier Reef island.

The Island

Hinchinbrook is the largest island off the Queensland coast, a magnificent, mountainous island cloaked in incredibly dense rainforest, soaring to 1121 metres high at the top of Mt Bowen and separated from the mainland only by the narrow but deep and mangrove-fringed Hinchinbrook Channel. The island stretches 34 km north to south and from the Bruce Highway or the sea it's often difficult to tell that it's actually divided from the coast.

Indeed when the *Endeavour* sailed by in 1770 Captain Cook did not realise he was passing an island. At that time Hinchinbrook may well have had a permanent Aboriginal population. Traces of the tidal fish traps constructed by the Bandjin Aboriginal tribe can still be seen near the campsite at Scraggy Point.

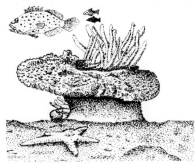

The island can be divided into three main areas. In the south, lush tropical rainforest on the mainland side rises to rugged granite peaks which form a backbone to the island. These towering mountains slope down to long sandy beaches and secluded bays on the eastern side. On the north-west peninsula there are lower, older volcanic rocks which slope down to the sandy beach at Hecate Point. The north-east peninsula, ending in Cape Richards, is notable for the eight km long strip of sand at Ramsay Bay, backed by the extensive mangrove forests of Missionary Bay. Ramsay Bay ends at Cape Sandwich and, round the corner from this cape, the long beaches of South and North Shepherd lead up to Cape Richards.

The whole island is a national park and most of it is untouched wilderness, some of it barely explored, but up at the northern tip at Cape Richard there's a small resort and also a camping area a couple of km south of the cape. Other camping areas are scattered around the national park, particularly at Zoe Bay although you can actually camp just about anywhere. The information that follows is divided into two parts: The Resort, which includes the Missionary Bay mangrove forests and the walk to Macushla Bay, and The Rest of the Island.

Information

The Queensland National Parks & Wildlife Service have two useful leaflets on Hinchinbrook and the islands to the north. Those planning to walk the coastal track from Ramsay Bay to George Point on Hinchinbrook should get a copy of the *Coastal Walk* leaflet. The *Hinchinbrook to Dunk Island* park guide is a small brochure full of fascinating information about Hinchinbrook Island, Goold Island, the Brook Islands, the Family Islands and Dunk Island. There's a QNPWS office and information centre right by the road, near the jetty in the middle of Cardwell, from where boats

North Shepherd Beach, Hinchinbrook Island (TW)

run across to north Hinchinbrook. They have an interesting rainforest display and the rangers can advise you about Hinchinbrook walks and climbing the mountains.

Hinchinbrook Island with text by Arthur and Margaret Thorsborne and photos by Cliff and Dawn Frith (Kevin Weldon Productions, McMahons Point, 1988) is a coffee table book on the wonders of Hinchinbrook with some superb photos and an engrossing text which reveals a real love for the island.

THE RESORT
The whole of Hinchinbrook Island is a National Park but the tip of Cape Richards is leased as a resort. From the resort guests can easily walk down to Macushla Bay and Shepherd Bay.

Information
The resort phone number is (070) 66 8585 and the address is Hinchinbrook Island Resort, PO Box 3, Cardwell, Qld 4816. Bookings can be made by phoning (008) 77 7021 toll free, direct with the resort or through the airlines or travel agents.

The resort has a small shop and a lending library of books.

Activities
The resort has a pool and canoes, sail boats, windsurfers, surf skis, fishing equipment and so on but this is not a heavy activity resort and nightlife means talking to people over dinner or in the bar.

Wildlife
Hinchinbrook has plenty of wildlife although visitors should come prepared for the small six-legged variety in particular. March flies are one pest you'll meet with if you come at the wrong season. They're ugly big monsters although fortunately so slow moving that you usually win every encounter. Mosquitoes and sandflies are also waiting to greet you at certain times of year. They're not a serious nuisance but insect repellent and, if

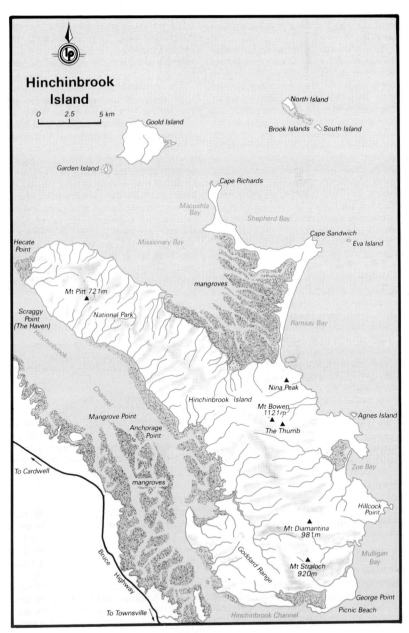

Hinchinbrook Island

0   2.5   5 km

Goold Island

Garden Island

North Island

Brook Islands   South Island

Cape Richards

Macushla Bay

Shepherd Bay

Cape Sandwich

Eva Island

Hecate Point

Missionary Bay

mangroves

Mt Pitt 721m

Ramsay Bay

Scraggy Point (The Haven)

National Park

Hinchinbrook Channel

Nina Peak

Hinchinbrook   Island

Mt Bowen 1121m

Agnes Island

The Thumb

Mangrove Point

Anchorage Point

Zoe Bay

To Cardwell

mangroves

Hillcock Point

Mt Diamantina 981m

Mulligan Bay

Goddard Range

Mt Straloch 920m

Bruce Highway

George Point

Picnic Beach

To Townsville

Hinchinbrook Channel

you react badly, some sort of treatment are a good idea.

There are other rather more interesting varieties of wildlife to be seen, particularly the very tame pretty faced wallabies which appear around the resort mornings and evenings. They've learnt that resort guests are often willing to hand out bits of apple and other goodies and put on a great act for children. Equally visible are the huge goannas that roam the resort area, scrambling up trees and hissing ominously if you approach too closely. There are lots of tiny lizards and skinks to be seen but the big, spotted, grey-black goannas are a fine sight. Other creatures you'll see around the resort include cane toads, echidnas, bush rats and bats.

The short stroll from the resort to Turtle Bay may well reveal why this little inlet gets its name. If you clamber up to the rocks above the bay you may see large turtles popping up in the waters, peering around myopically and then sinking beneath the waves again. Mud skippers, those strange walking fish, can also be seen at this bay.

Bird spotters will have a field day at Hinchinbrook. There's a constant background burble of bird noises and birds flit across the scenery continuously. Each of the cabins at the resort is named after a bird found on the island so you might stay in a cabin named Reef Heron or Boobook Owl. Scrub fowl or megapodes are one bird whose presence you'll often see signs of. This ground dwelling bird builds huge mounds of vegetation in which it lays its eggs. The heat of the decaying vegetable matter incubates the eggs. You'll often see these impressively large 'bumps' and the birds themselves, scampering off into the bush. Over 200 species of birds have been spotted on Hinchinbrook.

Mangroves

Missionary Bay is fringed by an extensive mangrove forest with twisting inlets leading in to it. The Australian Institute of Marine Science has constructed a boardwalk across from one inlet almost to the next one and you can walk this half km pathway and study this fascinating area. You can approach the boardwalk pontoon jetty in a dinghy borrowed from the resort or on a Reef Explorer tour.

The boardwalk stands a couple of metres above the muddy surface of the swamp and you can see bins, nets and instruments as evidence of numerous experiments being conducted in the mangroves. A constant background burble of noise indicates just how lively the mangroves are. Listen for the loud cracking of the snapping prawns, there's obviously a lot of them in there but, hidden in the mud, you won't see them. More visible are the numerous small mud crabs and the curious mud skippers, small square-faced fish who have adapted to life out of the water and skip across the surface of the mud using their front fins as 'legs'. They'll even climb trees! You may see them peering out of the little volcano-like mudhills they build to live in.

The mangroves, with their twisting and intertwined roots, are surprisingly varied in their form. In all there are 23 species of mangroves and the ability of these plants to live in saltwater creates a unique environment which scientists are now studying closely. Another boardwalk, right at the end of an estuary, leads to the long sand dunes which separate Ramsay Bay and the open sea from the sheltered mangrove forests of Missionary Bay.

Beaches & Snorkelling

Orchid Beach is as fine a sweep of beach as you could ask for and it's only a few steps from the resort cabins or the swimming pool. Apart from the rocky headlands at each end of the beach there's not much snorkelling potential around the resort, however. The trip across to the Brook Islands, where there is some fine coral and plenty of fish, is the popular snorkelling excursion. Hinchinbrook is close enough to the mainland that you should be cautious about box jellyfish during the November to March summer season, particularly on the coast side of the island.

Walks

Around the Resort There are a number of walks around the resort and further afield into the national park. From the resort you can take a couple of minutes stroll from the end of the beach up to the top of the rocky headland at Cape Richards. From there you have a fine view across to the misty outline of the Family Islands and Dunk Island, about 30 km away. In the other direction there's the idyllic sweep of Orchid Beach, the resort beach and as pretty a stretch of sand as you can ask for.

At the other end of Orchid Beach an equally short trail leads to tiny Turtle Bay, a rocky little inlet around the headland. Alternatively you can scramble around the headland to the bay.

To Shepherd & Macushla Bays A longer walk leads from the resort to North Shepherd, Macushla and South Shepherd. The

trail starts from the cabins and is signposted as a 40 minute walk to North Shepherd Bay although you can do the two km stroll much faster. The trail winds through the rainforest, climbing up to a ridge with fine views across to the Brook Islands before dropping precipitously down to the bay. North Shepherd is a long stretch of very wide beach with rocky headlands at each end.

It takes a good 20 minutes to walk the 1.3 km from one end of the beach to the other

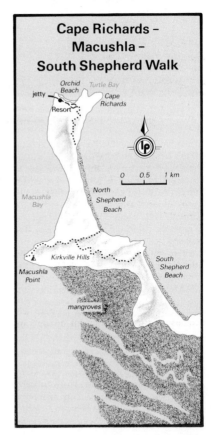

Rainforest, Hinchinbrook Island (TW)

and at the far or southern end the trail leads off to Macushla, crossing the peninsula to the sheltered beach on the calmer, coast side of the island. Look out for scrub fowl along this two km stretch of the walk, there seem to be plenty of them around. Skirting around the Kirkville Hills it only takes about 20 minutes to cross the peninsula to Macushla Bay. The beach is not always good for swimming as it's very flat and muddy at low tide but it is littered with countless tiny shells. A large camping area with toilets and tables but not much freshwater sprawls on either side of the headland. Mangroves start only a short distance north and south of the headlands.

The trail on to South Shepherd starts about half way across the peninsula between North Shepherd and Macushla. It's signposted as a 3½ hour walk but two hours is probably a better estimate for most walkers. Like North Shepherd, there's an endlessly long stretch of beach at South Shepherd.

Accommodation

There has only been accommodation on the island since 1975 and until recently the resort boasted that full meant 30 people. In late '89 the resort was closed down for major renovations and extensions. The original units were being retained and a further 15 units were being added so presumably the new 'maximum population' will be 60. Actually the resort could always accommodate more than 30 as with a real squeeze you could get six people into the larger units although two adults and two children was a rather more comfortable number. The resort is expected to reopen in mid 1990.

This is a very low-key resort but if you're looking for peace and quiet, not loud disco music, it may well be the perfect place. They push the fact that the guest population is low and that there are no heavy entertainment schedules – no entertainment director, no competitions and games, no disco. No TV or radio and only one phone too for that matter. It's popular with families with children and

Mushrooms, Hinchinbrook Island (TW)

with couples – the island is big enough and the resort population small enough that you can have as much solitude as you could wish.

There's nothing fancy about the resort, the older rooms are individual cabins, each with a deck out front, a kitchen-cum-bedroom with a couple of single beds, a bathroom and a bedroom with a double bed and a divan-sofa-whatever which could fold out to sleep a couple more. The older cabins are inelegant in the extreme and the furnishings equally straightforward but they're quite comfortable, with ceiling fans in the two rooms, and the resort rebuild will probably include some upgrading of the older rooms. The rooms were certainly well hidden. From the air or from the sea, even from just standing on the beach, there is absolutely no sign of the cabins at all. They're totally lost in the dense bush. The new rooms are still going to be simple but they will certainly be a lot more elegant than their predecessors.

The restaurant, bar and pool area are quite separate from the cabins. This area is close to the jetty, a couple of minutes walk along an unsurfaced road from the cabins which are scattered up the hillside above the beach. The restaurant is small but pleasant and the swimming pool, with a wide decking area around it, is just fine.

The cabins cost about $180 a night single or $170 a night each for two. Children are $70 a night. These rates include all meals and use of most equipment.

Food

Food at Hinchinbrook is surprisingly good, far better than at some of the large resorts. The restaurant is small, open air and pleasant and you simply sit down at any vacant space so, unless you're a big enough party to fill a table or desperately unsociable, you're constantly making new acquaintances. Breakfast is a serve yourself buffet with fruit, cereals (excellent muesli), juice and tea or coffee, Plus there's toast, great croissants and cooked breakfasts for the big eaters. Lunch might be in the restaurant (hefty mud-crabs one day), a poolside barbecue or if you're off on a walk they'll pack you a sandwich lunch.

At night they'll feed children early and the regular dinner starts at 7.30 pm with a four course meal offering a choice of main courses. Usually one is seafood, the other a meat course. The food seems to be consistently imaginative and well prepared, the ingredients were always fresh and top quality. A superb resort for eating, Hinchinbrook is a good small restaurant where big resorts like South Molle or Great Keppel are large fast service pubs.

There are no dress standards and, like other resorts, shorts and T-shirts are the usual rule although there's often a bit of dressing up at night time.

Getting There & Away
Hinchinbrook is about midway between Townsville and Cairns. Cardwell, the jumping off point for the island, is 192 km south of Cairns and 157 km north of Townsville.

Air Hinchinbrook is one of the most enjoyable of the islands to get to, if you take the Seair Pacific flight from Cairns ($115) or Townsville ($101). Seair's stable of amphibious aircraft includes an antique twin-engined Grumman Mallard, more modern De Havilland Beaver floatplanes and tiny Lake Buccaneers. From Townsville you take off from the airport and wing your way out over the sea between Townsville and Magnetic Island. Heading north you fly over various islands with the bulk of Palm Island, site of an Aboriginal reserve, looming to the east. You swoop down to land at Orpheus Island, the pilot dexterously parks the plane beside a pontoon while a boat motors out from the resort to collect arrivals.

Then it's off again to Hinchinbrook where a boat comes out to meet the amphibious aircraft while the floatplane can taxi right up to the pier if it's calm enough. The schedules vary with demand, it takes about half an hour to fly each leg of the Cairns/Hinchinbrook/Orpheus/Townsville route.

Sea The Hinchinbrook Booking Office (tel (070) 66 8539) at 91 Bruce Highway, Cardwell operates boats daily except Monday from Cardwell to the resort on Cape Richards. The crossing takes about half an hour and departs from Cardwell at 9 am, from the resort on the return trip at 4 pm. The boats are the MV *Reef Adventure II* and/or the MV *Hinchinbrook Explorer* and return cost is $35. Car storage facilities are available at Cardwell.

The same boat also makes day trips to the island. You can either spend a day at the resort and have lunch there or alternatively they will drop you at the resort and you can then make the walk from there to North Shepherd Beach and across to Macushla. At Macushla the boat will meet you again and take you up through the mangroves on Missionary Bay to the Ramsay Bay boardwalk. You'll have time to walk down to Blacksand Beach and even beyond towards Nina Bay, on the first part of the Hinchinbrook coastal walk. The trip up through the mangroves to Ramsay Bay depends on the tides so the trip may sometimes have to be done in reverse.

THE REST OF THE ISLAND
Although there's plenty to see around the resort and walks lead from the resort to Macushla Bay and North and South Shepherd Bay, that only touches on a small part of the island. The great bulk of the beautiful island is only open to intrepid bushwalkers.

The Coastal Walk
See The Resort section above for details on Cape Richards walks. A one km circuit track runs from the Scraggy Point camping area through the vine forest but the island's best walk is the 30 km coastal track from Ramsay Bay to Zoe Bay and on to George Point. This is probably the finest island walk along the Great Barrier Reef and can be completed in two hard days but allowing at least three nights camping on the island is a much better idea. The southern part of the walk between Zoe Bay and George Point was only opened in 1988 and many walkers still do just the

northern part as a Ramsay Bay-Zoe Bay-Ramsay Bay return trip.

The walk includes long sandy beaches, mountain streams, humid rainforests and magnificent mountain scenery. The trail is ungraded and includes some often challenging creek crossings. The maximum elevation along the trail is 260 metres, reached on Stage 8 between Upper South Zoe Creek and Sweetwater Creek.

Information The walking details that follow are southbound from Ramsay Bay to George Point but the walk can be done in either direction. Get a copy of the Queensland National Parks & Wildlife Service's *Coastal Walk* leaflet. The trail is rough and not always well marked although triangular orange trail markers, rock cairns and coloured tape may be found at some difficult spots. The trail is recommended for moderately experienced bushwalkers who should be adequately prepared and carry a map, compass and drinking water. Water is reliably available year round only at Nina Bay, Little Ramsay Bay and at the southern end of Zoe Bay. Between August and January water is particularly scarce and the trail can sometimes be closed to walkers.

Two creeks along the walk require special attention. North Zoe Creek (Stage 6) should only be crossed at low tides because of the theoretical, although unlikely, danger of an unpleasant encounter with a saltwater crocodile. The creek crossing can be completely avoided by taking the alternative inland route at this point. Diamantina Creek (Stage 9) can be swift and deep after heavy rain and great care should be taken when crossing it.

From November to May box jellyfish can be a danger, particularly at George Point, Mulligan Bay and Zoe Bay.

See the Getting There & Away section below for information on drop-offs at the beginning and end of the coastal walk.

Preparation Walkers intending to do the coastal track should be fit, experienced and well prepared. Water can be a problem. During the dry season from April to October

water may be very scarce and adequate supplies should be carried. If you find a dry creek or the water is salty it's often possible to find freshwater further upstream. During the wet season from December through March too much water can pose problems at the opposite extreme. The trail may be very slippery, creek crossings can be difficult and you should be prepared for heavy rainfall. In tropical conditions walking in a raincoat or poncho is likely to be very uncomfortable – better to simply get wet and have dry clothes to change into later.

At any time of the year it can be hot and humid during the daytime but from May through September the nights can be cold enough to require a sleeping bag. A good tent is necessary if there is heavy rain at night. Insects – mosquitoes and march flies – can be a nuisance so bring a good insect repellent. As anywhere along the Great Barrier Reef a good sunscreen and a shady hat are also vitally important.

Stage 1 – Ramsay Bay to Blacksand Beach, 1 km You reach the starting point on Ramsay Bay by going up the mangrove estuary from Missionary Bay and walking across on the boardwalk. It's about a km from the boardwalk at the south end of Ramsay Bay to Blacksand Beach. Look for the fossil crabs found along Ramsay Bay, they're thought to be 8000 to 10,000 years old, a relic of rising seas at the close of the last ice age.

Stage 2 – Blacksand Beach to Nina Bay, 2 km Between the months of January and June freshwater can usually be found at the small lagoons behind Blacksand Beach. From about two thirds of the way along Blacksand Beach and a little south of the second lagoon the trail starts from between three large paperbark trees and initially follows a small dry watercourse. It then turns left off the creek and goes through tall, open forest to the saddle to the east of Nina Peak before descending along a creek flowing south-east towards Nina Bay. The trail emerges on the mangroves behind the beach and at high tide these can be difficult to cross.

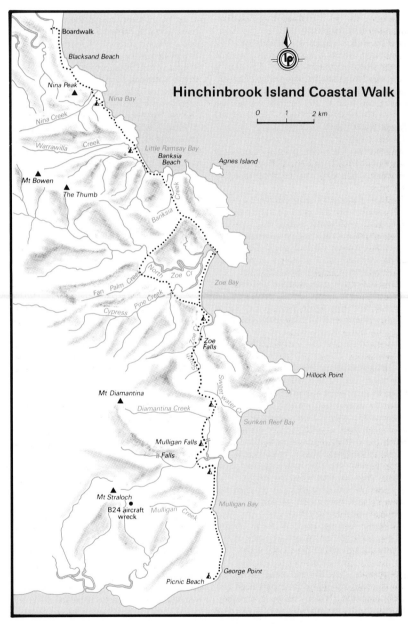

Hinchinbrook Island Coastal Walk

The track follows the western side of the mangroves and finally ends at the north end of the beach where there is a good place to camp.

It's an interesting, but steep and tiring, climb up Nina Creek to the pronounced top of Nina Peak. The views from the summit are superb.

Stage 3 – Nina Bay to Little Ramsay Bay, 2.5 km

From the rocks at the south end of Nina Beach you make your way around the headland and over a small cliff, following rock cairns to a rocky bay. Rock cairns mark the start of a well defined trail from the headland at the southern end of this bay. The trail goes south-east to the north end of Little Ramsay Bay. You can find freshwater in the creek which runs into the lagoon behind the beach here and the dunes on the south bank of the lagoon make a good campsite but watch out for crocodiles in the lagoon.

The shortest trail to the top of Mt Bowen, highest point on Hinchinbrook, runs along Warrawilla Creek from Little Ramsay Bay. Getting to the top really requires more than a day, you need to camp near the summit and make the final ascent on the second day. The longer ascent to the top along Pineapple Ridge takes the best part of three days.

Stage 4 – Little Ramsay Bay to Banksia Creek, 2 km

From the rocks at the end of Little Ramsay Bay it's only 50 metres or so to a very small beach and from the end of this beach the trail continues to a larger sandy beach. The trail bends east and climbs a steep slope before dropping down to Banksia Creek. The trail continues upstream on the western side to a waterfall then crosses to the eastern side and climbs a very steep slope to the top of the waterfall. The trail crosses back and forth over the creek and eventually reaches a large waterfall where water is usually available for much of the year. After August it may be dry until the rains come later in the year.

A short way up the trail from the second beach you can divert off to sandy Banksia Bay, also known as No Name Beach. From

Goanna, Hinchinbrook Island (TW)

here you can make your way round the coast to Agnes Island, which can sometimes be reached at low tide.

Stage 5 – Banksia Creek to North Zoe Creek, 3 km

From the waterfall the trail leaves the creek and heads south-east over a saddle then follows a dry watercourse through open forest, then into a stretch of rainforest. Soon after entering the rainforest the track branches. The left branch runs south-east to the mangroves on the coast and crosses North Zoe Creek at its mouth. The newer right hand branch runs inland around the Zoe Bay mangroves and avoids the need to cross the mouth of the creek.

Stage 6 – North Zoe Creek to South Zoe Creek, 3 km via coast, 5 km via inland

The coastal route involves crossing North Zoe Creek. This should only be done at low tide and with a wary eye for crocodiles. There are two possible crossing points but at either point remember that the narrower the creek the more deep it is likely to be. The one further up in the mangroves should only be attempted if the tide is extremely low. The second crossing point is further downstream where the creek is usually lowest, 100 to 200 metres west of a prominent reef of rocks jutting out from the north bank. You have to make your way around a thin fringe of mangroves and then select the shallowest route to the southern sandspit.

After crossing the creek the route follows

the beach to South Zoe Creek where you can camp on the north bank. A track leads along the creekside to permanent freshwater and a fine swimming hole below a waterfall. Zoe Bay, with its beautiful waterfall, is one of the most scenic spots on the island.

The alternative inland route runs uphill from the mangroves and crosses North Zoe Creek nearer its source before turning back down to the coast. Permanent freshwater can usually be found at Fan Palm Creek while Cypress Pine Creek has a good swimming hole just upstream from the creek crossing. If the water at creek crossings is salty or the creek is actually dry, it's worth heading upstream a few hundred metres. There is another good campsite near the North Zoe Creek crossing. The trail reaches Zoe Bay a little north of South Zoe Creek.

Stage 7 – South Zoe Creek via Zoe Falls to Upper Zoe Creek, 4 km From Zoe Bay the trail follows the western bank of the creek then crosses to the eastern side about 100 metres before the falls, 1.5 km from Zoe Bay. Above the falls the trail crosses back and forth over the creek then follows the western side of the creek through heavy undergrowth to Upper South Zoe Creek.

Stage 8 – Upper South Zoe Creek to Sweetwater Creek, 1.5 km Leaving South Zoe Creek the trail climbs a spur with good views of Mt Bowen to the saddle separating South Zoe Creek from Sweetwater Creek. At 260 metres this is the highest elevation of the whole walk. It then crosses the headwaters and runs parallel to the creek to the Sweetwater Camp, a short distance down a side trail. The creek usually has water.

Stage 9 – Sweetwater Creek to Mulligan Falls, 2.5 km The trail crosses a steep ravine and drops down a slope with good views of Sunken Reef Bay to Diamantina Creek. This creek rarely runs dry and can be difficult to cross after heavy rain. From the creek the trail climbs a ridge then drops down to Mulligan Falls where there is a good campsite

just south of the falls with a fine swimming hole below the falls.

Stage 10 – Mulligan Falls to Mulligan Bay, 2.5 km The trail skirts around the mangroves, crosses the creek and comes to Mulligan Bay, where there is another good campsite south of the mouth of Diamantina Creek. Fresh water is available about 300 metres before you reach the beach.

Stage 11 – Mulligan Bay to George Point, 4.5 km The trail continues along the bay crossing Mulligan Creek about half way along. The crossing can be difficult at high tide. The trail continues to the picnic area at George Point from where you cross to Lucinda. The six km long jetty, principally used for the bulk loading of sugar, is a Lucinda landmark. It's clearly visible from Orpheus Island.

It's possible to follow the creek from the south of the island up Mt Straloch. A USAF B-24 bomber crashed on the mountain during WW II and wreckage can still be seen below the summit. When you start to see wreckage by the creek turn off to the north. The climb and return can be made in a day.

Camping
Bush camping is permitted almost anywhere on the island except near the Cape Richards resort but you are requested to use the recommended sites wherever possible in order to minimise damage. Permits for camping should be applied for at least six but no more than 12 weeks in advance. Applications for the Macushla Bay and The Haven (Scraggy Point) sites and for bushcamping should be made to the Cardwell office of the Queensland National Parks & Wildlife Service. Applications for the sites along the coastal walk route can also be made to the Ingham office. Addresses are in the Facts for the Visitor chapter. The Macushla Bay and Scraggy Point sites are category B ($5 a night) while the other sites are category C ($2).

You can walk to the Macushla Bay site from the Cape Richards resort. A maximum of 35 campers can stay here and there are toilets, tables and fireplaces but no drinking water. The site at Scraggy Point is on Hinchinbrook Channel below Mt Pitt. As at Macushla Bay there is a maximum limit of 35 campers and there are toilets, tables and fireplaces but Scraggy Point also has drinking water available from Pages Creek.

Recommended camping sites along the coastal trail are on the north bank of the small lagoon on Blacksand Beach, on the dunes where the tracks meets the beach at Nina Bay, on the south bank of the large lagoon on Little Ramsay Bay and where the inland track crosses North Zoe Creek. On Zoe Bay on the north side of South Zoe Creek there is a site with toilets and a maximum limit of 30 campers. Further south there are sites at Sweetwater Creek, Mulligan Falls, Mulligan Bay and George Point.

Getting There & Away

It's relatively easy to arrange drop offs and pick ups for the coastal walk, the Cardwell/Ramsay Bay and Lucinda/George Point boat operators work together to drop and collect walkers at each end. At the northern end the Cardwell boat also operates day trips to Hinchinbrook and takes guests to and from the resort. Walkers can take the boat both ways for $35 or one way for $25. Contact the Hinchinbrook Booking Office (tel (070) 66 8539) at 91 Bruce Highway, Cardwell for full details.

At the other end the shorter Lucinda (Dungeness)/George Point, or vice versa, trip costs $15 one way or $25 return. Contact Hinchinbrook Wilderness Safaris (tel (077) 77 8307 or 77 8213 and ask for Bill or Kay) at 48 Patterson Parade, Lucinda. Although the MV *Searcher* is used as a pick up or drop off service by coastal track walkers it also operates day trips into Hinchinbrook Channel and exploring the southern end of the island including Scraggy Point and Deluge Inlet. Getting out of Lucinda to the main highway, 30 km away at Ingham, can be a little difficult although hitching is usually straightforward.

Campers at Macushla can reach the resort at Cape Richards by regular boats and flights and walk from there to the campsite at Macushla Bay or get dropped right at Macushla by the day trip boat.

Access to other points on the island is not so easy. There are no safe anchorages on the eastern (ocean) side of the island although boats can get in to Zoe Bay when conditions are favourable. Apart from the day trips to the northern and southern end of the island there are also trips with the MV *Tekin III* exploring Hinchinbrook Channel from Cardwell right down to Lucinda. The trip departs at 10 am, returns at 4.30 pm, costs $40 and is operated by Tekin Cruises (tel (070) 66 8000) at 141 Bruce Highway, Cardwell.

Islands near Hinchinbrook

Two national park island groups lie immediately north of Hinchinbrook. They are the large Goold Island, immediately north of Hinchinbrook, and the small Brook Islands group to the north-east. Further north are the Family Islands, also mainly national parks, and then the larger Dunk Island.

GOOLD ISLAND

Only 4.5 km north-west of Cape Richards and 17 km north-east of Cardwell the whole 8.3 square km island is a national park. The granite island is covered in eucalyptus forest with smaller patches of rainforest in the gullies. The noisy call of sulphur-crested cockatoos rings across the island and turtles and dugong are often seen feeding on the seagrass beds which spread across the shallow waters south and west of the island.

Just south of Goold Island is tiny Garden Island with a recreation reserve controlled by the local council. Unlike the national park restrictions which apply to Goold there are no restrictions on camping here and the island has a good sandy beach but, as usual, no freshwater is available.

Camping

The camping site on the western beach has toilets, tables and fireplaces but the creek at the northern end of the beach usually dries up between August and December so it is necessary to bring water. A permit from the Cardwell QNPWS office is necessary and there is a limit of 60 campers.

Getting There & Away
Charter boats operate to Goold Island from Cardwell.

BROOK ISLANDS
The four small islands of the Brook group are covered in dense vegetation and lie about eight km north-east of Cape Richards. South Island has a Commonwealth lighthouse but the other three islands – Middle Island, Tween Island and North Island – are all national park and cover a total area of 0.9 square km. There are regular charter boats operating to these islands from Cardwell and the Hinchinbrook Resort. The fringing reef around the three northern islands offers fine snorkelling and North Island's beach is a good picnic spot but there are no facilities on the island and camping is not permitted.

The islands are a nesting place for a huge colony of Torresian imperial-pigeons. Up to 20,000 of these black and white birds arrive here from Papua New Guinea in September to breed, departing with their offspring in

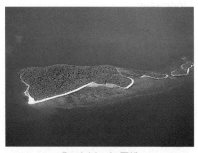

Brook Islands (TW)

February. The male and female birds take turns to incubate the eggs, while the bird enjoying a day off flies to the mainland where they feed on rainforest fruits. The summer months also find black-naped terns breeding on the island. During these months visitors to the island should take care to avoid nesting areas which are indicated by signs on the beach. The young pigeons are easily panicked and once out of their nests may not be able to return or may become entangled in the pisonia trees' sticky seeds. The tern's eggs are remarkably well camouflaged and can easily be accidentally stepped on.

Mangroves

My dictionary defines mangroves as 'Any tropical ever-green tree or shrub of the genus *Rhizophora* having stiltlike intertwining aerial roots and forming dense thickets along coasts'. They are a much maligned species, the word that usually follows *mangrove* is *swamp* and the image is of something dark, muddy, smelly, full of insects and gener-ally most unattractive.

In actual fact mangroves are an extremely interesting plant whose vital environmental importance has only been recognised comparatively recently. Mangroves are the advance troops, the first plants to reclaim land from the sea and they are able to do this because of their remarkable resistance to saltwater. Saltwater will kill most plants but mangroves thrive in it. They can either restrict its entry through their roots or expel excess salt through their leaves. Their remarkable adaptation to a hostile environment can also be seen in their extensive root system which enables them to grown in unstable tidal mud.

Gradually mangroves create new land but in the process they provide an environment for a host of other living things from oysters, crabs and snails to the mudskip-per fishes that prefer to scamper around on top of mangrove mud rather than swim in water, like any normal fish.

There are many interesting mangrove areas along the Great Barrier Reef including the huge and complex man-grove areas on the coast side of Hinchinbrook Island. A mangrove research facility has been established at Hinchinbrook and a boardwalk makes it possible to walk right through a mangrove swamp. Further north there are many cays where, once the mangroves become estab-lished, they take over the entire reef flat in one dense forest of mangroves.

The Great Barrier Reef region probably has the world's richest collection of mangroves. Australia has over 30 species of mangroves, compared to the four types found in southern Florida where the first important research on mangroves was completed. Tropical Asia also has a rich variety of mangroves but development is rapidly destroy-ing them. ∎

Boardwalk through the mangroves, Hinchinbrook Island (TW)

Mangrove seeds (TW)

Crocodiles

Films like Crocodile Dundee together with the odd tourist ending up as snack food have combined to make Australia's crocodiles very well known. There are two types and you're very unlikely to meet either of them, in the wild, along the Great Barrier Reef although both are found in Queensland.

The smaller freshwater crocodile is not dangerous to humans and in any case are found mainly on the Gulf of Carpentaria coast of Queensland, not on the Pacific coast except in the far north of the Cape York peninsula. As the name indicates freshwater crocodiles are generally found in freshwater – in streams, rivers and billabongs although they can be found in the tidal reaches of rivers. 'Freshies' live on insects, fish, frogs, lizards, birds and sometimes small mammals.

The dangerous crocodile is the estuarine or saltwater crocodile. 'Salties' have very occasionally been seen out at islands but generally they stick to the rivers and lagoons and particularly the tidal reaches of rivers. Saltwater crocodiles grow to a larger size than the freshwater variety, and can reach up to six metres in length although four metres is about as big as they are usually found. Their broad snout is the easiest way to distinguish a saltie from a freshie.

Although saltwater crocodiles can be found right along the Queensland north of Rockhampton it's only in creek and river mouths where you might spot this generally very shy creature. Hinchinbrook is the only Great Barrier Reef island where a watchful eye needs to be kept for crocodiles and even there it's really only bushwalkers crossing Zoe Creek who need to be careful. They could, of course, be found around the mangrove inlets on the inner side of Hinchinbrook. ■

Freshwater crocodile

Saltwater crocodile

Dunk, Bedarra & the Family Islands

The Family group consists of Dunk Island and the seven smaller islands to the south. They lie off the coast from Tully, about 30 km north-east of Cardwell. Dunk Island is about three-quarters national park, of the other islands five – Wheeler, Coombe, Smith, Bowden and Hudson Islands – are national parks while two – Timana (Thorpe) and Bedarra (Richards) Islands – are privately owned. Dunk has a large resort, Bedarra has two very small and very exclusive (read expensive) resorts while camping is permitted on Dunk and several of the other national park islands.

Dunk, the largest island of the group, is sometimes referred to as 'The Father'; Bedarra is 'The Mother'; Wheeler and Coombe 'The Twins'; Smith, Bowden and Hudson 'The Triplets'. The Family name was given to them by Cook when he sailed through the group on 8 June 1770. He sailed between The Twins and The Triplets and passed to the east (seaward) side of Dunk, which was the only individual island he named. Lord Montague Dunk was at that time the First Lord of the Admiralty and Cook made very certain of keeping important personages and possible patrons firmly on side! Lord Dunk was also the Earl of Sandwich and a very keen gambler. He is credited with inventing the 'sandwich' in order not to waste important gambling time by stopping for a meal!

Cook's journal comments that 'we saw on one of the nearest Islands a Number of Natives collected together, who seemed to

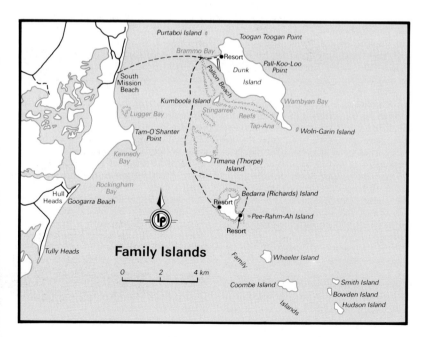

Family Islands

0   2   4 km

look very attentively upon the Ship; they were quite naked, and of a very Dark Colour, with short hair.' Although the Aborigines have now completely gone from the Family Islands E J Banfield, Dunk Island's 'Beachcomber', recorded their names for all the islands of the group:

Aboriginal Name	European Name
Coonanglebah	Dunk
Timana	Thorpe
Bedarra	Richards
Toolghar	Wheeler
Coomboo	Coombe
Kurrumbah	Smith
Budjoo	Bowden
Coolah	Hudson

Dunk apart, the Family Islands were given their European names by Lieutenant G E Richards when he came here on his survey ship *HMS Paluma* in 1886. The officers, engineer and surgeon of the ship each had an island named after him; double barrelled Lieutenant Bowden-Smith actually got two! The close relationship between Coomboo and Coombe indicates that Richards may well have been aware of the Aboriginal names of the islands. Timana and Bedarra are the only islands of the group which are still generally referred to by their Aboriginal names although it is thought that Banfield erred in his transcription of Bedarra and it should really be Biagurra. The island has also been known as Allason Island, after Captain Henry Allason, an early but brief European occupant.

The Family name neatly fits the group which all have one clearly similar family characteristic – each island ends in its northwest corner with a fine sandspit, a result of the prevailing winds and currents through the groups.

Climate

The Family Islands are cloaked in heavy rainforest, hardly surprising since they lie off the wettest area in Australia. Innisfail or Tully usually record the highest annual rainfall in Australia, generally around 3700 mm

or 150 inches. The temperatures in this tropical region are fairly even year round, averaging around 25 to 30°C in the warmer October to April months, dropping to 20 to 25°C in the cooler winter from May to September.

Rain, however, has a much more decisive effect on when to visit these islands. The wet season starts in December when the average rainfall is around 150 to 200 mm but in January, February and March the average figure is 400 mm or more, peaking in March before dropping dramatically in April. Although you can have dry, sunny days during the wet season it often rains every day and if you are unlucky it can rain all day every day. Visitors who come to these islands expecting tropical sunshine during the wet season can go home very unhappy!

Books

More words have been written about the Family Islands, and particularly Dunk Island, than any other islands on the Great Barrier Reef. In large part this is due to the activities of E J Banfield, Dunk Island's famous 'Beachcomber' who lived on Dunk from 1897 to 1923. During that time he wrote *The Confessions of a Beachcomber* (1908), *My Tropic Isle* (1911), *Tropic Days* (1918) and *Last Leaves from Dunk Island* (1925) which was published after his death. These books with their detailed and sympathetic observations of the island's natural history were immensely popular when first published and remain of great interest even today. *The Confessions*, his first and most popular book, has been regularly reissued and reprinted right down to the present day. The current Eden paperback published by Angus & Robertson, with a more recent introduction, should be on sale in the Dunk Island resort shop.

Equally interesting is Michael Noonan's biography of Banfield, *A Different Drummer* (University of Queensland Press, St Lucia, Queensland, 1983) which is also available in a paperback edition. This is an extremely readable account of his family's move to

Australia during the Victorian goldrush, his later career as a journalist and his life on the island. There have been various other books which dip into his writings. James Porter's *Beachcomber's Paradise* (Angus & Robertson, Sydney, 1983) is an attractive coffee table book with photographs of birds, plants, fish and other reef features, accompanied by Banfield's descriptions from his books.

Even without Banfield's books Dunk, and the other Family Islands, have been unusually well described. *Discovering the Family Islands* by James G Porter (Kullari Publications, 1983) is a small book on Dunk and the other islands of the group with chapters on the island's natural history, plant and wildlife, the Aboriginal history of the islands, their European discovery, the prolonged stay of E J Banfield and the islands' colourful collection of post-Banfield beachcombers, settlers, owners, artists and resort operators. The resort operators story is a continuing one as Bedarra's recent major revamp took place since the publication of this book, which you should find on sale on Dunk Island.

The other writer who has had some interesting things to say about Dunk is the poet Mark O'Connor who spent some time at the Dunk resort in 1976-77 working as its gardener. He wrote the *Dunk Island* chapter in *The Book of Australian Islands* and his poem *The Sunhunters* (published in *The New Oxford Book of Australian Verse)* is about the island's rich rainforest. More amusingly *Planting the Dunk Botanic Gardens* is a lengthy poem of the trials and tribulations of working as a resort gardener with some interesting insights into resort management, passing tourists and tropical lotus eating. It's published in his book *The Fiesta of Men* (Hale & Iremonger, 1983) and should also be on sale in the Dunk resort shop.

Finally the Queensland National Parks & Wildlife Service's *Hinchinbrook to Dunk Island National Parks* Park Guide leaflet has a great deal of interesting information about the island and its natural history.

Dunk Island

Area: 10 square km of which 7.3 square km is national park
Type: continental rainforest
High point: 271 metres
Maximum visitor population: about 400
Per person daily cost: $220
In brief: Dunk is a beautiful rainforest island, part of which is a national park. It's one of the larger resorts with accommodation for 400 guest but it has managed to avoid being too 'mass market'. It's operated by Australian Airlines, there are plenty of activities, some fine walking trails and children are well looked after during school vacations. The island is only five km from the coast and less than 30 km from the outer reef.

The Island

Dunk is a lush rainforest island with steep hills and some fine walks – 13 km of walking trails wind across the island. Over seven square km of the 10 square km island is set aside as a national park and the island is noted for its dense vegetation, prolific birdlife (nearly 150 species have been spotted here) and many butterflies. Some people say it's the most attractive of the Barrier Reef islands. The climb to the top of 271 metre Mt Kootaloo offers superb views over the other islands of the Family group and south towards the entrance to the

Walking track, Dunk Island (TW)

Hinchinbrook Channel and the jagged peaks of Hinchinbrook Island.

Dunk Island has also had one of the most interesting histories of any of the Barrier Reef islands. It was named by Captain Cook and at one time had an Aboriginal population who named many of the island's features. The island is, however, inextricably linked with the period from 1897 to 1923 when E J Banfield lived here and wrote *The Confessions of a Beachcomber* and his other books about the island and its natural history. Born in England in 1852, Banfield came to Aus-

tralia when he was only two years old during the Victorian gold rush. His father didn't find his fortune on the goldfields but he did as the publisher of *The Ararat Advertiser*, a Victorian country town newspaper which continues to publish to this day. Eventually Banfield moved north to Townsville where he worked as a journalist on *The Townsville Daily Bulletin*. He eventually became the paper's editor until overwork and ill health forced him to seek an alternative lifestyle.

His doctor had warned that he had only months to live if he continued working and

Dunk Island

0   0.5   1 km

PURTABOI ISLAND

Muggy Muggy

▲*Kootaloo*

Brammo Bay

Boat House   Resort

Golf Course

Airstrip

▲ *Tarn-coo-rah-ee*

● Dairy

▲ *Kut-tay*
Lookout

Pallon Beach

FARM

Toolguy-ah

DUNK ISLAND NATIONAL PARK

▲ *Tah-loo*

MANGUM GNACKUM ISLAND

● Bruce Arthur's Artists Colony

Coconut Beach
Coconut Bay

KUMBOOLA ISLAND

Stingray Reef

WOLN GARIN ISLAND

in 1897 with his wife Bertha he set up camp on Dunk Island, determined to follow the lead of the American writer Walden Thoreau and lead a life close to nature. For the following 26 years until his death from appendicitis in 1923 he lived on Dunk with only a handful of brief interruptions, the longest of which was in 1901 when he returned to his paper in Townsville for nine month. During those years on Dunk the Banfields lived a basically self sufficient life running a small farm and supplementing their income by the regular 'Rural Homilies' column he wrote for his Townsville paper and by the proceeds from his books about life on Dunk Island.

The books proved an instant inspiration to a host of other would-be-Robinson Crusoes, none of whom stayed the pace, but more importantly have been a continuing delight to the many people interested in this wonderful area's fascinating natural history. The 'Confessions', his first and most popular book, has been almost continually in print from the time of its first publication.

Banfield was worried that with his departure his beloved island would inevitably be spoilt but he would probably be delighted to find that despite the resort most of Dunk today has changed remarkably little from his early description. After his death Bertha stayed on the island with Essie McDonough, the Banfields' faithful housekeeper, for another year and returned several more times before her death in 1933. Her ashes were buried with the Beachcomber in his grave just above the resort.

After her death the Banfields' part of the island was taken over by their friend, Townsville businessman Spenser Hopkins and their bungalow became the main building in a small resort in 1934. A year later Hopkins sold most of the Banfield part of Dunk, keeping only the small section where today the artists' colony is located. During WW II the RAAF set up a radar station on top of Mt Kootaloo which played a part in the Battle of the Coral Sea, the turning point in the Pacific war. The rusty remains of the radar equipment can still be seen today. Various changes of ownership followed the war until in 1978

TAA, since renamed Australian Airlines, took over sole control of the resort.

The Resort

Dunk is a large resort owned by Australian Airlines. At peak capacity it accommodates about 400 people but despite this it manages to avoid being a real mass market resort like South Molle or Great Keppel – the food is better, the activities somewhat lower key, things are done with a little more taste and style. Perhaps it's some rub-off from the island's interesting history although poor Banfield's name is exploited shamelessly – you could imagine the Beachcomber turning in his grave, only a couple of hundred metres away, at the thought of the Banfield disco or island night at the Beachcomber bar.

The resort's comfortable style is also somewhat of a miracle when you look at its quite appalling architecture and planning. Whoever designed this one deserves to be pushed off the top of Mt Kootaloo. The rooms are out of the plonk-down-a-box style of architecture and the public rooms are straight from the nearest aircraft hangar design catalogue. Even the resort's fancy Banfield Restaurant occupies a corner of the games room and the whole resort looks as if it was planned on a plain piece of paper without a moment's thought to the island and its environment. It's no wonder that Mark Connor, the poet who worked for a time as the resort's gardener, wrote:

The architect said: 'Those huts
they had me build? For God's sake bury them!
Shrubs, creepers, trees, ferns, anything,
I'll back you to the hilt'.

It's enlightening to compare Dunk, with its urban-motel-square-box-style of the '60s and early '70s with the delightful (but very expensive!) merge-into-the-jungle late '80s architecture of nearby Bedarra.

Flora & Fauna

The Beachcombers long and enlightened study of his island has focused a great deal of interest on the natural wonders of Dunk and his writing forms a wonderful basis for a closer study of the island. Like the Aboriginals, for whom Banfield had so much respect, he was a keen observer of nature and his books provide anecdotes, lists, observations and insights into the island's luxuriant vegetation, numerous birds and other natural features. That Banfield was such a keen observer despite the handicap of having lost one eye simply makes you respect the man all the more.

Dunk's rainforest vegetation is a direct result of its heavy rainfall. The towns on the nearby mainland annually tot up the highest rainfall figures in Australia and although Dunk doesn't quite reach the same dampness it's definitely in the same league. When it rains in these parts it really rains. The result may be disheartening at times for holidaymakers chasing the sun but for the vegetation it's terrific.

The island harbours a rich variety of birds, in which the Beachcomber was keenly interested. The scrub fowl or megapode is one of the most interesting of the Family Island birds. A little smaller than a domestic chicken the megapode hen lays an enormous egg which it covers in a huge mound of decaying vegetation. The heat generated by the rotting leaves and other vegetable matter incubates the eggs. The mounds can be several metres across and a couple of metres high, so large that they're easily mistaken for some natural feature. You will often hear the megapode's loud cackle and may glimpse them scampering away as you approach.

The yellow-breasted sunbird is a complete contrast – 'sired by a sunbeam, born of a flower, gaiety its badge,' wrote an obviously entranced Beachcomber. The brilliant yellow little bird hovers like a hummingbird while dipping its long curved bill into flowers. A great many other birds can be heard in the rainforest or seen flitting amongst the trees in the resort.

The animal life on Dunk is as sparse as the birds are prolific. Despite the proximity of the mainland Dunk has no wallabies, no possums, no large mammals at all, introduced species like feral pigs apart. There are echidnas (spiny ant-eaters), bats, some rats including Banfield's own unique rat, the fruit-eating *Uromys banfieldi,* and plenty of lizards but that's about it in the non-aerial department.

Dunk does, however, have another aerial wonder and that is the wonderful butterflies seen all over the island including Australia's two protected insects, the Cairns birdwing and the Ulysses. The Ulysses has become the symbol of the island and although some fear they are not as prolific as during the Beachcomber's days if you're observant you should be able to spot some of these large and spectacular butterflies. The resort even does its best to aid butterfly spotting by way of its butterfly garden, complete with the flowers and plants a butterfly likes best and even butterfly feeding stations.

The Ulysses is a big butterfly with a wingspan claimed to often exceed 10 cm. The Ulysses's wings are edged with black and coloured deep, brilliant blue, like 'a flake of sky'. Apart from its size and bright colouring the Ulysses is also remarkable for its speed. This is no gently fluttering creature, it zooms across the sky like a hunting bird.

How time flies on Dunk Island.

Information

Reception is open from 8.30 am to 5.30 pm. If you're leaving the island outside those hours plan ahead, the resort is very much geared to visitors coming and going by plane. The resort phone number is (070) 68 8199. There are a couple of pay phones by reception but there are no phones in the rooms. A Commonwealth Savings Bank agency is operated at the reception desk and passbook withdrawals can be made.

There's a small shop next to reception with the usual island selection of toiletries, clothes, magazines, postcards and the like. There is usually a good selection of Dunk books including *Confessions of a Beachcomber*.

Children Dunk is a family resort and children are taken good care of, especially at school vacation time. A children's meal time is organised and there is free child minding during the following adult's meal time.

Beaches

Dunk has some fine beaches although at low tide the water is often far too shallow to be enjoyable, and weedy to boot. There's no great snorkelling around Dunk either. The main beaches include north facing Brammo Bay, the sweep of sand right in front of the resort. At the Spit the beach turns the corner and becomes Pallon Beach, an equally long and fine stretch of sand facing south-west. At low tide you can wade across to nearby Kumboola Island. Purtaboi, directly north of Brammo Bay, is off limits when birds are nesting there.

Only a short stroll from the resort is Muggy Muggy Beach, pleasantly quiet and secluded. The resort information booklet recommends it as a beach where you can 'get the kind of tan you can't show your friends'. Finally you can walk an hour or so south to the long stretch of Coconut Beach. There are other smaller beaches, like Naturist's Beach, which you can reach by rock hopping even further south.

Dunk is very close to the mainland and although reportedly the dreaded box jellyfish have not been spotted around the island it's conceivable they could get this far out from the coast during the November to March danger period. The resort doesn't make any fuss about them although the presence of large containers of vinegar kept by the beaches shows that somebody has been thinking about their possible presence. If jellyfish were present the beaches least likely to have them would be north facing Brammo Bay and Muggy Muggy Beach.

Walks

Dunk has 13 km of walking tracks and you can walk almost all of it in one 10 km circuit which is one of the most interesting and enjoyable walks to be found on any of the Barrier Reef islands. The walk runs most of the length of the island and includes the 271 metre summit of Mt Kootaloo, highest point on the island. Although the walk can be made in either direction it's probably best to walk

Banfields' grave, Dunk Island (TW)

it clockwise as you can then follow the steep climb to the peak and the long descent along the ridge which forms the island's backbone with a pleasant pause and swim at Coconut Bay. The walk takes about three hours but with a picnic break on the beach that can easily be extended to an all day stroll. If you're a guest at the resort they'll pack you a picnic lunch to take on your walk.

Starting from the northern edge of the resort the walk first of all stops by the Banfields' grave and almost immediately there's the turn-off to Muggy Muggy Beach. For a short time the walk follows alongside a deep gully – Dunk's heavy rainfall means the many streams run noisily for much of the year. The trail then crosses the gully by a picturesque swing bridge and then starts to climb the hillside. Occasionally there are views out over Brammo Bay and the resort but much of the time you walk in deep shade from the dense rainforest. During the January to March wet season it can be extremely humid and you can work up a prodigious sweat. By the time you reach the top of the peak your clothes will be soaking.

Eventually you reach a signposted junction where the trail meets the circuit track around the top of Mt Kootaloo. From here you can continue directly to Palm Valley, but the longer and more interesting way is following the Mt Kootaloo sign to the left. This takes you right around the peak to the turn-off to the actual summit before continuing on to Palm Valley. A sign here points out to Battleship Rock, Goold Island and Hinchinbrook Island. This is rather misleading as what you actually see so clearly in front of you is Kumboola Island, Thorpe Island and Bedarra Island! Battleship Rock is the bare rock rising just to the east of Bedarra and Goold and Hinchinbrook are far back in the background.

The short spur leads off from here to the summit, topped by the rusting, crumpled remains of a WW II radar installation. The trail actually continues beyond that point a short distance before fading out. Backtracking down to the circuit track you then turn right and descend steeply to a junction

signposted back to the resort and on, again, to Palm Valley. If you head back to the resort you soon reach the earlier junction where you started the circuit of the peak. The straightforward Resort-Mt Kootaloo-Resort round trip takes about two hours.

Continuing on the longer walk you follow the ridge line towards Palm Valley dropping down to a saddle then climbing up again, passing an easily missed turn-off back to the resort via the farm area and eventually reaching the Coconut Beach Lookout – where you may not be able to see the beach unless the vegetation has been cut back recently! From here the trail descends slowly following a stream bordered by palms in the aptly named Palm Valley. Eventually the trail reaches the coast and immediately doubles back towards the resort, running only a few metres away from the beach.

As at other Dunk beaches the water can be very shallow if the tide is low but this is still a pleasant place for a break. At the resort end of the beach there's a picnic table and here you will have to head back on to the trail as beyond the rocky headland the shore is fringed with mangrove swamps. The trail climbs around the headland, passes the entrance to the artists' colony and crosses a swiftly flowing little stream before running along the edge of the farm back to the resort. At the airstrip you can either walk along the roadway on the inland side or cross to the beach and walk down to the sandspit point along Pallon Beach.

This one walk encompasses almost all the walking track on the island. The other alternatives are to take the shortcut down from the ridge track through the farm to the resort or to rock hop along the coast from Coconut Beach south to Staff Beach and Naturist's Beach. The coastal track from the resort round to Muggy-muggy Beach is less than a km in length.

Banfield & the Gardens

Unfortunately very little trace remains of Banfield's time on the island. For a time his house was used as the basis of the small resort on the island in the '30s. As the resort grew the original structure was lost in extensions, renovations and rebuilds and at some time, probably in the 1940s, it disappeared completely. Similarly his carefully tended gardens have also disappeared although the overgrown area around his grave was once the homestead garden and keen botanists could probably find traces of the tropical fruit trees he spent so much time and energy growing. The stately avenue of palm trees which led up to his cottage do remain, they now lead from the resort up to the staff quarters. And, of course, the modern resort farm is a direct descendant of the small farm Banfield once tended.

At one time the resort gardener tried to follow Banfield's earlier aim to grow a wide variety of tropical fruit trees. Although that vision appears to have been shelved the resort's gardens are lush, colourful, carefully tended and a real delight. There's a weekly walking tour of the resort gardens and the garden staff are always happy to talk about their work.

Artists' Colony

The Family Islands seem to attract artists, with Noel Wood having spent many years on Bedarra, and Deanna Conti a long term resident on Timana. Dunk's artist is Bruce Arthur, a former Olympic wrestler, who has lived on Dunk Island since the early '70s weaving large tapestries. He leases an area of land beyond the resort farm together with a number of other artists who form a small artists' colony. The colony welcomes visitors on Tuesday and Friday mornings when they charge you $2 and give you a brief introduction to the island and their activities and an opportunity to purchase their work.

Activities

The resort has the usual range of resort activities including squash and tennis courts, a small golf course, two swimming pools and a variety of indoor activities. More unusual activities include horse riding, archery and a clay target shooting range. A weekly cricket match between staff and guests is organised.

Watersports activities includes wind-

surfers, catamarans and paddle skis (all free to guests) plus outboard dinghies, water skiing and parasailing (which cost extra). Visitors to the island who are not staying at the resort can still use some of the resort's equipment – windsurfers and catamarans are hired out for $10 an hour, paddle skis for $5.

The resort's farm runs a small herd of dairy cows which provide milk for the resort. Children enjoy a farm visit and at milking time (5 to 6.30 am and from around 3.30 to 4 pm) there are free milkshakes!

Cruises

The high-speed catamaran *MV Quick Cat* makes daily trips to Beaver Cay on the Great Barrier Reef. Departures are at 10.30 am, returning at 3.30 pm and the cost of $78 includes lunch. It takes about 50 minutes to get out to the reef where you can snorkel, observe the reef through a glass bottom boat or from a semi-submersible, or certified divers can get a couple of dives in.

Day cruises on the *Neptunius* operate around the Family Islands and cost $55. They also do a sunset cruise for $30 or fishing enthusiasts can get out on the *Hooker*. The water taxi operator which shuttles back and forth between Dunk and the mainland also does a daily 'Around the Islands' cruise which lasts about 1½ hours and costs just $26. Trips to the mainland are also arranged. Helicopter flights are made from Dunk out to the reef or scenic flights over Hinchinbrook Island and flights to Orpheus Island to see the clam research station.

Accommodation

The Resort The resort's 141 rooms are of three types, costs per person are:

	one person	two people
Banfield	$203	$168
Garden Cabanas	$227	$187
Beachfront	$262	$224

The tariff includes all meals in the Beachcomber Restaurant and most activities – generally it's the powered activities which cost extra. The older Banfield and Garden

Artists' colony, Dunk Island (TW)

Cabana rooms are mostly set back from the bayfront while the Beachfront units face the water. They all have attached bathroom, ceiling fans, a patio or verandah, a refrigerator and tea/coffee making equipment. Beachfront rooms have air conditioning as well as ceiling fans. There are laundry blocks with washing machines and driers. Although the rooms are basically straightforward boxes they're quite comfortable and the lush Dunk greenery certainly helps to hide them.

Camping Like Great Keppel, further to the south, Dunk is a resort island where you can also camp. Most of the island is national park and camping is permitted at the camp site right across from the jetty on the sandspit at the north-west end of the island. A permit is needed from the QNPWS in Cardwell. The site has toilets, tables and fireplaces and drinking water is available. There is a maximum limit of 30 campers at any one time and a maximum stay of three days.

Food

Dunk's dining possibilities should keep most people happy. There's always the risk at larger resorts of the food becoming an exercise in tropical island pub food. Mealtime in the main *Beachcomber* restaurant when the resort is busy can involve feeding 400 guests but fortunately they seem to cope with aplomb. Breakfast is the usual buffet style but there's plenty of fresh fruit, a wide choice of cereals and hot food from food warmers as well. Lunch is also usually a serve yourself affair with salads, cold meat and seafood, and the food warmers coming into operation again for hot dishes.

Dinner is served from a menu with a choice of starters, main courses and dessert. It's good food, pleasantly served and backed up by a solid if not inspired wine list with a variety of wines from around $18 to $26. Friday night at Dunk is seafood night which again is a serve-yourself operation with a mouth watering choice of food. Mud crabs, prawns, crayfish and lobster are all there in profusion and there's an equally mouth-watering choice of desserts. If you're worried about your waistline avoid Friday night at Dunk.

As well as the main restaurant Dunk has a second possibility in the smaller *Banfield's Restaurant*. There's a similar menu but with more inspired and exotic choices – lobster, buffalo, duck, even crocodile might feature on the menu and the food is excellent. Like everything else at Dunk the location and architecture don't do anything for the restaurant, in fact it's not even that easy to find the entrance to Banfields, but once you're seated it's fine. Dinner at Banfields costs a flat $27.50 per person – that's an additional charge to your otherwise food-inclusive tariff.

Banfields is not open every night so if you plan to eat there check first which nights it is open. In the Beachcomber you're likely to find the usual (for Barrier Reef resorts) short-age of tables for two – if you want a romantic tête-à-tête or simply don't feel like making new acquaintances it's wise to book a table at breakfast time, or earlier. Outsiders can also eat in the Beachcomber restaurant, meal costs are $10 for breakfast, $20 for lunch (not great value), $25 for dinner or $30 on the Friday seafood night.

Campers or day visitors to the island (or resort guests who can't last from one meal to the next) can also find food at the Jetty Bar where there's a typical fast food cafe featuring a variety of burgers from $2.50, fish, chips and salad for $5.50 and other similar possibilities. Resort guests who are hungry but not that hungry can also raid the coolers by the swimming pool and in the main bar which are kept stocked with a variety of fruit. Or there's tea, coffee, biscuits and fruitcake also on free call in the main bar.

Getting There & Away

Dunk is off Tully at Brammo Bay and also serves as the jumping-off point for neighbouring Bedarra Island.

Air Dunk has an airstrip and there are regular flights to and from Cairns (40 minutes, $75)

and Townsville (45 minutes, $83). Dunk is also the arrival point for guests bound for nearby Bedarra Island.

Sea Water taxis operate several times daily to Dunk Island from Mission Beach Resort (tel (070) 68 8310) at Wongaling Beach and from South Mission Beach (tel (070) 68 8333). The *MV Quick Cat* also operate Clump Point to the island prior to its daily Beaver Cay reef trip, and from the island to Clump Point after the trip. There are a couple of other services between Clump Point and Dunk each day. Any of these services to or from Dunk Island cost $7 one-way. There's also a Dunk Island hovercraft service.

Day trips to the island with the *Quick Cat* (tel (070) 68 7289) from Mission Beach cost $14 or $18 with lunch, children are half price. The MV *Lawrench Kavanagh* (tel (070) 68 7211) does Dunk Island trips from $11 or with lunch from $16 to $20. A longer cruise around other islands in the Family group costs $26 including lunch. Transport for children under 10 is free, they pay $2 for lunch.

Bedarra Island

Area: 1 square km
Type: continental rainforest, privately owned
High point: 107 metres
Maximum visitor population: 32 in each of the two resorts
Per person daily cost: $400
In brief: Two tiny and recently completely rebuilt resorts which are operated by Australian Airlines and aim to be exclusive, luxurious, sophisticated. They're also very expensive, no day visitors are allowed and no children under 15.

The Island

Bedarra Island is just six km south of Dunk and about five km offshore. The island is shown as Richards Island on marine charts but not on general maps. Like Dunk it's a rainforest island with natural springs and plentiful water. In fact the amount of fresh water which wells up from Bedarra's springs is quite out of kilter with the small size of the island. Bedarra is a rocky, hilly island cloaked in rainforest and fringed with some fine, sandy beaches, a short stretch of mangroves and wildly tumbled collections of giant boulders. Off the south-east end of the island is tiny Pee-Rahm-Ah Island, also known as Battleship Rock.

Like the other islands of the Family Group Bedarra has had an earlier history of Aboriginal habitation and it has subsequently had an interesting and varied European history. The publication of Banfield's *Confessions* (see the Dunk Island section) flushed numerous other would be beachcombers out of the woodwork including Captain Henry Allason who came over from England in 1913, sought Banfield's advice on a suitable island and purchased the whole of Bedarra from the Queensland Land Department for £20! They threw in Timana Island as well. Allason set up home near the sandspit where today you find the Hideaway Resort and soon became locally famous for setting out on long dis-

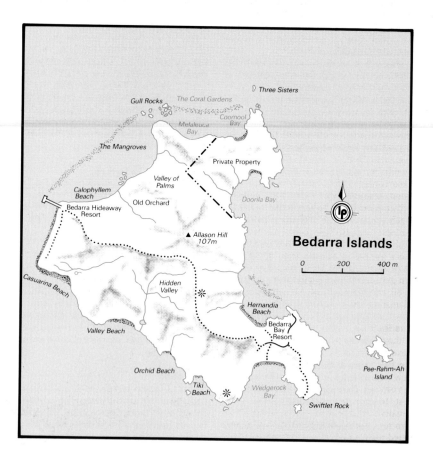

Bedarra Islands

tance swims from one island to another! Unfortunately for the captain his spell of island lotus eating was a short one. Only a year later WW I erupted in Europe, he was called up and was gassed in France during one of the notorious episodes of chemical warfare. Although he survived, the rest of his life was spent convalescing in Nice in the south of France.

Allason's £20 investment proved to be a sound one, however, as he sold the island during the 1920s to Ivan Menzies for £500. Menzies' plan to turn the island into a home for underprivileged English boys came to nothing and in 1934 he sold the island to a group known as the Harris syndicate. The Harris group also failed to make anything of their island ownership although in 1936 they did sell a corner of the island to the Australian artist Noel Wood. He built a home on the peninsula between Doorilla and Coomool Bay and over 50 years later, now an old man, he's still there!

The rest of the island went back and forth between various parties until in 1940 the Englishman Dick Greatrix and the Frenchman Pierre Huret bought the whole thing and established the gardens of the Hideaway Resort at the sandspit end. Meanwhile John Busst, another artist, leased the south-east corner of the island and his homestead eventually became the Plantation Resort, now Bedarra Bay. In 1947 Greatrix and Huret sold out to the Bussts and in subsequent years more owners came and went before TAA (now Australian Airlines) bought the northern part, including the Hideaway Resort, in 1980 and the southern part, including the Plantation Resort, in 1981.

The Resorts

Although Bedarra's two resorts have a long history with guests first staying here during the 1940s the current resorts are both brand new creations of the late 1980s. Both resorts are owned by Australian Airlines, both have just 16 individual cottages so full house usually means only 32 guests. Although the two resorts are totally separate they're marketed together and cost the same, so if you stay at one you're quite welcome to stroll over to the other for lunch, try out their swimming pool, lie on their beach or sail one of their catamarans. It's a 45 minute 'strenuous' walk between the two resorts so not many guests pop over to try the other one for dinner!

The two Bedarra resorts are small, exclusive and very expensive but they interpret the words 'all-inclusive' in a novel way. At other resorts the tariff may include all your meals and non-powered equipment like windsurfers and catamarans, some let you use powered equipment as well, but at Bedarra absolutely everything is included. The bar, for example, doesn't have a barman. If you feel like a bottle of Moet & Chandon champagne you just stroll over to the cooler and help yourself – and some legendary tales of Moet & Chandon consumption have leaked out of Bedarra! If you want to take an outboard powered dinghy to find your own private beach that's included too. The staff will pack you up a picnic Esky (complete with the Moet & Chandon if you wish!) and off you go.

Information

The postal addresses and phone numbers for the resorts are Hideaway Resort (tel (070) 68 8168) via Dunk Island, via Townsville, Qld 4810, and Bedarra Bay Resort (tel (070) 68 8233) Bedarra Island, via Townsville, Qld 4810.

There's a small 'shop' in each resort with essentials like suntan lotion, toiletries, cigarettes, postcards and the like. You help yourself and note what you've taken to be charged to your account.

Walking track sign, Bedarra Island (TW)

Walks

There's only one real walk on Bedarra and that's the 1½ km stroll from one resort to another. The walk through dense rainforest takes half an hour to 45 minutes and is rated by the resorts as 'strenuous', which it probably is for some of their elderly guests. It can also be rather slippery if there has been heavy rain but if you give the other resort a little warning you're quite welcome to stroll over to the other side in the morning, laze around and have lunch and if you don't feel like walking back there is often a boat going by in the afternoon.

Starting from the Bedarra Bay end the trail commences only a few steps beyond the dining room terrace and almost immediately climbs steeply upwards eventually reaching the resort's water tank and then continuing upwards to a lookout with a survey marker on a large rock beside the track. Through the trees you can see down over Hernandia Beach and the resort but this is the only view you glimpse on the whole walk. The entire rest of the way you are in dense, lush rainforest – which doesn't mean there isn't plenty to see. There are flowers, creepers, ferns, the twittering of birds, the towering mounds of megapode nests and if you're lucky an occasional glimpse of the bird itself.

From the lookout the trail undulates gently, passing a short distance to the south of 107 metre Allason Hill, the highest point on the island. At about the half way mark a sign nailed to a tree announces that you have crossed 'The Border' and the trail then drops gently down to the Hideaway Resort, coming out on the path up to the staff quarters, behind the resort. Very frequent yellow paint marks along the trail make it virtually impossible to lose your way and on what other bush walking trail in Australia will somebody phone ahead to make sure the champagne is waiting for you on ice?

A shorter alternative walk starts from just behind the Bedarra Bay tennis court and winds up to Swiftlet Rock overlooking Battleship Rock, Wheeler Island and The Triplets. It's a fine view across these other islands but you're asked not to climb on the rocks as this is one of the few nesting places of the grey swiftlet.

Beaches

Bedarra has some great beaches – Wedgerock and Hernandia Beaches, on each side of the Bedarra Bay resort, are particularly fine, as is the sandspit at Bedarra Hideaway. Doorila Bay, facing straight towards Hernandia and the Bedarra Bay resort, was commended by Banfield as the prettiest spot in the Family Islands but that's artist Noel Wood's private domain. There are several other small beaches around the western side of the island, accessible by dinghy. Officially the resort dinghies can only be taken 500 metres offshore but in practice they probably do tend to go a bit further afield on calm days. Nearby Wheeler island has a fine sandspit beach and it's certainly not likely to be too crowded!

Activities

Bedarra is not a heavy activity resort but the catamarans, windsurfers, paddle skis are all waiting right out front and since there are few people you rarely have to queue up to use them. There's also a tennis court at each resort and, of course, a swimming pool and spa. The lounge/bar area in each resort has a TV and video recorder although on rainy days you might wish they had a few more videos as well. The Hideaway Resort subscribes to the Great Barrier Reef Marine Park Authority's quarterly *Reef Report* videos which make interesting viewing.

Cruises

The resort will transfer you over to Dunk Island to join Barrier Reef cruises or helicop-

Wheeler Island, near Bedarra Island (TW)

ter flights from there and the fishing charter boat *The Hooker* and local island cruise boat *Neptunius* will also operate from Bedarra. These boats cost $750 a day but the resort often organises parties of six to eight for the fishing trips or 10 to 15 for the local island cruises.

Accommodation

Both resorts were rebuilt by Byron Bay architect Christine Vadasz and they're both delightful. Bedarra Bay was reopened after its total rebuild in 1986 and from the bay in front of the resort the 16 cottages are virtually completely hidden in the rainforest. Each cottage has a two level room with a sleeping area above and a living area below (a few steps lower in some, under a mezzanine level in others). Out front there's a verandah where you can laze, getting glimpses of the sea and the rocky island coast. The rooms are very pleasant indeed, luxurious enough but maintaining an island feeling. At Bedarra you know you're on an island, not in some faceless five star resort.

Bedarra Bay actually has two bays, the main resort building and most of the cottages overlook Hernandia Beach, a couple more cottages look out on to Wedgerock Bay on the other side of the peninsula. The two bays are only minutes walk apart so you can easily switch beaches as the sun, the wind or the mood dictates. They're both very fine beaches, Bedarra is blessed with some of the nicest beaches to be found on the Barrier Reef islands.

At the other end of the island the Hideaway Resort offers a very similar package. Again there are 16 units and although Vadasz was again the architect they're quite different in design although each room has it's own sleeping and living area and a verandah out front. There's a central dining and bar area and swimming pool. Bedarra Hideaway doesn't have two separate bays like Bedarra Bay but it does have that long golden sandspit so if the sun's off one side or the wind's on the other you only have to switch sides.

Daily cost at either Bedarra resort is $400 per person. As noted above that is very 'all inclusive', it's rather like being a guest at the home of a very rich friend!

Food

The Bedarra resort's small size and high costs are reflected in the food – they can afford to cater for personal whims and if you want to indulge yourself they'll go out of their way to help you. If your idea of tropical island eating is oysters and lobster for every meal I'm sure they'd lay it on for you. So the menu on offer need only be a starting point although most visitors will find it quite interesting enough.

Breakfast is the usual combination of serve yourself juices, fruit and cereals followed by toast, croissants, muffins or a full cooked breakfast if you wish. Tropical fruits, apart from the usual melons, papaya and passionfruit, might include exotics like tamarillos or slices of custard apple. Lunch is served from a menu with interesting light dishes like a cold champagne and fruit soup or an avocado and lime soup, followed by a spicy Thai salad or more conventional meat or fish dishes. Of course many guests take an outboard dinghy and picnic off to find their own beach, or cross over to the other resort to see how the other half live.

Dinner is usually preceded by drinks and hors d'oeuvres in the serve yourself bar and the resort's small guest list makes it a pleasantly social occasion. You can also scan the dinner menu at this point and decide what wine to take down from the shelf and into dinner with you. Again there's an interesting and imaginative menu, Bedarra may be expensive but few people complain that they don't get their money's worth.

Getting There & Away

Bedarra is reached from Dunk, a 20 minute boat ride away. The Bedarra boat connects with Dunk flights or the water taxis between the mainland and Dunk.

Other Family Islands

The five small national park islands of the Family Group are Wheeler, Coombe, Smith, Bowden and Hudson Islands. They cover a total of 1.2 square km and their tangled vegetation is strongly influenced by the prevailing winds. The windswept south-eastern side of the islands is covered in a tangle of casuarinas, wattles and eucalypts while the sheltered northern side has grander and more stately stands of figs, palms, milky pine, satin ash and other rainforest species. The prevailing winds and seas have also formed sand spits on the island's north-west sides; these provide convenient sheltered landing areas for boats.

Between Bedarra and Dunk lies privately owned Timana Island where Deanna Conti, an artist and wool tapestry weaver has lived for many years. There are also a couple of smaller national park islands just off Dunk.

Tiny Purtaboi lies just to the north-west, incoming or outgoing flights generally pass over it. Kumboola Island and Mung-Um-Gnackum Island, a mere dot on the map, are just to the south-west.

Camping

With a permit from the Cardwell QNPWS office you can camp on Wheeler, Coombe or Bowden Islands. There are tables and fireplaces at the campsites but no toilet facilities and only Wheeler has freshwater and then only during the cooler months. The maximum number of campers is limited to 20 on Wheeler Island, to 10 on Coombe and Bowden Islands.

Getting There & Away

Charter boats operate to these island from Clump Point jetty at Mission Beach or from Cardwell. There are also boat ramps at Hull River and Tully River.

Sponges

Sponges are amongst the most primitive of multi-celled creatures, in fact reefs were probably formed from sponge skeletons long before coral took over the reef construction business. Sponges still play a part in the growth of a reef as they bore into the coral as they grip it and are a major factor in breaking down the limestone in a reef to eventually form the sand which can grow into a coral cay.

Sponges feed by filtering bacteria out of the water which they do in amazing volume and with phenomenal efficiency. A sponge can typically handle their own volume of water every five to 20 seconds and continue doing that 24 hours a day. As the water passes through their body up to 99% of the bacteria is filtered out.

Despite this efficiency sponges have to look for additional ways to handle the nutrition they need. Some sponges have a form rather like a chimney and passing currents draw water up through the sponge. Most sponges also act as a home to blue-green algae, which pay rent by providing the host sponge with a share of their photosynthetic nutrient production. Other less welcome tenants also find that sponges make a good home – small crabs, shrimps, worms and even brittle stars often take up residence in a sponge's tubes and passages. ■

Yellow-red vasiform
sponge

Sea Cucumbers or Bêche-de-Mer

The sea cucumber, trepang or bêche-de-mer is another variety of echinoderm. They are typically cucumber like in shape but with a soft, leathery feel. There are a variety of types including *Holothuria*, *Stichopus* and *Thelonota*. You can see them scattered across shallow reef flats where they feed either on plankton or by filtering sand. Their mouth is at one end, their anus at the other and some varieties will, when alarmed, expel long sticky threads from their anus as a defence mechanism. Sea cucumbers are quite harmless.

Bêche-de-mer were one of Australia's earliest export industries, for sea cucumbers are a noted Asian delicacy and a ready market was found for them from the 1840s. The sea cucumbers were easily harvested at low tide and cheap Aboriginal and Torres Strait Islander labour then performed the messy task of gutting, boiling and smoking them. A 'nasty stinking business' commented the Government Resident on Thursday Island. ■

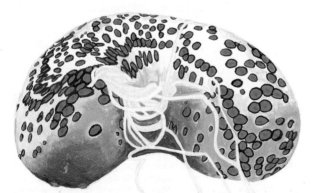

Leopard sea cucumber

Islands off Cairns

Cairns is the biggest tourist centre along the Great Barrier Reef and there is a constant stream of vessels heading out to the islands and reefs off the coast. Cairns has two popular islands, Fitzroy and Green Islands, both of which attract lots of day-trippers (too many some think) and some overnighters too. Just up the coast off Port Douglas is Low Isle, another popular cay for day-tripping although nowhere near as commercialised as Green Island.

There are also numerous reefs, popular targets for the hordes of scuba divers who every day head out from Cairns on diving trips. Tiny Michaelmas Cay with its huge population of seabirds is one of the most popular destinations from Cairns. Further north is Lizard Island – an expensive and exclusive hideaway and certainly not overrun by tourist hordes at all.

Getting There & Away

There is an armada of tourist operators out of Cairns but Great Adventures, who operate the resorts at Fitzroy and Green Islands and a fleet of high speed catamarans are the big name. They have numerous services and cruises operating to the two islands and to the other reefs and cays. Details follows under the relevant islands below.

If a high-speed catamaran or wavepiercer still isn't fast enough there are helicopter trips out to the reef as well. Contact Heliventure (tel (070) 53 5765) or Helijet (tel (070) 52 1244) for details. Cairns Seaplane Airways (tel (070) 50 5777) or Aquaflight Airways (tel (070) 51 3893 or 51 9566) will also wing you out to isolated islands and reefs in their floatplanes.

Fitzroy Island

Area: 4 square km
Type: continental
High point: 266 metres
Maximum visitor population: 144 in resort plus 50 campers
Per person daily cost: approximately $140 in the villas
In brief: A continental island close to the coast a little south of Cairns, principally a day trip island but with a small resort operated by Great Adventures.

The Island

Six km off the coast and 26 km south-east of Cairns, Fitzroy Island has been developed as a resort island since 1981 although there has been a lighthouse on the island and other activity from far earlier.

Fitzroy is a larger continental island with beaches which are covered in coral so they are not ideal for swimming and sunbaking. There's good coral for snorkelling only 50 metres off the beach in the resort area. The island also has its own dive school.

The island was named by Captain Cook after the Duke of Grafton, a noted politician of the era with a reputation for putting more effort into wine, women and horse racing than government. Phillip King stopped on Fitzroy in 1819 and his good report on the anchorage, freshwater and supplies of timber made Welcome Bay, where the resort is located, a popular shelter for passing ships.

In 1877 the island was made a quarantine station for Chinese immigrants bound for the north Queensland goldfields. New arrivals were supposed to stay there for 16 days to ensure they were free of smallpox and there were soon 3000 of them squeezed on to the island. Inevitably the miserable conditions led to a violent dispute with the colonial authorities and the island still has a number

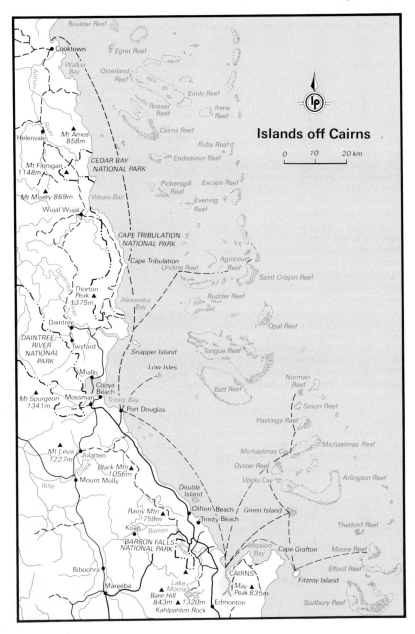

Islands off Cairns

0   10   20 km

of Chinese graves from that period. Fitzroy also had a bêche-de-mer business for a time.

Information

The resort phone number is (070) 51 9588, fax number is (070) 52 1335 and the address is Fitzroy Island, PO Box 2120, Cairns, Qld 4870. There are pay phones in the visitors' centre.

Activities

The resort has catamarans, windsurfers, paddleskis and other equipment for hire and there's a swimming pool in the main resort area but otherwise this is a resort where you make your own amusements.

Beaches & Snorkelling

Fitzroy's beaches are not ideal for lazy sunbaking and dabbling in ankle deep water. The Welcome Bay beach in front of the resort is made up of broken coral so it's not very comfortable for lying on. It also shelves off very steeply from the shore so you're out of your depth within a few paces. On the other hand there is some good coral for snorkelling only a few strokes out from the shore at both ends of the main resort beach.

A short walk round from the resort area to the south-west brings you to Nudey Beach. The sand here is much better and it's reputed to be a good place to collect an overall suntan.

For those not inclined to get wet the resort has a semi-submersible which conducts regular inspections of the island's excellent fringing reef for $12 (children $6).

Diving

Fitzroy can be a good place to do a diving course, safe from the day-to-day distractions of Cairns, with good diving water right offshore and the Great Barrier Reef itself not far out. Peter Boundy's Dive Centre offers a five dive, four day course for $240 or an eight dive, five day course including outer Barrier Reef dives for $290.

If you're coming out to Fitzroy to dive there are daily trips out to Moore Reef and hire of all equipment including one tank of air costs $36 per day.

Walks

Fitzroy has several good walks through the island's lush and often surprisingly dense rainforest or up the boulder strewn slopes to the peak.

Secret Garden Walk Starting from behind the Rainforest Restaurant a 20 minute stroll follows a damp valley running inland with dense rainforest vegetation embellished with ferns and creepers. The walk ends at a picturesque jumble of boulders topped by ferns.

Lighthouse & Peak Circuit A pleasant two hour walk will take you to the lighthouse at the north-east end of the island and on to the island's highpoint then back down to the resort. The walk starts past the bunkrooms and campsite and first of all passes the giant clam breeding centre. Here research is being conducted to commercially breed the giant reef clams whose numbers have been severely reduced by Asian poachers. After initially raising the clams in tanks they are transplanted to the reef just off the island.

The lighthouse walk runs up an often very steep paved vehicle track with glimpses of Green Island to the north. A lighthouse was originally established here in 1943 and rebuilt in 1959 and again in 1973. The most recent rebuild has left an extremely inelegant structure, seemingly designed by the Australian government's public toilet architectural team. It's one of the few manned lighthouses in Australia and inspections can be arranged from Monday to Friday between 10 am to 2 pm if you phone in advance. If you just walk up to the lighthouse all you'll find is an impressive collection of 'no entry' signs.

Retrace your steps down from the lighthouse and another paved vehicle track branches off east and climbs up to the site of a now demolished building. From here the walk is a real walking track and climbs steadily up the ridge line to the 266 metre peak which is Fitzroy's high point. There are good views northward from the huge boulders that are strewn around the top. Green Island is clearly visible.

From here the trail descends steadily towards the resort. There are some fine views down to the densely forested south-east end of the island. The slope here is littered with huge boulders and this part of the walk is known as The Boulders. At one point there are good views of the resort beach and the usual collection of yachts moored off the beach. Finally the walk leaves the drier high-altitude vegetation and re-enters the lusher rainforest close to the resort. Another lookout is reached just before the resort and you finally emerge directly behind the swimming pool bar.

Wildlife

The island has a wide variety of birds, butterflies, iguanas and even a kangaroo.

Accommodation

Although Fitzroy is to some extent a day trip island – fast catamarans shuttle out regularly from Cairns and the mainland is only a stone's throw away – there is also a variety of accommodation and the island is one of the few along the Great Barrier Reef with real possibilities for shoestring travellers. Overnight possibilities at Fitzroy come in three categories – Villas, Beach House Bungalows and the campsite.

The Villas Strung along the waterfront there are just eight of the villa units, straightforward but comfortable and quite attractive little units comprising a verandah out front, a bedroom with double bed, separated by the bathroom and the fridge and tea/coffee making area from a second mini-bedroom with a bunk bed unit. The units cost $158 as a single, $210 as a double and $53 for each

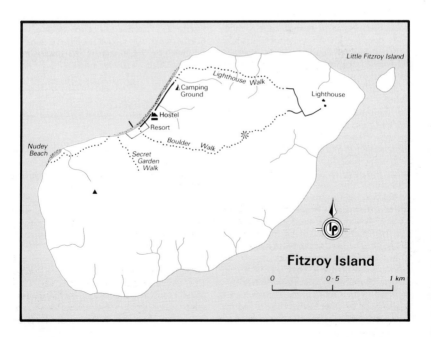

child. These costs include breakfast and dinner, you fend for yourself at lunchtime.

Beach House Bungalows Cairns is the backpackers' capital of the Queensland coast so it's only right there should be a backpackers' hostel on an island near Cairns. Fitzroy's Beach House Bungalows are typical bunkrooms for four; straightforward rooms with just two bunk units and a locker for each bed. Toilets and showers are shared and there's a kitchen and dining area plus plenty of fridge space.

Nightly costs are $24 for a bed or $85 if you take a whole room for four. Costs include bed linen (towels can be hired) but they are room only, meals are available at the visitors' area, the resort restaurant or you can fix your own food – either bringing supplies with you from Cairns or buying food from the rather limited supply at the island mini-market.

Campsite The villas and bunkrooms are both operated by Great Adventures, the island resort operator, but the campsite is managed on behalf of the local shire council. Daily rates are $10 for a site for two adults and two children. Permits must be obtained in advance from the Great Adventures Centre on Wharf St in Cairns.

Food
The mini-market by the bunkrooms sells a range of basic supplies for campers or backpackers intending to fix their own meals. Alternatively the visitors' centre around the swimming pool has a couple of mid-day eating possibilities. The kiosk is open from 8.30 am to 4 pm and does straightforward snacks and light meals of the fish & chips, reheated pizzas, pies, pasties and sandwiches variety. At lunchtime the *Flare Grill* does pub food like steak and chips, fish and salad and so on. There's also the *Mango Bar*, open from 10 am until late for drinks.

Villa residents have breakfast and dinner at the *Rainforest Restaurant* which is included in their room costs. The restaurant is also open to other island visitors and the food here is suprisingly good. For a complete meal of soup or starter, main course, dessert and coffee count on around $60 for two, plus drinks.

Getting There & Away
Great Adventures (tel (070) 51 0455), who operate the resorts at both Fitzroy and Green Islands, have a variety of excursions to Fitzroy. If you just want transport out to Fitzroy the return trip is $28, it takes about 45 minutes each way. A free pickup from your accommodation in Cairns is also included.

Day trip alternatives include a day out on Fitzroy including lunch and a trip on the semi-sub for $56. A trip out to Fitzroy with a two hour pause there, then continuing to Moore Reef (20 km further out), with lunch, use of snorkelling equipment and glass bottom boat coral viewing costs $66. Or you can combine Fitzroy and Green Islands – Cairns/Fitzroy/Green Island/Cairns with three hours on each island and lunch costs $70.

The *Reef Jet* does a $33 trip which visits Fitzroy and Green Island or you can take the *Reef Runner* for a visit to Fitzroy Island followed by 3½ hours on the outer reef. Phone (070) 51 8200 for either.

Green Island

Area: 13 hectares
Type: coral cay
High point: 3 metres
Maximum resident visitor population: 64
Per person daily cost: $180
In brief: small coral cay on the reef near Cairns, extremely popular for day trippers but also has a resort operated by Great Adventures. Major renovations are planned.

The Island
Offshore from Cairns, 27 km to the north-east, Green Island is a true coral cay. The island is only 660 metres long by 260 metres wide and rises only a few metres above sea level. The island and its surrounding reef is

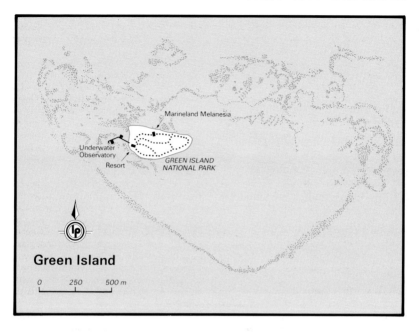

Marineland Melanesia

Underwater
Observatory

Resort

*GREEN ISLAND
NATIONAL PARK*

Green Island

0   250   500 m

all national park. The huge platform of coral debris which surrounds the island, and is indeed the island itself, is gradually being pushed north-westward by the prevailing currents. Green Island is by far the most accessible of the Barrier Reef's true coral cays.

The island was named by Captain Cook but not for its forest cover – Green was the chief astronomer on the *Endeavour*. In the 1870s, at the peak of the bêche de mer boom, the island was squabbled over by gatherers of that oriental delicacy and most of the island's trees were cut down for fires to boil the bêche-de-mer.

Local eccentric George 'Yorkey' Lawson later settled on the island which he claimed was haunted by victims of the bêche de mer battles. In the 1890s he started to develop the island as a picnic spot for Cairns residents and in 1937 the island, already suffering from over-use, was made into a national park. In 1974 the surrounding reef area was declared a marine park.

Although it also has overnight accommodation Green Island is essentially an extremely popular day trip from Cairns. Over 200,000 people a year visit the island! It's actually a really beautiful island although the down at heel resort certainly doesn't help it. That's all due to change as there are plans for a major redevelopment. Meanwhile, if you take a 10-minute stroll down to the other end of the island you can forget the tourist clutter is even there. The beach, right around the island, is beautiful, the water fine, the fish still reasonably prolific although the coral is not as extensive as it used to be in part due to that reef scourge the crown-of-thorns starfish. Although you can walk on the reef it's dependent upon visiting the island at the right tide time, check before you go if that is important to you. The island's vegetation makes an interesting contrast to the cays further south. Here it is denser, rainforest type vegetation, unlike the pisonia dominated cover of the southern cays.

Green Island (GBRMPA)

Information

The resort phone number is (070) 51 4644 and the address is Green Island Reef Resort, Cairns, Qld 4871.

Things to See

The time you get on the island on a typical day trip is quite enough to have a wander around it, go for a swim and see as many of the attractions as you need to. Even stopping at Green Island for just a couple of hours en route to Michaelmas Cay or the outer reef gives you enough time to have a reasonable explore of such a 'drop in the ocean'.

The man-made attractions start at the end of the pier with the now rather ancient and decidedly less than state-of-the-art underwater observatory where lots of fish can be seen around the windows five metres below sea-level. The old observatory was built in 1954 but it may soon be on its way out if the Great Adventure people manage to build their new underwater observatory which will be more

like a huge aquarium tank where visitors trundle round on what could be described as a semi-submersible on rails. If the design is approved it could be open in 1991.

Glass-bottom boats operate short trips from the pier too. On the island there's the Barrier Reef Theatre with films and Marineland Melanesia with a wide variety of fish and corals in aquarium tanks plus larger creatures (sharks, turtles, stingrays, crocodiles) in pools or enclosures, and a display of PNG art. Although there's an admission charge to each of these wonders of the reef if you come to Green Island on one of the day out trips (rather than the transport only trips) admission is likely to be included.

Accommodation & Food

The *Green Island Reef Resort* (tel (070) 51 4644) has Palm Units and slightly more expensive Tropical Units from around $280 for a double. This includes breakfast and dinner. The resort is primed for major renovations, just like the rest of the island.

Getting There & Away

Green Island is 27 km north-east of Cairns, about half way to the outer reef. There are a wide variety of day-trips to the island from Cairns, either simply to Green Island or combining it with Fitzroy, Michaelmas Cay or the outer reef.

Great Adventures (tel (070) 51 0455) are the main operator to Green Island and they will simply take you out and back for $20 by launch or $33 by fast catamaran. The return trip plus lunch and the various island activities will cost you $51. For $42 you can do a two island cruise which combines Fitzroy and Green Islands. Or for $70 you can have the same cruise but with lunch, underwater observatory, semi-sub ride and so on included. Finally you can go further afield, for $76 you can have two hours on Green Island plus a visit to Michaelmas Cay or for $95 you can have Green Island plus Norman Reef.

There are other operators to Green Island. The *Big Cat* (tel (070) 51 0444) does a straightforward return trip with five hours on the island for $20. The *Reef Jet* (tel (070) 51 8200) does a $33 day trip which visits Fitzroy and Green Island.

Other Islands from Cairns

A number of other islands are conveniently visited from Cairns as day trips. They include the Frankland Islands south of Fitzroy, Michaelmas Cay, a popular day trip north of Green Island, and the Low Islands, an enormously popular day trip from Port Douglas. Lots of diving trips head out to the reefs from Cairns, the fact that the reef is closer in to the mainland helps to make Cairns such a popular jumping-off point for these trips.

Diving Trips

There are numerous boats operating day or longer diving trips out of Cairns. Popular day trip targets out of Cairns include Moore Reef beyond Fitzroy Island, Norman Reef to the north of Green Island or the Agincourt Reefs reached from Port Douglas.

The Cod Hole, a dive site on the outer reef off Lizard Island noted for its huge potato cod or grouper, is a particular attraction. A typical trip would be three days and three nights aboard the MV *Explorer II* for $600 including equipment, dives and meals. Four days on the *Nimrod III* starting in Cooktown and finishing at Lizard Island or vice versa costs $650 including the flights from Cairns at the start and back to Cairns at the finish. If time is short, but money isn't, there are also a variety of seaplane tours to the reef. You can do a diving day trip to the Cod Hole providing you've got $500 to spare.

FRANKLAND ISLANDS

The Frankland Islands are a group of relatively untouched national park islands south of Fitzroy Island and about 12 km off the coast. They were named by Captain Cook after Admiral Sir Thomas Frankland. The islands consist of High Island to the north and four smaller islands – Normanby, Mabel, Round and Russell Islands – to the south. They're continental islands with good beaches and some fine snorkelling. On the day trips from Cairns the island time is usually spent on Normanby Island while divers go to Round Island.

Camping

Camping drop-offs can be arranged on High or Russell Islands but there are no facilities on the islands so you must come totally equipped. Usually campers go to Russell Island, High Island drop-offs are only made at peak periods (like Christmas) when Russell is full. A maximum of 15 campers are allowed on each island and permits are available from the Queensland National Parks & Wildlife Service in Cairns.

Getting There & Away

There's a $69 day trip to the islands operated by Frankland Islands Cruise & Dive, phone

(070) 55 4966 for details. You're taken by bus from Cairns to Deeral on the Mulgrave River from where you go out through the mangroves to the islands. A barbecue lunch is included in the cost. Divers pay $99 while the camping drop-off cost is $40 return from Deeral Landing.

MICHAELMAS CAY

North of Green Island and 40 km from Cairns, tiny Michaelmas Cay is a national park and popular rendezvous for trips out to the Barrier Reef. The cay is home to thousands of seabirds, in the summer peak nesting season 30,000 or more cram on to it. The island is still in an early stage of cay development, just a stretch of sand topped by low, scrubby vegetation. Behind the island a narrow strip of reef stretches for all of 10 km and there's good snorkelling and diving around the cay.

Visitors to the cay are kept strictly to one area of beach, you're not allowed to walk elsewhere on the island or into the vegetated area. At least 14 different species of seabirds have been sighted here and six are known to breed here. Noddies, sooty terns, crested terns and lesser crested terns are the most numerous nesting birds.

The sooty terns lay a single egg in a simple 'nest' which is really just a depression in the sand. Both parents sit on the egg and care for the chick. When it's about a week old the parents leave it to its own devices during the day and the sooty tern chicks soon form wandering groups known as creches. At least once a day the parents return to the island, call their chick out of the creche and feed it by regurgitation. It takes about 70 days from hatching before the sooty tern chicks can fly and they then spend three to six years wandering the world before returning to breed, often in their own original colony.

South of Michaelmas is Upolu Cay, a small cay to which some day trip operators go.

Getting There & Away

Great Adventures have a $76 day trip which includes two hours on Green Island en route to Michaelmas Cay plus a smorgasbord

lunch. The huge sailing catamaran *Ocean Spirit* (tel (070) 31 2920) also operates daily trips to the cay which cost $98 including lunch, snorkelling equipment and semi-sumbersible trips.

HASTINGS, NORMAN & MOORE REEFS

North of Michaelmas Cay, Hastings and Norman Reefs are a popular destination for day trips from Cairns to the reef. Great Adventures offers a $95 day trip to Green Island and then out to Norman Reef. Moore Reef is east of Fitzroy Island and Great Adventures do trips there as well. A number of other operators also do day trips to these reefs.

LOW ISLES

Off-shore from Port Douglas this extremely popular destination for day trippers has two islands. Low Island is a fine little coral cay topped by an incredibly well kept old lighthouse dating from 1878. On the other side of the reef Woody Island is an extensive area of the reef which has been claimed by mangroves. These mangrove islands become increasingly common if you continue north from here to Torres Straits. The Low Isles were named by Captain Cook in 1770 and in 1928 they were the site for C M Yonge's Great Barrier Reef Expedition. This detailed study took a year to complete and greatly advanced modern understanding of coral reefs.

A trip out to the Low Isles from Port Douglas gives you a day of snorkelling, glass bottom boat viewing, general lazing around and the obligatory smorgasbord lunch.

Getting There & Away

Quicksilver is the main operator to the Low Isles and their day trip costs $45 and gets you out to the island in just 20 minutes by fast catamaran. Departures are from Marina Mirage in Port Douglas, phone (070) 99 5500 for bookings.

Hardy' Courier (tel (070) 31 3006) sails you out there on a catamaran and also costs $45. The luxury trip to the Low Isles is on the wooden ketch *Willow* (tel (070) 99 0234

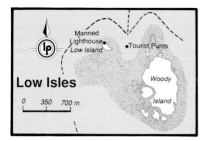

Low Isles

0   350   700 m

Manned Lighthouse
Low Island
Tourist Punts
Woody Island

or 99 5899) which takes just 12 people and costs $85 for the day. At peak seasons all the Low Isles trips are heavily booked so plan ahead.

SNAPPER ISLAND

This continental island is close to the mainland just off Cape Kimberley and the mouth of the Daintree River. It's national park and has some good fringing reef. Camping is permitted on the island with a permit from the Cairns office of the Queensland National Parks & Wildlife Service.

Getting There & Away

Snapper Island is popular for day trips, contact Snapper Island Cruises (tel (070) 31 1552) for information on their $69 day trips and $40 half day trips from Port Douglas.

AGINCOURT REEFS

Directly east of Cape Tribulation, on the outer edge of the Great Barrier Reef, the Agincourt Reefs offer some of the best diving in the region. It's the only outer ribbon reef reached in a day trip from the mainland. Quicksilver in Port Douglas operate daily trips to the reef in their wavepiercer catamarans. The cost is $85 and includes lunch, snorkelling equipment and semi-sub trips. For certificated scuba divers two dives cost an additional $50. For those who want to do it all you can also make a 10 minute, $50

helicopter flight over the reef from the Quicksilver landing pad.

ENDEAVOUR REEF

North of Low Island towards Cooktown is Endeavour Reef where Captain Cook's barque the *Endeavour* ran disastrously aground. See the following Lizard Island chapter for more information of their miraculous escape. In the desperate struggle to free the ship from the reef six cannons were pushed overboard along with a great deal of other heavy material.

Vince Vlasoff with his Cairns charter boat *Tropic Seas* began his ultimately successful search for the cannons in 1960. A chance meeting with American oil expert Virgil Kauffman introduced the technology needed to locate the coral encrusted objects. Kauffman raised $45,000 and organised sponsorship from the United States Academy of Natural Sciences and early in 1969 using a magnetometer the first cannon was located. All six were eventually recovered. Two years later the *Endeavour's* anchor was also recovered and weighed in at the Cairns game fishing wharf at 966 kg!

HOPE ISLANDS

North of Cedar Bay and south of Cooktown these two islands are on nearby reefs separated by a deep channel. The western island is mainly mangrove but the eastern one has a good encircling beach and in suitable winds there's a reasonably secure deep anchorage on its north-west side. You can camp on the eastern island with a permit from the Cairns office of the Queensland National Parks & Wildlife Service.

Getting There & Away

Access is by private boat or by seaplane from Cooktown, contact Cairns Seaplane Airways (tel (070) 50 5777) or Aquaflight Airways (tel (070) 51 3893 or 51 9566) about flying there.

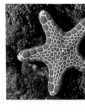

Starfish

Starfish or sea stars are the most visible members of the very large group known as *echinoderms*. There are five distinct types of echinoderms including sea urchins, from which the group's name is derived. The other four are starfish, brittle stars, feather stars and sea cucumbers or bêche-de-mer. It is difficult to believe that creatures as different looking as the starfish and the sea cucumber are closely related but the group all share three distinct characteristics. These are a five-armed body plan, a skeleton of plates and tube feet which are operated by hydraulic pressure. The five-armed plan of the starfish is easy to see and the sea cucumber has the same plan, although it's hard to believe.

Starfish or *asteroids* are bottom dwellers, like most echinoderms, and are very visible as they are often brightly coloured, do not move rapidly and in many cases do not hide away during the day. Generally they have five distinct arms although some may have more – crown-of-thorns starfish usually have 15 or 16 but may have even more. In other starfish, like the rotund looking pincushion sea star, the arms are not distinct at all but the five cornered shape is still immediately apparent.

The five arms of a starfish each contain the full quota of organs for respiration, digestion, motion and reproduction. Along the underside of each arm is a groove from which emerge the tiny tube feet. These hydraulically operated feet are the starfish's actual means of locomotion, not the much larger arms. The starfish's mouth, with a surprisingly complex jaw, is at the bottom centre but some starfish, including the crown-of-thorns, can also consume their prey by a method known as 'stomach eversion'. The stomach is pulled out through the mouth and wrapped over the prey which is digested before the stomach is pulled back inside. Most starfish are carnivorous and can even force open the shells of a bivalve like an oyster, then evert its stomach into the opening to digest the bivalve.

Echinoderms in general have strong powers of regeneration and can often regenerate the entire creature from a single broken off arm. A regenerating starfish is known as a comet since the newly regenerated parts do indeed look like a small star trailing a long, comet-like tail – the original larger arm.

The vivid blue starfish *Linckia laevigata* are widespread throughout the Pacific and easily recognisable by their distinct colouring but the brown sea star *Nardoa novaecaledoniae* is probably the most common. *Acanthaster planci*, the notorious crown-of-thorns starfish, is the best know of the Great Barrier Reef's starfish. ■

Lizard Island

Area: 21 square km
Type: continental but near outer reef
High point: 368 metres
Maximum visitor population: 64
Per person daily cost: $300
In brief: Lizard is a large island with a small resort where the emphasis is on seclusion. Its remote location, 240 km from Cairns, aids the isolation and the island has both historical interest due to Captain Cook's visit and fine diving and fishing possibilities. Children under five are banned.

The Island
The furthest north of the Barrier Reef resort islands, Lizard Island was named by Joseph Banks after Captain Cook spent a day here, trying to find a way out through the Barrier Reef to open sea. The islands of the Lizard group are the only high continental islands close to the outer barrier reef. The island has superb beaches (23 of them), great for swimming or snorkelling.

Lizard is one of the more expensive resorts and what you're paying for is not glossy sophistication – here your money buys you isolation and a location only 15 km from the outer edge of the reef. Furthermore the reef here is virtually untouched, as close to nature as you'll find. Naturally the diving is superb. The island has been a national park since 1939 and the other islands in the Lizard group were added to the national park in 1987. The resort was opened in 1972 and is now operated by Australian Airlines. The research station opened in 1975.

Lizard Island (GBRMPA)

233

Lizard Island
The jewel in the Reef
• A U S T R A L I A •

Cook's Visit

In 1770 Captain Cook, after his historic visit to Botany Bay, now in the southern suburbs of Sydney, sailed north along the coast of Australia. He named numerous places along the coast including Point Danger (near modern-day Surfers Paradise), Mt Warning (which should have warned him about Point Danger), the Whitsunday Islands and, between modern-day Port Douglas and Cooktown, Cape Tribulation.

Near the cape, and in sight of Mt Sorrow which he also named, his tribulations truly began. As the *Endeavour* had made its way up the coast the Great Barrier Reef, far out to sea, had not been sighted but Cook and his crew were certainly aware there was something out there from the unusual calmness of the sea and the frequent minor reefs they met with. Cook later noted that:

we have sail'd above 360 Leagues [more than 1700 km] by the Lead without ever having a Leadsman out of the Chains, when the ship was under sail; a Circumstance that perhaps never hapned to any ship before...

On the night of 11 June 1770 the *Endeavour* passed by, and Cook named, the Low Islands near Port Douglas, and:

My intention was to stretch off all Night as well to avoid the danger we saw ahead as to see if any Islands lay in the Offing, especially as we now begun to draw near the Lat. of those discover'd by Quiros [the islands of modern-day Vanuatu], for what reason I know not, have thought proper to Tack to this land. Having the advantage of a fine breeze of wind, and a clear Moon light Night in standing off from 6 until 9 o'clock, we deepened our Water from 14 to 21 fathoms, when all at once we fell into 12, 10 and 8 fathoms. At this time I had everybody

at their Stations to put about and come to an Anchor; but in this I was not so fortunate, for meeting again with Deep Water, I thought there could be no danger in standing on. Before 10 o'clock we had 20 and 21 fathoms, and Continued in that depth until a few minutes before 11, when we had 17, and before the Man at the Lead could heave another cast, the Ship Struck and stuck fast...upon the S.E. Edge of a reef of Coral rocks...

By heaving numerous items, including an anchor and six cannons, overboard the *Endeavour* was eventually freed from the reef which bears its name. A sail was hauled under the hull in an attempt to plug the gaping hole and then a miraculous drop in the breeze enabled them to limp up the Endeavour River to the site of present-day Cooktown. Here the sturdy barque was careened on the banks of the river and repaired. It was during this enforced interlude that Cook's party first saw that remarkable animal, the kangaroo.

Two months later the patched up *Endeavour* ventured out from Cooktown and set sail north. The presence of the reef was now very evident as here it creeps closer and closer to the coast and Cook and Dr Joseph Banks had been rowed out to Lizard Island in the ship's pinnace to try and find a way out from the reef. Banks later suggested the island's name due to the many large lizards he saw on the island. The two men climbed to the top of Cook's Look and from here:

To my Mortification I discover'd a Reef of Rocks laying about 2 or 3 Leagues [a league is about five km] without the Island, extending in a line N.W. and S.E., farther than I could see, on which the Sea broke very high.

Cook climbed the peak again the next morning to scan the horizon for some break in the reef but meanwhile the pinnace, which he had sent out to search for a passage, had located a safe route out of the reef to deeper water.

Other Early Visitors

Aborigines had been visiting Lizard Island long before Cook made his famous visit. Shell middens, where visiting Aborigines

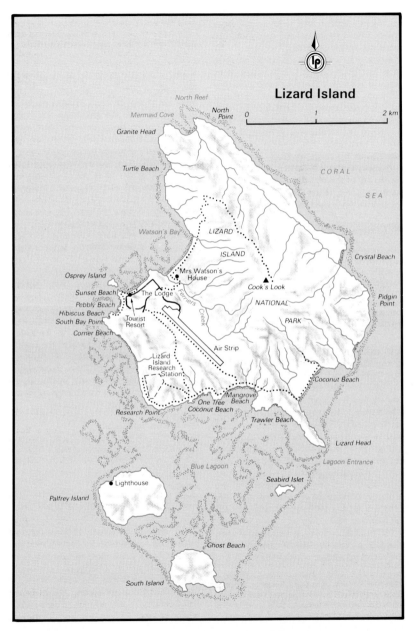

Lizard Island

0   1   2 km

North Reef

Mermaid Cove

North Point

Granite Head

Turtle Beach

CORAL

SEA

Watson's Bay

LIZARD

ISLAND

Crystal Beach

Osprey Island

Mrs Watson's House

Cook's Look

Sunset Beach

The Lodge

NATIONAL

Pidgin Point

Pebbly Beach

Hibiscus Beach

South Bay Point

Tourist Resort

Ferrers Creek

PARK

Corner Beach

Air Strip

Lizard Island Research Station

Coconut Beach

One Tree Coconut Beach

Mangrove Beach

Research Point

Trawler Beach

Lizard Head

Lagoon Entrance

Blue Lagoon

Seabird Islet

Palfrey Island

Lighthouse

Ghost Beach

South Island

feasted on shellfish, can be found at various points around the island and care should be taken not to disturb them.

Cook's comments on the island attracted other European visitors in subsequent years, many of whom wrote of their feelings as they climbed Cook's Look in the footsteps of their famous predecessor. Commander J L Stokes wrote of his visit to the island from HMS *Beagle* in 1839 while Joseph Jukes, the naturalist on HMS *Fly*, kept a chronicle describing his visit in 1843. Both their accounts were lyrical in their description of the beauty of the scene but Thomas Huxley, naturalist on HMS *Rattlesnake*, had a tougher climb to the top of the island:

The natural beauty of the scene was heightened by the recollection that one stood on ground rendered classical by the footsteps of the great Cook, who from this height sought some exit from the dangers which had so nearly put an end to him and his glory. I say "was heightened" Truth requires that I should substitute "ought to have been heightened", for in fact, the sun had been pouring on my back all the way up and my feelings more nearly approached sickness than sublimity when I reached the top.

A Queensland Tragedy

During Cook's visit Banks had noticed that 'the Indians had been here in their poor embarkations' and later visits also noted that Aborigines had visited the island, visits which were to lead to a Queensland tragedy. In 1881 Mary Beatrice Watson and her husband had built a small brick-and-stone cottage on the island in order to collect bêche de mer or sea slugs, a noted Chinese delicacy. Robert Watson left the island with his partner John Fuller to search for new fishing grounds, leaving Mary Watson with her baby, Ferrier, and their two Chinese servants Ah Sam and Ah Leong.

Her brief diary noted, with curious dispassion, the arrival of a party of Aborigines and the events which led to her death:

29 September Blowing strong S.E. breeze, although not as hard as yesterday. No eggs. Ah Leong killed by the blacks over at the farm. Ah Sam found his hat, which is the only proof.

1 October Natives (four) speared Ah Sam; four places in the right side, and three on the shoulder. Got three spears from the natives. Saw ten men altogether.

This part of her diary was found in the abandoned house and a subsequent diary with her body. At this point Mary Watson made the decision to leave the island and with some supplies, the baby and her wounded houseboy she paddled away in an iron tank used for boiling up the bêche de mer. For at least 10 days they moved desultorily from sand bank to island to reef to mangrove swamp, narrowly missing passing steamers or signalling unsuccessfully to them until eventually all died of thirst. Her last diary entry was made on 11 October.

Not until late January in the next year were the bodies of Mary Watson and her baby found on one of the Howick Islands. It was subsequently named Watson Island. They were still in their iron tank, which in the ensuing months had half filled with rainwater. Today visitors to Townsville can see the iron tank in the North Queensland branch of the Queensland Museum, at the Great Barrier Reef Wonderland where the superb Great Barrier Reef Aquarium is also located. Her two diaries are in Brisbane in the Oxley Memorial Library while in Cooktown you can see her tombstone with the inscription:

Five fearful days beneath
the scorching glare
her babe she nursed.
God knows the pangs that
woman had to bear.
Whose last sad entry showed
a mother's care.
Then – "near dead with thirst."

The tumbling walls of the old house can still be seen on Lizard Island today but near the top of Cook's Look there are also traces of stones marking an Aboriginal ceremonial area and it's possible that Mary Watson's unhappy end may have come because they had unwittingly strayed into an area sacred to Aborigines.

Watson's Bay, Lizard Island (TW)

Information

The resort's phone number is (070) 60 3999 and the address is Lizard Island, Private Mail Bag 40, Cairns, Qld 4870. The fax number is (070) 60 3991. The microwave phone link on the island was installed in late '88 and there's a pay phone at the research station which campers and yachties can use.

Lizard Island is on daylight saving time year round, thus it is one hour ahead of Australian Eastern Standard Time when the east coast states are not on daylight saving time. Queensland only tried out daylight saving time for the first time over the summer of 1989-90.

The Queensland National Parks & Wildlife Service puts out a *Lizard Island Group* information leaflet and the resort has a number of useful leaflets for their guests with information on birds, plants and fishing. *Lizard Island – Some of its History* by Allan McInnes is an interesting small book with extracts from the journals of Captain Cook and Joseph Banks, Mary Watson's diary and other interesting writings relating to the island. It's also supplied to guests at the resort.

Walking Preparations Don't set off on a walk on Lizard without sun protection including a hat and a good sunscreen. Take a water bottle as well, Lizard is hot and dry.

Zoning The waters immediately around Lizard Island are all zoned as Marine National Park where shell and coral collecting are not permitted. Around the northern part of the island it's Zone A, which permits limited line fishing. The southern part, including all of Blue Lagoon and the waters around Palfrey and South Islands and Seabird Islet, is Zone B where all fishing is prohibited.

Lizard Island Research Station

In 1974 the Australian Museum in Sydney founded the privately funded Lizard Island Research Station which pursues projects as diverse as marine organisms for cancer research, deaths of giant clams, coral reproductive processes, sea bird ecology, life patterns of reef fish during their larval stage and many other subjects. Funding has come from many companies in Australia and overseas, the station's 14 metre research catamaran *Sunbird* was provided by the Japanese company Suntory – *tory* means bird in Japanese. Tours of the station are conducted at 4 pm each Monday and Friday for guests at the resort and other island visitors such as yachties or campers.

The station can accommodate up to 15 visiting researchers and although preference is normally given to marine researchers (who usually pay $67 a night to stay at the station) high school and university student groups are also accommodated from time to time ($50 a night) and non-academic visitors ($90 a night). Information on the station can be obtained from The Co-Directors, Lizard Island Research Station, Private Mail Bag 37, Cairns, Qld 4871 (tel (070) 60 3977).

Island Wildlife

Lizard's most famous wildlife are, of course, the huge lizards which Cook and Banks commented on. The island has 11 species of lizards but it's the large sand goannas, often up to a metre in length, which are most interesting. They can often be seen around the resort and have become efficient scavengers at the resort's garbage dump. When young goannas are hatching out you will see many new holes dug by them in the sandy road between the resort and the research station.

Other terrestrial wildlife includes five species of snakes, none of them seen with any frequency, and a small colony of bats which may be seen winging their way over the resort soon after sunset.

More than 40 species of birds have been recorded on the island and a dozen or so actually nest there. The resort has a list of the birds which might be seen. Resident birds include the beautiful little sunbirds with their long, hanging nests. They even build them inside the small, open airstrip terminal! Bar-shouldered doves, crested terns, Caspian terns and a variety of other terns, oystercatchers and the large sea eagles are other resident species. Seabird Islet in the Blue Lagoon is a popular nesting site for terns and visitors should keep away from the islet during the summer months.

Cane Toads on Lizard

Bufo marinus, Queensland's ecological disaster, the rabbit of tropical Australia, first gained a toehold on Lizard Island in late '87. Cane toads were spotted near the resort's swimming pool and the discovery of dead goannas, possibly poisoned after they ate cane toads, added weight to the reported sightings. It was thought the invaders may have come over with plantings for a landscaping project at the resort. Fortunately the story is much happier than on the mainland where, since their introduction in 1947, cane toads have overrun all of Queensland and are threatening to move into New South Wales and the Northern Territory. Ten adult toads were caught almost immediately, four more were caught when tape recordings of mating toad noises were played to the randy reptiles and no further cane toad sightings were reported in 1988. You may spot pretty little green frogs around the resort but hopefully the hideous cane toads are gone.

Other Islands

There are four other smaller islands in the Lizard group. Osprey Island, with its nesting birds, is right in front of the resort and can be waded to. Around the edge of Blue Lagoon, south of the main island, are Seabird Islet, South Island and Palfrey Island with its automatic lighthouse.

The Watson House & Watson's Bay

It's only a short walk from the resort to the remains of the Watson house by Watson's Bay. The trail from the resort climbs up over Chinaman's Ridge which separates the resort from Watson's Bay. There are fine views over the bay where yachts can often be seen at anchor. A stream emerges from a mangrove swamp into the bay at its southern end and the trail follows a boardwalk through the swamp, with a neat little bridge arching over the stream. Two stout walls are all that remains standing from the Watson house but it's easy to trace the outlines of the foundations of what must have been a surprisingly large residence.

From here you walk along the beach to its northern end where there's excellent snorkelling on the fringing reef around the northern headland or the isolated heads slightly further out from shore. Apart from the usual selection of colourful fish the coral also has a phenomenal number of clams including many giant ones, some living, some just empty shells. There's also coral at the southern end of the bay, out from Chinaman's Ridge, and a superb clam garden in the middle of the bay.

The small campsite at the north end of the bay is also a popular barbecue spot for visiting boats including the *Queen of the Isles* and the *Noel Buxton* on their regular Cairns/Thursday Island/Cairns cruises. There's at least one large goanna which has learnt to pop up here at lunchtime and grab whatever handouts are going.

Cook's Look

The climb to the top of Cook's Look is undoubtedly the most popular walk on the island. The trail starts from the northern end of the beach, near the campsite. You can easily walk here from the resort, passing the Watson house on the way. Alternatively many resort guests take a dinghy, motor over to this point and by making an early start you can easily climb to the top and get back to the resort with a healthy appetite for breakfast. Occasionally the resort organises Cook's Look excursions complete with a champagne breakfast on the top.

From the extreme end of the beach the start of the trail to Cook's Look is clearly signposted and the trail, although it can be steep and a bit of a clamber at times, is easy to follow all the way with regular white or blue painted arrows. The trail starts off heading north then curves round and heads steadily south to the top, dipping down slightly into a saddle before making the final push to the top. The words 'Not Far Now', painted on a rock, urges you on over the last few hundred metres.

There are breathtaking views over Watson's Bay as you ascend and from the top, marked with a cairn and one of those 'X thousand km to all sorts of places' plates,

Lizard Island lizard (TW)

there are great views out towards the outer reef, 18 to 20 km away at this point. From the top on a clear day you can clearly see the opening in the reef where Cook made his thankful escape but in actual fact the reef at this point offers a number of passages. It's a popular outing for yachties cruising the Great Barrier Reef to exit through one of these passages, perhaps Cook's Passage, just to say they've sailed outside the reef, then come back in to the reef's protected waters through another passage.

The stroll to the top can take anything from half an hour if you run most of the way to 1½ hours at a very leisurely pace, 45 minutes is probably a good walk. It's worth contemplating Cook making his weary trudge to the top, 'with a mixture of hope and fear proportioned to the importance of our business and the uncertainty of the event'. Under the cairn there's a tupperware-type plastic box with an exercise book inside where you can write your name and any comments worthy of your own historic moment at the top.

In *Cruising the Coral Coast* Alan Lucas writes that down the north side of the slope a few hundred metres are some Aboriginal rock formations which, as noted in the section on Mary Watson, may have had a bearing on her death. They were only discovered in 1972 during the filming of *At Home on the Lizard*. Movie trivia buffs may be interested to know one of the first-timer film makers involved in this project was a Dr George Miller who was so inspired by this first attempt at film making that he packed in medicine and went on to become one of Australia's most financially, if not critically, successful movie makers with the Mel Gibson *Mad Max* series. Aboriginal ruins buffs may have less success finding the formation – there are an awful lot of jumbled rocks down the north side of the slope and just which ones might be a real formation is hard to tell.

An alternative to retracing your steps down the hill to Watson's Bay is to continue south to Coconut Beach. There's no trail most of the way down but the vegetation on Lizard Island is not dense and it's not too difficult to find your way down. A trail leads from the north end of Coconut Beach, following a creek through a small gully of rainforest part way up Cook's Look. You should allow most of a day to walk the complete loop from the resort to Watson's Bay, up to Cook's Look, down to Coconut Beach and back via Mangrove Beach.

Other Walks

There are several other interesting walks around the island and the dry, rocky and grassy coverage makes it pretty easy to walk almost anywhere. From the resort a trail leads down the side of the airstrip then continues directly from the end of the airstrip to Mangrove Beach and Trawler Beach, both on Blue Lagoon. A trail climbs up the side of the steep Lizard Head ridge and drops equally steeply down to Coconut Beach. Some real rock scrambling is necessary but Lizard Head offers superb views.

Another trail from the resort starts near the airstrip and leads to One Tree Coconut Beach

from where you can rock hop around the headland to Mangrove Beach. If you stuck to the trail, rather than turning off to One Tree Coconut Beach, it continues round to the Lizard Island Research Station. From the station you can continue around the bay and rock hop round the series of headlands and idyllic little bays back to the resort.

For those interested in the island's vegetation the resort has a *Plants Guide* report.

Beaches & Snorkelling

Lizard Island has the finest beaches on any of the Barrier Reef islands. Some islands have no beaches to speak of, or have been forced to create artificial beaches by bringing in sand, or have such severe tidal changes that their beaches are unswimmable at low tide. Lizard, by contrast, has superb beach after superb beach. There are long stretches of sand or perfect, picture book little bays, all of them lapped by glass-clear water with

Pebbly Beach, Lizard Island (TW)

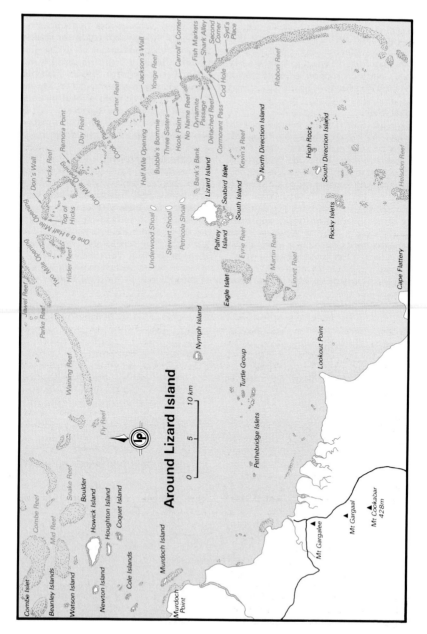

Around Lizard Island

magnificent coral. If you're a keen snorkeller Lizard is superb.

There's good snorkelling right in front of the resort, particularly along the north-east edge of Osprey Island. Immediately south of the resort are three postcard beaches – Sunset Beach, Pebbly Beach and Hibiscus Beach. They each offer great swimming, coral and snorkelling and despite their proximity to the resort (only a couple of minutes' walk) feel like they're light years away.

One Tree Coconut Beach, Mangrove Beach, Trawler Beach and Coconut Beach are all at the south-eastern end of Lizard Island and there is good snorkelling from the the latter two. Watson's Bay to the north of the resort is a wonderful stretch of sand with great snorkelling at both ends and a clam field in the middle. Other beaches round the northern end of the island are easily reached by dinghy and at Turtle Beach, Mermaid Cove or Crystal Beach you can really feel you've escaped from civilisation. They all offer good snorkelling.

At several good snorkelling places around the Blue Lagoon or North Point there are marine park mooring buoys where you can tie up your dinghy without damaging the coral by anchoring. The coral around the north-east side of the island has numerous caves in the reef edge.

Diving

Lizard Island offers some of the best diving along the Great Barrier Reef, in fact there's so much of it you're really spoiled for choice. There are good dives right off the island, particularly along the eastern side or on the southern side of South Island and at the western end of Blue Lagoon. With the outer barrier reef so close it's hard to resist the temptation of heading a little further afield, particularly to what is probably Australia's best known dive, the Cod Hole.

Despite the proximity of the dive sites diving at Lizard certainly isn't cheap – spectacular yes, economical no. Local dives cost $40 per person, inner reef dives $80, outer reef dives $100. A day's hire of regulator, buoyancy compensator, wet suit and two tanks of air will set you back another $40 so for a day's diving on the outer reef you're looking at $140.

Inner Reef Dives Immediately north of Lizard Island are a series of shoals – Underwood, Stewart and Petricola Shoals – plus Bank's Bank where a sand cay has formed on the shoal. There are wonderful coral formations and a great variety of reef and pelagic (open sea) fish. The diving off Bank's Bank is particularly good.

South east of Lizard there's good diving at Kevin's Reef and superb coral for diving or snorkelling off the northern side of North Direction Island. Rocky Islet, further south, also has good diving and snorkelling. Eagle Islet and Nymph Island to the west of Lizard are popular picnic spots and offer good snorkelling.

Outer Reef Dives It's only 18 to 20 km from Lizard Island to the edge of the outer reef where the ribbon reefs are cut by a number of openings. They include the historic Cook's Passage where the great navigator made his short escape to the outer ocean.

Starting from the northern end on Hick's Reef the Top of Hicks dive can be a fine drift dive along One & a Half Mile Opening. Outside the reef Don's Wall is a drop off where you may find patrolling reef sharks. Remora Point, on the outer corner of Day Reef, has very clear water and a wide variety of fish.

Day Reef is separated from Carter Reef, a research reef where no diving is permitted, by Cook's Passage. There are numerous dives around Yonge Reef, popular because of its proximity to Lizard Island. The dives include Half Mile Opening where there is also good snorkelling. Jackson's Wall is on the outer edge of the reef while other inner reef dives include Bubble's Bommie, the Three Sisters and Hook Point.

South again is No Name Reef with Carroll's Corner on the outer edge, and the Fish Markets and Dynamite Passage on the narrow pass between No Name and Detached Reef.

Top & Bottom: Featherstars on MacGillivray's Reef, Lizard Island (MN)

Separating Detached Reef from the long Ribbon Reef Number 10 is Cormorant Pass with the famous Cod Hole. It's a favourite destination for dive trips out of Cairns and dive boats from Lizard Island usually go here every second day. Its fame is well earned as a group of 15 to 20 huge potato cod live here and have become very familiar with the pleasures of being fed by visiting divers. The larger ones are up to two metres in length and will bump up against you or allow themselves to be stroked as they swim around looking for a handout. Merlin the friendly moray eel and a host of other fish also appear for their regular feeds. This dive can be equally good for snorkellers as the potato cod come virtually to the surface and the dive only goes down to about 10 metres. Round the corner from the Cod Hole is Shark Alley where you can see some other interesting large fish!

Outside Ribbon Reef, Syd's Place and Second Corner are vertical wall dives for the more experienced diver.

Fishing

Lizard Island is famed for its fishing as well as its diving, particularly heavy tackle fishing for which the annual competition over Halloween night (31 October) is a big attraction. September through December is the heavy tackle season. The Marlin Centre, at the north end of the resort bay caters for the many game fishing boats that use Lizard as a base at the height of the season. Its bar is renowned for extremely tall fishing tales.

Almost any boat trip from Lizard will involve dangling a line out the back (usually with some success) and light tackle fishing trips cost $135 to $200 per person per day depending on the size of the group. Half day or night fishing trips are $85 to $125 per person. Of course you can easily arrange your own fishing trip, all it needs is a dinghy and a line. The resort has an interesting *Fishing Guide* leaflet for their guests.

Activities

The resort has the usual sporting facilities including a tennis court and swimming pool.

All water sports activities including windsurfers, catamarans, outboard dinghies and water skiing are included in the daily tariff. Boating trips do cost extra and these are put on every day, either for fishing, diving and snorkelling, picnic and barbecue excursions to neighbouring islands, or combinations of these activities. The MV *Volare*, MV *Gamefisher* and MV *Kaihlua* are the boats most frequently used.

Accommodation

The Resort Lizard Island's accommodation is comfortable, modern and first class but in no way spectacular. Straightforward is the only way to describe the resort's design – there are no prizes for the resort's architecture! The rooms have air-coditioning and ceiling fans, fridges, tea and coffee making equipment and a telephone but no television or radio. Coming to Lizard is supposed to be an escape from the real world.

There are 23 double rooms at $275 per person per night including all meals and general equipment use and activities. Two larger suites cost $375.

Camping Camping permits for Lizard Island must be obtained from the QNPWS office in Cairns. There's a small category B campsite ($5 a night) at the north end of the Watson's Bay beach. The site has toilets, barbecues, tables and benches, and freshwater is available from a pump about 250 metres from the site, near the top of the mangrove swamp that extends in from the south end of the bay. Although campers are extremely unlikely to be welcomed with open arms at the resort the island's history, walks, fine beaches, excellent snorkelling and the research station make this an interesting island to stay on. No food is available from the resort or the research station, campers must be totally self sufficient. There is also no garbage collection, you must take it all out when you leave.

Food

The resort provides a buffet style breakfast while lunch and dinner are ordered from the menu. Although Lizard has a high reputation for its cuisine, the menu often aims a little too high and some rather simpler dishes might be appreciated and be more successful. There's an unexciting wine list with most wines from around $25. If you want to get away from it all for the day you can request a picnic hamper to take away in a dinghy.

Getting There & Away

It's a long way to Lizard Island, 240 km from Cairns, and this great distance adds to the resort's isolation and its expense.

Air Almost all guests at the resort arrive by air, Australian Regional Airlines has daily flights from Cairns and the hour-long flight by Twin Otter costs $124.

Sea There is no regular shipping or ferry service to Lizard Island but the Cairns/ Thursday Island cruise ships like the *Queen of the Isles* or the *Noel Buxton* may take passengers if there is room available. Count on around $70 or $80 for the overnight trip. A few cruise passengers have abandoned the ship at Lizard Island after a heavy bout of seasickness on the trip from Cairns.

Yachties usually anchor in sheltered Watson's Bay or in the Blue Lagoon and Lizard Island is one of the most popular anchorages right along the Great Barrier Reef. It's certainly the last really good anchorage before you get to Thursday Island. Intrepid madmen even come over to Lizard Island from the mainland in outboard powered 'tinnies'. It's about 30 km from Cape Flattery. The red carpet is not, however, rolled out to yachties by the resort.

The difficulty and expense of getting to Lizard Island puts off campers although a few do manage it. An interesting way of making a camping trip to the island would be to take one of the cruise boats up and continue on to Thursday Island on the same boat a week later, or fly out back to Cairns. Fortunately you do not have to bring freshwater to Lizard and you can burn driftwood.

A Prolonged Visit to the Reef

Lizard Island visitors flying to or from Cairns may spot a rusting ship, high and dry on Emily Reef about 40 km south-east of Cooktown. It's the MV *Debut*, sister ship to the ill-fated Greenpeace *Rainbow Warrior*, and she's been stuck there since 1987, with her captain and owner still on board! The *Debut's* owner had been kicking around the Pacific for over 10 years, scraping a living as best he could, until one day he ran out of money and fuel and drifted into Australian waters. Lent fuel by the Australian Navy the *Debut* limped into Cairns and tied up for a prolonged period, unable to raise the cash for fuel or port charges.

Finally, when the owner's visa expired and Australian immigration officials were closing in, the *Debut* again put to sea but before a role in a proposed *Rainbow Warrior* film could be settled a cyclone shoved the unfortunate ship to its current resting place. And there it remains with its owner demanding the right to salvage and sell equipment off the ship, the Australian government stating he can do no such thing without paying import duties and the marine park authority insisting they just want the rusting hulk taken somewhere else.

Islands around Lizard Island

There are a number of continental islands and small cays dotted around Lizard Island and south towards Cooktown. Camping is permitted on a number of the islands with a Queensland National Parks & Wildlife Service permit. The category C sites are all very basic and the permit costs just $2 a night.

ROCKY ISLETS

Immediately south of Lizard Island is Rocky Islet, wooded and with good beaches, and two adjoining islets, one covered in scrub, one bare rock. Day trips are sometimes made to the islets from Lizard Island and there is good snorkelling and diving there.

During the last century these islets played a part in the Queensland blackbirding business. Naive islanders from the Pacific were collected by unscrupulous labour recruiters to work on the North Queensland sugar cane fields or in the gold mines in conditions of near slavery. Rocky Islet was a slaver's barracoon where the hapless islanders were transferred from the ocean going ships to await collection by ships from the mainland. By this time blackbirding had been banned but the recruiters continued to smuggle labourers ashore by means such as this.

Camping is permitted on the north side of the main island between February and September.

SOUTH DIRECTION ISLAND
Just north of the Rocky Islets this island is scrub covered but without beaches. Yachts sometimes anchor here although it's not easy to get inside the reef.

NORTH DIRECTION ISLAND
This prominent island is another popular destination for day trips from Lizard Island. There's a good beach and sand spit and some fine coral for divers or snorkellers. Aboriginal rock paintings can be seen on the island.

EAGLE ISLET
Cook passed Eagle Islet and his log notes that his less than ecologically minded men killed the young eagles found in a nest. Fortunately the islet is still noted for its three eagle nests. From December to March it harbours a huge number of sea birds, particularly nesting sooty terns and white-crested terns. The small cay sits at the northern end of the large Eyrie Reef. It's only about eight km from Lizard and is a popular destination for day trips from the resort.

NYMPH ISLAND & THE TURTLE GROUP
About 25 km west of Lizard Island is Nymph Island, another good picnic spot with good snorkelling around the reef. Reportedly there have even been crocodiles in the island's inner lagoon. It's a good island for walking and camping is permitted.

Slightly south-west of Nymph Island are the islands of the Turtle Group, small sand and vegetated cays. Camping is permitted on three of the islands in the group.

THREE ISLANDS & TWO ISLANDS
Further south, camping is permitted on both these island groups. Three Islands are about 40 km north-west of Cooktown while Two Islands are 10 km further north again.

Stingrays & Manta Rays

Rays are essentially flattened sharks but their feeding habits are quite unsharklike. Stingrays are bottom feeders, equipped with crushing teeth to grind the molluscs and crustaceans they sift out of the sand. They are very common along the Great Barrier Reef, often lying motionless on the sandy bottom of their favourite shallow bays. It's fun to wade across such a bay, watching them suddenly rise up from the bottom and glide smoothly away. Just make certain you do scare them up, for stingrays are less than impressed when a human foot pins them down to the bottom and that barbed and poisonous tail can then swing up and into your leg with painful efficiency.

Manta rays are amongst the largest fish found on the Great Barrier Reef and a firm favourite of scuba divers. There's nothing quite like the feeling of sensing a shadow passing over the sun and looking up to see a couple of tons of manta ray swooping smoothly through the water above you. They are quite harmless, feeding only on plankton and small fishes, and in some places seem quite relaxed about divers approaching them closely. Manta rays are sometimes seen to leap completely out of the water, landing back with a tremendous splash.

Despite their shy nature rays do have one shark-like characteristic in that they generally give birth to live young. A baby manta-ray is born neatly wrapped up in its bat-like wings. ■

Lizard Island to Cape York

The tourist stretch of the reef ends abruptly at Lizard Island, there are plenty of interesting islands north of Lizard and the reef is more convoluted, complicated and close to shore than ever, but there are no resort islands. In fact there's not even another hotel, restaurant or bar until you get to Thursday Island, off the northern tip of Cape York, and Thursday Island is definitely no resort. The islands up here are generally not so attractive either. The south-east trades blow for most of the year and the islands are often windswept and barren. Nor are safe anchorages for visiting yachts easy to find, Lizard Island is the last really good anchorage heading north.

Getting There & Away
Even without your own yacht visiting the islands north from Lizard to Torres Strait is certainly possible. Two cruise ships, the *Queen of the Isles* and the *Noel Buxton* operate regular trips from Cairns to Thursday Island and back, stopping at a number of islands along the way. See the Cruising to Cape York account for a typical trip on the *Queen of the Isles*.

The *Queen of the Isles* is operated by Royal Tropic Cruise Line, Cairns Mail Centre 6900, Cairns, Qld 4870. For details phone (070) 31 1844, toll free (008) 07 9060 or fax (070) 51 9764. Departures are on Sunday night from Trinity Wharf in Cairns, arriving back on the following Saturday morning. Stops are usually made at Lizard Island, Cape York and Thursday Island plus whatever other anchoring places look interesting and are suitable for the conditions.

The 48 metre ship has a displacement of

Queen of the Isles (TW)

560 tons and a service speed of 12 knots. Fares include all meals and start from $550 in the six berth economy cabins and then advance through six berth family cabins, four berth cabins, two berth cabins, double sun deck cabins and finally, for $1250 per person, the double sun deck cabins with private toilet and showers. There are 23 cabins in all and a total passenger capacity of 78 but only the two most expensive doubles have private toilets and showers, everybody else shares. The ship is all air-conditioned, the food is surprisingly good, there's a bar and an observation lounge plus a popular sun deck. This certainly is not big ocean liner luxury cruising, but it certainly is a lot of fun.

The MV *Noel Buxton* is a smaller 35 metre vessel which operates very similar six day cruises to Cape York, Thursday Island and back. It's a bit cheaper and a bit less comfortable. Book through Cape York Relaxa Cruises, Wharf St, Cairns, Qld 4870. The phone number is (070) 51 7393 and the fax number is (070) 52 1408.

The *Tropical Trader* is a trawler mother ship that services the trawlers up the coast, stopping wherever the boats do. It can be found at Shed 5 on Cairns' Trinity Wharf, phone (070) 51 1470 for more details. They will take paying passengers if they're in the mood. The *Cape Trader* operated by Torres Islands Trading (tel (070) 69 1707 on Thursday Island, (070) 51 1044 in Cairns) carries passengers between Cairns and TI for $250. The *Atlantic Clipper* (tel (070) 31 2516) also goes up to Thursday Island. Try the Barrier Reef Hotel opposite the wharf in Cairns if you're looking for work on the trawlers. It's tough.

ALONG THE INNER PASSAGE

Remarkably despite the density of islands along the route north making landfall on them is often far from easy. Lizard Island is the last really secure island anchorage so which islands you visit on a cruise to TI depends on the prevailing weather conditions. It's a busy route with a steady flow of cruising yachts, prawn trawlers, container ships to and from Asia and bulk carriers

shuttling between Gladstone, south down the coast, and the Weipa mine on the west side of Cape York in the Gulf of Carpentaria.

The coastal route is fairly tightly prescribed – along this stretch the reef presses close to the coast so there's little option to zig zag and find your own route. Until a safe 'inner passage' was plotted sailing along the coast was usually done outside the reef with the considerable danger of finding a safe passage back into the sheltered inner reef waters at some point. Some of the more interesting islands north of Lizard include:

HOWICK ISLANDS

About 50 km north-west of Lizard Island is the Howick group where Mary Watson's ill fated escape from Lizard Island came to its dismal ending. Howick Island, the main island in the group, comprises a continental island with several prominent hills, while off to the west stretches a large reef flat which has been totally filled in by mangroves. Just to the north-east of Howick is Snake Reef, an oval-shaped reef, not snake like at all. While yachties and shallow draught boats sail west of Howick towards the coast, deep draught vessels have to take a tight dog-leg between Howick Island and Snake Reef, a route known as Snake Gully.

Watson Island is to the north-west of Howick, a low-lying ignominious little mangrove island. It was here that Mary Watson, her baby and the Chinese servant Ah Sam died. Noble Island, nearer to the mainland to the west, has a prominent mountainous peak rising to 122 metres. A brief gold rush took place here after surveyors unearthed a nugget, purely by chance.

FLINDERS GROUP

The Flinders Group in Bathurst Bay has two larger islands, Flinders and Stanley Islands, and a number of smaller islands. Flinders is said to have some Aboriginal cave paintings. This area was swept by cyclone *Mahina* in March 1899 causing great damage. Many ships had sheltered in the bay and a lighthouse ship, two pearling mother ships and 50 pearling luggers were sunk and in all 300

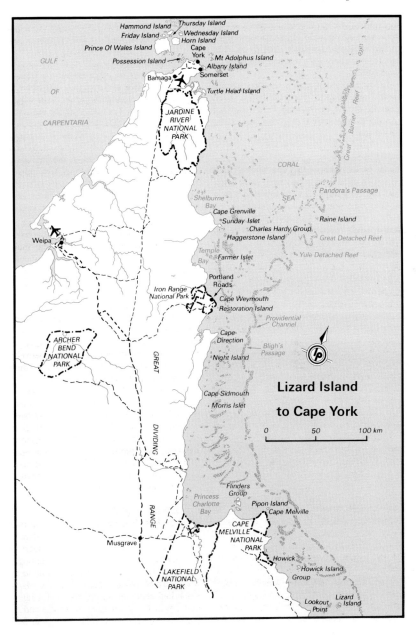

Thursday Island
Hammond Island
Friday Island — Wednesday Island
Horn Island
Prince Of Wales Island — Cape York
Possession Island — Mt Adolphus Island
Albany Island
Bamaga — Somerset
Turtle Head Island

GULF
OF
CARPENTARIA

JARDINE
RIVER
NATIONAL
PARK

CORAL

Shelburne Bay
Cape Grenville
Sunday Islet
Charles Hardy Group
Haggerstone Island

Great Barrier Reef

Pandora's Passage

Raine Island

Great Detached Reef

Weipa

Temple Bay
Farmer Islet

Yule Detached Reef

Portland Roads
Iron Range National Park
Cape Weymouth
Restoration Island

SEA

Providential Channel

ARCHER
BEND
NATIONAL
PARK

Cape Direction

Night Island

Bligh's Passage

GREAT

Lizard Island

to Cape York

0   50   100 km

Cape Sidmouth
Morris Islet

DIVIDING

Flinders Group

Princess Charlotte Bay

Pipon Island
Cape Melville

RANGE

Musgrave

CAPE
MELVILLE
NATIONAL
PARK

Howick

LAKEFIELD
NATIONAL
PARK

Howick Island Group

Lookout Point

Lizard Island

divers lost their lives. It is said that the seas were so high that dolphins were dumped upon the top of 12 metre high cliffs on Flinders Island. There is a cyclone monument on Cape Melville.

Today numerous prawn trawlers anchor around the islands, particularly in Owen Channel, during the daytime. Prawn trawling is a night-time activity and the crew sleep during the day.

MORRIS ISLET

About halfway between Cape Melville and Cape Direction is tiny Morris Islet, a small sand cay on a huge reef. At low tide a long sandbar runs north-east from the tip of the island for nearly two km. The cay is covered in low scrub, most of it needle sharp kapok plants, but towards the southern end is a single palm tree and under the palm tree is a 'diver's' grave, possibly the result of a pearl or trochus shell diver meeting his death at sea

on an old lugger. Floats, shells and other bits and pieces decorate the lonely grave.

NIGHT ISLAND

Like a number of other mangrove islands along this stretch of the coast Night Island is a tiny cay surrounded by mangroves which have spread to cover almost all the reef. The Low Isles, off Port Douglas further south, are somewhat similar. The island is a major nesting site for the Torres Strait pigeons who fly back to the island from the mainland every night. The island is only five km off the mainland and it was to this island that the bêche de mer gatherer Robert Watson was heading when he left his wife on Lizard Island.

BLIGH'S PASSAGE & RESTORATION ISLAND

About 250 km north of Lizard Island is Bligh's Passage or Entrance. In 1789 Captain

Morris Islet (TW)

William Bligh, having suffered the ignominious mutiny on his ship the *Bounty*, found his way through the reef here. The mutiny had taken place in the Tonga Islands and Bligh and his remaining faithful crew sailed 6000 km in a small 23-foot (seven-metre) open boat to eventually reach safety at Kupang on the island of Timor in the Dutch East Indies.

This remarkable voyage lasted 41 days and, despite having to contend with everything from violent weather to unfriendly natives as they sailed through the Fiji Islands, Bligh still found time to chart his route with such accuracy that aspects of modern maps are still based on his work.

Bligh made landfall at Restoration Island, just off Cape Weymouth and immediately south of Portland Roads, where today you will often see a group of prawn trawlers anchored. He named the island both for the fact that he and his men could 'restore' themselves after their long and difficult journey and because it was the anniversary of the Restoration to the throne of King Charles II.

PROVIDENTIAL CHANNEL

Not far north from Bligh's Passage is Providential Channel, where Cook, so recently a much relieved escapee from the Great Barrier Reef, made his way back inside it. Having sailed out from the reef through Cook's Passage near Lizard Island the unhappy captain found things were no better outside. The prevailing winds and currents were pushing him back on to the reef and when the wind died completely he found himself simply drifting towards the reef in water too deep to drop anchor:

...we both sounded now and several times in the night but had no ground with 140 fathoms of line. A little after 4 oClock the roaring of the Surf was plainly heard and at day break the vast foaming breakers were too plainly to be seen not a Mile from us towards which we found the Ship was carried by the waves surprisingly fast. We had at this time not an air of wind and the depth of water was unfathomable so that there was not a possibility of Anchoring, in this distressed situation we had nothing but Providence and the small Assistance our boats could give us to trust to...

Piper Reef Lighthouse, Farmer Islet (TW)

Despite launching the *Endeavour's* yawl and longboat and trying to tow the ship the reef still came closer and closer. By 6 am the *Endeavour* was less than 100 metres off the reef and the depth was still over 120 fathoms! The ship's pinnace, which had been under repair, was in the water as well by this time but:

At this critical juncture when all our endeavours seem'd too little a small air of wind sprung up, but so small that at any other time in a Calm we should not have observed it, with this and the assistance of our boats we could observe the Ship to move off from the Reef in a slanting direction...

Eventually the *Endeavour* was carried clear of the reef and the fortunate appearance of the narrow Providential Channel enabled them to duck back within the shelter of the reef:

...where we anchor'd in 19 fathoms a Corally & Shelly bottom happy once more to incounter those shoals which but two days ago our utmost wishes were crowned by geting clear of, such are the Vicissitudes attending this kind of service and must always attend an unknown Navigation.

CAPE WEYMOUTH TO CAPE GRENVILLE

North of Cape Weymouth in Temple Bay there are two small islets, Farmer and Fisher, on one part of the extensive Piper Reef. There's a good beach, coral and swimming on Farmer Islet and from here you can walk right out to the lighthouse at the tip of the reef at low tide. The shipping channel passing by here is the narrowest right down the Queensland coast.

Privately owned Haggerstone Island is just off Cape Grenville. The high, rounded hump of this continental island dips down to what looks to be a delightful sandy bay where two houses stand amongst the numerous palm trees. You could hardly think of a more remote hideaway. Just north of Cape Grenville there are more Bligh connections at Sunday Islet. Here the unfortunate captain nearly faced another mutiny when one of his crew challenged him. Bligh tossed the man a sword and suggested they sort the matter out there and then and his opponent promptly backed down.

Near the islands of the Charles Hardy Group off Cape Grenville the 313 ton barque *Charles Eaton* struck a reef in 1834. The crew and passengers escaped on a boat and two rafts and were taken aboard a large native canoe. The canoe then sailed to a nearby island and there the survivors were all slaughtered, except for two boys who lived with the tribe on Murray Island for two years until they were retrieved by the ship *Isabella*. This incident prompted the construction of a beacon on Raine Island.

RAINE ISLAND

Directly east of Cape Grenville and only about 35 km south of Pandora's Entrance this 30 hectare coral cay is, despite its minute size, of great interest for both its wildlife and

its history. The island measures less than a km long by less than half a km wide and is completely treeless. Its highest point is only six metres above sea level and high tides and cyclonic storms can wash waves right over the island. The island is on the outer edge of the reef, and close by the sea bottom drops to over 600 metres depth.

Outwardly it would seem like a very inhospitable little island yet for some reason this island attracts immense populations of turtles and birds. The island is a major breeding ground for the green turtle which comes to lay eggs here between November and February. Green turtles are found as far afield as the Caribbean to Borneo but today the Great Barrier Reef is their main habitat and Raine Island is their most important nesting rookery.

At times the turtles arrive here in unbelievable numbers. An 'invasion' took place in 1974 and again in 1984 when it was estimated 50,000 to 100,000 female turtles arrived to lay their eggs here and at nearby Pandora Cay. Observers counted over 10,000 turtles on the island at one time! Studies are being made of the migratory patterns of turtles from the island. The poor green turtle is the most popular turtle species for human consumption and many are captured around the eastern islands of Indonesia and shipped to Bali where they are an important delicacy.

Turtles, however, are not the only wildlife which finds Raine Island's meagre attractions irresistable. A variety of sea birds also nest on the island, some of them finding turtle eggs and newly hatched turtles a useful addition to their diet. It has been estimated that over 100,000 common and black noddys and sooty terns congregate on the island at one time and observers once counted 17,000 common noddy nests on the island. A variety of other sea birds visit this remote and tiny island, in some cases this is the only place in Australian waters where certain species have been sighted.

The island, which is thought to be only a few thousand years old, has also had an interesting human history. It was named after Thomas Raine, captain of the convict transport ship HMS *Surry* which he sailed to China from Australia in 1815, charting parts of the reef en route. Nearby Pandora's Entrance had claimed its most famous victim in 1791 but numerous other sailing vessels, trying to enter the the the reef, went down near Raine Island and in 1844 it was decided to build a stone beacon on the island to warn seafarers.

HMS *Fly*, which had done so much survey work along the reef, brought a convict party which erected a 15-metre-high tower. It was noted that the unfortunate convicts suffered not only from the heat, lack of water and lack of shade but also from lice which infested the island. A particularly annoying tick still lurks on the island today to irritate visiting scientific parties.

The tower, which was restored in the 1980s, was never lit as it was intended only to be a landmark visible in daylight. At that time the only light on the whole east coast of Australia was at the entrance to Sydney Harbour. As the inner route through the Great Barrier Reef became more popular the old outer route was soon abandoned and the tower eventually became redundant. Prominent though the beacon was, numerous ships continued to meet their fate around the island – 13 known and a number of unknown vessels went down between 1850 and 1860. Today few ships enter Australian waters at this point but in 1985 the *Kanai* managed to wreck itself on the reef here.

In the 1870s bêche de mer were harvested on Raine Island for shipment to China and a little earlier the island was first exploited for its considerable guano deposits. It's thought that tens of thousands of tons of guano were removed before the guano miners jetty and houses were dismantled when mining halted in 1892. The grave of Annie Eliza Ellis, wife of a guano miner who died in 1891, is a lonely reminder of that period.

PANDORA'S PASSAGE

Two years after Bligh came through the reef at Bligh's Passage in 1789, the *Bounty* saga played out another chapter 200 km further north at Pandora's Passage. Captain Edwards of the *Pandora* had been sent to the Pacific to track down the *Bounty* mutineers but his ship foundered when trying to enter the reef in 1791 and went down with 14 of the mutineers and 130 crew aboard.

The unfortunate mutineers had been kept on deck in appalling conditions in a three-metre long cell dubbed 'Pandora's Box'. As the *Pandora* started to sink Edwards repeatedly refused to allow the mutineers to be released but at the last moment the master-at-arms contrived to 'accidentally' drop the keys into the box. Most of the prisoners scrambled free but four, weighed down by their manacles, were lost with the ship along with 31 crew.

Once off the ship Edwards was scarcely less cruel to the mutineers permitting them only extremely limited water and not even allowing them to shelter from the fierce sun as the survivors huddled on a sand cay. Eventually using the ship's boats the survivors made their way to Kupang, following the route traced out by Bligh.

Even here Edwards maniacal character was to bring disaster to others. William and Mary Bryant with their baby son and young daughter had earlier escaped from Sydney together with seven other convicts. In a feat of seamanship scarcely less amazing than Bligh's they rowed and sailed their open boat the full length of the east coast, rounded Cape York and crossed open sea to Timor where they claimed to be shipwreck survivors. To their great misfortune Edwards' party arrived two weeks later, recognised them as escaped convicts, clapped them back in irons and shipped them off to Batavia (present-day Jakarta). There the luckless William Bryant and his son died and the heartless Edwards even refused his wife permission to visit her dying husband in hospital until over-ruled by the angry local Dutch community.

Tales of Edwards' single-minded cruelty were to pursue him the rest of his life but back in England Mary Bryant was befriended by the author James Boswell (noted particularly for his *The Life of Samuel Johnson*) and he eventually secured her release and personally provided her with an

Cape York (TW)

annual allowance of £10, a not inconsiderable sum in those days. The full story of the *Pandora's* fateful journey can be read in *Pandora's Last Voyage* by Geoffrey Rawson. In 1983 the wreck of the *Pandora* was located and various items salvaged by a party from the Queensland Museum.

ALBANY PASSAGE

Curiously, Albany Island, just south-east of Cape York, was once proposed as a 'Singapore of Australia' and a major trading port. A settlement named Somerset was established on the mainland side of Albany Passage. It was eventually abandoned in favour of Thursday Island and little trace remains of its historic past. There is a small cultured pearl project across the strait on Albany Island.

MT ADOLPHUS ISLAND

North-east of Cape York is Mt Adolphus Island, just south of which is Quetta Rock. Despite a number of surveys the shoal had

been completely missed until the steamship *Quetta* ran head on into it in 1890. The ship, with 290 passengers and crew, sank within three minutes with the loss of 133 lives. Thursday Island has a church built as a memorial to the shipwreck.

CAPE YORK

Eborac and York Islands stand just north of Cape York, the extreme northern tip of mainland Australia. There's a marker cairn to show that you are as far north as you can go.

POSSESSION ISLAND

To the west of the top of Cape York and south of Horn Island is Possession Island where Captain Cook took possession of all of the east coast of Australia. There's a monument on the north-west side of the island.

Cruising to Cape York

Maybe we're just used to the space age aluminium and plastic high-speed catamarans or 'wavepiercers' which are the standard means of getting about the Great Barrier Reef these days but for whatever reason the *Queen of the Isles* looked curiously old fashioned. It was hard to believe that she was only launched in the mid-60s and not 30 or 40 years earlier. Maybe we're just fooled by all that rich, dark looking wood and tightly packed little bunkrooms. Never mind, mid-60s or not, on board the ship it was easy to mentally dial the time back to 1930, 1880 or whenever you pleased.

And the *Queen of the Isles* had certainly packed plenty of colourful sailing into those mere 25 years. She had started her life with just that name, only the islands were not on the Great Barrier Reef, they were the Scilly Isles off Cornwall in England, to where she operated as a ferry. Then there was a change of ocean, ownership and name when she became the *Nukalofa*, the personal ship of the King of Tonga. Unhappily the Pacific's Friendly Isles weren't so friendly to her and she ended up at the bottom. Snide comments are made that it happened the first time the weighty king boarded her. Dragged up from the bottom she then became the MV *Gulf Explorer* and went to live in New Zealand, where at some point she also became a floating casino. Finally she reverted to her original name and took up cruising Australia's Great Barrier Reef from Cairns, the northern tourist centre on the reef, to Thursday Island, just off Cape York, Australia's most northern point on the main island.

Day 1 – Departure from Cairns

In fine Australian tradition we found the *Queen of the Isles* moored at Cairns' Trinity Wharf and overlooked by the verandah of a pub. We could watch the final preparations for departure while sipping a 'pot' of XXXX, Queenslanders' favourite beer. With the final drinkers chased on board we pulled out right on the dot at 8 pm, the customary streamers hurled to shore and the captain making a neat turn in the inlet, watched by an appreciative audience enjoying the free entertainment.

Once out of Cairns we were given our first briefing, told about the lifeboats and lifejackets and given the voyage's most serious warning – don't run the showers too long, we can't replenish the freshwater until we get back to Cairns and if we run out we run out!

The *Queen of the Isles* is a neat little ship and the air-conditioning, a necessity in summer in these parts, works almost too enthusiastically, but she's no floating luxury hotel. Only the two 'double staterooms' have en suite toilet and showers, for the rest of us it's a matter of making your way to the nearest shared toilets and showers, mostly not even on the same deck. The cabins are certainly tightly packed as well, sitting up suddenly in bed is likely to result in a crack on the skull whether you're in a top or bottom bunk. And if you're travelling solo you're likely to be booked into a four or six berth cabin and find yourself making some instant new friends.

No matter, our fellow passengers are a mixed bunch but all appear ready to give it a go. We range from young couples, a mix of solo voyagers and a more adventurous than usual collection of older cruise shippers. Gradually we drift out of the bar and make our way to our cabins, some unfortunates already wrestling with seasickness.

Day 2 – Lizard Island & the Howick Group

Next morning we meet again for breakfast at 7.30 am and at 9.30 drop anchor in Watson's Bay on Lizard Island. The stop at Lizard Island includes a beach barbecue complete with a visit from a large sand goanna. Most of us stroll down the beach to see the Watson house and a couple of us make a rapid ascent to Cook's Look, the weather is exceptionally clear and the view across to the outer reef is superb. It's no problem at all to pick out the passage Cook took to escape from the reef to the outer sea. The snorkelling right off the beach at Watson's Bay is exceptional with many giant clams and numerous large anenomes sheltering my favourite reef fish, the perky little clown fish.

Queen of the Isles lifeboat (TW)

In mid afternoon we shuttle back to the *Queen of the Isles* on the lifeboat we use for all our shore excursions, up anchor and head off north. In late afternoon we pass the Howick Group where Mrs Watson met her unhappy end after fleeing Lizard Island in a metal tank used to boil bêche de mer.

Day 3 – Portland Roads, Piper Reef & Haggerstone Island

All night we head north and in the morning pass by Cape Direction, where Bligh made landfall, after entering the reef waters through Bligh's Passage. Further north we can see Restoration Island, where he actually landed to 'restore' his crew. It's just off Cape Weymouth and immediately north of the cape we can see the prawn trawlers in Portland Roads.

Early in the afternoon we stop at Farmer Islet on Piper Reef, a long drying reef (one that surfaces at low tide) with some great snorkelling around the cay. I walk out to the very end of the reef where there's a lighthouse perched beside the channel. As I stroll back a huge container ship comes by, only a stone's throw from the reef. This is the narrowest shipping channel down the coast. Later that afternoon we pass Haggerstone Island with its mysterious houses. Who would live here, so far from anywhere?

Day 4 – Cape York & Thursday Island

We anchor at Cape York at 3.40 am and before dawn we're loading into the lifeboat again to scoot over to the cape. The sun rises as we drink champagne on the northernmost point of Australia. There's a campsite just below the cape and I talk with a couple who've just driven up to the top in a 4WD. The long road north is much better than it used to be and the difficult crossing of the Jardine River is now made on an Aboriginal run barge service. Not long ago you had to winch your vehicle across, or float motorcycles over on truck inner tubes.

Then it's on to Thursday Island, meeting the Torres Strait Pilot Service boat just before we reach the island. Thursday Island is a curious place, a meeting point between Australia and the Pacific where the town could be in North Queensland from one angle, in Papua New Guinea from another. There are a surprising number of pubs, some of them quite pleasant. After wandering the town we take a bus tour to the old cemetery with its graves of Japanese divers and the Green Hill fort. TI is such a compact little place we could just as easily have walked around as wasted time waiting for the bus.

Pulling out of Thursday Island in the afternoon we've reached the top and are heading back south.

Day 5 – Morris Islet

The weather turns distinctly rougher and colder overnight but we pass a number of cruising yachts, ploughing through the seas northbound. I'm a regular visitor to the bridge to study the charts and listen to the captain's tales of his many trips up and down the reef. As we near Cape Weymouth and Restoration Island, linked with the Bligh saga, what should we see but a replica of the *Bounty* captain's boat. Its crew are attempting to recreate his original journey and have just entered Australian waters.

Late in the afternoon we anchor off Morris Islet, a low-lying little cay with a mysterious 'diver's grave'. It's cold and blustery and only a handful of us opt to go ashore, the rest stay on board dangling fishing lines over the side. Our shore party circumnavigates the island but it's much too chilly to contemplate a swim.

Day 6 – Lizard Island

Once again we stop at Lizard Island, the uncooperative weather prevents us from trying alternative less secure anchorages but Watson's Bay at Lizard is fine. It's a repeat of our first visit with a larger party heading up Cook's Look on this occasion. Late in the afternoon we stow the lifeboat for the last time and head south to Cairns, and we're back outside the Trinity Wharf pub soon after dawn.

Pumice

Pumice stone, that lightweight volcanic rock which finds its way into many bathrooms next to the bar of soap and shampoo bottle, is an interesting item of flotsam right up the Great Barrier Reef. The air-filled stone is lighter than water so it floats with the tides but there are no live volcanoes on Australian soil today, so the pumice floats here from islands further east in the Pacific. Captain Cook also noticed the pumice on reef islands and deduced that he must, therefore, be downwind and west of the volcanic New Hebrides islands (Vanuatu today) which was first discovered by Portuguese explorer Queirós in 1606. Today volcanic eruptions in the these active islands are often followed some time later by fresh arrivals of pumice on Australian reef islands. ■

Shipwrecks

Even today with sophisticated navigation equipment and reliable charts, ships still get wrecked on the Great Barrier Reef so it is no surprise that the reef was once a real nightmare for early explorers, back in the days when Terra Australis was a big blank on the map. Captain Cook with his ship the *Endeavour* was, of course, the first recorded European explorer to tangle with the reef but Cook made a lucky escape, repaired his damaged ship at the site of present day Cooktown and sailed on back to report his finds. The cannons and ballast he jettisoned during his escape from the reef have been recovered by divers.

HMS Pandora, which sunk in 1791 while bringing captured mutineers from the *Bounty* back to England, wasn't so lucky and its discovery and investigation has made it one of the most interesting Barrier Reef wrecks. See the Lizard Island to Cape York chapter for more details.

Ships sailing along the Queensland coast basically had two choices. They could hug the coast and enjoy the protection the reef offered from the open ocean. The prospect of meeting an uncharted reef was the principal danger for this route. The other alternative was to sail outside of the reef and then enter the Torres Strait, north of Cape York, via the Great North-East Channel or Raine Island Entrance and Blackwood Channel. Again careful navigation was required and attempts to enter the reef at other points were fraught with danger.

Following either plan resulted in numerous shipwrecks over the years. The Capricorn-Bunker Group at the southern end of the reef claimed many boats while others, like *Pandora*, failed to find the key to Raine Island Entrance. Some of the interesting Great Barrier Reef wrecks from south to north include:

Golden City This American built clipper had operated as an immigrant ship from England to Australia and New Zealand but was wrecked on Lady Elliot Island while loading guano in 1865.

America A little further north the convict transport *America* had left its load of female convicts in Hobart and was sailing north to Batavia (Jakarta) in the Dutch East Indies when she struck a reef. The ship was abandoned on Wreck Island reef in the Capricorn Group in 1831.

Yongala This passenger steamer sank in a cyclone off Cape Bowling Green, south of Townsville, in 1911. All 120 on board were lost and it was not until WW II that the mystery of the ship's disappearance was finally solved. The ship lies in 30 metres of water and is a very popular dive site.

Foam This blackbirding schooner was wrecked on Myrmidon Reef, north of Townsville, in 1893. 'Blackbirding' was the collecting of Pacific Islanders to work on Queensland plantations. Supposedly they were recruited voluntarily and were free to return to their home islands at the end of their period of indenture but in practice they were often 'recruited' forcibly and worked under conditions of near slavery. The Islanders on the *Foam* were being returned home and all aboard were saved.

SS Gothenburg Originally named the *Celt* this iron steamer was also operated as a three-masted schooner and was carrying passengers, cargo and gold from the Pine Creek gold site near present day Darwin. She hit Old Reef off Ayr and sank with 106 people.

HMS Mermaid In 1829 this Calcutta-built teak schooner sank south of Trinity Inlet, Cairns. She had been used to survey the Australian coast between 1818 and 1820.

Morning Star Carrying cargo from early Australian colonies this brig sunk near Temple Bay, towards the top of Cape York, in 1814. The wreck has not yet been found.

Quetta The *Quetta* sank of Mt Adolphus island, near Cape York, in 1890 when it ran straight into an uncharted rock in the channel south of the island. She sank in less than three minutes, taking 133 of her 290 passengers and crew with her. ■

Thursday Island & the Torres Strait

The Torres Strait contains the scattering of islands which run like stepping stones from the top of Cape York to the south coast of Papua New Guinea. The islands are politically part of Australia although some of them are only a few km from Papua New Guinea. The population of the islands is about 9000 and the people are Melanesians, racially related to the peoples of Papua New Guinea.

History

The islands of the straits would seem, on paper, to have been an obvious conduit for early migration to Australia but in actual fact there seems to have been remarkably little movement across the straits and the dramatic differences between development in Papua New Guinea and amongst the Aboriginals of Australia is of great scientific interest.

Agriculture and animal husbandry are two of the most basic stages in human development but although these skills were known in Papua New Guinea about 4000 years ago they never crossed the straits to Australia. Gardening did spread to the eastern and central islands and to some of the western islands but it never got as far south as the islands close to the top of Cape York. Why this important development step only made it part way across the straits is an intriguing question.

By the 15th century vessels from Makassar in modern Indonesia and from China were regular visitors to the Arafura Sea in search of bêche-de-mer and a century later the Portuguese had made their way to the Moluccas or Maluku (the Spice Islands) while the Spanish had established themselves in the Philippines. In 1606 European eyes were first set on the Torres Strait from both east and west, but quite independently and with neither party aware of the other.

Dutch explorer Willem Jansz sighted the west coast of Cape York from his ship the *Duyfken*. He led a party ashore and could have claimed the honour of being the first European to set foot on Australia, except that he thought he was still on Papua New Guinea. Jansz continued east into the strait but currents and winds prevented him from crossing through into the Pacific and he continued to believe he was simply sailing into a bay and never realised that the land he had set foot on was separated from Papua New Guinea.

Meanwhile Spanish explorer Luiz Vaez de Torres was approaching the strait from the eastern side with his ship the *San Pedrico*. He had set out from Peru in company with another ship to search for *Terra Australis Incognita*, the Great South Land, and along the way to do as much converting to Christianity as he could manage. The party first stumbled upon the New Hebrides (Vanuatu) and thought they had found the mysterious land of the south.

The two boats were then separated and while Pedro Fernandez de Quiros, the expedition leader, sailed back to Mexico Torres continued east and would have reached the Australian east coast, or more likely foundered on the Great Barrier Reef, had he not given up the search only 200 km outside the reef. He turned north to sail for the Philippines but by this time he was already too far west to round the eastern end of Papua New Guinea and the same winds and currents that prevented Jansz from sailing east through the straits swept Torres in from the opposite direction. He landed on several of the islands and eventually inched his way through to the Arafura Sea and then looped around Papua New Guinea to reach the Philippines.

The Spanish, however, did not reveal Torres' historic discovery and for the next two centuries the straits separating Papua New Guinea remained a rumour until eventually Captain Cook confirmed their existence in 1770. After his involuntary halt at Cooktown to repair his damaged vessel Cook continued north and then, like Torres, was carried through the straits by the prevailing winds and currents. He paused long enough at Possession Island to claim the whole east coast of Australia for King George III.

Bligh, following the *Bounty* mutiny, passed through in 1789 and named Wednesday Island as he went by. The *Pandora* survivors (see the Lizard Island to Cape York chapter) came through the strait in 1791 but made no additions to the charts. In 1802 Matthew Flinders, during his epic circumnavigation of Australia, made the most systematic survey yet of the islands and channels of the straits and also named the straits after Torres, although remarkably little about his expedition was known even at this time.

By the mid-1800s the straits had become a major sailing route but the tricky waters led to frequent shipwrecks with often disastrous results. If the unfortunate passengers and crew survived the actual wreck they still had to face the less than friendly islanders who had often been terrorised by unscrupulous seamen and offered little mercy when the tables were turned. A settlement was estab-

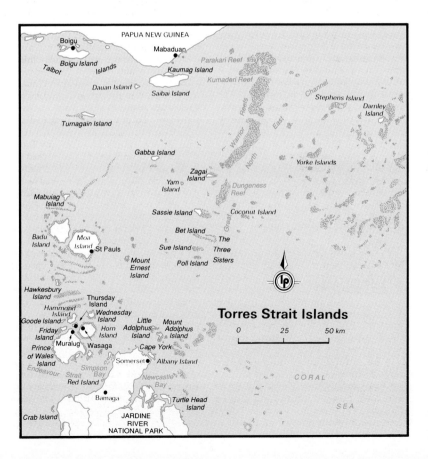

Torres Strait Islands

lished at Somerset, opposite Albany Island, in 1864 to police the straits. At that time bêche-de-mer were the main economic attraction but in 1869 the first shipment of mother-of-pearl shell from the straits was unloaded in Sydney and a rush for the valuable shells started soon after.

The easily reached pearl shells were soon exhausted and primitive diving suits came into use so that shells could be gathered at greater depth. A motley international crew of pearl divers descended upon the straits islands and fortunes were soon won and lost, murders committed, lives lost and general mayhem ensued. In 1872 Captain John Moresby reported from HMS *Basilisk* that 'anarchy and savagery' was the order of the day. The station at Somerset was proving to be a distinctly bad idea and in 1877 the settlement was shifted to Thursday Island.

Christianity, in the form of the London Missionary Society, arrived in the islands in 1871 when they set up a mission station on Darnley Island in the east of the straits. The missionaries had great success and Christianity still plays a strong role in the life of the islands.

By the end of the last century things were not going well for the Torres Strait Islanders and a number of the tribal groups had been all but wiped out. The Kauralgal people had been decimated by struggles with the British colonists while the Badulgal people had managed to pretty well wipe out the Moa. Thursday Island had become a prosperous centre, however, and gold was found on Horn and Hammond Islands. The pearl shell industry also continued to grow and at its peak 1600 men worked on the pearling fleets out of Thursday Island, Albany, Somerset and other ports. The pearling fleets used many skilled Japanese divers as well as islanders and a variety of other nationalities.

The Torres Strait was uncomfortably close to the bitter fighting in Papua New Guinea during WW II although remarkably Thursday Island was never attacked. The development of plastics after the war dealt a death blow to the pearl shell industry. Mother

Thursday Island pub (TW)

of pearl was extensively used for button making and soon buttons were all made of plastic and the pearling industry simply disappeared. Farming artificial pearls brought a little employment to the region but in the main the choice was between returning to a traditional lifestyle or emigrating to the big cities of Queensland. There are now large islander communities in Cairns, Townsville, Mackay and Brisbane.

Geography

The islands of the straits are of three types and in total 17 of them are inhabited. At the western end of the straits the main Torres Strait islands are flooded mountain tops, a final northern fling of Australia's Great Dividing Range. During the last ice age when sea levels were much lower Australia and Papua New Guinea were joined by dry land. Rising sea levels cut this land bridge about 7000 to 8000 years ago but even today the straits are very shallow, in some shipping lanes minimum depths are as little as 10 metres. The shallow water, narrow straits and often ferocious tidal currents makes the straits a difficult place for navigation.

Inhabited islands in this western group are the tight cluster of Thursday, Prince of Wales, Horn and Hammond Islands. Those four are close to the top of Cape York. A little further north Moa (Banks Island), Badu (Mulgrave Island) and Mabuiag (Jervis Island) are also inhabited. A final three inhabited islands – Boigu, Dauan and Saibai – are very close to the Papua New Guinea coast. Interestingly Thursday Island, the administrative and population centre of the islands, was uninhabited prior to the European arrival. Its native name, *Waiben*, means 'no water', which may account for this.

The second group of islands in the straits are a scattering of coral cays on the reefs to the east of the main islands. Inhabited islands here are Sue, Yam, Coconut and Yorke Islands. Finally there are a group of volcanic islands, cloaked in luxuriant vegetation, to the extreme east of the straits. In this group Mer (Murray Island), Darnley and Stephens are populated.

Pilot Boat, Thursday Island (TW)

THURSDAY ISLAND

Area: 3.25 square km
Type: continental
High point: 104 metres
In brief: This is not a resort island. Thursday Island is right at the top of Australia and the population of around 2300 is mainly Torres Strait Islanders. The island has had a long and interesting history.

The Island

'TI', as it is usually known, is the best known of the Torres Strait islands. It's only just over three square km in area and 39 km off the top of Cape York. At one time Thursday Island was a major pearling centre and pearlers' cemeteries tell the hard tale of what a dangerous occupation this was. Some pearls are still produced here, from seeded 'culture farms'. Although Thursday Island has lost its former importance as a stopping point for vessels, it's still a popular pause for passing yachties. It's an interesting and easy-going little place although the island itself is somewhat dry and unpreposessing.

History

Nearby Wednesday Island was certainly named by Captain William Bligh during his *Bounty* misadventures but how Thursday Island got its name is less certain. Various explanations have been advanced but the most likely is that it was named by Captain Owen Stanley during a surveying voyage on HMS *Rattlesnake* in 1848. Curiously he appears to have named Thursday and Friday Islands in reverse order but some tidy minded individual later switched them around so that Wednesday, Thursday and Friday fell in neat east to west order.

Thursday Island's busy European history started with the establishment of a settlement there in 1877. The opening of the Suez Canal had made the northern route around Australia

a far more economic proposition than the old route around the south of the island. The route was shorter and the advent of steam ships meant the old problem of prevailing

1	Old Quarantine Area
2	Japanese Pearl Memorial
3	Green Hill Fort
4	Quetta Memorial Church
5	Sacred Heart Mission
6	Torres Hotel
7	Court House
8	Jumula Dubbins Hostel
9	Federal Hotel
10	Torres Memorial
11	Australian Airlines
12	Grand Hotel
13	Custom's House
14	Post Office
15	Government Jetty
16	Pilot House

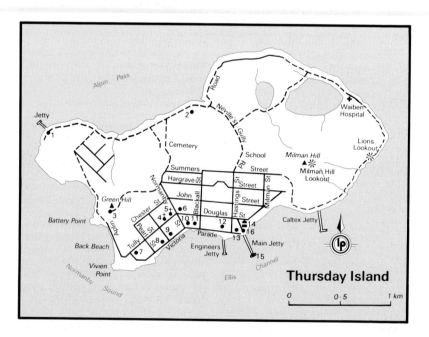

winds was no longer a factor. The reefs certainly were a problem, however, and numerous ships went down around Cape York, including the *Quetta* which sank on an uncharted reef in 1890 with the loss of 133 lives. Thursday Island soon became an important port for the pilots who guided ships through the perilous reef waters.

At the same time the pearling boom continued, particularly from 1885, when restrictions on using the island as a pearling base were relaxed. At that time the population was only a few hundred but within 10 years it had increased to over 2000. The first Japanese divers, who were to be the mainstay of the diving force, arrived in the straits in 1883 and there were soon thousands of men working on the pearl luggers. TI was a very cosmopolitan place with Torres Strait Islanders, Europeans, Japanese, Melanesians, Aborigines, Polynesians, Malays, Micronesians, Chinese and many other nationalities adding to the mix.

Pearl diving with the primitive equipment of the time was desperately unsafe and over 1000 divers, a very large proportion of them Japanese, lost their lives. The Thursday Island cemetery has the tombstones of about 500 divers. In this cut throat economic struggle the poor Torres Strait Islanders were completely forgotten and were actually banned from living on Thursday Island until after WW II. It was part of the paternalistic mood of the times as the authorities believed that allowing the islanders to live on TI would expose them to alcohol and other forms of European exploitation.

The pearling business continued until first the Great Depression, then WW II and finally the invention of plastics made pearl buttons, the main use of Mother of Pearl, an unnecessary anachronism. There was a brief resurgence in the pearl business when artificial pearls were cultivated in the 1960s, again an activity where the Japanese led the way, but the enterprise failed and today frozen prawns and crayfish are the islands' economic mainstay.

At the time of Papua New Guinea's independence in 1975 there was some dispute over where the boundary should be drawn and whether some of the islands should go to PNG but they ended up remaining Australian.

Pilot Services

The operation of a pilot service was a prime reason for the establishment of the settlement at Thursday Island and today, despite jumbo jets and container ships, the Queensland Coast & Torres Strait Pilot Service still operates with a sense of Victorian ritual that seems strangely out of place today. The 40-odd pilots who operate the service are all co-owners and on average pilot a vessel to or from Thursday Island twice a month. Each night the pilots dine together, moving up towards the head of the table each time a passing ship collects a pilot. Eventually, after a three day wait on average, a pilot reaches the head of the table, chooses the menu and wine for dinner that night, and departs on the next vessel to arrive. The service was established in 1884 and over 100 million tons of shipping are piloted each year.

Pearl Shells

Despite the popular image pearls were not what pearl divers sought. The pearl shell itself was the thing of value, pearls were just an occasional lucky bonus. Pearl shell or Mother of Pearl was used for buckles, jewellery, inlays, cutlery handles and, most important, for buttons. The gold lip and silver lip pearl shells of the Torres Strait are the most valuable pearl shells found although the silver is actually worth more than the gold. Pearl shells are graded from AA or 'chicken' shells down through A to E.

The old pearl diving luggers have disappeared with the decline in the industry. Originally they were indeed luggers, carrying two masts with a jib and two lug sails. The later diving boats were ketch rigged but the name 'lugger' remained. Although it is uncertain when pearl diving started the first big shipment of pearl shells was taken down to Sydney in 1869. Diving suits and hand operated air pumps started to be used in 1874 and by the late 1870s over 100 vessels were operating in the Torres Strait. By 1913 there were over 1000 men working on the pearling boats and almost half this number were Japanese. The Thursday Island cemetery speaks clearly of the dangers of pearl diving.

Information

Old TI by M J O'Riley and I B Wallace is a readable little sketchbook of interesting places on the island. You should be able to find it on sale in TI or in Walkers Bookshop in Cairns. The *Torres News* is a weekly news-

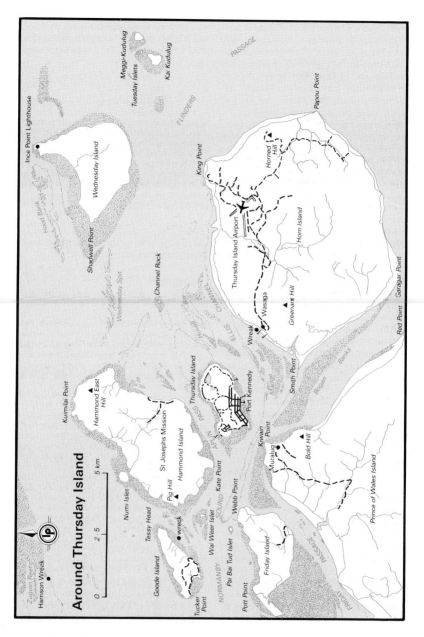

Around Thursday Island

0   2.5   5 km

paper which labels itself 'The voice of the islands'.

Thursday Island has a post office, shops and a healthy selection of pubs for those in need of a cold beer. There's a bank opposite the post office.

Quetta Memorial Church

The Quetta Memorial Church was opened in 1893 as a memorial to the British Indian Steamship *Quetta* which went down near Thursday Island in 1890 with the loss of 133 lives. See the Mt Adolphus Island section of the Lizard Island to Cape York chapter for more details. The church has a number of relics from the disaster including the ship's bell, a porthole, the ship's riding light and a copper jug near the font.

There is also a *Quetta* stained-glass window and various other connections with the ship. The pews with swinging seat backs were retrieved from the wreck of the *Volga* and the church's font is a memorial to James Chalmers, a missionary who was killed on Goaribari Island in Papua New Guinea in 1901. See the Lonely Planet book *Papua New Guinea – a travel survival kit* for the full story on that incident.

Other Interesting Buildings

At the south-west end of the island the old Court House actually predates the establishment of TI as the administrative centre for the islands. It was built in 1876 and is still used by the local government.

Right in front of the main jetty the original Customs House was built on this site in 1889. The present building dates from 1939 but the original building can still be seen on John St. Adjacent to the Quetta Memorial Church, the Catholic Sacred Heart Church dates from 1885 and is the only TI church which remains unchanged from its original construction.

The magnificent old Metropole Hotel was burnt down during WW II but the fine old Grand and Federal Hotels still overlook the waterfront.

Cemetery

The Thursday Island cemetery on the north side of the island has many picturesque graves of Okinawan and Japanese divers and the Japanese Pearl Memorial to the many divers who worked here. The islanders graves are also very interesting. The Torres Strait Islanders hold a Tombstone Opening ceremony when they have managed to save up enough to erect a suitable headstone and unveil it at a special ceremony.

Green Hill Fort

Thursday Island's strategic importance led to the decision in 1891 to build the fort on top of Green Hill. It was abandoned in 1939 but a number of the rusting guns still remain in position and the fort itself is now used as a weather station. Curiously Thursday Island was never attacked by the Japanese during WW II. Local legends relate that it was because a mysterious Japanese princess was buried on the island, but in actual fact it may

Japanese diver's grave, Thursday Island (TW)

have been because the Japanese forces thought that the many Japanese pearl shell divers were still on the island.

Wongal Trees

The Wongai, a native tree of the Torres Strait Islands, is said to have magical powers and anyone who eats the tree's fruit is bound to return to the islands. A very famous Wongai tree once stood in front of the Federal Hotel on Victoria Parade but it was blown down by a cyclone in 1977.

Accommodation

The *Jumula Dubbins Hostel* on Victoria Parade is principally for use by Aborigines and Torres Strait Islanders.

The *Federal Hotel* (tel (070) 69 1569) has air-con motel rooms with attached bathrooms for $50, hotel rooms for $35 and $45. At the *Torres Hotel* (tel (070) 69 1141) accommodation costs $20/35 for singles/doubles. The *Grand Hotel* (tel (070) 69 1557) claims to be 'Somerset Maugham's old haunt'.

Food

The various hotels have counter meals Monday to Saturday while a barbecue often features on Sunday. The *Torres Hotel* claims to have the most comprehensive menu on TI and on Sunday evenings they have *Crabbies Steakhouse*. The *Grand Hotel* has counter meals and *Anchors Restaurant* in the evening. At the *Federal Hotel* it's the *Pearl Lugger Restaurant* for evening meals.

Tarie's Snackbar, the *Chat 'n Snack* and *K&B Snackbar* have ice creams, snacks and takeaways.

Getting There

Air The TI Airport is actually on neighbouring Horn Island. Australian Regional Airlines have regular flights between Cairns and Thursday Island. The fare is $245 and the flight takes two hours direct, longer if it goes via Weipa or Bamaga. On TI the Australian Airlines office (tel (070) 69 1264) is on the corner of Victoria Parade and Blackall St. Their Cairns number is (070) 50 3777.

Sunbird Airlines also have flights from Cairns to Thursday Island for $245. Their TI numbers are (070) 69 1353 and 1506 while in Cairns they're on (070) 53 4899. Falcon Airlines also fly between Cairns and TI. Their TI number is (070) 69 1761 while in Cairns they're on (070) 53 7111. Spirit Air fly Cairns/TI either via Weipa or via Weipa and Bamaga. Their TI number is (070) 69 1264.

Sunbird fly an extensive network around the islands of the Torres Strait. Flights from Cairns include: Thursday Island ($245 one-way); Boigu, Coconut, Darnley, Mabuiag, Moa, Murray, Warraber and Yam Islands (all $326) and Yorke Island ($282).

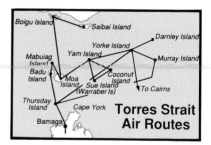

Sea The *Queen of the Isles* and the *Noel Buxton* operate regularly Cairns/Thursday Island/Cairns. Although most passengers take the round trip cruise you can also travel one way. See the Lizard Island to Cape York chapter for more details. Torres Islands Trading (tel (070) 69 1707) carry passengers between Cairns and TI on the *Cape Trader* for $250.

There are regular ferry services between Bamaga and Thursday Island. Phone Peddells Ferry Services (tel (070) 69 1551) on TI for details – they have morning and afternoon services on Monday, Wednesday and Friday, afternoon only on Tuesday and Thursday. The fare is $45 same-day return or $30 one-way. Torres Islands Trading operate to other islands in the straits as well as their service to Cairns.

Intrepid travellers have, in the past, continued on from the Torres Strait Islands to Papua New Guinea by finding a fishing boat across the straits to Daru, from where you can fly or ship to Port Moresby. These days you will probably run into severe visa problems if you try this since Papua New Guinea officials frown on this unconventional entry point.

The Torres Strait's south-east trade wind is the strongest and longest lasting trade wind in the world. Combine this with numerous reefs and islands plus fickle tides and currents and it's easy to see why this is frequently not an easy area to sail through.

Getting Around

Peddells operate a regular ferry service between Thursday Island and Horn Island, where the TI airport is located. The fare is $5 one way and it operates Monday to Saturday, more or less on demand although there's usually a service about every two hours.

Around TI there are taxis and sometimes there's a bus, it usually operates a tour of the island when the cruise boats come by. You can rent small Daihatsu Charade cars from R&F Rent-a-Car opposite the post office. The cost is $10 an hour or $58 a day. TI is small enough to walk around quite easily.

Fishing

Although much of the Great Barrier Reef waters are marine park there is an important fishing industry. Prawn trawling is the most important commercial fishing operation along the coast with prawn trawlers operating the entire length of the east coast of Australia and around into the Gulf of Carpentaria. Scallop trawling is also important in the southern reef waters. Fish are also important economically with barramundi, salmon, coral trout, red emperor and sweetlip all economically important. Fish are also caught on the reef for aquariums and that gourmet's delight, Queensland's revered mud crab, can't be forgotten.

Of course there is more than just commercial fishing along the reef. Queensland has a huge sport fishing industry ranging from hanging a line off a dinghy to chasing marlin off Cairns. Traditional Aboriginal and Torres Strait Islander fishing is another area and the Great Barrier Reef also suffers from a variety of illegal fishing activities. Over the years Queensland has acquired quite a fleet of confiscated Asian fishing vessels, caught illegally poaching in Australian territorial waters. The protected giant clams are a favourite for some of these fishermen and if you visit the underwater observatory off Great Keppel Island you can see a confiscated Taiwanese fishing boat, sunk beside the observatory to provide a haven for fish. ■

Coral trout (GBRMPA)

Dugongs

The dugong, a sirenian or sea cow, looks rather like a decidedly overweight and lethargic dolphin. Like dolphins they are mammals but have adapted to spending their entire lives in water. They are gentle, slow moving creatures which live mainly on sea grass, unlike dolphins which are carnivorous predators.

The Great Barrier Reef is probably the world's major habitat of this rare and endangered creature. They are protected except for hunting by Aboriginals and Torres Strait Islanders from native communities. Their flesh is said to taste like veal. The main danger to the dugong is drowning after accidentally becoming entangled in fishing nets. Shark proof netting on swimming beaches along the Queensland coast also poses a danger to them.

Dugongs live to about 70 years of age and breed very slowly. A calf is produced every three to seven years and stays with its mother for the first two years of its life. Dugongs suckle their young from mammary glands under each flipper, positioned much like human breasts. It is thought that dugongs may have inspired the ancient seamen's tales of mermaids although they are a very long way from the traditional glamorous mermaid pinup! ∎

Index

Map references are in **bold** type

MAPS

Temperature

To convert °C to °F multiply by 1.8 and add 32
To convert °F to °C subtract 32 and multiply by .55

Length, Distance & Area

	multiply by
inches to centimetres	2.54
centimetres to inches	0.39
feet to metres	0.30
metres to feet	3.28
yards to metres	0.91
metres to yards	1.09
miles to kilometres	1.61
kilometres to miles	0.62
acres to hectares	0.40
hectares to acres	2.47

Weight

	multiply by
ounces to grams	28.35
grams to ounces	0.035
pounds to kilograms	0.45
kilograms to pounds	2.21
British tons to kilograms	1016
US tons to kilograms	907

A British ton is 2240 lbs, a US ton is 2000 lbs

Volume

	multiply by
imperial gallons to litres	4.55
litres to imperial gallons	0.22
US gallons to litres	3.79
litres to US gallons	0.26

5 imperial gallons equals 6 US gallons
a litre is slightly more than a US quart, slightly less than a British one

Guides to the Pacific

Australia – a travel survival kit
The complete low-down on Down Under – home of
Ayers Rock, the Great Barrier Reef, extraordinary
animals, cosmopolitan cities, rain forests, beaches. . .
and Lonely Planet!

New Zealand – a travel survival kit
Magnificent scenery, fresh open air and outdoor
activities are New Zealand's feature attractions. It's
not a big country, but for sheer variety it's hard to
beat.

Fiji – a travel survival kit
Whether you prefer to stay in camping grounds,
international hotels, or something in-between, this
comprehensive guide will help you to enjoy the
beautiful Fijian archipelago.

Solomon Islands – a travel survival kit
The Solomon Islands are the best-kept secret of the
Pacific. Discover remote tropical islands, jungle
covered volcanoes and traditional Melanesian villages
with this detailed guide.

Tahiti & French Polynesia – a travel survival kit
Tahiti's reputation as an idyllic island paradise
continues to enchant travellers. . . and after you have
explored Tahiti, more than 100 other islands await you
across the crystal clear water.